ZEPPELIN
OVER
DAYTON

guided
by
voices
album
by
album

JEFF GOMEZ

for jasper, my son cool

A Jawbone book
First edition 2020
Published in the UK
and the USA by
Jawbone Press
Office G1
141–157 Acre Lane
London SW2 5UA
England
www.jawbonepress.com

ISBN 978-1-911036-59-3

Printed by Everbest Printing Investment Ltd.

1 2 3 4 5 24 23 22 21 20

CONTENTS

'What I wrote was based on passionate listening, research, and interviewing, and, of course, the kind of speculation that we inevitably apply to anything, or anyone, whom we admire from a distant shore.'

PETER GURALNICK
*Last Train To Memphis:
The Rise Of Elvis Presley*

INTRODUCTION

*Would you like to know
how he came from Ohio?*

uided By Voices are the best band America's ever produced. In their
more than three decades of existence, they've rocked harder, been more
productive, and exhibited more creativity than any other band in the
country. R.E.M.? Talking Heads? Ramones? They're good, but they're not
Guided By Voices. And yet GBV should never have existed. Singer and
main songwriter Robert Pollard should have been an athlete, should
have played in the major leagues. He should be known for baseball, not
rock'n'roll. That's where he was headed, and it's what he'd been groomed for
since childhood. And yet, like so many other things in Pollard's life, things
took an unexpected turn.

As a child who came of age in the 1960s (he was born in 1957), Bob grew
up during a golden era of pop music. His first big cultural experience was
seeing The Beatles on *The Ed Sullivan Show*. 'My entire family watched it,'
Pollard later recalled. 'It was a huge event for everyone except my dad. He
wasn't so impressed.'

Robert Ellsworth Pollard Sr. wanted his oldest son to play sports and
make big bucks. But it was too late. The Beatles, and all the other bands
that followed in their wake—The Rolling Stones, The Who, The Kinks—
aroused something inside of Bob. And so, even though he continued with
sports throughout grade school and after high school—he attended Wright
State University on a baseball scholarship—Pollard Jr. never lost his love of
music and the desire to do what The Beatles did: write songs, make records,
play concerts. And while most famous or successful songwriters start in their
teens, having been either child prodigies or—at the very least—precocious

youngsters who picked up an instrument early, Bob didn't start playing guitar until college. But that never got in the way of his imagination.

Throughout his teen years, Pollard invented bands, songs, album titles. He went so far as to create make-believe covers for the make-believe records by his make-believe groups. Bob and his friends even wore homemade T-shirts for their fake bands. He would later breathe life into this fantasy by writing words and music to go along with the song titles of his youth, not to mention actually forming and fronting some of the imaginary groups he'd daydreamed, including Guided By Voices.

But that was all later. Right out of college, Pollard married his high-school sweetheart, bought a house, had two kids. He got a job teaching fourth grade at a nearby school. This meant short days and long vacations, giving him more time to do what he'd finally become serious about: writing songs. After joining a local songwriters' group, he amazed them by bringing in tune after tune. But while these early years of honing his craft basically boiled down to Bob with an acoustic guitar, his main ambition was to be in a band.

Over the years, he formed various groups with various friends. And while none of them stuck—Anacrusis, The Crowd, Mailbox, The Needmores—the songs kept coming. He wrote them all the time and recorded them whenever he could, using whatever gear or players he had on hand at the time. Crude sketches, song snippets, and sometimes—despite the low fidelity of the recording—pop masterpieces. Many of these early attempts can be heard today on Acid Ranch records, or as part of the *Suitcase* series.

And yet, even though the dream was slowly becoming real, Pollard never expected much to happen. He was from Ohio, a flyover state. Dayton was a blue-collar town in the middle of nowhere. It was filled with people who worked in factories. Nobody famous came from Ohio except the Wright brothers, and that was more than a hundred years ago. Sports were all people talked about, or aspired to, and Bob was done with all that. Plus, Pollard was from a part of Dayton known as Northridge. It was almost an Appalachian community, filled with hillbillies and rednecks, briars. Elvis may have been born in Tupelo, but he went to high school in Memphis. Memphis was the epicenter of a vibrant cultural and musical scene, and he drove by Sun Records every chance he could get. Dayton wasn't anything like that. There wasn't any sort of scene, and bands that played in the town's few clubs stuck to covering hits.

So, for years, Bob and his buddies recorded songs in their basements. Early experiments at playing in front of crowds only reinforced the idea that Ohio didn't want, or wasn't ready for, what Pollard had to offer. He and the band stayed underground, literally, retreating again and again to the sanctuaries beneath their homes. A place where they felt safe, where they could escape wives, kids, responsibilities. Bob nicknamed his basement the Snakepit, and it gave birth to hundreds of songs.

From the very beginning, Guided By Voices were about recording. EPs, LPs, double records. Bob was sitting on a mountain of tunes. This led him and a few of his friends, in 1986, to finally introduce their music to the world. The fruit of their labor was the debut Guided By Voices release, a seven-song EP called *Forever Since Breakfast*.

Even though the record didn't get much attention, and Bob only unloaded a handful of copies on family and friends, he and his collaborators were undeterred. An LP soon followed. Nineteen eighty-seven, in fact, saw the release of not one but two Guided By Voices albums. Even though the band had no following and no fans, and their families thought they were wasting their time, Pollard insisted on releasing a pair of records in one year (just like The Beatles). It would be the beginning of a three-decade journey that Bob's still on.

Even after the band broke in 1994, the albums kept coming. It didn't matter if he was touring or had to make videos or give interviews. It didn't matter that fans were still wrapping their brains around the last GBV record. Nothing could stop Bob from making albums. Whether it was as Guided By Voices, a solo artist, or one of a dozen side projects, the records just kept on coming. And now, with over a hundred full-length LPs under his belt, Pollard shows no sign of stopping.

While I love some of GBV's EPs, compilations, and live records—not to mention music made by other people associated with the band, such as Tobin Sprout—I believe the best way to tell the story of Guided By Voices is through their studio albums. By going through them, one at a time, we see the arc of the band: their rise, fall, and rise again.

Looking at GBV album by album also provides the most complete picture possible of Robert Pollard. Because he's a guy who makes things. Bob's constantly producing stuff—creating collages, writing songs, or releasing music. By looking closely at what he makes, we begin to see his fingerprints. Pollard's defined by what he creates, and the aim of this book is to examine, analyze, and celebrate his most accomplished body of work: the full-length albums of Guided By Voices.

Without a doubt, GBV have released a lot of material. Hundreds and hundreds of songs. Decades of records. More words and melodies than are possible to remember (even for Bob). And while it may seem daunting to approach such a vast catalogue of work, there's only one way to start such a journey. At the beginning.

01 DEVIL BETWEEN MY TOES

nineteen eighty-seven

M ost groups release a debut record to meet a need. It's part of a process that goes like this: band plays around town, band gets fans, those fans want a recording of the songs the band plays live. That sequence of events is one almost every group follows. Not GBV. *Devil Between My Toes* was the answer to a question nobody had asked.

Citing indifference from hometown audiences, the band had stopped playing live. And because everyone in the group had jobs and marriages and careers, hitting the road and trying to become known on a national level was out of the question. Besides, Pollard didn't have a stable lineup. He played guitar, and his childhood friend Mitch Mitchell played bass, but drumming was split between two people: Kevin Fennell, who was married to Pollard's sister, Lisa (although they would divorce the year this record came out); and Peyton Eric, whose real name is Timothy Payton Earick. Tobin Sprout, whose contributions would prove crucial half a decade later, was around, too, but he was focusing instead on his own band, Fig. 4. So GBV became a studio band. And, even though the group's first release, the 1986 EP *Forever Since Breakfast*, didn't set the world on fire, Pollard was undaunted. He'd spent too many years just imagining bands and having the record sleeves he designed be fantasies. It was time to make the dream real.

Mitchell and Fennell were guys Pollard knew from the neighborhood. They all went to Northridge High, but Mitch and Kevin are two years younger than Bob. Another thing Pollard and Mitchell have in common is that both of their birthdays fall on holidays: Mitch's is on Christmas and Bob's is on Halloween. The three were in a variety of bands together, with different names, until Bob settled on Guided By Voices in the early 1980s.

Pollard's younger brother, Jim, plays additional guitar on the record. He also has four co-writing credits, and Mitch has two. Jim's the youngest of the Pollard kids. They also have older sisters. Like Bob, Jim was an amazing high-school athlete. He was a legend around Northridge, referred to only as 'the man.' He averaged thirty-six points a game his senior year and holds the Dayton-area single-game scoring record with fifty-seven points. Many people felt Jim was good enough, and was destined, to play in the NBA. He was such a big deal that, when he got into college on a basketball scholarship, it was reported in the *Washington Post*. In a 1980 article entitled 'College Recruiters Look to Next Year,' John Feinstein wrote, 'Arizona State signed an excellent guard in 6-2 Jim Pollard from Dayton, Ohio.' However, after being plagued by a series of injuries at Arizona State, he dropped out of college and returned to Dayton in 1982. Bob promptly asked him to join GBV.

By the time Pollard got around to making his debut LP, he was thirty years old and teaching fourth grade, and he had been married for years, with two kids and a house. When you imagine bands starting out, you picture kids in their twenties. The Who playing the Marquee Club, or The Strokes on the Lower East Side of New York, hanging out with models. You don't usually think of thirty-year-old schoolteachers who have kids. This would later prove an irresistible angle for journalists, and is one of the reasons why GBV broke so big, but at this point it was just another thing standing in Pollard's way.

By comparison, R.E.M.'s Michael Stipe—lead singer of a band Pollard liked and admired—was three years younger than Pollard. In 1987, Stipe was twenty-seven, and his group had already released five LPs. By the time Stipe turned thirty, R.E.M. would be one of the biggest bands in the world. And by the time the guys in The Beatles were thirty, they'd already broken up. So Pollard had a lot of catching up to do.

Forever Since Breakfast had been recorded at an expensive studio in Kentucky, costing Pollard and the guys three hundred dollars a night. And since that record failed to sell, or get any kind of attention, Bob had to find a cheap alternative to a high-end recording studio. The solution arrived in the form of a nearby eight-track studio called Nemesis Records run out of a garage. Owner Steve Wilbur, a Dayton local who was into bands like Iron Maiden and Megadeth, charged a reasonable fifteen dollars an hour. Plus, the fact that he lived right around the corner from Pollard, in an area known as Dixie Estates, was an added bonus. All or most of the next four GBV records would be recorded at Wilbur's. However, at least one song on *Devil Between My Toes*—the opening track— was recorded in Pollard's basement. This would pave the way for many more basement recordings, and offered a peek at what was to come for the band.

Bob produced the record, although, as time went on Wilbur provided input and even played guitar on subsequent albums. And while the overall sound of the LP is rough, it's not without its charms. Even though early GBV is usually compared to R.E.M., on *Devil* there's more of a post-punk influence. Another interesting thing is the way Pollard sings on the record. The English accent hasn't yet shown up, and there's no real affectation in his voice except a bit of country twang.

The original name of the record was *The Future Is In Eggs*. The title that was eventually chosen comes from the rooster that's seen on the cover. The rooster's name is Big Daddy. Pollard had bought the rooster for his son, Bryan. But when the rooster started misbehaving, he gave it to his neighbor, an older woman named Nana. The rooster continued to bother Pollard (at one point, Bob even called the cops on it) and the title came from that: Pollard was being pecked and said, 'I've got a devil between my toes!'

The cover—back when the LP was called *The Future Is In Eggs*—was going to be artwork done by a high-school friend featuring a cockfight, with a bunch of weird people in the audience. But Pollard couldn't locate the guy to draw it, so instead he settled on Mitch Mitchell's picture of Big Daddy. The photo's kind of blurry because it was taken through a chain-link fence, and the rooster was trying to attack Mitch when he took it. This same rooster comes up later in 'Don't Stop Now,' a song from 1996's *Under The Bushes Under The Stars*, when Pollard sings, 'Woke up one morning, saw a rooster struttin' by my house.' In the next verse, Pollard references the rooster directly, asking, 'What keeps Big Daddy happy?' This is only slightly different from the *Devil Between*

My Toes subtitle, which is printed right on the cover of the record, 'What makes Big Daddy happy?'

The cover also has a drawing, but it may have been cut out of something and just pasted on. It isn't credited on the sleeve. Not counting the compilation record *King Shit & The Golden Boys*, which was part of the Scat box set in 1995, *Devil Between My Toes* is the only GBV cover that's just black-and-white.

The back cover features an illustration of a guy pulling a mule. It's not a Pollard collage, but it has a sort of 50s textbook vibe, like the boxers on the back of *Propeller*. Maybe Pollard thought that the man's struggle was what he was feeling as he tried to make a go of being in a band. Or maybe he just liked it as an image. Either way, the GBV visual aesthetic was beginning to form.

Pollard issued *Devil* on Schwa Records. *Schwa* is a phonetic term; it's that upside-down and backward *e* you find in dictionaries (it signifies the sound of an *a* in *alone* and *sofa*). There was already another Schwa Records, out of Chicago, that released punk records in the early 80s and put out a cassette as late as 1985. The LP was initially released only on vinyl, and each of its two sides had names, instead of just being labeled A and B or 1 and 2. The sides are named 'Buckeye' and 'Briar.' A buckeye is a North American tree or shrub related to the horse chestnut. It's also the state tree and the mascot of Ohio State University. A briar is a prickly plant or shrub. It's also slang for somebody who's a hillbilly, including the 'mountain men' Pollard sings about on the record.

Since nothing prior to 1993's *The Grand Hour* received any sort of national distribution, *Devil Between My Toes* was available only at a few local stores: Gem City, Renaissance, Goldenrod Records, and Omega. Pollard mentioned only one person, his assistant principal, buying the record and liking it. And just to place *Devil Between My Toes* into a musical context, some of the big college rock records of this year were The Cure's *Kiss Me Kiss Me Kiss Me*, Depeche Mode's *Music For The Masses*, The Smiths' *Strangeways Here We Come*, R.E.M.'s *Document*, and U2's *The Joshua Tree*. *Devil Between My Toes* doesn't match up to any of those bands, except possibly R.E.M. This shows that Pollard, for most of his career, has existed outside of any sort of popular scene or contemporary influence. Even later on, when they were lumped in with lo-fi bands, or even the indie-rock scene in general, Pollard and GBV had their own sound and aesthetic. And it all started with this LP.

SIDE ONE

Track one: *'Old Battery'*

This is the one song on the record that was recorded in Pollard's basement. It makes total sense that the first song on the first GBV album is a basement recording. Bob's voice actually reminds me of Devo (specifically, Gerald Casale singing 'Beautiful World'). Pollard has talked a lot about his love of Devo, and it's an influence you hear a bit in GBV. Bob's said that 'Old Battery' is about mortality and how people find religion late in life, just in case. He's also mentioned that when he played the song for Tobin Sprout, Toby immediately asked him to play it again.

Track two: *'Discussing Wallace Chambers'*

Wallace Chambers was a football player who played for the Bears and then the Buccaneers in the 70s. For college he went to Eastern Kentucky University, and since Kentucky is just south of Ohio and Pollard played sports growing up, it makes sense that Bob would know who Chambers was. This is another song that's similar to Devo, especially the background vocals.

Track three: *'Cyclops'*

This song features a spidery guitar and a martial drumbeat, as Pollard sings of a cyclops with 'no depth perception.' But this isn't the creature of Greek mythology who was born with just one eye. Instead, this is a regular guy named Tom who has 'one eye on the mend' and 'one eye on his watch.' He knows that time is running out, and even though his parents try to reassure him, telling him, 'Don't worry, Tom, there's plenty of jobs in the big city,' Tom knows how difficult it's going to be to find work while injured. This is Pollard in empathetic mode, writing with real insight and sympathy for those who are deemed different by society. It's a theme that crops up again and again in his work, as recently as 2019's 'Send In The Suicide Squad,' not to mention classics like 'Redmen And Their Wives' and 'Xeno Pariah.'

Track four: *'Crux'*

This is the first of five instrumentals that appear on the record. And while some of the others are impressionistic sketches, this one feels very much like a backing track that Pollard could have easily put vocals to. It's puzzling why Pollard would include instrumentals on his debut album, not to mention so many of them. *Sandbox* would be recorded that same year, so he presumably had those songs written and ready to go. Plus, this is the guy with the 'suitcase' full of songs, so why have nearly a third of the record be instrumental? My guess would be that he was trying out different sounds in the studio, experimenting with forms and genres. GBV were still a young band, and maybe Pollard hadn't decided which way to take them. He had an abundance of influences—Wire, The Rolling Stones, King Crimson, The Kinks—and was still in the process of deciding what he would take, and what he would ignore, from his various heroes, and you hear that searching all over the album.

Track five: *'A Portrait Destroyed By Fire'*

At 5:09, this is by far the record's longest song. It's also the most interesting, with an opening that sounds very Joy Division or early Cure. But the background vocals on the verses make it sound sort of prog. Even within one song, you hear Pollard trying out a variety of styles. Lyrically, Bob's said the song is about spousal abuse: 'Yelling and hitting and that sort of thing.' In the line 'Rings of gold and rings of blue,' he explains, 'those are bruises.' There's a chilling point in the track where the abuser, having long rationalized away his actions by telling his wife, 'It hurts me worse than it hurts you,' finally realizes 'that's not true.' Spousal abuse also made an appearance on the final song of the *Forever Since Breakfast* EP, 'The Other Place,' where Pollard writes, 'A little boy stepping in front of his mom when his dad starts to beat her.' Since this kind of realism wasn't dealt with again beyond these first few records, you have to wonder whether Bob later retreated into more surrealistic language to escape the depressing reality he saw around him.

Track six: *'3 Year Old Man'*

This short instrumental closes out side one. And unlike the earlier track 'Crux,' which felt a bit more fully formed, this one feels like an exercise or sketch. It's nothing but a heavily reverbed guitar and some bass.

SIDE TWO

Track one: *'Dog's Out'*

This track, coming after the last four songs on side one, which leaned heavily toward a cold, post-punk sound, returns to the poppier territory of the album's opening. It features some strong vocal harmonies and lyrics that chronicle the plight of the workingman, Pollard writing that he 'must get high working that line.' Bob knew plenty of people, including his own brother, who worked in factories and on assembly lines. And, while he's often espoused the benefits of alcohol to get through tough times, here he's saying that getting stoned also helps deal with a difficult reality.

Track two: *'A Proud And Booming Industry'*

This is the shortest instrumental on the record. It's also one of the barest, being just a minute of moody electric guitar. A different song with the same title was intended to be the B-side to a single for the track 'Captain's Dead.' That version—which finally saw the light of day on *Suitcase 2*—borders on kitchen-sink parody, with its lines about 'union reps' and an 'industrial town in the morning.' And even though Pollard's often been dismissive of Bruce Springsteen, in the alternate version of 'A Proud And Booming Industry' (also known as 'Industrial Morning'), he's tapping into the same blue-collar struggles that the Boss has often chronicled.

Track three: *'Hank's Little Fingers'*

This is easily my favorite song on the album, with some driving guitar, a great vocal by Pollard, and an insanely catchy chorus. It's about a guy he knew, named Hank, who had a birth defect. He had little fingers on his right hand, and he played guitar by attaching a pick to his hand with a rubber band. The fact that he was good—and didn't let his disability stop him—inspired Bob to play guitar, not to mention write the song. But it's also about paying respects to people that Pollard knew while growing up in Northridge. He knew how people looked at rednecks, not to mention how the rest of the country looked at Ohio. Think of a song like 'The Big Country' by Talking Heads, where David Byrne writes, looking out the window of a plane, 'It's not even worth talking about those people down there.' It's that classic 'flyover state' mentality.

But Pollard, here and elsewhere, defends these people, challenging, 'Unless you got the answers, don't patronize the mountain man.'

Track four: 'Artboat'

This two-and-a-half-minute instrumental has almost a Throbbing Gristle or Einstürzende Neubauten vibe. It's genuinely odd and is probably the least GBV-sounding song to ever appear on a GBV record. And to think that Bob was shooting for rock stardom, and yet was putting things like this on his band's debut LP, shows a stubborn (if not suicidal) adherence to an aesthetic vision that would appear time and time again over the course of his career.

Track five: 'Hey Hey, Spacemen'

Bouncing back from the dourness of the previous track, this fun song is jaunty in an 'Echos Myron' way. I'm not sure if the 'Jimmy' referenced in the lyrics is Pollard's brother, but it probably is, since Jim has four co-writes on the record and was a big part of the band during these early years. In its praise of 'camaraderie,' the song's connected to other GBV anthems about brotherhood and solidarity, the most famous being 'A Salty Salute.' But it also cites a 'carefree world of opportunity' and meeting up after school, showing how such groups get together in the first place; the Monument Club got its start as a tree house.

Track six: 'The Tumblers'

This sleepy song has some interesting effects that sound like a Martin Hannett production. The drums have no cymbals, just toms, and the guitar has a free-flowing sort of jangle that wouldn't be heard again until Doug Gillard joined the band a decade later. Some of the lyrics begin to hint at the wordplay that would end up becoming Pollard's trademark, such as 'Don't mistake your mistake for my mistake.'

Track seven: 'Bread Alone'

This is the final instrumental on the record. It's basically just a song sketch on an acoustic guitar. Just to show how full circle things have come for Pollard, it's not at all dissimilar to the title track from 2019's *Zeppelin Over China*.

Track eight: *'Captain's Dead'*

Of the fourteen tracks on the record, this is the most widely known because it's also on 2003's GBV best-of, *Human Amusements At Hourly Rates*. It's also the one track on the album that hints at the band's eventual sound. Because while they'd sometimes return to the musical playfulness of 'Hey Hey, Spaceman,' or the lyrical ideas found in 'Hank's Little Fingers,' the hard-charging rock of 'Captain's Dead' is what GBV—over their thirty-year career (and counting)— would become known for. You can hear echoes of 'Captain's Dead' in later classics like 'Game Of Pricks' and 'Cut-Out Witch.' Meanwhile, the moody post-punk instrumentals that cropped up throughout *Devil Between My Toes* would disappear completely. Bob seemed to have found, on this song—if not the whole album—the sound he was looking for.

02 SANDBOX

nineteen eighty-seven

T he band's second album was their bid for stardom. It has a slick cover and was meant to look like a release from a major label. This is how and where the band were going to go legit: with a polished power-pop record. And yet, even though the LP didn't quite achieve what Pollard and the band hoped— like every other pre-*Propeller* album, *Sandbox* didn't sell more than a handful of copies—and despite Bob later decrying the album as overproduced, it has some quality songs and is a solid listen throughout. The sound and tone don't at all match GBV's later work—on more than a few songs, Bob's singing in a Southern accent—and yet you can still find kernels of the classic Guided By Voices aesthetic all over the record. 'Barricade' shows off Pollard's burgeoning love of wordplay, and is in several different parts, which means it foreshadows future prog-inspired classics like 'Over The Neptune / Mesh Gear Fox.'

GBV also produced two LPs in one year, which proves that Pollard had begun to love recording and making records. It was something he was determined to do, despite the fact that no one had positively reacted to either *Devil Between My Toes* or the *Forever Since Breakfast* EP. He didn't care. He was now on a quest to capture what he heard in his head. And if the results weren't perfect, that's okay, because *Sandbox* spurred Bob on to push himself and try harder.

Unlike *Devil Between My Toes*, which was released on Schwa Records, *Sandbox* was issued on another newly minted Bob label, Halo. The Halo logo, as Pollard designed it, is the word in a kind of italic script beneath what looks like a hand-drawn halo with some light emanating from it. I'm not sure if this is a tongue-in-cheek reference to religion or whether Pollard's sincere in his belief—and promotion of halos and angels. Because while he's never shown himself to be devout, religious symbolism—both overt and merely alluded to—have cropped up in his work repeatedly.

Another change from the previous album is that Tobin Sprout had nothing to do with it. He's 'thanked,' but he doesn't play on any of the songs. Also gone from the last record is drummer Peyton Eric. Instead, Kevin Fennell drums on all the album's twelve tracks. Mitch is still on bass, while Bob again handles almost all the guitar. And even though producer Steve Wilbur plays lead on a few tracks, and Bob's brother plays on a lot of the songs, this is about as small as Guided By Voices would ever get. The band's essentially a power trio, with Bob on guitar and vocals, Mitch on bass, and Kevin on drums.

The band photo on the cover was taken by Bruce Greenwald. Bruce would later be listed as 'crew' on the *Get Out Of My Stations* EP, and he also gets thanked on *Bee Thousand* and the *Forever Since Breakfast* EP. The picture shows Bob, his brother, Mitch, and Kevin lounging on a lawn. There's some stuff in the background, including a statue and a windmill. Of the four, Kevin looks the coolest, leaning back and resting on his elbows, with bare feet. Pollard's looking at the camera, kind of skeptically. He's holding a bottle of wine, or maybe it's a big bottle of beer. Whatever it is, it's certainly not a can of Miller Lite, the drink that later became associated with the band. Mitch looks very 80s in a yellow polo shirt. His hair's also kind of short; he actually looks sort of preppy. Jim, wearing a striped T-shirt, is barely in the photo. The front also has a drawing of a nymph, which was done by Mark Greenwald, who is presumably Bruce's brother. He's also the same guy who did the drawing of the sun on *Forever Since Breakfast*.

The back cover features four more photos of the guys. These were probably taken the same day as the cover photo, since they're all wearing the same clothes (and Kevin's still not wearing shoes). The photos aren't too bad, and the song titles, displayed in a big font, look kind of cool. As a package, it definitely looks more like a professional record than their debut.

During the recording of *Sandbox*, Pollard started hanging around with Greg Demos. He was the bass player who—along with Tobin Sprout, Mitch

Mitchell, and Kevin Fennell—would later form the so-called classic lineup. At the time, Demos was playing guitar in a band called The New Creatures. Bob had met him at a New Creatures show in 1986, and, by 1987, Demos's band were recording at Steve Wilbur's studio while GBV were making *Sandbox*.

The New Creatures are thanked on the *Sandbox* sleeve, along with a whole bunch of other people, including Bob's wife and kids. Pete Jamison, an old friend of Pollard's, is listed as the group's manager. He didn't manage much on a day-to-day basis, since they weren't playing live, and Bob wouldn't let anyone do anything promotional for the early records. Still, Jamison was hugely important to the story of Guided By Voices. Even Pollard has admitted this, saying that, without Jamison, GBV wouldn't exist. That goes for *Sandbox*, too. Because, to pay for *Sandbox*'s thousand copies, Bob, Jimmy, and Pete took out a loan from the Teachers Credit Union. After being initially turned down, Pete remembered that his mom had a mortgage with the bank, which meant that her signature was on file. So he asked, 'What if my mom's name was on the loan?' And the manager, who was also in bands, took pity on them. That loan not only paid for *Sandbox* but would be renewed and repaid over and over again, supplying the capital for the rest of the band's self-released recordings.

Sandbox is credited on the sleeve as 'A Production Of … Gotham City Music.' There was also an insert that said, at the top, 'Gotham City Music Presents.' Below this were photos and descriptions of all the GBV and GBV-related releases up to that point, in addition to records by The New Creatures and Tobin Sprout's group Fig. 4. As Matthew Cutter writes in *Closer You Are*, 'Lacking a scene, they made their own.'

The scheme partly worked, since *Sandbox* is the only one of the five self-released records to get any kind of contemporary reviews, including a mention in *Spin*. This was in the January 1989 issue, and was part of a column named 'Underground,' which took a monthly look at independent bands all across the country. The column was written by Byron Coley, who normally wrote for the zine *Forced Exposure*. The zine's now long gone, but the Forced Exposure name lives on as a mail-order website.

The *Spin* column that featured Guided By Voices also included several other bands that would become important to the indie scene, such as Beat Happening, Galaxie 500, and Screaming Trees. Coley describes GBV as 'one of the sharpest sounding angle-pop bands out of the Midwest.' He also writes that GBV play 'the hardball pop game like a field of kangaroos, hopping from stroke to riff.' He finally refers to them as 'Beatlesesque.'

At the time, *Spin* was a big magazine, with a circulation of a couple hundred thousand (U2 were on the cover of the issue GBV was featured in). And, while it wasn't as big as *Rolling Stone*, *Spin* was a lot hipper. This would be the biggest and best press mention GBV would get until they started getting reviews for their Scat releases in 1993.

Another interesting bit about the Gotham City insert is that it mentions a Pollard release that never came out. A six-song EP called *The Everlasting Big Kick* was going to be credited to just Robert Pollard, not Guided By Voices. This was about ten years before his actual solo debut LP, *Not In My Airforce*. Among the six songs that were going to be included on the EP were 'Stumbling Blocks To Stepping Stones,' 'Once In A While,' and 'Bird.' 'Once In A While' can be found on the first *Suitcase* compilation, but the others aren't widely available. And, just to show how interconnected the Pollardverse is, the phrase 'everlasting big kick' would crop up later in the song 'The Enemy,' from 2001's *Isolation Drills*. Everlasting Big Kick is also the name of a Guided By Voices cover band operating out of New York City.

SIDE ONE
Track one: *'Lips Of Steel'*

This track starts with a guitar that sounds a bit like 'You Really Got Me' by The Kinks. And while the bass is kind of cheesy, the drums feature lots of fills and a 4/4 beat. Gone are the post-punk experiments of *Devil Between My Toes*. The song seems to be partially about a band, saying, 'Let's go see the show,' and ending with an announcement hyping a group, Pollard declaring—in a sort of radio DJ voice—'Ladies and Gentleman, back by popular demand for your entertainment and spiritual enlightenment, Electric Jam Soul Aquarium!' Also, the line 'We're on our way' is answered later with 'We're finally here' in 'Echos Myron.'

Track two: *'A Visit To The Creep Doctor'*

This is a strong track that shows drummer Kevin Fennell putting in a great performance with fill after fill. Pollard's Southern accent makes the track reminiscent of R.E.M. circa *Lifes Rich Pageant* (which had been released the previous year). With strong rock songs like this, it's hard to believe that GBV couldn't get any traction on the local scene.

Track three: *'Everyday'*

The opening to this track sounds just like the 1985 song 'Love Vigilantes' by New Order, while the guitars, especially on the verses, are again similar to R.E.M. The straightforward nature of the song's subject matter, and the way Pollard presents ordinary life, stand apart from almost everything he ever wrote. The opening line, 'Clouds of industrial waste rise up to obscure God's very blue sky,' is also interesting in terms of how Bob's writing about religion.

Does Pollard actually believe in God, not to mention that God's the one who made the sky blue? A few lines later, he says, 'Lines of shopping mothers grabbing their kids, pushing up to the front / Rows of pretty little houses and lawns, I want you to have a beautiful one.' Ten years later, on *OK Computer*, Radiohead would talk about 'such a pretty house, and such a pretty garden.' That song is about the deal you make with the system to get what you want; that 'handshake of carbon monoxide' will make you happy today, but it might kill you tomorrow. Pollard's talking about that here, too. Whether you're paying for it directly, like when Pollard writes about 'money burning through the exhaust pipe,' or in a larger sense by having to live with industrial waste that blots out the blue sky.

Track four: *'Barricade'*

At four and a half minutes, this is the longest song on the record. It's also, with its various parts, another example of Pollard showing his prog influence. The lines in a middle section, 'Little child, little child, won't you dance with me?' are a direct lift—you can't even call it a reference—to The Beatles' song 'Little Child' from 1963, which starts with those exact lines. Pollard's talked a lot about loving The Beatles, and, when compiling his top ten records of all time for *Jane* magazine, he listed two Beatles LPs, *The White Album* and *Abbey Road*.

They're definitely an influence you can hear later in GBV, in both the short poppy songs and the way he sings with an English accent. In fact, he's almost getting to that accent on some of this song. The track also has a guitar solo from Steve Wilbur, which adds some welcome melodic color as it fades out.

Track five: 'Get To The Know The Ropes'

This slower song recalls some of the post-punk vibe of the band's debut, with the kind of gated reverb snare sound that's all over Joy Division's *Unknown Pleasures*. And, since the group from the first song, Electric Jam Soul Aquarium, is recalled at the end this track, it harkens back to *Sgt. Pepper*, where the fictitious band is introduced at the album's opening and then given a reprise at the end.

SIDE TWO

Track one: 'Can't Stop'

This rocker is another song wherein Pollard has a decently pronounced Southern accent. There are some strong melodic moments, like when he sings, 'You never really had to look through me' over jangly guitar. The track also captures Bob's ambivalence toward being in the band; 'I know I'm wasting time,' he writes, and yet he just 'can't stop.' This sentiment would also be reflected in later songs such as 'Don't Stop Now' and 'Keep It In Motion.' But, with its repeated use of the words 'baby' and 'babe,' you can see that Pollard, at this point, was still writing within standard rock'n'roll idiom.

Track two: 'The Drinking Jim Crow'

The way Bob sings this, dragging out the beginning of the lines 'I have emotional scars' and 'I don't understand what you're saying,' is very similar to the way he'd sing 'Everywhere With Helicopter' more than two decades later. The title, 'The Drinking Jim Crow,' is both a pun on Jim Beam whiskey as well as a reference to the 'Jim Crow' laws, which kept segregation in place for a large part of the United States in the late nineteenth and early twentieth centuries. And while it's not exactly in good taste for a song that already has a reference to slavery in it to mention 'the master of races,' as Pollard does here, he seems to signal which side he's on by calling America, earlier in the track, a 'nasty little nation.'

Track three: 'Trap Soul Door'

This brief song—at 1:15, it's the shortest track on the album—is similar to 'Game Of Pricks.' In that track, Pollard writes, 'I never asked for the truth, but you owe that to me,' while in this song, over a sparse musical accompaniment, he declares, 'I'm still wrong, but you're still a liar.'

Track four: 'Common Rebels'

For the first minute of this 2:03 song, Pollard sings in an exaggerated and clipped manner he wouldn't employ on any other GBV track. The music's also abrupt and staccato, with the drums sounding like a faster version of Joy Division's 'Atmosphere.' The lyrics are also out of the ordinary, with Pollard referring in the opening line to 'Pab Picasso,' and then making a fun joke, 'Count the *quesos*.' And while the track's an experiment that doesn't quite work, it's interesting to hear Bob and the guys try out different styles.

Track five: 'Long Distance Man'

This gorgeous folk song, with its layered harmonies, sounds a lot like a number of acoustic Beatles tracks from the mid 60s, such as 'You're Gonna Lose That Girl.' And the title, of course, is similar to 'Nowhere Man.' And while, at 1:17, the song feels somewhat incomplete, it's a pleasant and solid track.

Track six: 'I Certainly Hope Not'

This song's a plea to someone to not give up, Pollard first asking, 'Are you quitting?' and instantly following this with the repeated and soaring chorus of 'I certainly hope not.' Since Pollard's a guy who would later pack his songs with fantasy imagery and surreal wordplay, I love the realism and the plainspoken language of some of these early songs. And, similar to the sentiment found in the next track, even though people try to help by giving advice, all that just gets 'in the way.'

The song ends with the repeated refrain, 'Attracted to the light, where everything will be alright.' This could be taken two ways. Light is often used to represent passing over into death (people who have had near-death experiences say that dying is like going into a bright white light). And, of course, once you're dead, your troubles go away. So Pollard might mean that the only relief or escape for his character is death. However, 'light' here could also be a metaphor for knowledge; perhaps, by attaining that knowledge, the character achieves freedom.

Track seven: *'Adverse Wind'*

This fast song features great drumming and an anthemic chorus. The only bad thing about it is the production. The overall sound is tinny, and the drums just don't pack the wallop you know they did when they were played live. Despite this, it's an enjoyable track. If it were slipped into GBV's current live set, it wouldn't at all sound out of place. Lyrically, 'Adverse Wind' touches upon a theme Pollard's written about his entire career (not to mention in the prior song), which is how we're all defenseless in the face of fate. We all want to be free, and have smooth sailing in our lives, but that's hard to do when you're facing the 'adverse winds' Pollard writes about here. The subject of the song is a crying woman who lives 'in solitude.' He can't reach her and, more importantly, he can't help her. Instead, she's 'dying,' because, similar to 'I Certainly Hope Not,' she's 'relying' on what 'the people say.' Pollard, always a skeptic, mistrusts the status quo, not to mention the same old advice everyone gives, and yet he's a 'lifetime away.' He can only watch as she wrestles with, and tries to make her way through, life.

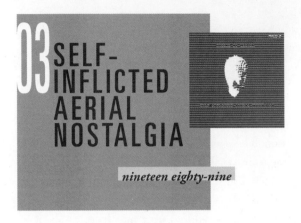

03 SELF-INFLICTED AERIAL NOSTALGIA

nineteen eighty-nine

G BV didn't release anything in 1988, but they returned the following year with their third LP. Big college-rock records that same year were The Cure's *Disintegration*, *Doolittle* by the Pixies, The Jesus & Mary Chain's *Automatic*, and debut records by Nine Inch Nails, The Stone Roses, and Nirvana. The year prior had even seen one of Pollard's favorite bands, R.E.M., make their leap to a major label, signing with Warner Bros to release their sixth album, *Green*.

Warner Bros would end up being one of the labels that lobbied hard to sign GBV after their own success with *Bee Thousand*. Pollard could have followed in R.E.M.'s footsteps, but instead he opted to sign with Matador, the indie-rock powerhouse that was founded by Chris Lombardi the year *Self-Inflicted Aerial Nostalgia* was released. In fact, this same year saw the debuts of a number of bands that GBV would later be compared to, and lumped in with. The Grifters, known at the time as A Band Called Bud, released the cassette full-length *Dad* on Doink Records; Sebadoh's first LP, *The Freed Man*, came out on Homestead Records, which was run at the time by Gerard Cosloy, who would join Matador the following year; and Pavement's debut EP, *Slay Tracks*, released on their own Treble Kicker label, also came out in 1989.

So, even though GBV existed outside of any scene and seemingly had no contemporaries, the groundwork was being laid for their eventual success. Not, of course, that the group knew it at the time. Because, even though their previous LP had received a bit of attention, the band still weren't playing live, and Bob had forbidden manager Pete Jamison to lobby too hard on the group's behalf. Pollard had been stung by early reactions in Dayton, not to mention from his family (who seemed to have no faith in him or his abilities), all of which gave this period a weird push-pull dynamic. Bob obviously wanted to make it as a band and as a musician, yet he lacked the confidence to put himself out there. Even when GBV finally got their big break in 1992, it would be not because of Pollard's promotional efforts but rather in spite of the lack of them.

Aerial Nostalgia was not actually slated to be the band's third record. In 1988, GBV were set to release an LP called *Learning To Hunt* (in true GBV fashion, the song 'Learning To Hunt' wasn't on the album; it wouldn't show up until 1997's *Mag Earwhig!*). The album was mixed, mastered, and ready to go before Pollard pulled the plug. However, five of its proposed fourteen songs ended up on what became their next record: 'Slopes Of Big Ugly,' 'Paper Girl,' 'The Qualifying Remainder,' 'Liar's Tale,' and 'Short On Posters.' The remaining *Learning To Hunt* tracks ended up on either *King Shit & The Golden Boys* or else on one of the *Suitcases*. Bob's said of the proposed LP, 'It might have been a better album than *Self-Inflicted Aerial Nostalgia*.'

Pulling a record at the last minute, or else changing it drastically, is something Pollard would go on to do throughout his career. This means he might make a double record a single, or change out half an album's songs. The Guided By Voices database (located at gbvdb.com) has a section called 'What if,' listing all the aborted and work-in-progress GBV projects. It's a long list, since Pollard has done this dozens of times. This shows that Bob actually *does* have an editor. That he's *not* just slapping stuff together and putting out every song he records. Since the *Suitcases* hold four hundred songs at this point, there's a whole bunch of stuff he's leaving off records. He could make *every* album a triple record if he wanted to.

That's not to say that everything he releases is a gem. Not by a long shot. But whatever Pollard puts out is part of his vision. You may not like his vision, or understand it, or want to experience every single bit of it, but it's all done on purpose. The records are just how Pollard wants them, warts and all.

As with all of the pre-Scat records, *Aerial Nostalgia* was available in only a handful of record stores in and around Dayton, not that they ever sold much. Pollard made note of the lack of traction for these early records in a later interview. 'Well, a few years back I went to collect consignment on some of our records in a Columbus store and some smart-ass chick there remarked with a smirk on her face that we hadn't sold any.'

Originals of those early LPs are now worth hundreds of dollars. But while it's great for an artist to receive eventual recognition for their work, that's cold comfort during the period when people just don't get it. Alfred Hitchcock once said that all of his films went from being failures to masterpieces without being successes. The same could be said for the first part of GBV's recording career.

Aerial Nostalgia appeared on Halo Records, a holdover from the last LP. The record was released on black vinyl, but only five hundred copies were pressed.

The same Gotham City Music insert from *Sandbox* was included with *Aerial Nostalgia*. (The back cover also has the Gotham City Music logo.) However, it hadn't been updated to include the most recent GBV record, and Gotham City Music would never again be mentioned after this album, so Pollard's tenure as the Dayton version of Tony Wilson seems to have been a short one.

The band lineup had shifted yet again. Kevin Fennell is gone, and Peyton Eric is back on drums (along with Bruce Smith, who plays on one song). Mitch Mitchell's not even there, with Steve Wilbur playing bass. That being said, both Kevin and Mitch are credited with 'additional musical assistance.' Guitar's handled by just Bob and his brother. The liner notes are the usual assortment of thanks to their friends at the time. Writer Byron Coley, who wrote the *Spin* piece about *Sandbox*, is also thanked.

The album was recorded yet again at Steve Wilbur's eight-track studio. This is probably because, even though he'd been part of the first record, Tobin Sprout had moved to Florida with his family during this time. And since Tobin had the most experience of recording at home—he was the one with the four-track—they kept going to Wilbur's eight-track studio because they had to. This meant that, in addition to paying for the production of the actual records, they were also spending money while recording. Sure, it was cheap, but even at fifteen dollars an hour, that's going to add up.

Clocking in at 37:48, *Aerial Nostalgia* would be the longest GBV album until *Alien Lanes* in 1995. One reason for the record's duration is longer songs. Only two of *Aerial Nostalgia*'s fourteen songs are under two minutes, whereas about seven were that short on *Sandbox*. Another factor was that Bob wanted to use the best tracks from the unreleased *Learning To Hunt* LP. Plus, since it'd been two years since the band's last album, he had been stockpiling songs.

The LP's cover is also a total 180 from the previous record. Whereas *Sandbox* had a photo of the band, along with more shots of Pollard and the guys on the back, *Aerial Nostalgia* just has a big splash of yellow and the band's name, and the record's title in a typewritten font. In the center of the cover there's a photo of an object that looks like a piece of sculpture or a mask.

The mustard-yellow background on the front cover makes this the brightest of all the GBV sleeves. The back, by contrast, is in black-and-white. The song titles are in the same font, and they're flanked on either side by photos of rows of houses or buildings. At the very top—floating over the songs—is the figure of a man who's either flying or falling. And while the three elements are far apart, that they've been cut out of a magazine, or from a larger photo, is a nod toward the collages Pollard would use on future GBV records. This is also the first GBV LP to solely credit Pollard with the art.

The title doesn't seem to have any real meaning; I think it's just another example of Pollard leaving literal language behind and having words be either purely poetic or surrealistic. Songs like 'Everyday' or 'The Other Place,' with lyrics that sketch scenes from everyday life, were beginning to appear less and less. Instead, we're getting glimpses of fantasy and myth, with mentions of kings and wizards and some of the stuff that GBV would later be associated with, for better or worse.

SIDE ONE

Track one: *'The Future Is In Eggs'*

This post-punk track—the drums once again sound like Joy Division's 'Atmosphere'—is a puzzling choice for the album opener. It's slow and doesn't have any discernible structure, and right in the middle there's a forty-second segment where nothing happens except electric guitar slashes that sound like Jonny Greenwood's right before the choruses in Radiohead's 'Creep.' The phrase 'the future is in eggs'—which had been the working title for GBV's first LP—is repeated a few times, as is the word 'smiling' and the phrase 'all coalition, some nutrition.' It doesn't add up to much.

Track two: 'The Great Blake Street Canoe Race'

The vocals throughout this song are double-tracked, with Pollard providing some pleasant harmonies, especially on the chorus. The lyrics show Bob once again in a reflective mode, writing about daily life 'falling apart before our eyes' and how all that's left for him to do now is learn old things, repress his feelings, and 'fake' his mind away. It's as if he's wondering, a few years into his thirties, 'Is this all there is to life?' The title's taken from a street where the tough guys hung out in Pollard's hometown.

Track three: 'Slopes Of Big Ugly'

Like the album opener, this improvised song doesn't go anywhere, and it's not a lot of fun to listen to. Even at this early stage of the band, Pollard knew how to write fully formed songs, and yet I think he liked including unfinished material like this to challenge the listener. It's something he has done throughout his career (a tactic perhaps reaching its zenith on the ultra lo-fi Teenage Guitar records). He's often cited Wire's somewhat-difficult third record *154* as being his all-time favorite, so I see the inclusion of this kind of track as a sort of homage.

Track four: 'Paper Girl'

After a thirty-second abrasive opening featuring distorted guitar and drums, this turns into a quiet folk song with Pollard on acoustic guitar. It sounds very Beatles-esque, with tambourine and background vocals. *Suitcase 2* features a different version, with more of a full-band sound. Another difference is that on the *Suitcase* version Pollard doesn't flesh out the metaphor of the title. On *Aerial Nostalgia*, Bob says that the 'Paper Girl' falls 'apart so easily' and is going to 'blow away.' Whereas, on the *Suitcase* take, the lyrics paint a more straightforward scene of romance gone wrong.

Track five: *'Navigating Flood Regions'*

This hard rocker, with its one-string riff, is awfully similar to the later classic 'Postal Blowfish.' Pollard's hometown of Dayton was founded along the Great Miami River, with most of downtown Dayton built in the river's natural floodplain. In the nineteenth century, Dayton experienced major floods every decade. The worst flood ever was the Great Dayton Flood. During one week in late March 1913, over 65,000 people were displaced, 20,000 homes were destroyed, and over 360 people died.

Track six: *'An Earful O' Wax'*

A buildup of earwax can lead to sudden or partial hearing loss, which the song seems to be partly about, since Pollard sings, 'Hey, man, what was that you said? I'm going deaf.' It's an engaging song, and an interesting one, since it goes through a few different sections, and, at one point, Pollard's voice is treated with so much tremolo it's almost unrecognizable. Toward the end there's a guitar solo, courtesy of Steve Wilbur. There's also some strong drumming by Bruce Smith.

This song has never been played live, which is a shame, since this would rock in a concert setting. Also, at 4:22, it's the longest track on the record. The song provided the name for a GBV compilation put out by the German label Get Happy!! in 1993. And since 'wax' is also a slang term for vinyl, the LP's title takes on an additional meaning.

Track seven: *'White Whale'*

With its jangly guitar, this track sounds very R.E.M. And, with its mentions of 'dying for freedom' and marching with 'true soldiers,' it fits into the mold of Bob's many 'call to arms' songs. But, in a subtler way, it's about Pollard's own quest to become a musician and to be known for something other than being a fourth-grade teacher. He writes, 'You were nobody, now you're somebody.' Even though he hadn't managed to escape his hometown, Bob knew there was more to life than what was around him. And yet making that escape isn't going to be easy, since he adds, later in the song, 'You can't change the plan when it's made, but we have changed it.' You're presented with a plan for your life, and it sometimes appears to be set in stone. And yet, Pollard here is saying that he and the guys have 'changed it.' They're going to alter the small-town fate that's been assigned to them. They're in control.

SIDE TWO
Track one: 'Trampoline'

With its mention of a 'cooler of beer,' this may seem on the surface like a typical GBV tune, but a mention late in the song of an 'orgone machine' ties it to Pollard's interest—usually presented in his graphics—with medical fads and pseudo-science (the next record would have a phrenology diagram). Wilheim Reich developed his ideas about 'orgone' being a spiritual force in the 1930s. According to the website *Natural News*, 'Reich believed that traumatic experiences blocked the natural electrical flow of life energy in the body; this produced body armoring and in turn led to physical and emotional disease.'

Orgone accumulators, machines, or full-sized orgone boxes—which people would sit inside—were supposed to 'trap and then radiate' the 'magical orgone energy into a concentrated area.' The list of notable celebrities and intellectuals who dabbled with an orgone machine or box includes Allen Ginsberg, Henry Miller, William Burroughs, Norman Mailer, Saul Bellow, and Albert Einstein. Even fellow Ohioans Devo claimed that their iconic red energy-dome hats were designed to capture this mythical force, Mark Mothersbaugh saying, 'You probably know this very well, but your orgone energy goes out the top of your head and it dissipates out the top, but if you wear an energy dome it recycles that energy.' Even though the science around Reich's theories and the resulting devices have long been disputed, you can still buy a variety of orgone machines today.

Track two: 'Short On Posters'

This is a melodic song in the vein of some of GBV's early R.E.M.-influenced work. It's interesting to think about what would have happened to Guided By Voices if they'd stuck with or tried to push this sound for the rest of their career. The Paisley Underground scene was already out of steam by the late 80s, and, by this time, even R.E.M. had left behind their early sound. Grunge was just around the corner, and bands were getting heavier, not more jangly. So it's a good thing GBV took the turn they did.

Track three: *'Chief Barrel Belly'*

Pollard's said this song is about organized religion and being against it. Or at least against the idea that if you're immoral all week but then you go to church on Sunday, you're absolved of your sins. Musically, the track is sort of like Black Sabbath, although the chorus, which states that love's 'the one thing we need in all the world,' is similar to The Beatles' song 'The Word' from *Rubber Soul.*

Track four: *'Dying To Try This'*

This short song, featuring just Bob and an acoustic guitar, sounds like it was recorded at home. Also, the line 'Cigarette in one hand and a beer in the other' offers a perfect portrait of Pollard. However, the narrator never makes it clear exactly what it is he's 'dying to try,' making the track feel unresolved.

Track five: *'The Qualifying Remainder'*

Jim, Mitch, and Kevin all get a co-writing credit on this odd and tuneless track, so it was probably just some weird studio jam that Pollard set lyrics to. Musically, it's another one of GBV's early post-punk songs. For some reason, especially at the beginning, it makes me think of Siouxsie & The Banshees. I could see her belting out the lyrics, with Budgie behind her, pounding out the beat.

Track six: *'Liar's Tale'*

This is a slow and gorgeous song that features Pollard singing over a strummed electric guitar with a lot of tremolo. The opening perfectly sets the scene:

> *Let me tell you a story*
> *Conclusive, based on fact*
> *Long ago in the morning*
> *She left, did not come back*

Bob later interrupts his own story with a sort of meta commentary on its contents, writing, 'This tale is too long, the plot is weak and the characters wrong.'

This is one of the rare early songs that GBV played in their later concerts. It was part of their set lists from 1998 to 2004, with recorded versions appearing on *Live In Daytron* and on at least one bootleg. On a version posted to YouTube, Pollard mistakenly identifies it as being from their 1990 record *Same Place The Fly Got Smashed*, although he changes that title to *Same Place Michael Stipe Got Trashed*. The mistake is understandable, since GBV have so many records, and also because Bob sounds quite drunk in the clip.

Track seven: *'Radio Show (Trust The Wizard)'*

This track reminds me of The Who's mini-opera 'A Quick One While He's Away,' especially in the 'Alone he's alive he's alone he's alive' section. And, of course, toward the end, with the backward tracking, it sounds like The Beatles circa '66 or '67. Since the song's called 'Radio Show,' perhaps Bob meant for the disparate parts to sound like standalone songs you might hear while listening to the radio, with the Wizard being the DJ (again, Pollard favorites The Who made a whole record sound like a pirate radio show on *The Who Sell Out*). The last minute of the song consists of some strummed guitar that ends the song, and the record, on a perfect note (or, rather, chord).

04 SAME PLACE THE FLY GOT SMASHED

nineteen ninety

T his record is where the GBV sound—and the template for their later LPs—begins. It stands head and shoulders above the three other pre-*Propeller* records and is, in my mind, the first truly great Guided By Voices album. But it's also a bittersweet one, because Pollard would never be more discouraged about the band, or feel like more of a failure, than when he was making this record. He was getting increasingly pressured by his family to give up his expensive hobby. No one around him really liked his music, let alone understood his obsession. Pollard had lost money on everything GBV released, and they had nothing to show for all their effort except boxes of records Bob wouldn't let anyone hear and a couple of reviews, which were now a few years old.

But Pollard also knew that he was talented. He knew his songs were something special, and that if people could only hear them, he'd find the audience he was sure he deserved. Not that anyone else believed him. One day, during an argument with his parents, he said, 'I'll tell you what the fucking problem is. It's that I'm a fucking genius and nobody gives me any fucking credit for it.' To which his mom replied, 'At what?'

They had no idea what music meant to him, or even how good he was.

They thought he was just being Bobby, making up silly names for make-believe bands. Clinging to teenage dreams and living with his head in the clouds. He needed to wake up and face reality, be a better son, husband, and father. But Pollard wasn't quite ready to give up on his dream, so he kept on making records.

The thing that set this LP apart from the earlier albums is that it's a concept record. It deals with the life, and death, of an alcoholic. The website *Consequence Of Sound* talks about the record as 'not quite a rock opera, but certainly a concept album of sorts.' The concept, or thematic through line—while certainly there—is a bit hard to follow. Then again, so are Pollard favorites *Tommy* and *The Lamb Lies Down On Broadway*.

The fact that the record's about an alcoholic, with a whole bunch of songs touching on the subject, makes this as good a time as any to talk about how alcohol fits into the history and work of Guided By Voices.

Nick Mirov of *Pitchfork*, in a 1999 review of the Robert Pollard and Doug Gillard record *Speak Kindly Of Your Volunteer Fire Department*, talked about seeing GBV live: 'The band is drunk, the audience is drunk, the soundman is drunk, and the guy who sells the T-shirts is drunk.' It's one of the first things you hear about the band, that they play with a cooler onstage, and they're always swigging beers and tequila. One of their concerts even had a bartender onstage, serving the band shots. Lou Reed only mimicked shooting heroin onstage in the '70s—it was just an act—whereas Bob and the guys get wasted for real, right onstage before your eyes, every night. For some people who go to see the band in concert, that's probably part of the appeal. The idea that the whole show, at any moment, could go sideways, and Bob will fall over. Or else the concertgoer wants to be the one to get drunk and fall over. That certainly happens at GBV shows.

Some people might even say that Pollard and the group's love of alcohol gives them inspiration, and indeed fuels not only their concerts but their songwriting and recording. In his book *The Thirsty Muse: Alcohol And The American Writer*, Tom Dardis writes, 'It seems reasonable to ask if some link exists between alcohol and creativity.' He does this by looking at four American writers, all of whom were alcoholics: Eugene O'Neill, Ernest Hemingway, F. Scott Fitzgerald, and William Faulkner. Dardis concludes that contrary to helping their creativity, these writers drank because they couldn't be creative. The more Faulkner and Hemingway saw their powers diminish, the more they drank. Alcohol didn't fuel their best work. Instead, they drank because they knew their best work was behind them. Of the group, only Eugene O'Neill managed to quit drinking. Once he did, he wrote powerful plays about the danger and horrors of addiction, including *The Iceman Cometh* and *Long Day's Journey Into Night*.

Pollard's obviously never hit that sort of rock bottom, but I think it's dangerous to assume he needs to get drunk to do what he does. And, while *Same Place The Fly Got Smashed* certainly glorifies some aspects of alcoholism, that it ends in murder and death certainly shows the darker side of GBV's rock'n'roll good time. *Glide Magazine*'s Morgan Enos later acknowledged this, writing, 'Pollard would go on to populate his internal universe with elves, demons and robot boys to much applause, but [*Same Place The Fly Got Smashed*] is as real as it gets from a bunch of drinking buddies in Dayton.'

The record's title is one of the few where we know the origin and what it means, even though it seems like the usual Pollard non sequitur. According to GBV insider Rich Turiel, the title comes from a true story. 'Apparently somewhere in Bob's basement was a fly that was smashed against the wall. Several weeks later, Bob looked up and there was a dead spider in that spot but no fly. Hence, the spider was located in the same place the fly got smashed.' The phrase also appears on the record, in a song called 'Local Mix-Up.' And, because the subject of the record is alcohol, the word 'smashed' takes on a double meaning.

Same Place was released on yet another Pollard-created record label. Gone are Schwa and Halo; instead, *Same Place* appeared on Rocket #9 Records. Rocket #9 didn't last long. Pollard only issued one album—this one—on the imprint. There's a Sun Ra song called 'Rocket Number Nine Take Off For The Planet Venus,' from a 1966 record called *Interstellar Low Ways*. The name of that song was later shortened to just 'Rocket #9,' and it was re-released as a single on Sun Ra's own Saturn label in 1982. It was later covered by Yo La Tengo. And, while Pollard has never professed much love for jazz, I would think he'd find Sun Ra a kindred spirit. He was a maverick who followed his own path, released his own records, and, more importantly, built around him a complete universe of backstory and myth. Also, Pollard's lyrics, like Sun Ra's, are filled with references to aliens, spaceships, and UFOs. Another interesting coincidence is that the record on which the Sun Ra song first appeared, *Interstellar Low Ways*, was supposed to be called *Rocket #9*, and the sleeve featured a red-and-white drawing very similar to *Same Place The Fly Got Smashed*. On the GBV album, the drawing is of a person smoking. There's also a drawing of a clown, but it looks to have been cut out of something. It's one of the uglier GBV covers, sloppy and amateurish (even for GBV).

The back, also in red and white, features a series of circus tents (maybe the circus that the clown escaped from). Inside one of the tents is an illustration of an octopus. The band's name is also on the back in the same handwritten style as the cover. The octopus and the hand-drawn band name would go on to feature on a T-shirt design in the 90s that was brought back years later. Five hundred copies of the record were made, that number holding steady from the last release.

There wasn't a Gotham City Music insert this time around, and, in fact, there's no mention of Gotham City Music anywhere on the record. There was, however—for the first time—a lyric sheet. The design mimics the back cover of the LP, with the handwritten lyrics fitting inside the same circus tents that are seen on the back of the record. Despite this, words to three of the LP's songs are missing: 'When She Turns 50,' 'Club Molluska,' and 'Starboy.'

In terms of album personnel, Kevin and Mitch, frustrated that GBV weren't going anywhere, had left to join another local group. Fathom Theory were a hardcore band led by a guy named Frank Harmon. Harmon, the singer, would go on to be in a few other hardcore bands in Ohio, including Pawn and Twenty Third Chapter. Fathom Theory put out only one record, the seven-inch EP *Blinded By Hatred*, in 1992. The cover is a cheap approximation of Raymond Pettibon, the artist behind Black Flag's illustrations, while the back features a photo of the band. In the picture, Kevin looks kind of puffy while Mitch, along with the other two guys in the group, has a shaved head. Mitch and Kevin were replaced by the rhythm section from The New Creatures, Greg Demos on bass and Don Thrasher on drums. Also, since Tobin Sprout had returned to the area, he plays guitar on 'Blatant Doom Trip.' His contributions would prove crucial to the next five GBV records.

Same Place lists two producers, Fingston Redwing and Spider Blackhead—pseudonyms for Bob and Greg. The album was again mostly recorded at Steve Wilbur's eight-track garage studio in under a week. Three additional songs were recorded in Pollard's basement. It was Greg Demos's idea to pan the vocals and instruments so that, in some songs, you have the bass on the left channel and the vocals on the right. Bob initially hated the results, but now he likes it.

SIDE ONE

Track one: *'Airshow 88'*

The album kicks off with a snippet from a TV movie starring Lindsay Wagner called *Shattered Dreams*. The film, based on a true story, is about a battered wife who finally decides to leave her husband after years of abuse. That the film's about spousal abuse ties it to two songs from previous GBV records, 'A Portrait Destroyed By Fire' and 'The Other Place.' Once the song starts, we hear Pollard in full who-gives-a-fuck mode. His vocal is gloriously unhinged as he sings against an electric guitar. You almost get the sense that he's making up the words as he goes along. He also introduces the LP's theme of alcohol here by writing, 'We began drinking to forget about our jobs.'

Track two: *'Order For The New Slave Trade'*

Sound-wise, this is night and day compared to the first song. It features a full band, with new member Greg Demos adding a super-melodic bass line. The story continues, with the narrator saying, 'While crossing the parking lot a stranger approached me, handed me a gun.' This sets the stage for the death that leads to the later song 'Murder Charge.' The slow pace, and the song's general feel, foreshadows 'Circus World' on the band's next album, *Propeller*.

Track three: *'The Hard Way'*

This strong rocker has a lot going on in the lyrics, although when you're listening with headphones, the hard panning of the instruments and vocals is a bit distracting. Greg Demos has another incredible bass line in the track, proving quickly what an asset he was going to be to the band. I'm not sure how the lyrics relate to the story or concept of the record, but the chorus, 'Doing everything the hard way,' could be applied to GBV. Nothing was really going their way, and they weren't following the typical steps that bands follow to be successful. They had sort of given up, retreating to their basements and cheap garage studios.

Track four: 'Drinker's Peace'

This beautiful track, which is essentially a love song to liquor, features spare fingerpicked guitar and a great melody and vocal by Pollard. Bob talks here about the numbing power of alcohol, stating that, after a few drinks, he 'can't remember what the problem was.' It's a way to escape when life gets too real, or too hard to face. Pollard's characters are blue-collar workers who have been passed by for the American dream. His own brother almost became a professional athlete but now worked the night shift at General Motors. These were tough lives, people facing tough realities, so who can begrudge them having a few drinks to help them forget? Alcohol also lets them off the hook, making everything seem not so bad, Pollard writing that drinking reduces his 'felonies' to just 'misdemeanors.'

An alternate version of 'Drinker's Peace' was put out in 2015 by the Chicago label Bloodshot Records. The new version is interesting in that it's a bit faster and features a string section. If you ever wondered what a Robert Pollard version of 'Eleanor Rigby' would sound like, give it a listen.

Track five: 'Mammoth Cave'

In this full-band rock song, Pollard sings, 'You can dig my grave in Mammoth Cave.' Mammoth Cave is a real location. It's in Kentucky and consists of a series of underground caves and tunnels. It's about 250 miles from where Pollard lived and grew up. It's described, on the National Parks website, as a 'grand, gloomy, and peculiar place,' which means it fits in just right on this record.

Track six: 'When She Turns 50'

If you crank the volume on this acoustic song, or listen with headphones, it's like Pollard's right in front of you. Lyrically, it adds to the theme of the record with its mention of taverns and vodka.

Track seven: *'Club Molluska'*

This super-simple song—it's just electric guitar and vocals—is quite effective. Bob's ragged and heartfelt belting out of the refrain at the end, 'It's a runaway world,' shows why he's one of the great rock'n'roll singers. Lyrically, the song fits in well with the concept of the record, the narrator asking, 'Have you seen that girl with the bloodshot eyes?'

SIDE TWO

Track one: *'Pendulum'*

Pollard has called these lyrics his favorite ever, going so far as to add that, lyrically speaking, *Same Place The Fly Got Smashed* is his favorite album. The track opens with, 'Come on over tonight, we'll put on some Cat Butt and do it up right.' Cat Butt were a Seattle band who only existed for a few years. They formed in 1987 and broke up in 1990, putting out only one full-length record, *Journey To The Center Of.* It was produced by Jack Endino, who produced a bunch of important Seattle bands, including Green River, L7, The Gits, Soundgarden, and, of course, Nirvana. Pollard has said that, years later, someone from Cat Butt wrote to him to thank him for mentioning the band in the song. He's also claimed that *Same Place* was partly inspired by grunge, although the scene didn't yet have that name. When GBV were featured in that 1989 issue of *Spin*, they were mentioned alongside Seattle bands such as The U-Men, Screaming Trees, and Girl Trouble, so maybe that's where Pollard's interest in the scene started. He also had a Tad poster in the Snakepit.

Later in the song, Pollard writes:

When the pendulum swings and cuts
When the big door swings open and shuts
Yeah, we'll be middle-aged children, but so what?

Tying the image of the back-and-forth motion of a pendulum to a door opening and closing is a brilliant way to turn the cycle and repetition of life into a metaphor. On the song 'Everyday,' from the second GBV album, Pollard writes about the circular nature of life, 'Moving in circles out on the freeway, coming and going to everyday.' And, later on, he'd write, 'As we go up, we go down.' So, the idea that our fate is something that swings or fluctuates, and that we're just along for the ride, is something Pollard would refer to throughout his career. The mention of 'middle-aged children,' meanwhile, is a nod to how Pollard felt about himself at the time. He felt pressure from everyone to be more responsible. He knew that he should act more like an adult, but he just wanted to play music with his friends. But this is more than just a tongue-in-cheek admission about growing up. By couching this language within the context of an album about murder and madness, it shows that he was aware of the corrosive effects of his dreams.

Track two: *'Ambergris'*

Even though Pollard would later proclaim that this short track was 'the worst song we ever wrote,' it's about an arcane and interesting subject. Ambergris is a substance that's found floating on the surface of the ocean; for a long time, people didn't know what it was. It wasn't until the 1800s that it was finally traced to sperm whales. There are disputes about how ambergris actually exits the whale, although both are unpleasant: it's either vomited up by or passed through the whale. As it dries, ambergris begins to take on a musky smell that's not unpleasant. Because of this, for hundreds of years, it was used to make perfume. This is why Pollard's narrator asks, 'What's that you're wearing that smells so good?' But he seems to be aware already, quickly adding, 'You don't want to know.' The music was created by Jim Pollard turning the tuning pegs as Bob played.

Track three: *'Local Mix-Up'*

This is two different songs, with slow verses and a fast chorus. It's also the longest song on the album, at 4:40. The chorus refers to the title of the record:

> *You as a person have got to think fast*
> *'Cause this is a party that's not gonna last*
> *And this is the same place the fly got smashed*

He's playing again here with the idea of fate, likening the ups and downs of humans to insects, saying it's just as easy for us to be swatted by life as it is for a fly.

Track four: *'Murder Charge'*

The character in the song has, I guess, committed a murder, and this song is about him being sentenced to, and dying in, the electric chair. The lyrics mention him being 'strapped' into a chair, with reporters there to witness the event until, finally, 'his ticker stopped' in what Pollard punningly calls an 'electrifying conclusion.' That phrase would be resurrected for GBV's farewell tour in 2004. The use of the electric chair for capital punishment in the United States lasted from 1924 to 1976, when it was replaced by lethal injection. The GBV video *The Devil Went Home And Puked* shows Pollard recording this song—as well as 'Pendulum' and 'Mammoth Cave'—at Wilbur's studio. In the footage, you can see Pollard belting out the lyrics, both hands securing the headphones as he strains to hit the notes.

Track five: *'Starboy'*

This song starts off as a multitracked a cappella before switching abruptly to what sounds like Pollard playing and singing in his basement while someone walks around in the background. It's another short song at a bit over a minute long.

Track six: *'Blatant Doom Trip'*

This is the only song that Tobin Sprout played on, having just moved back to the area. After a couple of short and spare songs, this is a long, full-band rocker clocking in at 4:00. It's an okay track, except it doesn't have much of a tune beyond a melodic bass line. The word 'fags' makes an appearance as part of the line, 'Scags, fags, and scallywags,' which is not a lot of fun to hear. *Blatant Doom Trip* was later used as the title for a 1998 tribute record put out by Simple Solution Records. Simple Solution was a label that operated out of the Dayton record store Trader Vic's Music Emporium, which was run by Pollard's friend, Trader Vic. You can see him and the store in the documentary *Watch Me Jumpstart*.

Track seven: *'How Loft I Am?'*

This is another acoustic track, with Pollard singing over strummed guitar. His voice sounds awesome, and it's just a great all-around tune. It's a short song, at just a minute long, but I could listen to it for another three or four minutes. It's the perfect way to end the record.

05 PROPELLER

nineteen ninety-two

Even though it's not necessarily their best record (although it's almost that, too), in terms of how it changed Pollard's life, *Propeller* is where the GBV story begins. What's ironic is that it was actually meant to be the story's end. Bob's 'final statement' is the thing that launched his career.

Going into 1992, GBV had existed for almost a decade. They'd recorded four full-length albums and an EP, but nothing was happening. They were barely even a band. There was no consistent lineup, and two of the guys, Kevin Fennell and Mitch Mitchell, had joined a local hardcore group. Meanwhile, Pollard's family thought he was selfish—if not just plain nuts—for pouring money and time into what they thought was just a hobby. It had gotten to the point where he agreed with them. 'There were people who told me I should focus more of my efforts on teaching. That I shouldn't be using money on music when I should be spending it on my family, so I finally thought I was going to have to become—as some people put it—"responsible."'

Not only was Pollard in debt from the previous records, but so were his friend Pete Jamison and his brother. 'I realized that we didn't have enough money and couldn't keep financing these records,' Pollard later said. 'We were done. It was settled.'

Not content to let the group go out with a whimper, Bob resolved to make one more album. It would contain his best songs and be recorded again in a professional studio. The LP would be called *Propeller* because it was going to 'propel' the band to stardom. It was meant to be an ironic (if not outright sarcastic) title. No one involved with the group—Bob included—thought it would amount to much. And, at first, it didn't.

When the album was done, everyone associated with the band took their copies, and Bob kept on teaching. That was the end of Guided By Voices. Except, of course, it wasn't. Within the next year, they'd get signed, start playing shows, and receive rave reviews in national publications. Pollard's dream—the one he'd been carrying around inside of him for decades—finally began to come true.

What happened is that 'manager for life' Pete Jamison didn't just hang on to his copies. He sent them to labels, magazines, and tastemakers. In a typewritten note, charming with grammatical errors, he wrote, 'Here is a copy of "Guided by Voices" new LP Propeller. Please listen to it and consider it for a review in your publication.' And while press coverage ended up being nonexistent and distribution was still limited to local outlets—most people wouldn't hear the record until the following year, when it was included as part of the CD release of *Vampire On Titus*—those who came into contact with *Propeller* were blown away.

One of those people was musician Matt Sweeney. He was living in New York at the time, getting ready to start his band Chavez. Chavez would go on to release a few records on Matador before breaking up and getting back together in 2017. Sweeney reached out to Bob, writing he was 'embarrassed' by how much he liked *Propeller* and that a 'creepy obsession with the record immediately seized me and everybody I've played it for.' He also wrote that 'GBV is way too great for me to put into words.' (Sweeney would not only become friends with Pollard but, for a short time, was the band's bassist.)

Reactions like this, not to mention a growing buzz among musicians on the Ohio scene, would soon land a copy of *Propeller* in the hands of Scat Records founder Robert Griffin. 'From note one of *Propeller*, which was the first thing I heard, I was like, *Oh my God, this is the shit*,' he later recalled. 'I played that record so many times.' He was drawn in because of the band's influences, not to mention the production, which meant the album sounded great loud. 'It's so anthemic and well sequenced, but varied,' Griffin said. 'There wasn't one part of it I didn't love.' He would soon reach out to Pollard, signing the band shortly thereafter.

This amazing chain of events wouldn't have happened if Jamison had just kept his copies, filing them away instead of sending them around the world. If Pete hadn't worked to get the word out about the album, then Robert Griffin would have never called Bob to ask for a single. And with no *Grand Hour*, there's no *Vampire On Titus* (not to mention there's also no *Bee Thousand*). Guided By Voices would have left behind just those early records, the boxes of which would have sat unopened in Bob's basement, stacked in the same place where some of the songs had been recorded.

We all have our *what-if* moments. Intersections where we're faced with choices that stand to have huge consequences. What if we do this instead of that? How will our lives be different? It's interesting to think what would have happened in Pollard's life if Jamison hadn't sent out those copies of *Propeller*.

But all that happened later.

At first, before Pollard decided *Propeller* was going to be his grand artistic statement, it was just another album. Bob's working title was *The Corpse-Like Sleep Of Stupidity*. It was set to contain twenty-three songs, most of which consisted of four-track basement recordings. From that initial track list, only six made it onto what finally became *Propeller* ('Some Drilling Implied,' 'Red Gas Circle,' 'Unleashed! The Large-Hearted Boy,' '14 Cheerleader Coldfront,' 'Particular Damaged,' and 'Lethargy'). A few early versions of classics that would later appear on *Bee Thousand* were also included ('Buzzards And Dreadful Crows,' 'Tractor Rape Chain,' and 'The Goldheart Mountaintop Queen Directory'). Most of the remaining songs would see the light of day on subsequent EPs (*Get Out Of My Stations* and *Fast Japanese Spin Cycle*) or else as part of the *Suitcase* series. And just to make things even more confusing—much like the aborted *Learning To Hunt* album from 1988—the follow-up to *Same Place The Fly Got Smashed* was first intended to be an LP called *Back To Saturn X*. It was all ready to go, complete with art, before Pollard declared the record 'fatally flawed' and pulled the plug. Snippets from the LP can be found on the *Propeller* track 'Back To Saturn X Radio Report,' but other than these brief passages, no complete songs from *Back To Saturn X* appear on *Propeller*.

The scattered nature of the album's conception ensured that a wide range of Pollard's collaborators ended up taking part. Mitch Mitchell played guitar, as did Jim Pollard. Tobin Sprout contributed more than ever, including recording a number of tracks. Don Thrasher played drums, and Greg Demos stuck around, playing bass. A new addition was Dan Toohey on bass. He had played previously in Tobin Sprout's pre-GBV band Fig. 4 (and was also part of Tobin's post-GBV band Eyesinweasel).

While the past four records were recorded in Steve Wilbur's garage, for *Propeller* the band returned to a big studio, Encore, to record on sixteen-track. However, as with their first EP, this meant they ran into engineers who didn't approve of the band's recording methods. They also recorded at Cro-Magnon's eight-track studio, in addition to recording a bunch of stuff in their basements on four-track. This means that the sound is much more varied than on previous GBV albums. And this in turn sets the template for their best records, including *Bee Thousand*.

No one's credited as producer, but the liner notes say the LP was 'lovingly fucked with' by Mike 'Rep' Hummel. Mike Rep is a musician himself, having been at it even longer than Pollard. He recorded his first seven-inch, *Rocket To Nowhere*, in 1975. It was released in 1978 and has since been reissued. And, like Pollard, Mike's had his own band and been part of numerous other groups and side projects over the years. As Mike Rep & The Quotas, he's released three full-lengths and a bunch of singles. Their 1996 release *A Tree Stump Named Desire* was described in a review as 'the warm, fuzzy distortion of a 4-track with all its meters pegged in the red producing a rich, noisy, yet harmonically pleasing listening experience.' Sound familiar?

'We took it to Mike Hummel in Columbus to re-EQ everything and give it that "in the room" sound,' Bob has said. 'Mike's very good at that, and he taught us a lot.' It turned out to be a crucial ingredient missing from their previous records. It also showed that GBV's much vaunted 'lo-fi' sound was much more of an aesthetic choice than merely the by-product of recording on a four-track or in a basement. Pollard *wanted* these early records to sound raw and unpolished, and he was willing to go to sometimes-absurd lengths to achieve this. This aesthetic would reach its zenith on the band's next LP, *Vampire On Titus*.

Propeller was also different from the previous four GBV records in that it initially had no cover. While past sleeves featured glossy photos of the band or Pollard's artwork, *Propeller* was delivered in plain white sleeves that Bob and the band, along with some friends, decorated by hand. It took about a month to finish all five hundred covers. This means that each copy of the initial pressing of *Propeller* is a unique work of art (most of them were also numbered). Since owning one is like owning an original painting, one of these copies will today cost you somewhere in the neighborhood of $5,000. In the most recent Scat reissue, there are two covers to choose from, featuring designs from *Propeller* numbers 1 and 14. The CD reissue has a booklet with a bunch of different covers, so you can essentially choose whichever one you want.

SIDE ONE

Track one: *'Over The Neptune / Mesh Gear Fox'*

Similar to their previous LP, *Propeller* opens not with a song but with voices. Exuberant fans chant 'GBV!' as the band ask the standard concert question, 'Is anybody ready to rock?' only to be answered, seconds later, by Pollard, who flatly declares, 'This song does not rock.' It sounds, of course, like a live recording of the group playing a triumphant gig for a mass of adoring fans. But it's an illusion. Scott Kannberg of Pavement asked Bob a few years after the record came out, 'What concert was that?' Bob just laughed and told him it was faked in the studio by the band and some friends. 'We weren't even a live band at that point,' Pollard said. 'We'd quit playing live; we hadn't played live for, like, five years.'

While the chants and the cheers may have been faked, the stage banter is real. It's taken from 'Lion W/ Thorn In Paw,' a bonus track on 2005's *Briefcase 2 (Suitcase 2 Abridged—The Return Of Milko Waif)*. 'Lion' is a live recording of an early incarnation of the band, playing an instrumental version of what would later become 'Sheetkickers,' off *Under The Bushes*. Pollard, indulging in a bit of mythmaking, invented the 'GBV!' chant and grafted it onto what was an otherwise-tepid reception by the crowd. However, that chant of 'GBV!' is now a real thing. You hear it when you go to their shows. The illusion has become real. Pollard, by not giving up, and by having a bit of luck, has managed to make his dream a reality.

What follows is not only a great track to open this album but one of the best openings to any album by any band. It's an anthem; it soars, it rocks. But it's not just a song; it's a mission statement, one that eventually set the course—if not predicted—the future of the band. Pollard writes:

Hey, let's throw a great party
Today for the rest of our lives
The fun is just about to get started
So throw the switch
It's rock-and-roll time

Bob's inviting us all to a party, with GBV as the house band. And yet it's a fantasy, because there was no band and there was no party. It's like how Oasis sang about being 'rock'n'roll stars' on the first song of their first record. They *weren't* rock'n'roll stars. They were nobodies from Manchester on a small label. But in no time they were the biggest group in England. What they were singing about came true. And yet, Pollard's invitation isn't all glamour. He admits to his fellow travelers, 'You must be willing just to ride along with me. You must be happy just to do the job for free.' It might be fun, but it's fun on Bob's terms. And, as Pollard repeatedly cites in his work, it comes at a cost. It's 'yours for the taking,' but only if you 'follow certain rules.' Rules that Bob and the band had constantly refused: playing live, getting out of Dayton, or just plain dropping the whole daydream of being in a group. But Pollard then sticks up for himself, and his vision, protesting, at the song's most anthemic point, 'I'm much greater than you think.' This is Bob singing directly to his parents, his wife, and anyone else who didn't believe in his talents.

In the song's swooning second half, Pollard turns uncharacteristically sentimental, telling someone he wants to marry them. But even this comes at a price, as he adds, 'No use changing now.' It's marriage on his terms. Bob can only be himself.

Sonically speaking, this is the best GBV had sounded up to that point. Bob's finally approaching the arena-rock ambition of his heroes The Who. Pollard's vocals sound amazing (the English accent is beginning to kick in), the drums sound huge (with fills left and right), and you can clearly hear a twin guitar attack. At 5:41, it's one of the longest songs GBV ever recorded. But, as written, it was actually longer. The original track, 'Special Astrology For The Warlock Tour,' was eleven minutes (that's longer than several of the band's early EPs).

In demo form, the first two parts of the song were the same as what's on *Propeller*, while the third section is essentially 'Circus World' from side two of the album. This then segues into a version of 'Tractor Rape Chain' (known as the 'Clean It Up' version, since that's what he says at the end). From there, it goes into 'Class Clown Spots A UFO.' This song wouldn't be properly recorded or released until twenty years later, in 2012, for the album of the same name. 'Over The Neptune / Mesh Gear Fox' was played often once GBV began to tour nationally in '95 and '96. It was also the first song the band played on the last date of their farewell tour in 2004, as part of the marathon New Year's Eve show that was later issued on DVD.

Track two: 'Weedking'

As this song begins, the violin from the opening track is back. The first line, 'Long Live Rockathon,' has proved prophetic, since Rockathon is still around as a label and online entity for the group (its current website can be found at rockathonrecords.com). For Pollard, a guy who was desperately trying to change his circumstances and what people thought of his music, the line, 'The history book has lost its binding, pages everywhere' is intriguing. Bob isn't trying to rewrite history but, instead, wants to banish it. If we're never told how the story ends, maybe we can rewrite history and come up with something better.

When Bob later sings, 'We conjure ghosts and then we feed them,' he's giving a nod to the 'fantasy creeps' we'll meet on side two. He'd had a dream about being in a band, and making it big, for so long that it'd curdled into a ghost that was haunting him. And yet, he still couldn't give it up. In fact, he's 'feeding' it—giving it just enough nourishment to keep it alive. A minute into the song, it just explodes; Pollard's voice sounds spectacular as the track turns into a fist-pumping anthem. Its placement as the second track provides a one-two punch of opening songs. The only thing odd to me about it is—coming after a whole record about alcohol—it feels incongruous for Pollard to be singing the praises of weed.

Track three: 'Particular Damaged'

This is definitely a four-track song, if not straight from Bob's boom box. I have no idea what it's about, since Pollard's voice is maxed out with distortion and I can't tell, half the time, what he's singing. But it's still fun to listen to, and it acts as a bridge between the second and fourth tracks.

Track four: *'Quality Of Armor'*

This is one of the oldest songs Pollard's ever put on a GBV album, with the opening snippet dating back to 1979. It was written around the time he was trying to get a group going with locals Nick Weiser and John Dodson. They were a bit older, and the band—called 86—didn't last long. Sonically, this track sounds amazing. The line 'Oh yeah, I'm going to drive my car' paid off sixteen years later, when automaker Nissan licensed the track to appear in a Canadian commercial. The commercial's fun, featuring five young kids in a car, bouncing along to the GBV track. And while bands had in the past been accused of selling out when licensing tunes to advertisers, after the collapse of the record industry it became one of the easiest ways for groups to get some cash, and fans didn't seem to mind. For some groups, it would prove instrumental in helping them get an audience. The Black Keys, for one, credit having their songs in commercials as part of their eventual success. Pollard had wanted to make a deal like this for a long time, telling *Magnet* magazine's Eric Miller in 2007, 'I've always said to my manager, You need to get some of my songs in commercials, especially car commercials.'

Track five: *'Metal Mothers'*

It's hard to believe that, when the band finally got a big audience a few years later, with *Alien Lanes*, nothing on that album would sound nearly as good as this, and yet this record wasn't heard by anyone when it first came out, Pollard's gone so far as to declare this the best song on the album. And while I wouldn't quite go that far, it is indeed a solid track. The lyrics mention a rock star who finds 'time to get laid' and 'get paid.' Whether this was Pollard daydreaming about himself, or he was just writing in a general rock style (the whole first side of this LP boils down to sex, drugs, and rock'n'roll), it's a bit ironic, since at the time he was a married father of two who, by day, taught fourth grade.

Track six: *'Lethargy'*

This short heavy rocker is a lot of fun, with Pollard absolutely shredding on the vocals. When I saw the band in New York, on the reunion tour of the so-called classic lineup in 2010, Mitch Mitchell sang this while wearing a football helmet. The line 'I wish I could give a shit, just a little bit' is classic Pollard.

There's also a line about 'The book of instructions to the rusty time machine.' For a while, the working title of *Bee Thousand*, when it was intended to be a double album, was *Instructions To The Rusty Time Machine*. Ending side one with this song helps to ensure that the first half of *Propeller* absolutely kicks ass.

SIDE TWO

Track one: *'Unleashed! The Large-Hearted Boy'*

This is a fun song, although Bob's vocal is a bit sloppy throughout. The track kicks off with an infectious Jim Pollard bass line that Bob's called, with obviously no trace of bias, 'One of the greatest bass riffs of all time.' The song seems to be about freedom and being able to choose your own destiny, Pollard writing, 'It's up to you to stay put.' He's saying you have the power to 'unleash' yourself. If not, you'll be 'driven to the fields' and 'whipped like a slave.' This song would later provide the name for the website *Largehearted Boy*, which looks at literature and music.

Track two: *'Red Gas Circle'*

GBV go back to the four-track for this quiet, acoustic song that provides the first relief from the overall heaviness of the record. And the shift from 'Unleashed' to this—the variety of sounds—is why a lot of people like the band, especially the early stuff.

Track three: *'Exit Flagger'*

This is just Bob and Toby, Pollard having called up Sprout all excited one morning to tell him he had a great new song. 'We went down to my basement and threw it together,' Sprout later said. 'He played drums and I played pretty much everything else.' The whole process, from start to finished track, took under an hour. Pollard has identified the subject of the song to be death, with the exit flagger being the Grim Reaper. The narrator says he promises to meet the exit flagger 'one of these days,' just not today.

Track four: *'14 Cheerleader Coldfront'*

This is the only song Pollard and Sprout ever wrote together, Sprout having the melody and Pollard supplying the lyrics. The two of them worked out the song on the spot and recorded it onto Bob's boom box. It's a lovely song, and a much-deserved fan favorite. Bob and Toby later collaborated outside of GBV as Airport 5, but that was the same as the rest of Pollard's collaborations: Sprout did the music on his own, and Pollard later provided vocals. The song's title came to Pollard while he was at a high-school basketball tournament. He counted all fourteen cheerleaders on the court, and, because they seemed sort of stuck up and more into themselves than the game, Bob said, 'Look at the fourteen cheerleader coldfront.'

Track five: 'Back To Saturn X Radio Report'

This is actually a bunch of snippets from tracks the band had recorded up to that point, most of which would appear on later releases, such as *Bee Thousand*, *Alien Lanes*, and the compilation *King Shit & The Golden Boys*. It's a fun listen, sounding a bit like *The Faust Tapes*. This same year, They Might Be Giants did something similar, stitching together twenty-one short snippets as 'Fingertips' on their record *Apollo 18*. The title *Back To Saturn X* was in the running to be the name of either an LP or an EP in 1992.

Track six: 'Ergo Space Pig'

This ramshackle punk song finds Bob's vocal mostly distorted and unintelligible, as on 'Particular Damaged' from side one. It's an okay song, although the wah-wah guitar solo toward the end wears out its welcome.

Track seven: 'Circus World'

After a string of lo-fi four-track songs, this one sounds like it was recorded in a studio. Lyrically, it's sad and angry. A lot of the songs on the second side were written as they were recording the album, and since this was a period wherein Pollard had basically decided to give up the band, many of these final tracks depict his mindset. He talks here about almost reaching his limit, saying, 'If I were a freak who self-destructs.' He then rails against the establishment— all those 'painted sluts training monkey men.' The song also speaks to his frustration of not being able to achieve his dreams, or to penetrate the music business: 'I call to the door, but they won't let me in.' It's a castigating, score-settling song in the same vein as Dylan's 'Positively 4th Street.'

After a faster middle section, the song ends in an almost-sentimental mood, Pollard lamenting, 'There's too many people involved in the game,' the dour music implying that he's not one of them. Or, rather, he is playing the game, but he's losing.

Track eight: 'Some Drilling Implied'

This title later inspired the name for GBV's now out-of-print home video *Some Drinking Implied*. Similar to 'Circus World,' this is a bitter and angry song. Pollard—who felt betrayed by his family, and had probably stopped sharing anything GBV-related with them—writes, 'I dare not say the way I feel.' Why talk about your dreams if everyone's just going to put you down? He also talks about dying and about being chewed up and spit out.

The song ends by addressing the 'fantasy creep.' 'Fantasy Creeps' was one of the song snippets featured in 'Back To Saturn X Radio Report.' In that track, Bob says that the 'fantasy creeps' are 'here to hound you.' This is a reference to his own dream of making it as a musician. He was, at this point, on the brink of giving up on that fantasy. But he was savvy enough to know that he'd never get away from it, that the dream would always be there, gnawing at him, 'hounding him.'

Track nine: 'On the Tundra'

The record goes out on a total high note after a couple of heavy and depressing songs. And yet, even though it's more upbeat than the previous pair of tunes, it deals with some of the same themes. It starts with Pollard and the guys trapped and alone, literally 'on the tundra,' a cold and unforgiving place that finds them 'going under.' This is the end not only of the record but of the band. They've been to 'vicious places,' staring down 'dark and punished faces.' And yet even these trials can't make the group 'shake' or 'outgrow' their need to write songs, make records, and dream about making it big. Whereas in the opening song Bob promised a 'great party' that would last forever, here he merely hopes for it. Pollard knows the band's a joke, but he still believes in it. And he suspects that GBV may yet have their moment in the spotlight. Maybe the fantasy will somehow become real. What's amazing is that he was right, and this record is what put all that into motion.

06 VAMPIRE ON TITUS

nineteen ninety-three

Since this was their first album to be released by a proper label, and not just something made up by the guys, it's a historic record in the history of Guided By Voices. It meant getting distribution for the first time. And, even though the initial pressing was still small—just one thousand LPs and two thousand CDs—Scat managed to get *Vampire On Titus* into independent record stores all across the country. The band also received numerous reviews and played shows for the first time in years. After a decade of mere fantasy, GBV were becoming a real band.

What led to this was their previous album. Whereas, in the past, each new LP saw the band starting from scratch, *Propeller* actually managed to break out of the group's orbit. People outside Ohio were finally hearing the group, and they liked what they heard. This included people like Sonic Youth's Thurston Moore, and Mark Ibold from Pavement. Ron House from Ohio's Thomas Jefferson Slave Apartments was also a fan, and he told Bob to send a copy to Robert Griffin, who ran a small label called Scat. Griffin loved *Propeller*, to the point where he was listening to it at full volume at least once a day. His first instinct was just to help Bob sell some of the older GBV albums, but then he decided he wanted to release something by the band.

The only problem was that Bob had broken up what was left of the group. Guided By Voices no longer existed. *Propeller* was meant to be their last record, and, for a while, it was. So when Griffin called to offer to put something out, Bob relayed the news, telling Griffin there was no band. And while that was technically true, there was more to it than that. GBV had never been a coherent group. There'd never been formal practices; there were no shows, and no real shared vision. GBV was Bob. So why did Pollard hesitate when Griffin offered to release something? It was because he'd made a vow. Bob's family had been hassling him for years to give up the band and quit pissing away his money. They wanted him to concentrate more on his teaching and his family, and he'd finally listened. GBV was over. And yet, he couldn't quite let go. A week later, Griffin received the cassette for *The Grand Hour*. (Since mastering engineers were wary of working with standard audiocassettes, throughout Griffin's relationship with the band, whatever Pollard sent had to be transferred to a different format. This later led to the use of Pro Tools, which the band and the label used to great effect for *Bee Thousand*.)

Scat Records, at that time, was based in Cleveland. It later moved to St. Louis, where it remains to this day. Label founder Robert Griffin was also the guitarist in the band Prisonshake. In '93, when he began working with Pollard, Griffin, at twenty-seven, was about ten years younger than Bob. He had modest ambitions for the label. 'I don't expect everything to make money,' he later said. 'I don't expect everything to break even.' That he was also in a band, and just wanted to follow his artistic instincts, made him a perfect patron for Pollard.

Signing to Scat was a big deal for Bob. After all those years of not being taken seriously, having someone believe in his vision meant the world to him. It wasn't quite as momentous to his family, but it was taken as welcome news. His wife's response was, 'At least you don't have to pay for it anymore.'

The material that Bob put together for the first legitimate GBV release, *The Grand Hour*, spanned six songs. (The name of the EP was actually meant to be *The Golden Hour*, but Griffin misheard Pollard over the phone, and Bob liked the new title better.) Similar to *Propeller*, it consisted of tracks recorded at home and at the sixteen-track studio Encore. Its most well-known song is also the most polished, 'Shocker In Gloomtown.' Clocking in at 1:25, it's a perfect slice of indie rock that was covered by The Breeders the following year. They even made a video for it, which featured a cameo by GBV. Pollard and Kim Deal, both being indie-rockers from Dayton, struck up a friendship around this time, though it wouldn't last long.

The EP's a glorious mess. A ragged, unpolished gem. GBV's introduction to the world couldn't be truer to Pollard's musical vision. It signaled that if the band were going to achieve any sort of success, it was going to be on Bob's terms. Two tracks on the EP provided the names of the next two GBV albums, with 'Alien Lanes' appearing on the first side and 'Bee Thousand' closing out side two. 'Bee Thousand' has to be one of the weirdest GBV songs ever.

The full-length follow-up, *Vampire On Titus*, was just as ragged, if not more so. James Greer, in the excellent *Guided By Voices: A Brief History: Twenty-One Years Of Hunting Accidents In The Forests Of Rock And Roll*, describes it as 'the noisiest, messiest, most poorly recorded record Bob had ever done.' Which makes me wonder, why did Bob turn in what he turned in? Why send in stuff that sounded so raw? He had plenty of songs left over from previous recording sessions. Tracks that certainly sounded better than those on *Vampire On Titus*. The compilation album *King Shit & The Golden Boys* alone collects no less than seven songs that predate 1993, some of which sound quite good. So why not just put together an LP from stuff he already had? This was, after all, his big chance. He was finally signed. The fact that *Vampire On Titus* was so ragged and lo-fi shows that Bob believed in himself and his vision. He basically said, 'Fuck it,' and put together the record *he* wanted to make.

When Griffin got the final cassette, it was not love at first listen. 'I was definitely taken aback by it,' he told me. 'There wasn't the same sort of arena-rock vibe as *Propeller*, so it was quite a departure.' But Griffin stuck with it, and, while staying at his girlfriend's, he would listen to the cassette loud on a boom box while taking a bath. He had previously listened to the record on a proper stereo without making a real connection to it. But after hearing *Titus* within the natural echo of the bathroom, he got it. The acoustics of the small, tiled bathroom perfectly suited—and seemed to amplify—the album's sonic universe. Its shabby sound actually made it stand out against everything else that was out there at the time. Griffin told himself, 'I can't think of anything else that sounds like this.'

After the success of *The Grand Hour*, and with Griffin finally succumbing to the ragged charms of *Titus*, it was time to put out a record. And yet, even though his label was beginning to do well, Griffin was running low on funds.

To get the cash he needed to press albums he'd promised to his artists, he entered into a short-term agreement with Caroline Records to release *The Roaring Third* by his band Prisonshake, as well as *Out Of Sight, Out Of Mind* by My Dad Is Dead. He also offered them *Vampire On Titus*. Caroline passed.

Undaunted, Griffin sought to obtain a loan of $8,000 from a sympathetic couple with some extra money who were friends of Douglas Enkler, the singer of Prisonshake. To convince them to hand over the cash, Griffin had to put together extensive budgets and projections, and there was a good deal of haggling over the final legal agreement.

This infusion of cash also allowed for Griffin to hire 2:30 Publicity to help get the word out about the album. 'They were very connected, had worked in various aspects of the independent music industry for a few years, and were very cool people, and only represented shit that was cool.'

Another thing that helped was that Scat was distributing its records—as well as those from a number of other important indie labels, such as Drag City—directly to over a hundred stores around the country. 'At least half of those were like *the* record store in that town,' says Griffin. And all those cool record clerks were turning their customers on to the band. 'It was a really organic kind of thing. Like, just about anybody with taste who heard the shit knew it was brilliant.' Scat also had a thriving mail-order business.

Titus was played and recorded by just Bob, his brother, and Tobin Sprout. Bob played guitar and drums, Toby played guitar and bass, and Jim's credited on the sleeve with 'guitar and amp noise.' Kevin and Mitch may have been off playing with Fathom Theory, but what about Greg Demos, Dan Toohey, and Don Thrasher? Had Bob run out of favors from these guys, or was he too proud to ask? Either way, this marks one of the slimmest incarnations of GBV until the 2016 record *Please Be Honest*, where it's just Bob.

The cover's a great indicator of the sound found inside. It's handmade, and the band's name and the record's title are pasted onto thin poster board. The yellow of the cover is from a highlighter; if you look closely, you can see the ink strokes. The original art was only four by four inches, which is why—when it was blown up by the primitive technology of the day—it looks a bit pixelated in the LP format. The illustration of the animals coming out of the plants goes back a few centuries. It first appeared in 1499, as part of *The*

Travels Of Sir John Mandeville. What's pictured is a cotton plant with lambs coming out of the stalks. It must be a famous illustration, because it's popped up in a number of places, including on the title page of Cormac McCarthy's screenplay *The Gardener's Son.*

The back cover has the tracks in burgundy type placed against a blue photograph. It's hard to make out the titles; that's probably why, for the 1996 reissue, they were printed in yellow. The back also features a photo of Bob in a T-shirt, drinking a beer, with a guy standing behind him. The guy is Randy Campbell. Campbell's co-written eight songs with Bob, including *Bee Thousand's* 'A Big Fan Of The Pigpen,' to which he also contributed backing vocals. The photo is credited to Bruce Greenwald, the friend who took the cover photo for *Sandbox.*

The sleeve also includes a credit for the album's title, which goes to Pollard's friend Jim Shepard. Like Mike 'Rep' Hummel, Shepard was an Ohio musician who played in a number of bands, among them Vertical Slit, V-3, and Ego Summit. He also did lots of recording at home, and had been releasing his own music since the 70s. Like Bob, he had also attracted the attention of tastemakers like Thurston Moore and Byron Coley, so you could see how he and Pollard would form a quick and fast friendship. One night, in awe of Bob's ability to write songs and come up with melodies, Shepard said that Pollard was 'like a vampire on Titus, sucking songs out of the earth.' Titus was the street Bob was living on at the time. (Shepard committed suicide in 1998, at the age of forty-four. Bob later paid his respects to his friend by contributing a beautiful version of Shepard's song 'Bristol Girl' to a 2001 tribute record entitled *Matter Dominates Spirit.*)

Being on a real label meant GBV received the first real reviews of their career. And they had to be pleased by their reception. In *Spin's* 'Heavy Rotation' section, Craig Marks begins his review by asking, 'Where in God's name did these "out there" spacemen come from?' It described the band as a trio and compared them to such other 'gifted loons' as Syd Barrett and Roky Erickson. It went on to describe the songs as 'absurd sci-fi yarns … beautifully stored in chunks of overmodulated treble,' and also cited the record's 'offhanded, winsome melodies.'

Even more remarkably, Tom Sinclair of *Entertainment Weekly* gave the record an A+, writing that 'it's a low-fi tour de force, featuring songs and fragments of such casual brilliance ... that you know the majors will soon come sniffing.'

Another thing that would bring the labels 'sniffing' was GBV's high-decibel live show, which made its debut that summer. After agreeing to put out the band's records, Griffin talked a reluctant Bob into playing a gig in Manhattan as part of that year's New Music Seminar. They would be part of a Scat and Thrill Jockey showcase alongside Griffin's band Prisonshake, as well as New Bomb Turks, Zipgun, Gaunt, and Soul Vandals.

It had been six years since GBV had last played live, and they'd never played in New York City before, let alone at a historic venue like CBGB. There was also the pesky fact that Bob had no band. But he didn't let that stop him. He got back Dan Toohey on bass, Mitch Mitchell on guitar, and Kevin Fennell on drums, along with Sprout on second guitar. And, even though he played guitar on the records, for the show Bob wanted to just sing (something he's stuck with ever since). Pollard's first choice to play drums was actually Don Thrasher, who'd played on *Propeller*, but Thrasher said no because his wife was pregnant. It was the first but not the last time Bob would lose a band member to domesticity. His brother also turned down the opportunity to be in the band, thinking that his skills weren't sufficient.

Even those who Pollard had convinced to play weren't that confident. They were all nervous about the show—Bob most of all—and unsure about what their reception would be in the Big Apple. It probably didn't help that Henry Rollins had muscled his way into fitting in an early secret show at the venue, thus pushing back the Scat/Thrill Jockey showcase by a couple of hours. This meant more time to hang around, and more drinking time to squash the growing nerves.

The stars had aligned for a packed crowd, which also included movers and shakers like the Beastie Boys. Prisonshake were in their prime, New Bomb Turks were blowing up, and *The Grand Hour* had been a success, selling a couple of hundred copies in New York City alone. A few weeks before the show, advance copies of *Titus* had begun making the rounds. Chatter about the band was growing, and this was everyone's first chance to see them live.

As Bob has said, 'We did like twenty songs bam-bam-bam-bam, Ramones style, out of nervousness. I didn't say anything between songs.' They performed some of their best and most muscular tunes, including 'Postal Blowfish' and 'Shocker In Gloomtown.' The crowd was blown away by the volume and the energy of the performance. This was nothing like the records. According to Griffin, 'Even at that early date, it became clear that with GBV the records were one thing, and the live show something else altogether.' People kept coming up to Griffin after the show, telling him, 'Wow, I didn't even realize they were a rock band!'

Since *Titus* is the rawest of GBV's lo-fi records, it's appropriate to look at lo-fi as a sound and as a movement. The phrase 'lo-fi' invariably comes up in every review or mention of GBV. If you know only one or two things about the band, the first is that they drink a lot and the second is that they're lo-fi. (If you know a *third* thing, it's that they've released a lot of albums.) When GBV broke in the early 90s, they were lumped in with the lo-fi movement, along with bands like Pavement, Sebadoh, and The Grifters. To me, that doesn't make sense. Pavement's first couple of singles were abrasive, but does that mean they're lo-fi? Big Black are abrasive, but they're not lo-fi. Those first couple of Pavement singles were recorded in the same sixteen-track studio where they recorded their debut record. In fact, *Slanted And Enchanted* sounds like *Dark Side Of The Moon* compared with *Vampire On Titus*. So how can you call Pavement lo-fi? And by the time Pavement got to their fifth record, they were produced by Radiohead collaborator Nigel Godrich. GBV's fifth record was recorded in a basement. The same as records six through eight. (The first four were recorded in a garage.)

Early records by Sebadoh and The Grifters were lo-fi, but by the mid 90s both of those bands had cleaned up their sound. They were recording in studios, not at home or on a four-track. Either band could still be noisy, or loose, or ragged, but that's not lo-fi; that's just the way they played. GBV *chose* to be lo-fi. Bob loved the way the limited dynamic range of the TASCAM made his vocals sound, and the ease of recording at home matched both his general impatience and his desire to capture the initial excitement of a song's creation. It wasn't just about finances or circumstances, although those certainly played a part (at least in the beginning). It was also about how Bob wanted to present himself and his music: raw, unfinished, rough around the edges. It's how he saw the world. As he has said, 'It was with the four-track that we came closest to getting the sound that we had in our heads.' Writing about *Propeller* for *Pitchfork* in 2005, Stephen M. Deusner would note that GBV's 'lo-fi sound is essential: it preserved the illusion of connection between performer and listener.'

Of all the groups initially tagged as 'lo-fi,' GBV stuck with it the longest. And not out of some dogmatic ideology (the mid- and hi-fi records they made, and continue to make, bear that out). They stuck with the sound for the same reason they chose it in the first place: because it's in their DNA. It's who they are.

SIDE ONE
Track one: *'Wished I Was A Giant'*
Much like *Vampire*'s DIY cover, this song is the perfect calling card for the seventeen songs that follow. The drumming, by Bob, is rudimentary at best, but the guitar sounds okay. And, yeah, the lyrics are hard to hear, but so what? I've listened to plenty of bands where I never know what they're saying. The point is that it all fits together. Even when Bob's just wailing and screaming at the end, and the guitar's seesawing back and forth, it works.

Track two: *'#2 In The Model Home Series'*
This is a bare song with some interesting lyrics. It has some sort of Oedipal/sci-fi thing going on, as if Philip K. Dick had written The Doors' song 'The End.' Pollard writes about an all-seeing 'automated wife' and his favorite 'cyber-son' finding his gun, and, now that he has, 'the fun begins.' It's a chilling and effective song.

Track three: *'Expecting Brainchild'*
This track begins with a found-sound recording of an older woman saying, 'Bob, would you and Living Praise Choir please lead us into "God Be The Glory?"' The song that follows is an effective rocker, even though the drums are awfully basic (Don Thrasher, who played on the previous LP, is sorely missed). That being said, the song doesn't lose much by being simple. The chorus of 'It's time to draw the line' could be seen as autobiographical, since Bob found

himself at a crossroad in his life. He knew that he was leaving behind one period of his life and about to enter another. However, it's disturbing to hear the word 'faggot' used in the song, as Pollard lists 'scholars and flunkies' along with 'faggots and junkies.' (The word reappears on 'Hit,' from *Alien Lanes*.)

Track four: *'Superior Sector Janitor X'*

This is a super-short song at just thirty-seven seconds. It seems to hint, like the second song on the LP, at some sort of dystopian future, Pollard writing about a 'bitter world' where people are 'known only as a number.' The narrator, who transforms himself into Superior Sector Janitor X, might be some sort of drone or slave, like the workers who toil underground in Fritz Lang's *Metropolis*. And yet, even though the character's 'coats' are 'blue,' his 'visions' are 'white.' Like Winston Smith in *1984*, the narrator sees himself as a free man because he still has the power to imagine. Except that it may be too late, since he begins to doubt himself, asking for confirmation about what he sees. But an answer doesn't arrive, and the song is soon over.

Track five: *'Donkey School'*

This is a Tobin Sprout track—the first time he got his own song on a GBV album. I've always found that his subject matter and his voice are the perfect companions to Bob's material. His presence would prove to be a welcome addition to GBV, and his contributions to records like *Bee Thousand* and *Under The Bushes Under The Stars* go a long way toward making those LPs the classics that they are. This is also the song that Strokes guitarist and GBV super-fan Albert Hammond Jr. mentions as being the point at which he first encountered, and fell in love with, the band. It happened when he was a young kid, barely a teenager. He was at the house of a friend of his who was a few years older: 'He was playing *Vampire On Titus*. There was this one night at his house where we played "Donkey School" 100 times in a row.' The Strokes would later open for the band and invite GBV to be in one of their videos, while Hammond Jr. often covered 'Postal Blowfish' in concert when performing as a solo artist.

Track six: 'Dusted'

The music here, again, is basic. The drumming's just pounding, and I don't hear much beyond one distorted guitar, except at the end, when there's a solo that plays the song out. The lyrics, though, are amazing. They're written in an almost archaic style, as if Pollard wanted the language to match the antiquated woodcut of the LP's cover. If it began life as a poem, I wouldn't be surprised. Bob writes about 'fear' and 'ignorance,' 'truth,' and the 'windows of our youth.' It's as if Pollard was wondering—now that his dreams were coming true—whether it'd all be worth it: 'And larger though we grew in size, not a thing was gained.' A different version appears on the 1994 EP *Fast Japanese Spin Cycle*.

Track seven: 'Marchers In Orange'

Jim Pollard gets a co-writing credit on this, so it might be him providing the instrumental backing. According to Robert Griffin, the instrument being played is a 'portable Magnus chord organ. Six buttons on the left would play chords, and there was a two-octave keyboard on the right. Every other kid's house had one in the 60s and 70s. It generates sound very similarly to an accordion or harmonium in terms of physics, hence the tonal similarities.' The lyrics are very impressionistic; it's not quite Bob at his most surreal, but they're more a collection of impressions and images than a narrative or story. And even though this song would be re-recorded in a full-band version for the *Fast Japanese Spin Cycle* EP, I prefer this one.

Track eight: 'Sot'

This Pollard/Sprout co-write is the most polished and melodic song on side one, if not the whole record. It has a dynamic lead line and bass, and it sounds a lot more fleshed out than the other tracks. GBV have only played it once, at that first show in New York at CBGB. But Tobin played it a handful of times in 2004, when he opened up for GBV on the Electrifying Conclusion tour. The refrain, 'There's nothing I'd rather do than be here right now,' could relate to the band—the sort of rallying cry/mission statement that was all over *Propeller*, if only ironically. However, since the word 'sot' means a habitual drunkard, it might just be another love song to alcohol. Either way, it's great.

Track nine: *'World Of Fun'*

This short acoustic song clocks in at just under a minute. It's an okay song, even though it feels like just a sketch.

SIDE TWO

Track one: *'Jar Of Cardinals'*

This song is super melodic, with jangly guitar and a vocal melody that goes up and down. From the lyrics, I can't tell if it's about a bird, or from a bird's point of view; Pollard croons, 'Hush now seedling, don't you cry, maybe I'll be coming home quite soon for you.' The final line twists that last bit to 'quite sinful you.' This song was brought back for the first reunion tour in 2010. In fact, there's a fun video on YouTube of Bob showing the band how to play it.

Track two: *'Unstable Journey'*

This song doesn't do much for me; the drums at the beginning are off the beat, and overall it just seems willfully sloppy. It also doesn't hew to any sort of structure; it's just a succession of verses.

Track three: *'E-5'*

This track's title is the baseball term for an error at third base. It's also another sloppy song. All three guys get a co-write, so maybe that's Jim playing guitar and Bob and Tobin making up words on the spot. Thankfully, it's short, at a minute and a half

Track four: *'Cool Off Kid Kilowatt'*

This is another short, lo-fi song where all three guys get a writing credit. And, again, it sounds like Bob's just making up any old thing to sing on top of a tune that's not really there. In the lyrics, he asks, 'Isn't it interesting? Isn't it odd?' Odd, maybe, but not too interesting.

Track five: *'Gleemer (The Deeds Of Fertile Jim)'*

Toby's voice just sounds so good, and is so welcome, on this and the next couple of records. When he sings, 'Could this be a brand-new low,' it's the most transcendent moment on the album. As much as I love the post-Toby

GBV records, I do think they suffer from not having Sprout as a counterpoint to Pollard. GBV have played this live a lot, and Tobin continues to play it in his solo concerts.

Track six: 'Wondering Boy Poet'

This is another track where Bob's commenting on his new life, and his chance at fame and fortune. 'The cup is only being filled, for a chance to have it spilled.' He knows that every dream has a dark side, and that just because your fantasy comes true, you won't necessarily live happily ever after.

Track seven: 'What About It?'

Another super-bare song; Sprout comes in toward the end, although I could do with more of him throughout. Otherwise, it just sounds like Bob making up words while Jim makes noise in the background.

Track eight: 'Perhaps Now The Vultures'

Even though this is a raw track, it's one of the few on the album where I can hear any bass guitar. The line 'Consider this a failure, so be it,' could be Pollard's challenge to the listener about this song, if not the whole record.

Track nine: 'Non-Absorbing'

Like the last couple of GBV LPs, *Vampire On Titus* goes out on a total high note; this is a fun song. The repeated refrain of 'Do you see me, like I see you?' is insanely catchy, and it always manages to get stuck in my head whenever I hear it. It was the only song from the record to be featured on the 2003 best-of *Human Amusements At Hourly Rates*.

The year this record came out ended up being a sort of *annus mirabilis* for Bob and the band. They released their best record, Pollard was able to quit his job, and, due to the success of their previous album, indie labels everywhere were asking him for material. In 1994, the band released an LP, four EPs, and three split singles, and contributed to a soundtrack. Everywhere Bob turned, someone asked him for a song or to put out an EP. And since he'd been so frustrated for so long, with his family not understanding his passion (not to mention recognizing his genius), Pollard said yes to everything. Most of the stuff he put out that year was worth hearing. *Fast Japanese Spin Cycle*, *Clown Prince Of The Menthol Trailer*, and *Get Out Of My Stations* all quickly became—and remain today—fan favorites. GBV were entering their imperial phase. They were everywhere. They could do no wrong. But even though it probably seemed like everything was going great, all was not well.

'Around the time we were putting *Bee Thousand* together, I was freaking out,' Bob later said. 'We were giddy because we'd made music for so many years while no one gave a shit and then all of a sudden they did. It was a very exciting time, but a confusing one, too.'

Pollard had a crucial decision to make. Now that he had an audience, what did he want to sound like? What was his vision for the band? *Vampire On Titus* had been the most raw-sounding GBV record ever—and it was a success. But how would he follow it up? 'I was wondering what to do next. What direction we should take it. Then it hit me … I should take all the best ideas that I hadn't used over the years—segments of songs, pieces of songs—and throw them together like a patchwork.'

It was basically an extension of what he'd done on *Propeller*: record a couple of new songs and mix them in with a bunch of older tracks and reworked material. The result would be, as Pollard put it, 'fitting a puzzle together to make a complete picture.' The picture that Bob and the band would finally assemble would prove to be their masterpiece. But it would be a long journey with many detours.

The earliest version of what became *Bee Thousand* was an LP entitled *All That Glue* that Bob had put together for Engine Records. When Robert Griffin got wind that Bob was going to put out a GBV album on another label, he wasn't happy. Bob pulled back and gave Engine just an EP, *Fast Japanese Spin Cycle*. He then began reworking *All That Glue* for Griffin, as the band's follow-up to *Vampire On Titus*.

Glue was the usual Pollard stew of demos, new tracks, and unreleased songs. Of the initial seventeen tracks, only three eventually wound up on *Bee Thousand* ('Queen Of Cans And Jars,' 'Smothered In Hugs,' and 'The Goldheart Mountaintop Queen Directory'). Griffin suggested turning the record into a double ten-inch. Pollard liked the idea of a double but wanted both discs to be proper LPs, so he set to work coming up with four sides of vinyl. By August of '93, Pollard had sequenced a thirty-three-track double LP called *Instructions To The Rusty Time Machine* (named after a lyric from *Propeller*). A DAT was put together, and Bob started handing out cassette copies to his friends. Reviewing the proposed double album when *Bee Thousand: The Director's Cut* came out in 2004, *Pitchfork*'s Eric Carr wrote, 'This original sequence is so bafflingly unsatisfying that it might've kept Guided By Voices in the basement for another decade had clearer heads not eventually prevailed.' Thankfully, by winter, Bob was back to tinkering and had soon trimmed enough songs that it was back to a single disc.

By December, Pollard was calling his LP-in-progress *Bee Thousand*. He'd added 'Don't Stop Now,' which wouldn't resurface until *Under The Bushes Under The Stars*, and 'Crocker's Favorite Song,' which would be re-recorded and released in 2012 as 'Class Clown Spots A UFO.' The album's title was a typical Pollard construction, with help from his brother. Jimmy had come up with *Zoo Thousand*, but around the same time Bob had passed a drive-in theater playing the family film *Beethoven*, only they'd used a *u* instead of a *v* on the marquee. This led Bob to come up with *Bee Thousand*. He also liked that if you said the title while holding your tongue, it sounds like 'Pete Townshend.' All of that being said, it was a title he'd come up with years before, since it's the last song on the EP *The Grand Hour*. It was also during this period that Bob wrote 'I Am A Scientist' and 'Gold Star For Robot Boy.' The plan was to issue them on Scat as a single.

But Pollard still wasn't finished. He sent Griffin a fifth draft, still called *Bee Thousand* but now sporting the subtitle *Hardcore UFOs*. This was the most hodgepodge version yet, stripping away more than half a dozen GBV classics and fan favorites, such as 'Tractor Rape Chain,' 'Queen Of Cans And Jars,' 'Echos Myron,' and 'Buzzards And Dreadful Crows.' In their place were a handful of tunes rescued from the abandoned double LP. Proposed side two opener 'Zoning The Planet' is a ramshackle mess, while 'I'll Buy You A Bird' from side one is a pleasant song in the vein of 'Paper Girl.' 'Rainbow Billy' is an acoustic track that sees Pollard doing a passable white-soul falsetto for just about the first and last time in GBV's existence. Unfortunately, it sounds like a rehearsal or sketch; if Pollard had taken another crack at it, it could have been an interesting song, but in the proposed state, compared to 'Tractor Rape Chain,' it's pure *Suitcase* material. A track new to version number five, 'Break Even,' is a full-band mess. If *Bee Thousand* had indeed been issued with these tracks, it would have basically been *Vampire On Titus II*. And while that would suit some fans just fine, it would have all but enshrined GBV as nothing more than a novelty band in the vein of Half Japanese.

Griffin was nonplussed by the latest incarnation of the LP. 'It was very much focused on shambling, first-take songs. It could totally pass for a Nightwalker album.' What Griffin missed were the 'insanely brilliant songs' from earlier versions. He knew that a great record was in reach; Pollard just needed to be pointed in the right direction. As Griffin recounts in the liner notes to *Director's Cut*, 'I plucked up my courage, wrote Bob a letter and sent a cassette to Dayton with my proposed sequence.'

Pollard approved, and, with just a small amount of back-and-forth (swapping out Toby's track 'Scissors' for 'Mincer Ray,' and adding 'Yours

To Keep'), the final sequence was decided. Griffin's suggestions, as well the inclusion of 'I Am A Scientist' and 'Gold Star For Robot Boy,' are what make the record a classic. The final piece of the puzzle was added in February of '94, when the band came to Cleveland to play a show. Griffin used the opportunity to finalize the art and assemble the master. To get the sequence just right, Griffin, Pollard, and Sprout went to Landmark Records (a fitting name, given what the album later became) and used the then relatively unknown computer program Pro Tools to cross-fade and add small bits from other songs to the tracks. And while this would end up being the icing on the cake—pulling together all the various bits and snippets to produce a masterful mosaic—the decision to use Pro Tools was one of necessity.

'The band's cassette masters often had the tracks spaced very closely together,' says Griffin. 'Although I could've assembled a proper master on the more traditional quarter-inch two-track tape, that would've meant losing a generation of fidelity, so digital transfers became the norm with GBV.' Griffin hadn't requested any changes to *Vampire On Titus*, so it was transferred to DAT straight from the source tape. But since the material for *Bee Thousand* had been spread across so many cassettes, transferring it to DAT proved difficult. 'Bits of the beginnings and endings of songs kept getting snipped off, due to both the cassette and the DAT machines being imprecise and slow to respond. But if we put all the cassettes into Pro Tools, that not only solved that problem but also allowed us to get the time between tracks—when there was any—exactly right. Add the ability to cross-fade and insert additional material, and we were off to the races.'

Ironically, it was Bob's adherence to primitive technology—sending Griffin the tracks on cassette—that pushed the band toward the most advanced technology of the time. 'If Bob had sent masters on quarter-inch tape,' says Griffin, 'I never would've considered using the digital domain at all, would not have learned about the existence of Pro Tools, and *Bee Thousand* would've been quite different, though no doubt still great.'

Griffin also pushed Bob on the cover. The art Bob initially delivered was a collage featuring a headless man placed against a red, blue, and yellow splatter painting. There's a train coming out of where the man's head should be, with the band's name hand-drawn on the side. Griffin later doubled this image and used it as the cover of the *Director's Cut* edition of the album.

What ended up on the final *Bee Thousand* sleeve was initially just meant to decorate the inside. 'The wizard image was provided to me for use on the lyric sheet,' says Griffin, 'but I thought it was the most evocative of the album as a whole, and I convinced Bob to let me run with that for the front cover. I edited it pretty heavily.'

The picture was taken from a 1990 story in *National Geographic* entitled 'The Cajuns: Still Loving Life.' The original photo showed participants celebrating Courir de Mardi Gras in Mamou, Louisiana. The conical hat, known as a *capuchon*, has its origins in medieval Europe. Designed to resemble the tall, pointy hats worn by noble women, they were often paired with elaborate costumes and masks intended to conceal the wearer's identity. The image has been cut out and taped over a new background (if you look closely, you can clearly see the horizontal lines of Scotch tape). The oval above the figure is a street lamp—Griffin edited out the pole (and as much of the tape as he could) to make it suggestive of a UFO. Griffin also made the colors a bit more saturated. The horizontal strip removed from the bottom of the image was intended to match the dropouts in the songs, where a guitar or another sound might suddenly disappear.

Griffin, who studied art in college as part of a double major, wanted 'to communicate visually what I thought was in the album.' The back cover, with its swaths of red and blue, was similarly striking.

'I always felt *Bee Thousand* was a profoundly psychedelic album,' says Griffin. 'Not so much in playing to tropes like extreme panning or backwards guitar solos, but in the most essential, time-distorting way. A disorienting journey. Things happen very quickly, and sometimes the changes and shifts are so sudden that the listener is like, *Hey, wait, is this the same song? Where am I? How long ago did that other thing happen?* I wanted the type to reflect that, too, so the band's name is upside down, and all of it is a bit rough, distorted, and off-kilter, just like the recording.'

The red, white, and blue color scheme was reinforced throughout the design, with side one being 'The Red Room' and side two being 'The Blue Room.' Naming the sides like this harkened back the 'Buckeye' and 'Briar' sides of GBV's first LP, *Devil Between My Toes* (and was used again on 2019's

Warp And Woof). Griffin also designed the lyric sheet, with each song given its own image (which Bob and Toby supplied). Each song title's also in a different font. The whole package was miles ahead of their previous records.

Griffin knew he had something special on his hands. 'Shit started to happen really, really fast before the record even came out. There was definitely a sense that this record is going to do really well and this band is going to do really well.' He was proved right as soon as the LP was released. 'It did really well out of the gate and then just kept selling.'

The reviews were uniformly positive. *Spin* gave *Bee Thousand* it's highest ranking, one that told readers to 'Go directly to your local record store. Buy this album. Immediately. Kill if you must.' The review's first paragraph is all about lo-fi, mentioning bands such as Pavement, Sebadoh, and The Grifters. The review also mentions the band's age, saying that they're 'old' (it should be noted that the issue in which this review appeared had Beck on the cover, and he looks like he's about fourteen). Pollard, with his 'batty lyrics,' again gets compared to the 'fried synapses' of Syd Barrett and Roky Erickson, along with Daniel Johnston. While there's certainly a through line from 'Arnold Layne' and 'See Emily Play' to 'Echos Myron' and 'Chasing Heather Crazy,' I find this comparison insulting. Each of those musicians had serious mental illnesses, having to either spend time in mental institutions or ultimately abandoning music because they went insane. Pollard, by contrast, just has a vivid imagination.

Michael Azerrad, author of the underground rock bible *Our Band Could Be Your Life*, gave *Bee Thousand* four stars in *Rolling Stone*. He called the record 'remarkable' and declared it a 'tour de force by a good old-fashioned American basement genius.' Being called a 'genius' by the most important music magazine in the world had to make Pollard feel vindicated. *Bee Thousand* would later come in at number 79 on *Rolling Stone*'s list of the 100 best records of the 90s (one spot above *Last Splash* by The Breeders, which must have made the always-competitive Bob smile).

Perhaps more important than getting positive reviews, Bob was finally being embraced by his peers. When musician and early GBV fan Matt Sweeney was in town, he and Bob brought an advance cassette of *Bee Thousand* to Kim Deal's house. The Pixies bassist and Breeders founder had grown up in Huber Heights but now lived in Oakwood. They all got stoned, played the album, and everyone loved it. It was reactions like this that persuaded Pollard to make the biggest leap of his life: quitting his job and pursuing music full-time. Not that it was an easy decision. Pollard had been teaching for fourteen years—he had benefits, and a family to think about. But he knew this was something he needed to do.

Even a staunch supporter like Griffin had his doubts. 'I wasn't sure if it was the best thing for him personally, not that I knew him well enough to make such a judgment, but, you know, it was an older guy with kids and a wife and all that.'

The record also changed Griffin's life. The cash that started coming in because of the album allowed him to pay off some debts and leave Cleveland— something he'd been wanting to do for a while. He moved to St. Louis to be closer to a girl (to whom he's still married, by the way).

While there wasn't an advance single from *Bee Thousand*, after the record was released Scat put out the *I Am A Scientist* EP. This included a re-recorded version of 'I Am A Scientist' along with three non-LP tracks. The sessions were produced by Andy Shernoff, founding member of punk band The Dictators. He'd produced Griffin's band Prisonshake and was eager to work with GBV. At this session, the band also cut a blazing version of 'My Valuable Hunting Knife' that's miles above the two versions released later. The original plan was to record material for just a single, with 'Scientist' as the A-side and 'Hunting Knife' as the B-side. Two things put an end to that idea: Bob wanted 'Hunting Knife' to have 'more of a Devo feel,' and he was excited about the new songs he'd recorded and wanted them on the record, so it ballooned to an EP.

The band also made a video for 'I Am A Scientist.' Directed by Banks Tarver, who would go on to make the GBV documentary *Watch Me Jumpstart*, it features a slightly beefier mix than what's on the album. It contains mostly black-and-white footage of the guys, including Pollard playing guitar and wearing a blazer. The footage at the band shell was shot at Dayton's Island MetroPark. The band shell was built in 1940 and has played host to a number of popular entertainers, including comedians Abbott & Costello, who performed there in 1942. It's now part of GBV history, also making an appearance in the 2017 video for 'Five Degrees On The Inside.' The clip for 'Scientist' is simple and raw, which means it matches the song, and the band, perfectly. It was shown several times on MTV as part of its legendary alternative-music show *120 Minutes*, which aired late on Sunday nights. And just to show how ubiquitous GBV were becoming around this time, both 'I Am A Scientist' and The Breeders' version of 'Shocker In Gloomtown' were once shown during the same episode of *120 Minutes*. Perhaps more importantly, MTV News did a segment on GBV around this time, interviewing the band, showing them in concert, and documenting their rags-to-riches success story. The boys were fast becoming a legitimate phenomenon.

The other big indie-rock records of the year were Pavement's second LP, *Crooked Rain, Crooked Rain*, and Superchunk's best album, *Foolish*. It was the era of Generation X and slackers. Bob and the guys didn't belong to either category. They were too old for Generation X, and they had real jobs, so couldn't be considered slackers. Hell, their bass player had just graduated from law school. The 90s stereotype put in place by films like *Reality Bites*, where good-looking twentysomethings hang out all day in coffee shops, had nothing to do with Guided By Voices. These guys were parents. They owned homes. They were, as you heard over and over again, old. And yet, GBV not only made an impression on indie rock but became one of the defining acts of the period.

It was something that Pollard himself had a hard time believing. Talking about the first time they played in New York, he said, 'Afterwards I went off the stage and I went back in this little dressing room … and all of a sudden I got mobbed by people from Pavement and the Beastie Boys … and I was freakin' out a little bit. I was going, really? Are you shittin' me? You actually think we're good?'

While the band's backstory continued to prove irresistible to journalists, and GBV seemed to be everywhere you turned, the main reason *Bee Thousand* connected with people is because it was good. The album went way beyond just the lo-fi scene; GBV were operating on a whole other level. No one had the influences they did, and no one sounded like them. Pavement threw up a bunch of clones, and lightweight grunge bands were a dime a dozen in the wake of Nirvana, but no one successfully followed in GBV's footsteps. And no one has since managed to equal, or emulate, *Bee Thousand*. Not even the band that made it. 'I'm not trying to create another *Bee Thousand*, because I don't know how to do that,' Bob later said. 'It's got to be an accident, I guess. *Bee Thousand* was an accident.'

SIDE ONE

Track one: 'Hardcore UFO's'

True to Bob's intention of recycling older material, this is a reworked song from the 1980s called 'Walls And Windows.' It was slated to go on an abandoned record from 1984 called *Pissing In The Canal*. Bob kept the melody and some of the words, but otherwise wrote new lyrics. You can hear the original version on *Suitcase 4*. It's a great way to open the record, especially when the guitar disappears about two-thirds of the way through due to a recording glitch. It's Pollard's way of letting you know you're not in Kansas anymore. And the question 'Are you amplified to rock?' sets us up for the journey that follows.

Track two: 'Buzzards And Dreadful Crows'

Bob reworks older material here once again to great effect. The snippet collection from *Propeller*, 'Back To Saturn X Radio Report,' opens with a few lines from a different version of the same song. Bob's grouped this with other tracks he's written about the fear of death. Evoking the 'Exit Flagger,' Pollard's said, 'Death's coming to get you, waiting like cats.' The song dates from around 1990, and was written along with the batch of tracks that ended up on *Same Place The Fly Got Smashed*. The line 'There's something in this deal for everyone' is fun to hear, since the success of *Bee Thousand* not only changed Pollard's and Griffin's lives but allowed band members like Mitch Mitchell and Kevin Fennell to finally achieve the rock-star dreams they'd been harboring since high school. Live, 'Buzzards' is amazing, and not in a balls-to-the-wall way like 'Cut-Out Witch.' Instead, it turns into an amazing communal experience that gets the whole room singing. Live, or on record, this has to be seen as one of GBV's all-time best songs.

Track three: 'Tractor Rape Chain'

By this point, you're getting the effect that Griffin was going for in the sequencing, with three amazing songs appearing in a row. You're just hooked and want to hear more. While the lyrics hint at an ecological message, it also charts something more personal—the dissolution of a relationship—Pollard asking, 'Why is it every time I think about you, something that you have said or implied makes me doubt you?' The lines in the chorus about 'parallel lines on a slow decline' are as depressing and evocative as anything Ian Curtis wrote in 'Love Will Tear Us Apart'; even though we love someone, it's easy to drift out of sync.

Like *Bee Thousand* itself, this track went through a myriad of versions. The opening lines come from an early track called 'Tell Me.' The romantic nature of the song is reinforced by the chorus: 'You gotta tell me how you feel about me.' The ecological aspect first appeared in 'Clean It Up,' which contains the final track's eventual chorus, but also ends with Pollard admonishing us to 'Clean it up, clean it up right now' ('it' presumably being the Earth). This version can be heard on *Suitcase 4*. A much longer recording of the song, now called 'Tractor Rape Chain,' was included as part of the Darla 100 box set. It's notable for being twice as long as the early versions. A portion of the track ('In the chance I took on the broken horse, I'm the one who's no good in your eyes') was included as part of *Propeller*'s 'Back To Saturn X Radio Report.' And if all that wasn't enough, the acoustic intro included on the *Bee Thousand* version was originally part of an early song called 'South Rat Observatory,' which you can find on *Suitcase 3*. It all adds up to another one of those shout-at-the-top-of-your-lung sing-alongs that's always a blast. If you're at a GBV show and you don't end this song with your arm around someone else's shoulder, you're doing it wrong.

Track four: *'The Goldheart Mountaintop Queen Directory'*

Even though the record slows down a bit with this quiet tune, it's another absolutely gorgeous song, which has since become a fan favorite. Pollard says he wrote it while he was on acid. The song had been part of the *Bee Thousand* track list since the beginning, appearing even on *All That Glue*. It was, however, one of the songs removed for the fifth draft of the album, only to be returned by Robert Griffin. Also, the phrase 'hallway of shatterproof glass' would provide the name of the 2010 reunion tour of the so-called classic lineup.

Track five: *'Hot Freaks'*

The instrumental track was done by Tobin Sprout, with Bob singing over it. It took him only one take, and it's probably the best example of Pollard's surreal lyrics ('I met a non-dairy creamer explicitly laid out like a fruitcake'), which he says were inspired by King Crimson's Pete Sinfield. The vocals were recorded on a day when Sprout's wife was having a yard sale, and Bob was in the basement, shouting 'Hot freaks!' over and over, which must have been comical to the people looking at picture frames and dishes. A snippet of the song can be heard at the beginning of Toby's track 'Off The Floor,' from *The Grand Hour*. It's a great track, and I especially like how Bob doesn't come in until twenty seconds into the song; letting the initial bars breathe goes a long way toward establishing the funky groove Sprout created.

Track six: 'Smothered In Hugs'

This is an absolutely gorgeous song; you don't listen to it as much as you ride the tune like a wave. The verses are hypnotic in the way Pollard almost slurs the words before going into a soaring chorus. He's said the song's about the long-standing apathy he'd received from his family, as well as 'watching interesting possibilities slip away.' He also uses his experience of being on his school's textbook committee to draw a parallel between how the establishment declares history's winners and losers. These are the people who have, as Pollard writes, 'decided you should be left out—not even mentioned.' It was the fate he'd always feared for GBV, although he now saw the opposite happening.

Track seven: 'Yours To Keep'

This is an edit from a longer version that originally clocked in at 1:50. It was slated to be released on a single in 1993, along with a track called 'Alright' (not the same one that ends *Alien Lanes*) and 'Big Fan Of The Pigpen.' The version on *Bee Thousand* is beautiful and effective. Bob fumbles with a note here and there on the guitar, but that doesn't matter; it sounds close and intimate. And even though the lyrics lean toward prog/fantasy, with a mention of slaying a beast and a 'necklace of 50 eyes,' Bob conveys real emotion and longing in the way he delivers the lyrics. Albert Hammond Jr. titled his first solo record, released in 2006, *Yours To Keep*.

Track eight: 'Echos Myron'

This super-fun and poppy track is the perfect way to end side one. The bass line is amazing, and the lyrics are a victorious declaration of GBV's success, Pollard writing, 'We're finally here, and shit, yeah, it's cool.' That being said, he's realistic about the fate of the band, singing, 'What goes up must come down.'

Early versions of the *Bee Thousand* track list had this as 'Echoes' with an *e*, like the Pink Floyd song. An early demo of the song, with Pollard singing over two acoustic guitars, had a much more romantic message, Bob declaring, 'I never knew what it's like to be loved until I found you.' In this version, the eponymous character is never mentioned, and lyrics from the final version appear in different form, for example, 'Man of wisdom and man of compromise, man of weak flesh in an armored disguise' was initially 'Man of wisdom and man of big disguise, man of wealth and enterprise.'

Fellow Ohio band The National paid homage to the track by including the line 'Towers to the skies, an academy of lies' in the title track to their 2019 album *I Am Easy To Find*. Lead singer Matt Berninger, in a 2008 interview, admitted being obsessed with GBV, and this record. 'As far as learning to sing, I remember just listening to *Bee Thousand* on repeat and just realizing you don't really need to have … well actually Bob Pollard does have a great voice. But that if you sing with gusto, you can pull it off.'

SIDE TWO

Track one: *'Gold Star For Robot Boy'*

This spectacular song is a great way to start the side. It's also one of the few songs that was written around the time the record was being put together; it wasn't based on older or reworked material. Bob said, 'I wrote "Gold Star For Robot Boy" when I was in the process of making a decision about whether I should continue to teach or quit to become a recording artist. [It] was a way of putting that question to myself. What should I do? Should I go for the gold star just like some of the kids in my class do? I became the robot boy.'

Pollard's also castigating, yet again, all those people who'd never believed in him, as well as giving them a bit of an 'I told you so.' He writes, 'If I waited for you to show me all the actions I should take, would I get my break?' And, of course, he didn't wait. He chose his own path, and it ended up working pretty well for him.

Track two: *'Awful Bliss'*

This is the first Tobin Sprout song on the record, and while it's hard to argue with the results, if I have any complaint about the sequencing of the album, it's that all four of Toby's songs appear on the second side, with two, this and the next one, appearing in a row. I would have preferred to have Sprout's tracks spread across both sides. Apart from that small quibble, this a lovely track that's a great example of how a song can be short and yet still feel complete.

Track three: 'Mincer Ray'

This Tobin Sprout track is more of a full-band song, which is maybe why it doesn't sound too weird coming right after another of Toby's songs. It was a late addition to the record, replacing Sprout's 'Scissors,' which had been part of the single-disc edition of *Rusty Time Machine* and the first version of *Bee Thousand*. 'Scissors' is a fun song—a slow, chugging track that would have fit in perfectly next to 'Buzzards' and 'Tractor' on side one. It finds Toby declaring, 'All my life I've wanted scissors, not the kind that are so forgiving.'

The voices you hear in the middle of 'Mincer Ray' are from the beginning of 'Way To A Man's Heart,' which had appeared as part of the proposed LP *All That Glue*. That song starts with Pollard strumming a guitar while a phone rings in the background, causing Bob to drawl, 'Tell him I'll call him back if it's for me.' Jim then relates that their dad had called, asking for cash. Money, and basically the lack of it, was a point of contention between Pollard and his dad for years. Pollard senior had wanted both Bob and Jim to play professional sports, Bob later saying, 'He had dollar signs in his eyes.' It must have been a disappointment when both his boys, who were star athletes in high school, turned their backs on sports and instead became interested in, and pursued, music. Even though both of Pollard's parents are now deceased, they lived long enough to see Bob and his band become a success.

Track four: 'A Big Fan Of The Pigpen'

The music for this song was recorded during a jam session with Bob, his brother, and their friend Randy Campbell, the guy seen behind Bob on the back of *Vampire On Titus*. The song has the line 'An impeccable arrangement by the soft rock renegades.' In 2001, Pollard released a record named *Choreographed Man Of War*, credited to Robert Pollard & The Soft Rock Renegades.

Track five: *'Queen Of Cans And Jars'*

The riff that runs through most of this song is just great, and the whole tune has a warm vibe. The lyrics lean a bit toward Bob's prog side, but it's a perfect song at just under two minutes. It's also one of the best examples of how the guys managed to sound good recording in a basement on a four-track.

Track six: *'Her Psychology Today'*

This is one of the weirder songs on the record, with a bunch of different sections and some spoken-word stuff in the middle that you can't quite make out. Putting this song on side two was part of Griffin's plan to emulate the second side of the final Beatles record: 'The shortest songs reminded me of side two of the Beatles' *Abbey Road*, and I started to fiddle with a sequence of my own along those lines, with more developed rock songs on side one, pop fragments and weirdness blending together to form a suite on side two.' Yet another aspect played a part in the song being on the album. As Griffin explained, 'I included this track in the final running order mostly as a nod to the band as a whole. Songs credited to the whole band were rare.'

Track seven: *'Kicker Of Elves'*

It probably goes without saying that, lyrically, this song comes from Bob's fantasy/prog side. This was something that rubbed a lot of indie rockers the wrong way when the record first came out. Eric Davidson from the Columbus band New Bomb Turks referred to this kind of thing as GBV's 'star-spangled elf shit.' Remember, this was the 90s. The *Lord Of The Rings* movies wouldn't appear until the next decade, and Harry Potter was still a few years away. Hipsters were wearing flannel and sporting goatees, trying to look serious and edgy, so singing about elves and wizards was just not what was done if you wanted to be taken seriously. That being said, this is a fun song. Pollard's called it the 'boldest statement' he makes on the record, saying that it's 'about nationalism and flag-waving, jingoism, bullies, maybe the US.'

Track eight: *'Ester's Day'*

This Tobin Sprout track starts with a short clip from the Pollard song 'At Odds With Dr. Genesis.' 'Dr. Genesis' was one of the tracks Bob had added to the

Hardcore UFOs edition of the LP, only to see it axed by Griffin. Later included as part of the *King Shit & The Golden Boys* compilation, it's an interesting song. While the lyrics are typical Pollard prog fare ('Steel-headed giants roam the land and feed on chocolate syrup'), the instrumentation comes from a Casio or similar kind of keyboard. Bob has never included that sort of sound on GBV records, and only sparingly included keyboards or drum machines, so it's fun that it crops up here. Tobin's said that his song is about escape, the title character tempted by a 'flying car' to 'just get out of here.' On *Alien Lanes*, Pollard would tell his fans to just 'motor away,' but Sprout here is basically saying the same thing.

Track nine: *'Demons Are Real'*

This short and weird song was slated to be the opening track on both the double LP version of *Rusty Time Machine* and the first incarnation of *Bee Thousand*. While I don't mind it as part of the weird songs of the second side, it's not a great choice to begin an album, so I'm glad that wasn't the case for the final version of the LP.

Track ten: *'I Am A Scientist'*

This is a serious song that shows Pollard laying out his thoughts and ideas. For as whimsical or off the cuff as the band may appear, or present itself, a whole lot of Bob's songs and lyrics say something. This track's charm also comes from how simple it is. It starts with a basic guitar riff, and doesn't get much more complicated than that. That simplicity turns into an invitation to listeners, rather than keeping them at bay. In terms of the sequencing, it's kind of amazing that—even though this was more or less the 'single' off the record—it comes so late on the album. Then again, maybe that was another shrewd move, especially since both of the band's previous LPs started to run out of steam late into their second sides. Pollard's called this a 'kind of a self-analyzing song. I'm a scientist studying myself. I'm a journalist and reporting what I find.' What he finds is that, 'In the end, rock and roll's the religion, the source of redemption. The way out.' The song came in at number 19 in *Spin* magazine's 100 best alternative rock songs of 1994.

Track eleven: *'Peep-Hole'*

This is a rewrite of an early track called 'Sleeper,' which was intended to be part of a cassette from 1985 called *Rifle Games* (you can see the cover in the *Suitcase 2* booklet). And, even though Bob's called the original version 'hokey,' it's a sweet and effective song, the track's narrator admitting, 'Maybe I hurt you bad' and 'Maybe I won't come back.' It's Pollard at his most plaintive. The rewrite keeps the general nature of the song intact, Bob admitting in the final line, 'I love you, I must confess.' He felt this was 'much more heartfelt and poignant' than the first version. And even though Garrett Martin of *Paste* would note that this 'might be the record's saddest song,' I hear a lot of hope and acceptance. For example, when Pollard sings, 'I'm looking inside your brain, and Christ it's a cluttered mess,' he immediately follows this with the line cited above.

Bob has said 'humans are imperfect,' and his whole body of work not only allows for imperfection but embraces it. Those imperfections get pushed to the forefront to such a degree that they become an integral part of the entire experience. A mistake isn't something you sweep under the rug; it's not even a mistake. That's just what the song becomes, and, without it, it's not the song. We're the same way. We don't love our spouses or children in spite of all the little imperfections about them, but rather because of them.

Track twelve: *'You're Not An Airplane'*

Since Toby was instrumental to the sound and feel of this record, I love that he gets the last word. Plus, the ethereal nature of this song makes it perfect to end the record. Sprout actually has a pilot's license, and has loved planes all his life. This is why aircraft imagery appears throughout his work (there's also 'To Remake The Young Flyer' and 'Waving At Airplanes'). Also, since GBV is thought of as a guitar-heavy rock band—which they indeed are, most of the time—I love that their best LP ends with just piano and voice. Plus, the final line, 'The race is yet to come,' is perfect. It's like Tobin's saying the band is just getting started (which, at that point, they kind of were). And yet, it wouldn't always be a smooth ride; Sprout later called this the last 'innocent' GBV record. 'After *Bee Thousand* I think we slowly lost it,' he said, quickly adding, 'not lost it, exactly, but it had become something else.'

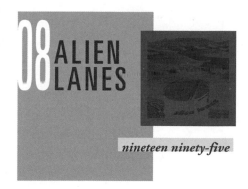

08 ALIEN LANES

nineteen ninety-five

A fter the release of what was widely heralded as the group's masterpiece, *Bee Thousand*, in 1994, GBV were coming off their biggest year ever. They also—due to the positive reception given to their 1993 record, *Vampire On Titus*—were asked to release a bunch of singles and EPs on a variety of labels. The group that once had to make up their own record companies now had labels from all over the world wanting their songs.

They also embarked on their biggest and longest tours ever, one stint of which was as part of the still mostly popular Lollapalooza tour. They appeared along with friends and fans The Breeders and Beastie Boys, not to mention a dozen other groups such as Smashing Pumpkins, Nick Cave, Green Day, and The Flaming Lips. And while 1995 wouldn't prove quite as momentous as the previous year, it still held a number of milestones for the band, the biggest of which was signing a six-figure record deal.

This was also the year GBV began to be caught in a bit of a backlash. The band had been written about so often, and in such glowing terms, that they were beginning to wear out their welcome. Journalists hadn't been able to resist Bob's tale of a decade-in-the-making overnight success, something Marc Woodworth, in his book about *Bee Thousand*, calls 'one of the great long-shot stories of rock and roll.' But all that attention began to rub some people the wrong way. In some circles, the band were snarkily referred to as 'Guided By Critics.' Two years prior, no one knew who they were. Now people were getting sick of hearing about them.

This was also the age of irony and slackers. Kids wore T-shirts that said 'LOSER' and got their clothes at thrift stores. The more beat-up the Dr. Martens, the better. No one was supposed to give a shit, something that Bob—on the surface anyway—seemed to endorse. The lo-fi records and the drunken live shows attested to that (not to mention he once sang, 'I wish I could give a shit, just a little bit'). Beavis and Butthead, while watching a Pavement video, said of the band, 'It's like they're not even trying.' And if you ever saw Pavement live, it's kind of hard to argue against that.

Strokes guitarist Albert Hammond Jr. later talked about the difference between the indie-rock scene he grew up in versus the one he later joined. 'In the mid-90s, it was like it was cool to not be successful. It was the opposite when we were coming out a few years later.' But Guided By Voices were different. 'I know for sure,' says Hammond, 'that [GBV] wanted to be successful.'

The first step they took in trying to reach that wider audience was to switch labels. The timing was right, since the band were getting so much attention. The two serious contenders that eventually emerged were Matador and Warner Bros. Matador's Gerard Cosloy had been a fan of the band since he witnessed GBV's second CBGB show. Plus, since Matador had a production and distribution deal with Scat, they were already working with the band, albeit indirectly.

Meanwhile, out in California, Geoffrey Weiss from Warner Bros pursued the group, going so far as to visit them in Dayton, as well as flying Bob and Jim out to Los Angeles. And while it may seem like a cynical move on the part of Warner Bros—a huge label trying to grab the last bit of the post-Nirvana alternative gold rush—Weiss's heart was in the right place. The website *Dust And Grooves* described him as 'the world's best record collector.' At Warner Bros he'd worked with plenty of bands similar to GBV, including Dinosaur Jr., Built To Spill, Pavement, and Mudhoney. And, of course, The Flaming Lips have had a long and fruitful relationship with Warner Bros, while Bob's 80s heroes, R.E.M., were also on the label.

One of Pollard's conditions for signing to a label was that it had to release the band's next record as-is. Bob had compiled a cassette of random tracks he was calling *Scalping The Guru*, and he was insistent it be the follow-up to *Bee Thousand*. He gave copies of it to the prospective record companies that wanted to work with the band. The scratchy-sounding cassette caused a publicist at Warner Bros to tell Pollard, 'This lo-fi shit's gone too far!'

As it turns out, Weiss and the others never had a chance. Pollard later said, 'A lot of the labels came around, and I personally told most of them that I'd had my mind set on Matador from the beginning.' Matador ended up paying a $100,000 advance for *Alien Lanes*, a figure that even label founder Chris Lombardi admitted was 'insane.'

An interesting thing about the deal with Matador is that it specifically spelled out that Bob was the band. He, and not the other guys, was Guided By Voices. That was put right into the contract. As Bob explained, 'I write all the songs, have all of the imagery and concepts; it's my creation.' This is something he would put into practice over the years by hiring and firing members, not to mention retiring or resuscitating the name whenever he felt like it.

The label they were leaving, Scat, would continue to work with the band, but would never release anything new by Pollard or GBV. The year *Alien Lanes* came out, Scat released a box set containing all the self-released LPs, as well as a compilation of unreleased songs. *Rolling Stone*, in a four-star review, called these mostly unheard records 'a kind of indie-rock version of Dylan's *Basement Tapes*.' Scat would later reissue *Propeller* as a standalone CD in 1996, as well as *Bee Thousand: The Director's Cut* in 2004. And while GBV's creative relationship with Scat was fairly short—barely two years— Robert Griffin, by being the first to sign GBV, and releasing their first proper records, plays a large and indispensable role in the story of Guided By Voices.

For their new record, GBV stuck to the template they'd followed with *Bee Thousand*. Old tracks were mashed up against new tracks. Everything was recorded at home, and fast, most of the sessions happening in Toby's basement (listed in the liner notes as Collider X-L). The four-track Sprout owned was a TASCAM Porta One Ministudio, which made its debut in 1984. TASCAM was the first company to produce a four-track that recorded on standard cassette tapes. That milestone happened in 1979 with its TEAC 144 Portastudio, which retailed for $1,100. Before this, people who recorded at home had to use unwieldy reel-to-reel machines. Once TASCAM introduced the TEAC 144, other companies—such as Fostex and Yamaha—followed suit with four-track cassette recorders of their own.

The fact that these new machines operated on standard audiocassettes, and were super simple to use, meant that anybody could cheaply record themselves or their bands. This led to an explosion of musical creativity. Whereas punk taught people that anyone could be in a band and release a record, four-tracks moved the recording studio into the bedroom, giving rise to a whole new wave of bands and labels.

The first title, *Scalping The Guru*, came from a song off the *Clown Prince Of The Menthol Trailer* EP. The eventual name of the LP, *Alien Lanes*, was from *The Grand Hour* EP. An early track listing for *Guru* had twenty-five songs; almost everything on *Guru* would appear on *Alien Lanes*. The five songs that weren't on *Scalping The Guru*, but which eventually made their way onto *Alien Lanes*, were '(I Wanna Be A) Dumbcharger,' 'Game Of Pricks,' 'The Ugly Vision,' 'Chicken Blows,' and 'Little Whirl.' And while it's inconceivable to think of *Alien Lanes* without 'Game Of Pricks,' most of those other songs don't add much. Why Bob felt the need to add yet more tracks to what was already a twenty-five-song record almost boggles the mind. *Uncut* has called GBV's vision and aesthetic 'so heroically DIY it borders on the professionally suicidal.' *Alien Lanes* is ample evidence of that.

The producer was listed as Mr. Japan, who was really just Bob, and the engineer was the Red-Nosed Driver, who was Sprout. The record was mastered, however, by recording industry legend Bob Ludwig. He's worked on records by seminal bands and artists such as Eric Clapton, Rush, Neil Young, and Pollard's favorite, The Who. Before Ludwig got started with *Alien Lanes*, Tobin asked if he'd worked on any records recorded on a four-track. Bob answered that he had: Bruce Springsteen's *Nebraska*. But while that's technically a four-track record, it's not in the same universe as what GBV were doing. A better comparison would have been Lou Reed's infamous *Metal Machine Music*, which Ludwig mastered in 1975. Also recorded on a four-track, it was described in a Reed biography as 'four vinyl sides of nonstop, reverberating, distortion-laden clamorous guitar feedback,' not to mention 'a screeching fuck-you not only to Reed's record company but to his fans.' And yet Ludwig, who knew and admired avant-garde composers like Stockhausen and Xenakis, took Reed's project seriously. So he was probably open to, and intrigued by, what Pollard and the guys were doing.

As with *Bee Thousand*, the single and EP that were associated with *Alien Lanes* featured re-recorded versions of what appeared on the LP. The reason for this was simple: to break the band out of the lo-fi ghetto and get them played on something other than college stations. In a story that came out prior to the record's release, *Billboard* wrote that 'Motor Away' was being re-recorded to 'help make *Alien Lanes* more appealing to radio.' And, in terms of *Tigerbomb*'s version of 'Game Of Pricks,' Jim Greer has said, 'We were asked by the record company to re-record it as a possible single for radio play.'

Kris Gillespie, Matador's director of radio promotion at the time called the band 'relatively new' in the same *Billboard* article quoted above, and said, 'For a lot of commercial radio stations, this is the first time that they have heard the band, despite all the press.' It seems like a long shot to try to sell GBV, and especially *Alien Lanes*, to any sort of audience beyond an indie or college-rock crowd (not to mention to try and get them on the radio).

'Motor Away' was re-recorded at a studio in Ohio and issued as a seven-inch. This is the version that appears on *Human Amusements At Hourly Rates*. I much prefer the version on *Alien Lanes*. On the re-recorded version, Bob's vocal is too affected, and the reverb on his voice makes him feel far away. When I hear the first version, I feel like I can take on the world. When I hear the second version, I just think, 'Eh, that's not a bad song.'

The single's B-side was 'Color My Blade.' It was recorded in Chicago by Steve Albini, who's credited on the sleeve as 'Fluss.' The sleeve also gives special thanks to Kim Deal for helping with the arrangement of 'Color My Blade.'

The band made a video for 'Motor Away,' although it uses the *Alien Lanes* version and not the one on the seven-inch. The video also includes the song that immediately precedes it on the album, 'Auditorium.' (Speaking of Kim Deal, the Pixies did something similar in 1990 with a video that included both 'Dig For Fire' and 'Alison.') The 'Motor Away' video features all the guys in the band, as well as 'manager for life' Pete Jamison, and Nate Farley, who was just a roadie at the time but would later step in as a full-fledged member.

Later in the year, the *Tigerbomb* EP would have re-recorded versions of two tracks from *Alien Lanes*, 'My Valuable Hunting Knife' and 'Game Of Pricks.' The band also made a video for the re-recorded version of 'Hunting Knife.' The cover of the 'Motor Away' single features Mitch Mitchell, while *Tigerbomb* featured Bob's brother. So, even though Pollard was the main creative force in the band (legally and spiritually), he was willing to give others the spotlight.

The cover for *Alien Lanes* was designed by Matador Records' in-house designer, Mark Ohe, with help from Bob (who's credited, in an act of sibling solidarity, as Bob Ohe). Ohe was one of Matador's earliest employees, starting at the label when there were only a handful of staffers. In addition to coming up with Matador's logo, he's designed a bunch of records for bands such as Pavement, Yo La Tengo, Cat Power, and many others.

'I enjoy collaborating with other people,' Ohe has said. 'Using the talents I have to further their ideas, and working together to come up with something new that neither of us … would have come up with.' He helped design most everything GBV put out on Matador, working closely with Bob to do so. Ohe's website features a number of Pollard-esque collages, so I can see how these two were kindred spirits with the same aesthetic vision.

The cover for *Alien Lanes* features a sort of collage, with a photograph of a drum (which is also on the back cover) and a wavy, rainbow-like pattern over the drumhead. The pattern was taken from the cover of *Tune In, Turn On*, a jazz LP by Benny Golson released in 1967, where it appeared as the screen of a TV sitting in a desert. The background on *Alien Lanes*, sand dunes and dried brush, is awfully reminiscent of the Golson sleeve. The desert background featured on *Lanes* would later be used on Circus Devils' double record *Sgt. Disco*. The *Alien Lanes* cover is an okay cover, although it looks dated and 90s in a way that *Mag Earwhig!* does not.

The back of *Alien Lanes* shows the band at the time: Mitch Mitchell, Kevin Fennell, Bob, Toby, and new bassist Jim Greer. They're all sitting on an old couch in Kevin's basement. There's some musical equipment—drums, drumsticks, and an amp head—as well as assorted basement miscellany, like a bag of golf clubs and a tub of laundry detergent. The band members have a cool and weary look, with only Greer and Mitchell looking at the camera. Bob's head is pointed up with his eyes closed, and Toby and Kevin look away with thoughtful stares.

Jim Greer is the author of the official GBV biography, *Hunting Accidents*, which came out in 2005. The book covers the origins and rise of the band, following the group up until the breakup in 2004. (The 2018 authorized bio of Pollard called *Closer You Are* covers the same time frame.) Greer's written novels, short stories, screenplays, music criticism, and journalism. He met GBV while writing about them for *Spin*. The idea that Greer liked the band so much after profiling them that he stayed on as a member has a wonderful cult-like aspect to it, like how in *Apocalypse Now* the first guy they sent to take out Kurtz actually switched sides and joined up with him. However, Greer was engaged to Kim Deal at the time, and was hanging out a lot in Dayton, so his joining the band wasn't as out-of-left-field as it appears. (After his brief stint with Guided By Voices, Greer went on to be in other bands, most recently as the duo DCTV, who released four records and had a video directed by GBV fan Steven Soderbergh.)

Once again, the reviews were mostly positive. *Spin* gave the LP a seven out of ten, writing, 'There are definitely some classic GBV stylings here,' and stating that, for new fans, 'The chaotic 28-song *Alien Lanes* offers a rockier introduction than last year's *Bee Thousand*.' The review also cites the record's 'self-interrupting breathlessness,' as well as the audio 'throwaways' and 'bric-a-brac' that accompany the 'five or six songs' that are as 'perfect as perfect can be.'

One of the lone dissenting voices in 1995 was legendary *Village Voice* critic Robert Christgau who, having already labeled GBV 'pop for perverts' the year before, proclaimed *Alien Lanes* to be a 'dud.' I have to agree. As much as this record is loved, for me it doesn't hang together nearly as well as other GBV LPs. Bob had called *Bee Thousand* a puzzle. The songs may have been in pieces, but they formed a coherent picture once they were put together. After all, puzzles get solved. Whereas *Alien Lanes* sounds to my ears like a haphazard collection of tracks, some of which just aren't very good.

Bob's stated intent with *Alien Lanes* was to 'create a double album's worth of songs on one record.' The problem is, as with most double LPs, there's a ton of filler. And while I realize I'm in the minority here—most people love this record and put it forth as one of GBV's best—there's at least one person who agrees with me: Kim Deal.

'Kim Deal hated *Alien Lanes*,' Pollard admitted. 'She said it was just too fragmented, too short, but that was the concept. You can finish the songs, yeah, but the point is those songs are finished. I didn't have any intention to make them any longer, that's what they were.'

The problem isn't that the songs are short. I like plenty of short songs, by GBV or any other band. The problem is that the songs are bad. That's not to say there aren't some great moments on *Alien Lanes*. There are. There are lots of them. But in between are a bunch of half-baked fragments that detract from the overall focus and quality of the album.

Another thing I have against the LP is what it did—or rather didn't do—for the band. In 1994, GBV were everywhere. They'd just released their best album and were media darlings. They could have written their own ticket. They were like Orson Welles coming off his *War Of The Worlds* broadcast or The Beatles on their way to America for the first time. The band had a huge amount of artistic capital, and by insisting their next LP be a substandard batch of poorly recorded songs and snippets, they completely squandered that capital. *Alien Lanes* put a stop to the band's momentum, not to mention any chance they had of reaching a wider audience; it all but assured their status as a cult band. And, despite repeatedly rejecting the tags 'lo-fi' and 'indie rock,' which were constantly assigned to the group, Pollard doubled down on them with the release of *Alien Lanes*. He had the opportunity to shed those labels forever but chose not to. He was like an animal that rails against its cage and yet, when the door is left open, stays inside.

Sure, the LP has rabid fans today, and even when it was released some people loved it. But when I look at *Alien Lanes*, I see a missed opportunity. That's not to say the only point is to sell copies or get big; by that metric, Maroon 5 are a thousand times more successful than GBV. That's not how I keep score. What I'm saying is that *Alien Lanes* is, for me, a symbol of cockiness and hubris as much as it is an album. It's the point where Pollard was faced with two paths, took one over the other, and gradually discovered the road he'd chosen only got smaller and smaller the further he traveled.

SIDE ONE

Track one: *'A Salty Salute'*

This rousing call to arms is the perfect way to start the record. With its references to 'proud brothers' and ideas of group identity and deliverance, it's pretty much GBV's pledge of allegiance. The final declaration that 'the club is open' even becomes a meta comment about the record itself. It's an invitation to everything that follows, and a sly nod to the opening track of *Sgt. Pepper*, which served a similar purpose.

Like 'Hot Freaks' from the previous album, the song began as an instrumental by Tobin Sprout. The opening riff—which sounds like a bass—was originally played on a six-string guitar. The phrase 'the club is open,' along with the 'GBV!' chant that opened *Propeller*, has since entered into GBV mythology. You can even get your own 'THE CLUB IS OPEN' neon sign for under $200 from a variety of online sources.

Track two: *'Evil Speakers'*

The placement of this song makes me miss the touches that Robert Griffin brought to *Bee Thousand*. Whereas Griffin ensured that record had an amazing one-two-three opening punch, *Alien Lanes* falters right out of the gate with this fragment that sounds like Bob free-forming over a lackluster instrumental.

Track three: *'Watch Me Jumpstart'*

This is another great song in the mold of heroic mission-statement songs like 'Over The Neptune / Mesh Gear Fox,' Pollard here promising to 'bulldoze every bulldozer away.' But it also has the usual sober skepticism that Bob injected into even his most anthemic rallying cries, stating, 'Where it's going it's hard for me to say' and 'Don't look now, I'm a phase.' No matter how 'white hot' he might be, Pollard can only be himself: 'I can't pretend to be something I'm not.'

The song also provided the title for Banks Tarver's film of the same name, which was available separately and as part of the *Hardcore UFOs* box set. Tarver's brother, Clay, was in the band Chavez, which was started by early GBV fan Matt Sweeney. The documentary started as a film-school project for Tarver, who was around the same age as the guys when the movie was made. Tarver attended Harvard as an undergrad and went to Berkeley for law school. After working as a civil-rights attorney in Texas, he attended film school at Stanford. He later worked for MTV, and now has his own production company based out of New York.

Track four: 'They're Not Witches'

This short throwaway sets up a pattern on *Alien Lanes* of a fleshed-out song sandwiched between a fragment or snippet. This effect dulls the LP's momentum.

Track five: 'As We Go Up We Go Down'

This brilliant song is Bob at his most pragmatic. His band had spent the past couple of years being media darlings, but he was wise enough to know that whatever rises must fall—as we go up, we go down. And yet, even though he acknowledges the vagaries of fame and fortune, he looks to protect himself, stating, 'I speak in monotone, leave my fucking life alone.'

Track six: '(I Wanna Be A) Dumbcharger'

This song doesn't do much for me, and the line 'Temptation creeps to you like rapists in the night' seems needlessly shocking. If you're interested, a dumb charger is a device used to recharge 'dumb' batteries ('dumb' batteries being ones that have no internal electronic circuitry, as opposed to 'smart' batteries, which have an internal chip that can communicate with a 'smart' charger).

Track seven: 'Game Of Pricks'

While I prefer the longer and faster version on *Tigerbomb*, this is still a great rendition of one of GBV's best songs. Everything about it is perfect. It's a rocking tune with great lyrics, and Bob sings it perfectly. The line 'I've entered the game of pricks with knives in the back of me' is similar to the Morrissey line 'I've been stabbed in the back so many times I don't have any skin.' And yet, for as serious and heavy as the song is, it's a joy to listen to, and it's always a raucous favorite when they play it live.

Track eight: 'The Ugly Vision'

This slow song has subtle piano and acoustic guitar. The line 'Sell yourself to the man' could be seen as a reference to Pollard's recent dealings in the music industry, the same as 1997's 'I Am Produced.'

Track nine: 'A Good Flying Bird'

This fast song by Tobin Sprout is different from his *Bee Thousand* tracks, which were slow and acoustic. Since Toby had called the band's prior album GBV's last 'innocent' record, the lyrics here could be seen to be about the group. 'Many years we spent unpressured' could refer to GBV's early wilderness years. And yet, as isolated as the band was, and no matter how many wrong or weird decisions they may have made, they never gave up. Bob's written a bunch of songs in this vein, but it's cool to hear these sentiments from Toby as well. And, of course, the repeated cries of 'yeah, yeah' at the end are reminiscent of 'She Loves You' by The Beatles.

Track ten: 'Cigarette Tricks'

This is the album's briefest track at a mere eighteen seconds. It's a complete throwaway. The only reason I can see that Bob included it was to achieve his stated intention of having the feel of a double album on a single disc.

Track eleven: 'Pimple Zoo'

This is another fragment (it's not even a minute long) that's annoying even though it's awfully short. Pollard spends most of track barking out the line, 'Sometimes I get the feeling that you don't want me around.'

Track twelve: 'Big Chief Chinese Restaurant'

While this song's not nearly as annoying as the previous two, it adds nothing to the overall album except to pad out its length. It's also emblematic of the problem I have with *Alien Lanes*. These short songs, which aren't satisfying on any level, get in the way of what could have been a run of amazing songs. Imagine if the record went 'A Salty Salute,' 'Watch Me Jumpstart,' 'As We Go Up We Go Down,' 'Game Of Pricks,' 'A Good Flying Bird,' 'Closer You Are,' and then 'Motor Away.' Bam. Side one. Seven songs instead of fifteen.

Track thirteen: *'Closer You Are'*

This fast and poppy song is everything you want from GBV. The opening line, 'Chain smoke rings like a vapor snake kiss,' is perfect. There's also a reference to being 'stoned at the Alamo tonight.' Of course, as everyone knows, there's no basement at the Alamo, so don't even ask.

Track fourteen: *'Auditorium'*

This song, which also began as a Sprout instrumental, is decent. The lyrics at the beginning are surreal and kind of fun, Bob spitting out, 'Post-punk X-Man parked his fork-lift, like a billion stars flickering from the grinder's wheel.' But there's not much of a tune, and Pollard's singing seems unconnected to the music in the background. Thankfully, it only lasts a minute, and then we're into the next track.

Track fifteen: *'Motor Away'*

This is quite simply one of the best songs on this or any other GBV album. As Bob has said, 'It's another one of those "fuck you" songs.' In it he talks about 'belittling every little voice that told you so' and, finally, just getting in a car and getting the hell out of there. He obviously still had a lot of anger and resentment left over from the years when his family didn't believe in him. But it's not just about the past. It's about the present, too, Bob reminding himself of what's at stake and what kind of opportunity the band's been given. 'You can't lie to yourself that it's the chance of a lifetime.' It's a truly great song, and one of the most inspiring and anthemic ones Pollard's ever written. It doesn't lose anything by being in this four-track basement version. This song's actually been recorded a bunch of times; the Guided By Voices database shows four different demo versions, one of which was released on *Suitcase 4*.

SIDE TWO

Track one: *'Hit'*

At a mere twenty-three seconds, this is the second-shortest track on the record. It's also one of the worst. The fact that it was included on GBV's only official best-of, *Human Amusements At Hourly Rates*, is a joke. It's also not fun to hear Bob sing about 'giggling faggots.' Why Pollard, or anyone at Matador, thought this 'song' should be included on anything is beyond me.

Track two; 'My Valuable Hunting Knife'

Unlike 'Motor Away,' I prefer the re-recorded version from the *Tigerbomb* EP. But even in this primitive form, it's a lot of fun. The title may have been inspired by a Jim Morrison poem from the book *The Lords And The New Creatures*:

A knife was stolen. A
valuable hunting knife

Track three: 'Gold Hick'

This track—which is just six lines of nonsense—is another of the throwaway song snippets that litter the LP.

Track four: 'King And Caroline'

Bob injects the lyrics here with some strong melodies, but it feels half-baked, even for GBV.

Track five: 'Striped White Jets'

This song shows how heavy you can be on a four-track in a basement. It's another track about aviation, which Pollard has chalked up to being from Dayton, the birthplace of aviation. The song was later covered by Cobra Verde, whose version came out on both a seven-inch and the *Blatant Doom Trip* tribute record. I'll talk more about them when we get to 1997's *Mag Earwhig!*

Track six: 'Ex-Supermodel'

The only thing I can say about this annoying fragment is that the snoring is from an old high-school friend of Bob's whom Pollard had christened 'the narcoleptic truck driver.'

Track seven: 'Blimps Go 90'

This simple tune sounds like 'Bohemian Rhapsody' compared to the rougher tracks on side two. It could once again be read as a statement on where the band found themselves at this stage of their careers. GBV had been in the spotlight for the past two years, but that shine was beginning to wear off, and both Bob and Toby were beginning to get a little nostalgic for when the band was their own personal secret, Bob here writing, 'Oftentimes I'm reminded of the sweet young days.' But then he made it, he was 'knighted,' and people started giving him all kinds of advice. He was also beginning to realize what a commitment he'd made: 'This is not a vacation.' Everything has a hidden price. The song also mentions sipping 'Gentleman Jack,' which is a type of whiskey made by Jack Daniel's.

Track eight: 'Strawdogs'

This lo-fi track goes back to the 'sandpaper' sound of *Vampire On Titus*. I'm not sure if the title is a reference to Sam Peckinpah's 1971 film *Straw Dogs*. The lyrics don't directly reference it, but the line 'We've been sent in defending the one thing because it's our duty' is somewhat reminiscent of the film's plot.

Track nine: 'Chicken Blows'

This fun song had been around for a while. It was originally supposed to appear on the *Back To Saturn X* EP. That never happened, but a snippet of it was part of the track 'Back To Saturn X Radio Report' from *Propeller*. It was then included on a compilation seven-inch that came with a magazine. In the documentary *Watch Me Jumpstart*, the song is playing while Bob's driving around Dayton, and he remarks that the track is 'Beatles-esque,' adding that some people don't like The Beatles but he loves them. In 1995, not a lot of bands in the indie-rock world would have admitted to liking The Beatles. The Fall, The Stooges, and The Velvet Underground, yes. But the lovable moptops from Liverpool? Not so much.

Track ten: 'Little Whirl'

This fast song by Tobin is almost punk rock, with Sprout screaming over and over again that he doesn't care. It was one of the few songs not originally part of *Scalping The Guru*.

Track eleven: *'My Son Cool'*

This song is, of course, about Pollard's son, Bryan. Bob would write a song for his daughter, 'Your Name Is Wild,' on next year's *Under The Bushes Under The Stars*. And while it's not exactly Cat Stevens's 'Father And Son,' it's touching that Pollard refers to Bryan as 'my love.'

The theme seems to be the independence that all kids must achieve when they grow up, Bob writing that 'the rope has been severed' and that his son must 'decide now' his own path in life.

Track twelve: *'Always Crush Me'*

This song had also been around for a while, appearing the previous year on a split seven-inch with the band Belreve. It doesn't do much for me, especially as the twenty-seventh track on a record with twenty-eight songs.

Track thirteen: *'Alright'*

Only Bob would make the last track of a twenty-eight-song record the longest. It's practically an instrumental, with the first two and half minutes being a solid groove with Bob occasionally shouting 'All right!' Even on *Scalping The Guru* this was the last song, so Pollard had obviously wanted to end his new record with this song for some time. It's a fun way to end what's a stubborn, confounding, and ultimately iconic album.

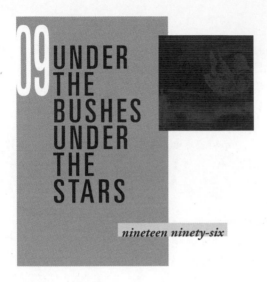

09 UNDER THE BUSHES UNDER THE STARS

nineteen ninety-six

G BV became the band that fell to Earth. Instead of everything going right for the group, things began to go wrong. Bob's indecisiveness about what kind of record he wanted to make set the group back, they started to have trouble with their label, and the current lineup would be dissolved. All the glory that came with the six-figure deal for *Alien Lanes*, and the endless news stories, disappeared. Pollard began to doubt himself, and his relationships with indie-rock royalty like Kim Deal and Steve Albini soured.

None of this, of course, stopped Bob or Guided By Voices from releasing material. It was the opposite, and that was kind of the problem. In 1996, they released what would be their longest record until the 2017 double album *August By Cake*. They also released two EPs, a fan-club-only LP, and two singles. This year also saw the release, on the same day, of solo records by Pollard and Tobin Sprout. Bob's was noisy and experimental, Toby's confident and polished.

As usual with all the band's albums, what provided the initial spark for the new LP was all but extinguished by the time it was finally released. The follow-up to *Alien Lanes* was initially a concept record called *The Power Of Suck*. It was going to be loosely based on the rise of GBV, complete with a short story by the band's bassist at the time, writer Jim Greer. In 1995, MTV reported that the record would have nineteen tracks, including 'Deaf Ears,' 'Newton's Hopeless Marriage,' 'Systems Crash,' and 'Delayed Reaction.' In true Pollard fashion, none of those songs appeared on *Under The Bushes*. Those weren't even *Power Of Suck* songs. 'Deaf Ears' was eventually a B-side on the 'Official Ironmen Rally Song' single, while 'Systems Crash' led off the *Plantations Of Pale Pink* EP. In the *Watch Me Jumpstart* documentary, you can see Bob and Sprout recording 'Systems Crash' in Toby's basement.

The original producer of the record was going to be Kim Deal, with whom, by this time, Bob had formed an important friendship. She'd been a fan of the band for a few years, and she and Pollard had worked together on a few different projects. She was also engaged to GBV's bassist, which ensured that she was often in the band's orbit.

A few years prior, Deal and Pollard contributed a hauntingly lovely duet of 'Love Hurts' to the soundtrack for the film *Love And A .45*. (Kevin's wearing a shirt for the movie in one of his *Watch Me Jumpstart* interviews.) Pollard later said that his wife, also named Kim, hated his involvement with Deal, thinking that the two of them were in love, which Bob admitted, 'We kind of were.'

On Marc Maron's podcast, Kim Deal talked about her relationship with Pollard, at first audibly sighing in annoyance when Maron brought him up. Deal insisted that she 'didn't want to produce' GBV's next record, but that Bob persisted, saying, 'But I love your guitar sounds,' so Deal said yes. The problem is that Pollard didn't want to put in the time to get that great sound. Plus, that the band had to rehearse the songs for hours grated on the guys, who'd never spent much time recording their songs, let alone rehearsing them. In a cover story in the CMJ magazine that appeared around the time of *Under The Bushes*, Mitch Mitchell talked about the LP's preparation. 'We rehearsed in Kim's basement for, like, a month, every day, six hours a day. And it began to feel too much like a job.'

By the time the band got down to legendary Easley Studios in Memphis, they were already sick of the material. Plus, the famously impatient Pollard quickly tired of Deal's exacting process. After just a handful of tracks were recorded, Bob decamped back to Dayton, supposedly to watch his son's basketball game. Deal was not happy. It was the first crack in a relationship that would soon be irretrievably ruptured. The final straw was a show in Cincinnati where Deal's band The Amps were opening up for GBV. Guided By Voices hadn't left Deal's group enough time to sound-check. Deal, thoroughly pissed off, proceeded to punch Pete Jamison in the stomach, causing him to double over. Pollard and Deal never spoke to each other again.

Around this time, the band worked again with longtime Deal associate Steve Albini. The iconoclastic producer had reached out to Matador, wondering why GBV hadn't been in contact. Bob may have been flattered, but he was reluctant to get in touch, wondering, 'Why would Albini, who makes these big, fucking hard-assed records, want to work with us and our little, squeezed-down four-track songs?'

Pollard and the band went to Chicago. They recorded a few songs over the span of three days and, even though they all got along well, Bob wasn't happy with the results. 'The thing about the stuff we did with Steve is, I think we gave him inferior songs,' Bob later said. 'I like what he did, but I don't much like the songs we did with him.' The only songs that Albini worked on that ended up on the band's next LP are 'It's Like Soul' and 'Sheetkickers.'

After recording with Albini in Chicago, the band left for a tour overseas. By the time they came back, Bob had decided to say goodbye to most of the songs from the previous sessions, as well as *The Power Of Suck*. 'We went to Europe and did our tour, and when we came back I had decided to shitcan the concept album, and I wrote a bunch of new songs, like eighteen or twenty songs, and I thought they were better. They were more spontaneous and more free, they weren't geared toward a concept of anything, so we decided to record them in Dayton.'

Rather than fully retreat to the safety of their basements and just mash together the studio stuff with four-track stuff, like they'd done on *Propeller*, GBV went into Dayton's Cro Magnon studios to record what Bob had written while on the road. Once the concept album idea was jettisoned, Pollard considered a number of new titles, among them *The World Series Of Psychic Phenomena*, *Plantations Of Pale Pink*, *The Flying Party Is Here*, and *Under The Bushes Under The Trees*.

After the record had been turned in, Matador decided to put the album's final six songs on an EP that would come with the vinyl record. The LP came in a gatefold sleeve, with an eighteen-track record on one disc and the six-track EP as a separate twelve-inch. This seems odd, since Matador had had to continually battle with the band about how much stuff Pollard released. In an article in *Billboard* a few months prior to the release of *Under The Bushes*, Patrick Amory, Matador's director of national sales, said, 'We have to stop them from giving us new records.' He added that the label did everything they could to 'hold back' the band from releasing more than one LP a year. So why confuse things by packaging an EP with an LP? On the CD, the last six songs of the EP were 'bonus' tracks, resulting in a twenty-four-track album that's almost an hour long. The CD itself doesn't even list the final six songs, since they were initially axed by Matador, but then added later on.

The seeds of the band's eventual break with Matador seem to have been sown around this time. Bob, for a long time used to being the captain of the GBV ship, was unhappy to be limited in terms of the group's output. Matador, however, had a point. Bob's desire to flood the market with product is a horrible idea for a band that wants to last and for a guy who wants to make being a musician his career. But Bob wasn't thinking in terms of shifting units, or even radio play. After being denied an outlet for his music for so long, he just wanted to get stuff out there.

All the indecision swirling around the record, from Pollard's usual tinkering with the track list to Matador's confusion about what in the hell to do with the band, would seem to imply that *Under The Bushes* adds up to a schizophrenic listening experience. However, this is GBV we're talking about. All their records are schizophrenic listening experiences. That's why a lot of people, me included, like the band. So the hodgepodge nature of the record's creation, and its track list, doesn't strike my ears as odd or out of place. That being said, the length makes it difficult to enjoy in one sitting, and the amount of songs does seem excessive. This was reflected in the LP's reviews and general reception, which seemed muted after the response to *Bee Thousand* and *Alien Lanes*, both of which were hailed as almost-instant classics. *Rolling Stone*, in the band's first three-star review, gave the record tempered praise, with Michael Corcoran writing, '*Under the Bushes* searches for something new in the pop-rock ruins and finds that the quest is the thing.'

Chuck Stephens of *Spin* gave the record a paltry six out of ten, calling the

LP 'brittle' and 'overbaked,' and stating that '*Under the Bushes* manages to showcase but a single new lo-fi trick: the art of carrying a tune while holding your nose.'

Lorraine Ali, in a two-star review in the *Los Angeles Times*, wrote, 'Although *Under the Bushes* offers twenty-four songs free of rock'n'roll pomp and ultra-polished production, the album still can't help but feel self-conscious and contrived.'

The sleeve is one of GBV's least interesting covers. The front features some found art of a landscape, with a picture of a guy contained within a circle. The guy in the circle—taken from the December 1963 issue of *National Geographic*—is just plopped onto the rest of the cover; it isn't integrated into the overall collage. That it's a circle pays a visual homage to the record or CD found within—this element was used as the basis for a limited-edition picture-disc seven-inch released in the UK.

The back cover's also bland, featuring just an out-of-focus photo of a woman and a young boy. It's a picture of a pawnshop window in Germany. Inside the pawnshop, Pollard and Matt Sweeney found the postcard that features on the cover of the *Sunfish Holy Breakfast* EP.

The inside cover's a bit more engaging. The song titles are listed in all caps in a bold, sans-serif font, black on white. The album's credits are placed against a cool photo of a building that has mannequins attached to the outside. The perspective of the photo, not to mention that one of the mannequins has a creepy head that's staring right at the viewer, makes it an eerie and effective image. This same image is on the cover of the book *100*, which features the front and back of Pollard's first hundred full-length releases.

Probably the most momentous thing about this record, and what happened to GBV in 1996, is that the band—what's come to be known as the 'classic' lineup—dissolved. This means no more Toby, no more Mitch, and no more Kevin. Bassist Greg Demos is also mentioned as being part of this lineup, even though he never toured regularly with the group, having chosen to become a lawyer rather than join the band full-time.

Toby left first, feeling the pull of family life and responsibility. Creatively speaking, his departure was the biggest blow to the band. His voice, and his songs—not to mention his technical prowess with a four-track—provided the perfect counterpoint to Pollard. I would also say that, by this point, Sprout didn't *need* GBV. He'd created and carved out his own audience; this would be the year that saw the release of his first solo record. The time was right for him to strike out on his own.

In terms of Kevin and Mitch, this loss was probably a bigger deal to Pollard on an emotional level. They'd been with Bob from the beginning. Since before the beginning. They were old friends from Northridge and had known Pollard from high school. Kevin had been Bob's brother in-law. These were ties that went beyond just the band. Kevin's resurgent substance-abuse problem, long held in check, had become an issue during the band's European tour. His subsequent behavior brought matters to the point where Pollard looked upon Fennell's dismissal as a foregone conclusion. 'I didn't fire Kevin,' Bob later said. 'He fired himself.' Bob tried to keep Mitch in the band, initially moving him to bass as the guys from Cobra Verde joined the group as the new lineup, but Mitchell thought of it as a demotion. His interest waned to the point where Pollard felt he had to let him go, even though they'd been in bands together for decades.

The breakup was big enough news that it was written about in the *Dayton Daily News*, with Pollard quoted as saying, 'The good ship Guided By Voices will continue on, but the existing personnel has decided to split. We were getting a little sick of looking at each other. And there are certain things—personal goals—people need to do.' It was the end of an era.

SIDE ONE
Track one: *'Man Called Aerodynamics'*

That it just starts, and then ends, with no real structure, makes this song sound unresolved and not the best one to open the record (especially when there are so many other great tracks on the LP). Bob plays all the instruments, as he did on *Vampire On Titus*. The line 'Look it up in the book mobile' seems to harken back to Pollard's days as a schoolteacher, while the next, 'Look it up in the gun rack,' speaks to some of the working-class characters he would chronicle in several of the LP's songs.

Track two: *'Rhine Jive Click'*

This is a great example of the record's mid-fi sound. The buzz and hiss heard on earlier records is nowhere to be found. It's not as slick as they'd get in a few years, but it's miles ahead of their last couple of albums. The opening line, 'Crowded gymnasiums, no shortage of knock-outs,' recalls the inspiration behind '14 Cheerleader Coldfront.'

Track three: *'Cut-Out Witch'*

This awesome song has an effective buildup. The only downside is that the sound is thin and doesn't at all convey what a monster it is live. At any GBV show, if the pit isn't already going nuts, this is the song that's going to kick things off. The lines 'Do you suppose you could change your life?' and 'If you could, then I wish you would' were taken from an Acid Ranch track called 'Edison's Memos.'

Cutouts, in terms of the recording industry, refer to records or CDs that have been discounted or remaindered. According to the blog *Music Weird*, 'Cutouts took their name from the physical cut on the album cover that indicates that they are deleted titles. Over time, manufacturers also identified cut-outs by drilling holes in records, stamping a message on the covers, or cutting off a corner of the album cover.' Sometimes, promo copies were also notched or given the 'cutout' treatment. When it comes to CDs, a circle cut into the barcode means that it's a promo, whereas, when the side of the jewel case is cut, or notched, it's overstock. Now that Bob was on a bigger label and was part of the actual Recording Industry, he had to worry about stuff like this. It's something he'd write about even more explicitly on the *Mag Earwhig!* tune 'I Am Produced.'

Track four: *'Burning Flag Birthday Suit'*

This starts out as a minimal song, with Pollard singing against a lone electric guitar in a way that wouldn't sound out of place on the pre-Scat LPs. But then, about a minute in, the whole band comes in and it sounds great. The lyrics are also a lot of fun, showing Bob at his most surreal and inscrutable.

Track five: 'The Official Ironmen Rally Song'

This is one of GBV's all-time best songs. It's a great tune, Bob sounds great, the band's fantastic — it ticks all the boxes. The guitar solo was played by Tripp Lamkins from the Memphis band The Grifters. GBV had toured with The Grifters and were friendly with them—plus, they were always being compared to them. 'Ironmen' was the first single off the record, and it was accompanied by a video by Banks Tarver, the filmmaker who, around this time, was making the documentary *Watch Me Jumpstart*. The video, with its archival photos of Bob and the guys, brilliantly captures the twin strains of melancholy and joy that run through the song. However, if the label was at all concerned about the band seeming old, at least to an indie-rock crowd, highlighting a bunch of photos from the 70s, when Mitch Mitchell's wearing a ruffled shirt and Bob looks like he's headed to the prom, probably wasn't the best idea.

The only bad thing about this track is that, since this is one of the Kim Deal–produced songs, it makes me long for the full-length record the band could have made if they'd only stuck with it. Plenty of groups have gone through the wringer to make great records, and I wish Bob had stuck it out for a couple more weeks. It would have been worth it.

Track six: 'To Remake The Young Flyer'

The one-two punch of this song next to 'Official Ironmen Rally Song' is amazing, since this is one of Sprout's best songs right next to one of Bob's best. It features a great riff, with the vocals coated in chorus and flange. It sounds totally psychedelic. And while a few bands are playing in that space today—groups like Animal Collective or Tame Impala—in the 90s that sound was embraced only ironically. Bands like Jellyfish wore floppy hats and bell-bottoms, The Pooh Sticks pretended to be the second coming of *The Partridge Family*, and Redd Kross covered the Carpenters. It was all a bit tongue-in-cheek. For the most part, 90s bands were more interested in being monochromatic than colorful. That's why Charles Peterson's black-and-white photographs have ended up being the perfect documents of the era. But Bob and Toby, given their ages, were coming to these influences firsthand; it's just the stuff they heard while growing up. There was no trace of irony when they embraced these sounds.

The subject matter of this song pays yet another tribute to Dayton's history of flight, not to mention Sprout's own long-standing interest in planes and flying. The only bad thing about the track is that it's short, at under two minutes.

Track seven: 'No Sky'

This is a fine mid-tempo, mid-fi rocker that has a great vocal by Pollard. It's only been played live once, back in 2006, as part of a Robert Pollard solo show.

Track eight: 'Bright Paper Werewolves'

This sounds to me almost like a sequel to 'The Goldheart Mountaintop Queen Directory.' *Magnet* called the song's first line, 'Come on polluted eyeballs, stop scouting out the fields,' 'maybe the best opening line of Pollard's life.' What Bob's referring to with the title, and in the song, are lottery tickets. Basically, people trying to get rich with 'bright, eye-catching' scratch-off games, which Pollard calls 'bright paper werewolves.' It's another instance of Bob seeing the underside of the dream, and the tradeoffs that come with happiness. Sure, a lottery ticket might bring you millions, but it's actually a wolf in sheep's clothing. It appears friendly and benevolent, but it's just out for your money. All you're going to get out of the experience are 'obscurity and misery.'

Track nine: 'Lord Of Overstock'

This song seems tied to 'Cut-Out Witch,' in terms of being about the downsides of being in a band. By 1996, Pollard had had a few years of being a professional musician, a process—from recording in big studios to dealing with album release schedules—he didn't seem to like. He now had to deal with issues like cutouts and overstock (overstock being excessive inventory, or the records that didn't sell). *Alien Lanes* wasn't quite the success the band or the label had hoped it would be, and some of that reality was creeping into Bob's lyrics.

This song also seems a kindred spirit to the opening track off *Revolver*, 'Taxman.' Where George Harrison's rapacious taxman condescended to his citizens—'Be thankful I don't take it all'—thirty years later, Pollard's 'lord of overstock,' along with his minions of 'overfed rats,' declare, 'We'll … take every cent you earn.'

SIDE TWO

Track one: 'Your Name Is Wild'

The construction of this song's interesting in that It's Just one minute that the band basically plays twice; the second half of the track is exactly the same as the first, except with some added harmony on the vocals. The subject is Pollard's daughter, Erika. (*Alien Lanes* had a song about Bob's son, Bryan.) It's a sweet song, with Pollard saying that he's paid the angels to keep his daughter safe. Pollard was just about to turn forty, and his kids were growing up, so he must have been going through some reflections about being middle-aged.

Track two: 'Ghosts Of A Different Dream'

Before seguing into a fast rocker, this starts out as the most jangly GBV song in years, recalling the R.E.M. influence that cropped up on most of the self-released LPs. The subject matter seems to recall side two of *Propeller*, where Bob was wrestling with his ambitions and desires, singing about how his fantasies were 'hounding' him. After the success of GBV, Pollard knew firsthand that every dream has a downside, even the ones that come true. Everything exacts a price. The song also makes mention of an 'ogre's trumpet blaring.' *Ogre's Trumpet* would later be used as the name of GBV's 2018 live record, capturing a show from Asbury Park.

Track three: 'Acorns & Orioles'

This acoustic track has the repeated refrain 'I can't tell you anything you don't already know.' Given where Bob was in his life at the time, a professional recording artist who was having his songs critiqued and pulled apart for meaning, this could be seen as an attempt to demystify or short-circuit any attempt to find significance in his work. As Cormac McCarthy writes in *Blood Meridian*, 'Your heart's desire is to be told some mystery. The mystery is that there is no mystery.'

Track four: 'Look At Them'

This spare and angular track takes us back to the post-punk experiments of the band's early albums. It doesn't sound bad—Bob's vocal is slathered in echo and sounds huge—but the song goes on for way too long, something that isn't helped since it blends into the next song.

Track five: *'The Perfect Life'*

This is just an outro to the previous track.

Track six: *'Underwater Explosions'*

This starts out with Bob drawing out the words, recalling 'Smothered In Hugs' from *Bee Thousand*. It then goes into full-on pop-song mode, and it sounds great when it does. The line 'Something passes through me' predicts an even poppier GBV tune, 'Glad Girls,' where Pollard sings about 'the light that passes through me.'

Bob's profile at the time was high enough that he was approached to write a song for a Tom Hanks movie called *That Thing You Do*. The movie's about a fictional band, a one-hit wonder that, in the mid-60s, rises and then falls based on the strength of one song, also called 'That Thing You Do.' Bob was approached to write the group's one-hit song, only he refused. 'They told me that Tom wanted the title track to sound like "a cross between 'La Bamba' and 'Twist And Shout,' as played by the Rascals." Huh? I just said, "Fuck that!" The Rascals? I don't write that kinda shit.'

With all due respect to Pollard, he's out of his mind. He's written dozens of songs that sound like The Rascals (including this one). Besides, he has songs coming out of his ears. He releases them in batches of a hundred at a time. Bob could have knocked that song out in ten minutes, and been paid handsomely to do it. So why didn't he? Plus, the tagline of the movie was 'In every life there comes a time when that dream you dream becomes that thing you do.' That was Bob's life! How could he not connect to that? Adam Schlesinger from Fountains Of Wayne eventually wrote the title track for *That Thing You Do*. The song ended up getting nominated for both a Golden Globe and an Oscar. It was yet another opportunity Pollard missed to expose his work to a wider audience.

Track seven: *'Atom Eyes'*

This is a perfect track from Tobin Sprout. His songs for GBV had blossomed over the past couple of records. The short, acoustic tracks on *Bee Thousand* gave way to the faster, electric guitar tunes on *Alien Lanes*, and, on this record, he's got a full band sound on what were arguably the best songs he'd ever written. The title most likely comes from breaking apart the word 'atomize' into 'Atom Eyes' (there's also a line in the song where Sprout writes, 'atomizer sprinklers are spraying perfume'). A different version was included on a 2002 charity record, and it was also played during a Peel Session from 1996, where it sounded amazing.

Track eight: 'Don't Stop Now'

This is one of GBV's all-time best songs. And that's what sort of makes *Under The Bushes* an odd record. I never consider it as one of GBV's best, and yet some of my all-time favorite GBV songs are on it. This track had been around for a while, with an early, stripped-down acoustic version included on *King Shit & The Golden Boys*. The first verse refers to the rooster, Big Daddy, pictured on the cover of *Devil Between My Toes*. It's another one of the songs Kim Deal produced at Easley in Tennessee. It's also up there with 'A Salty Salute' as a contender for being the band's theme song. It's a gorgeous tune that, once it kicks in toward the end, with the whole band joining in, shoots into the stratosphere. The strings on the song are by Shelby Bryant. Bryant, at the time, was part of a Memphis synth band called The Clears.

Track nine: 'Office Of Hearts'

This is an okay song, but coming after three amazing tracks, it ruins a run of impressive tunes, not to mention, if you're listening to it on vinyl, it's kind of a poor song to end the side. That being said, it's not without its charms. The line about an 'octopus caveman' having 'a girl on every arm' is awfully funny. But, overall, it definitely feels like a minor track. This is also where the eighteen-song LP ends.

EP SIDE ONE
Track one: 'Big Boring Wedding'

This is another one of the leftovers from the Kim Deal sessions, and, like everything that they recorded in Memphis, it sounds great. The song has the line 'Thank you for such delicious pie.' The phrase 'delicious pie' would show up later on the *Hardcore UFOs* box set, as part of the title of a disc of unreleased songs, which was called *Delicious Pie And Thank You For Calling*. The chorus,

'Pass the word, the chicks are back,' is taken from a 70s commercial for Carter Hall tobacco. The commercial is a cartoon where a guy smoking a pipe talks about different brands of tobacco, and how the smell drives women away. However, thanks to the pleasant aroma of Carter Hall, 'The chicks are back.'

Track two: 'It's Like Soul Man'

This is one of the few songs to make the LP from the Steve Albini sessions. It sounds okay but is kind of muddled. As amazing a producer as he is, pairing Steve Albini with Tobin Sprout doesn't make a lot of sense. That being said, I think it's a great song, and, once again, Sprout contributed amazing tracks to this record; if he's George Harrison to Pollard's Lennon/McCartney, then this record was his *Abbey Road*. It's also another song that had been around for a while—at one point, a four-track version was included on a working version of *Bee Thousand*. Sprout would go on to record the song yet again for his solo record, *Carnival Boy*, which was released just a few months after *Under The Bushes*.

Track three: 'Drag Days'

This is another of the Kim Deal songs—it sounds great. How something like this—or any of these final half-dozen songs—ended up as bonus tracks is just nuts. It was written by Bob when he was young, just twenty or twenty-one, and originally called 'In A Germantown,' Germantown being an area southwest of Dayton.

EP SIDE TWO
Track one: 'Sheetkickers'

This is another song Albini recorded, as well as one that had been intended for *The Power Of Suck*. It's an okay song but sounds a bit 90s. A shorter version, entitled 'Cocksoldiers,' was included on early versions of the LP, when it was still called *The Flying Party Is Here*.

Track two: 'Redmen And Their Wives'

This is one of the most beautiful and humane songs Pollard's ever written. It's another one of his thoughtful reflections on where he comes from, like 'Hank's

Little Fingers.' In that song he defended the 'mountain men,' and here he's lamenting the fate that befalls 'redmen and their wives,' by which he means rednecks (not Native Americans). He's writing about the lack of choices that are given to young adults in rural, blue-collar towns. You grow up and get married right away. As Pollard has said, 'Have kids, have a family, get a job and everything ... that's what you do. You don't even know what else there is.' Even Bob didn't know, since that's the path he followed. As he writes in the song, your life is 'issued' to you. You have no say in the matter. And the people to whom this is happening are too passive or depressed to resist, muttering to themselves, 'So then be it.'

This is Bob at his empathetic best. It's not the Pollard of wizards and elves and spacemen; it's Bob as an intelligent songwriter with things to say. Musically, the song's also amazing. It starts off spare and melancholy, and yet, by the end—once the whole band kicks in—it turns into a fist-pumping anthem.

Track three: 'Take To The Sky'

This is an odd choice to end what Bob has said is a 'more serious' record, since it's a short and silly song that has what seem to be nonsense lyrics. It was part of track lists for the LP going back to 1995, so it's a song Pollard had wanted on the record since the beginning, though I don't know why. The mention of the 'Chinaman' isn't terribly PC today, and, quite frankly, would have seemed out of place even in 1996. Even when Devo had a character named that in the 70s it felt out of date, and was used more or less for shock value, so I'm not sure why Pollard's used it here. It's a slightly underwhelming ending to a record that boasts some of the best and most mature songs the band had recorded up to that point—and, quite frankly, would ever record.

10 MAG EARWHIG!

nineteen ninety-seven

t'd been a decade since the band put out their first LP, 1987's *Devil Between My Toes*. In that time, Guided By Voices got signed and toured the world, and Pollard was called a genius in all kinds of publications. Bob had a lot to be proud of at this point in his career. He'd proved all the doubters wrong. He was living the dream. But he was also discovering that the dream was not all it was cracked up to be. He even began to long for the days when the success he'd achieved was out of reach. 'When it was just a fantasy for GBV, when it was just a make-believe kind of game that we were playing,' he later said, 'it was much more fun.'

The release of the band's previous record, *Under The Bushes Under The Stars*, had not been much fun. Bob ended up reworking all the material he'd recorded with two indie-rock icons, Steve Albini and Kim Deal. On top of all this, Matador muddled the packaging of the album, and, finally, after it was turned in, Pollard disbanded the lineup, leaving him without a band.

Meanwhile, the indie-rock scene was beginning to run out of steam, even if the big groups from earlier in the decade were still around and releasing records. Pavement's *Brighten The Corners* was a welcome return after 1995's disappointing *Wowee Zowee*, The Grifters released *Full Blown Possession*, and Sebadoh's *Harmacy* had come out the previous year. But as fine as their recent albums were, each of these bands was dealing in sounds people had heard before. They were treading water, and none of them would last into the next decade.

In England, it was the beginning of the end of Britpop, with Oasis's bloated third record appearing and Blur actually turning to American groups like Dinosaur Jr for the harder edged sound of their self-titled record from this year. More important was Radiohead's *OK Computer*, which was not just one of the best records of this year but one of the best records of the decade. *Pitchfork* would later name it as *the* best record of the 90s. (If you're keeping score, *Bee Thousand* came in at ten on *Pitchfork*'s list, and *Alien Lanes* was twenty-seven.) Speaking of Radiohead, the *Los Angeles Times* quoted Thom Yorke as saying that *Mag Earwhig!* was his favorite record of the year. Elsewhere, he said that Guided By Voices were 'the only band who have sussed recording and are happy to make things as long as my limited attention span will allow.'

But before Yorke could like *Mag Earwhig!*, Bob had to record it. The biggest barrier to him doing so was that he didn't have a band. Instead of trying to recruit new members, holding tryouts and auditions and all that kind of stuff, Pollard simply co-opted another band and called it Guided By Voices.

Named after the 1987 Werner Herzog film, Cobra Verde were born out of the ashes of an earlier Ohio band, Death Of Samantha (who, in turn, took *their* name from a Yoko Ono song).

Death Of Samantha were around for most of the 80s. They released three LPs and a handful of EPs and singles on Homestead Records, before breaking up and reforming as Cobra Verde in the 90s. According to the *New York Times*, 'Both bands sacrificed promising material to mediocre playing; less sloppiness and more dynamic variety would have made the songs hit home.' Since that sounds like it could also be applied to GBV, I can see how Bob thought he'd found the right group of guys. Pollard had indeed been a longtime fan of Death of Samantha, and the first time he met Doug Gillard, he complimented him on some of the riffs he'd created for that band. Pollard was also a big fan of John Petkovic, Cobra Verde's singer and guitarist, calling him 'the coolest guy in the world.'

Cobra Verde were on GBV's first label, Scat, and the bands had toured and gotten to know each other during the Insects Of Rock tour. Once Bob secured them as his new backing band, he became inspired to write material to match their sound and abilities. 'I knew that finally I had a chance to record some stuff in a big capacity and make some big booming-sounding, room-filling music.'

An added benefit to working with Cobra Verde was that bassist Don Depew had his own recording studio, a sixteen-track setup in a suburb of Cleveland. Once it became apparent that Mitch Mitchell, whom Bob had tried to keep around after the last record, wasn't going to be happy switching from guitar to bass, Depew also jumped in as the band's new bassist.

Even though Pollard was excited and energized by the new setup, he was also nervous. 'It was a little scary,' he said. 'They have a lot of experience. These guys have been around since '83. They've been in the limelight a little bit, people have known about them. They've always had a great sound, and GBV always just kind of tinkered around in the basement.'

It was awkward for the guys in Cobra Verde, too, Depew saying, 'It was weird because it's one thing to record people who just come in and you can look at them objectively and try to make a record of this object that just walked in. It's another thing when you're participating in the thing too. And it's an even harder thing when you've got to be a participant, record it, and it's somebody you liked before and it sounded a lot different then. Bob's easy to get along with, but it was still a weird thing.'

Bob felt the weirdness, too. 'It was not real comfortable at first. Don knows what he's doing, but he's sometimes a little difficult to communicate with.' Pollard also knew he was part of the problem. 'Because I'm difficult to communicate with, it's hard to articulate what I want. With my old band, they'd been with me for four or five years; I could grunt, and they'd understand what that meant.'

According to Depew, the band didn't know or work on Pollard's songs before they were recorded. 'We just had a cassette of Bob singing and playing an acoustic guitar. We never played the songs before. Bob basically ran through them with Dave [Swanson, Cobra Verde's drummer], and then we put everything else on it later.'

Pollard gave the band the freedom to do whatever they wanted, asking them to just 'make it good.' However, even though they recorded an album's worth of material at Don Depew's studio in Cleveland, Matador balked at releasing an entire LP of what was essentially 'Cobra Verde with Bob.' This prompted Pollard to record yet more material back in Dayton, as well as with Tobin Sprout using Toby's new Yamaha MT8X eight-track. At Sprout's they recorded 'Can't Hear The Revolution,' 'Are You Faster?' and 'I Am Produced.'

The old lineup's actually all over the LP. Tobin's credited on the record with bass, backing vocals, guitar, and drums. Mitch Mitchell plays on five songs, and Kevin Fennell drums on three. Even Bob's brother is back, playing on three songs.

Like all GBV albums, the record went through the usual changes of title and track list. An early version of the record was even called *Do The Collapse*. Another name for the album was *Panic On Landlord Street*. What finally appeared as *Mag Earwhig!* was the usual GBV hodgepodge of tracks, musicians, and locations. But when it came time to play the songs live, it was indeed basically Bob fronting Cobra Verde. And that's when there was trouble.

It started with John Petkovic wanting to turn the tour into an opportunity for Cobra Verde. This included suggesting having Cobra Verde be GBV's opening band for a few shows, as well as selling Cobra Verde merchandise. Bob didn't like either of those ideas. Things went downhill from there. 'We weren't getting along as well as we were in the beginning,' said Bob. 'At first, there was all this enthusiasm and excitement, which ended up dwindling and dying.'

As the tour went on, Pollard knew he was going to sack the band, something he told to a writer from the website *Addicted To Noise*. The problem is that word got back to the Cobra Verde guys before Bob had a chance to tell them himself. This obviously didn't sit well with Petkovic or the others—something that was evident during the final, tense show of the tour.

In early November of '97, Petkovic was quoted in an MTV News article about the breakup. 'I don't think any of us have a problem with the outcome of what happened, but we wish that it would have been done in a more upfront, friendly manner.'

Bob was pragmatic about the situation, admitting, 'It just didn't work out.' And while the whole thing was messy and undoubtedly a drag for all involved, of the Cobra Verde guys, Doug Gillard remained in the lineup. He's since worked with Pollard on and off for the past twenty years, right up to today— he's currently in the most recent incarnation of the group.

Bob, of course, didn't waste any time getting a new band back together. Another MTV News article, from late November, saw him announcing yet another lineup.

At the time *Mag Earwhig!* came out, a press release proclaimed that the LP was a 'conceptual rock opera,' declaring, 'Pollard is the main character in this sprawling narrative, an insectile cartoon figure named the Magnificent Earwhig, who interacts with a wild cast of characters in songs evoking nostalgic memories of an Ohio boyhood, starting one's first band, and inhaling American roadside pop culture.' That's all bullshit, Bob later admitting, 'It isn't a concept album. It doesn't mean anything.'

The record's cover features a gorgeous Pollard collage entitled 'The Astral City Slickers.' The band's name and the record's title are in an elegant and understated sans-serif font. The 'face' in the collage was taken from an illustration of the sun from the sixteenth-century text *Splendor Solis*. It's one of the best GBV covers ever. However, the back cover and inside are lackluster. There's no thematic or visual through line, and, when you look at the front and then the back, they could be two different records.

A new graphic element for the band was introduced around this time, making its first appearance on the *Sunfish Holy Breakfast* EP in 96, but it was also part of the 'Bulldog Skin' single and the *Mag Earwhig!* cover. It's what's come to be known as the 'rune,' that diagram of a triangle intersecting with some thick lines. It's the closest thing the band has to a logo, and it continues to be used today. The design's based on a drawing that Pollard made, and it's supposed to be a paper football sailing through a goal.

'Bulldog Skin' was released as a seven-inch and CD single a few weeks before the record came out. The band also made a video for the song. The video, which was probably cheesy even at the time, has not aged well. I'm also not a big fan of the song. 'I Am A Tree' would have been a much stronger contender as a first single, and as a calling card for the record. Instead, 'I Am A Tree' was the album's second single, released in July. It was dedicated to Tim Taylor, lead singer of the Ohio band Braniac, who had died that May in an automobile accident in Dayton.

At the time *Mag Earwhig!* was released, it received mixed reviews. *Rolling Stone* loved the record, giving it four stars (prior LP *Under The Bushes Under The Stars* had only received three). Reviewer Ben Kim noted that Cobra Verde 'simply [rocked] harder than the old GBV, scrapping the off-handedness that goes hand in hand with low-fi.'

The *AV Club* was respectful, Stephen Thompson writing, '*Mag Earwhig!* sounds like the work of a great band that, while not making any drastic changes in formula, continues to improve.'

Taking a later look at the record, Jeff Terich, writing for the website *Treble* in 2016, concluded, 'The thing about *Mag Earwhig!* is it sounds like two albums. Two-thirds of it is this muscular new Guided by Voices, and the other third comprises weird Pollard lo-fi exercises, for the most part. They don't all make sense together.'

Less charitably, in a feature on the *Spectrum Culture* website devoted to 'weak albums by strong artists,' Brian Wolowitz wrote that, with *Mag Earwhig!*, 'Pollard turned in the GBV oeuvre's weakest batch of songs, a turgid mess with little persona.' He added that the record 'comes close to being a front-to back stinker.'

While I wouldn't go that far, Wolowitz made a good point when he wrote, 'This album began Pollard's trajectory as pop music's Pinocchio: eager to shed his wooden lo-fi style and become a "real" rock band.' That idea hits the nail on the head, in terms of what was happening with Bob and the band. Pollard kept saying he wanted a big rock sound, but, as we saw with what happened with Kim Deal, he didn't want to put in the effort. He was also caught between different ideas and sensibilities. Should the record be a concept album? Should he go for a slick sound? Should he just hunker down in a basement with Toby, like he used to? All these warring factions within him meant that a number of GBV records from around this time suffer from a clear lack of vision, *Mag Earwhig!* included. It's an okay album, but it doesn't hang together the way a satisfying LP should. And especially coming after *Under The Bushes*, which had some of Bob's best songs ever, *Earwhig!*—whose best song was written by someone else—can't help but pale in comparison.

SIDE ONE

Track one: *'Can't Hear The Revolution'*

For an album that was billed as being recorded with a new band, this sounds an awful lot like the old band—Tobin Sprout's on backup vocals—and while I'm fine with confounding expectations, this is just not a very good song. It was recorded in Toby's basement, and it sounds like Bob and his brother just kind of screwing around. Maybe that's how they struck gold before, but it's not working here.

Track two: 'Sad If I Lost It'

After the opening fragment, this track properly kicks off the LP. The line 'I'll wear my maroon blazer all the time' is a reference to Bob's high-school years. The basketball team would wear their maroon blazers on game day, along with a tie, something Pollard loved to do. Bob's been into these kinds of tribes or groups all his life, whether it was the sports teams of his youth, the revolving membership of Guided By Voices, or the drinking buddies of Dayton he's dubbed the Monument Club.

Track three: 'I Am A Tree'

This song is an absolute blast. The drums sound amazing, the guitar is awesome, and it's probably the most polished heavy rocker the band had recorded up to that point. Their basement recordings, or even the stuff done at Steve Wilbur's, just didn't have this kind of bite. And even though Pollard had been drawn to work with Kim Deal because of her guitar sounds, the songs she produced that made it onto the previous GBV LP—tracks like 'Don't Stop Now' or 'Official Ironmen Rally Song'—were ballads. The guitar sound on this song, however, is absolutely massive; Pollard was finally getting to that warm, heavy guitar sound made famous by some of his 70s idols.

The interesting thing about the song is that it wasn't written by Pollard. Doug Gillard had written it years earlier. And while there are plenty of examples of Pollard singing over other people's instrumental tracks, he'd never sung someone else's song in Guided By Voices. Gillard wrote it when he was in a short-lived band called Gem, which he'd formed in between the end of Death of Samantha and the start of Cobra Verde. When it came time to record the band's debut record, Gillard chose not to include it, having a 'stigma about nonsensical lyrics.' Pollard—who has no such stigma—heard the song, loved it, declared that it sounded like The Who, and wanted it for GBV. The rest is history. Gem's version of 'I Am A Tree' was later released on an EP by Scat.

Track four: *'The Old Grunt'*

This is a short, mostly acoustic song with free-form lyrics. It's not bad, but coming after the one-two punch of 'Sad If I Lost It' and 'I Am A Tree,' the LP loses a bit of steam here. The lyrics could be autobiographical, since it seems to reference a somewhat-cynical musician who writes 'buzzing one-stringers' and who is 'quite the singer.'

Track five: *'Bulldog Skin'*

This is my least favorite GBV single. The lyrics are weak, with rhymes like 'I took a car, I drove it far' and 'I crashed my nerve, I made it swerve.' Even though some of those lines are a callback to *Propeller*'s 'Quality Of Armor,' here they sound terrible. And, yeah, the guitar solo's kind of impressive, and it sounds heavy overall, but it's just a meathead track. *Magnet*, normally a huge admirer of Pollard and his work, was also not a fan, writing, 'You have to have bulldog skin to not skip this clunker.'

Track six: *'Are You Faster?'*

At a minute long, this song, recorded in Sprout's basement, is a fragment. It's almost in the song-snippet territory of *Alien Lanes*. It's from that era—back in 1995, 'Are You Faster?' was part of the initial track list for *The Power Of Suck*.

Track seven: *'I Am Produced'*

This is Bob's most direct comment on where he found himself as a recording artist, writing that he felt 'pressed, printed, stomped,' and 'shipped out.' Their earlier records, like *Propeller*, saw the guys literally touching every copy. But being on a real label, and being sold all over the world, meant that Pollard was 'strategically removed,' not to mention 'trapped' and 'tricked.'

Track eight: *'Knock 'Em Flyin''*

This feels like a practice run for what could have been. It has an engaging tune and some interesting lyrics, but halfway through the tempo changes and it just fades out. It's one of the songs Bob recorded in Dayton, with Kevin Fennell on drums. There's also a demo version on the 1996 fan club release *Tonics & Twisted Chasers*.

Track nine: *'Not Behind The Fighter Jet'*

This song sounds heavy, and features a catchy tune. When it ends, you instantly want to hear it again. The imagery, with its fighter jets, goes back to the themes of aviation, planes, and flight that run through a lot of Pollard's songs. It's another of the tracks he did with Cobra Verde in Cleveland. That being said, of the ten songs on the first side of *Mag Earwhig!*, only three were recorded with his new band. As with the Kim Deal songs on *Under The Bushes*, it makes me wonder what a whole LP recorded with Cobra Verde would have sounded like.

Track ten: *'Choking Tara'*

This is more understated than the GB-Verde stuff found elsewhere on the record, with Bob singing against just an electric guitar. A demo version of the song exists as part of the *Hardcore UFOs* box set, and a full-band version, known as the 'creamy' version, appeared on the Matador compilation *Everything Is Nice*.

SIDE TWO
Track one: *'Hollow Cheek'*

Bob's back in Dayton with this spare snippet (the shortest track on the album) that doesn't match the others he'd recorded up in Cleveland. The lyrics harken back to some of the fantasy/prog stuff that had appeared on other records, Pollard writing, 'The mightiest toughman leads into the skeleton forest on cold ass western wheels.'

Track two: *'Portable Men's Society'*

You can tell right away that this is another one of the Cleveland songs recorded with Corba Verde. It's a big, bold track that sounds amazing. There's also some cool stuff going on in the background, either synth strings or a drone. It's a real tribute to Don Depew's production. Lyrically, I can't tell at all what the song's about, but who cares; it sounds good.

Track three: *'Little Lines'*

This is another scorching GB-Verde song. As *Magnet* wrote, 'Pollard can do prog and he can do pop and he can do all sorts of weird musical idioms better than anybody. But once in a while, he can also unapologetically do straight-ahead sledgehammer arena rock. The muscular "Little Lines" is one of the best of the bunch.' Pollard also gives the track a great melody, especially when he draws out the repeated refrain, 'Change now.'

Track four: 'Learning To Hunt'

This gorgeous song features minimal production and a restrained vocal by Bob. He can belt it out like Roger Daltrey when he wants to, but he's also great in these quieter moments. The lyrics are sincere and romantic, with Pollard's line 'no one will care half as much as I care about you' being maybe the most touching thing he's ever written. The song's also pragmatic and mature, Bob admitting he's only 'learning to hunt' for the object of his desire; he doesn't have it yet. The track was actually intended for his first solo record, 1996's *Not In My Airforce*. *Learning To Hunt* is also the name of a proposed record that was meant to be released in 1988.

Track five: 'The Finest Joke Is Upon Us'

This is another song that was part of the initial working versions of *Not In My Airforce*. It's an elegant track, with one of the most soaring choruses in GBV's discography, which—given Pollard's knack for melody—is saying something. When Bob draws out the lyrics, 'Words of smoke distorted, never broken, paradise is open but I choke,' it becomes, for me, the best moment on the LP. This, along with the three preceding tracks, creates an impeccable quartet of songs.

Track six: 'Mag Earwhig'

At thirty-nine seconds, this is the second-shortest song on the record. It's another one of Pollard's fragments. It doesn't do much for me.

Track seven: 'Now To War'

This acoustic song finds Pollard sounding a lot like Paul McCartney; I almost expect to hear Bob break into 'And I love her.' The lyrics, though, are serious, Pollard declaring, 'There is no boy in me now' and 'there is no time and I'm alone.' He also compares a relationship to combat, writing, 'But this is you and this is war, it makes me drink even more.' The acknowledgment here that Pollard doesn't just drink Miller Lite with his buddies to have fun seems like a serious admission, getting back to the dark undercurrents of *Same Place The Fly Got Smashed*. An electric version of the song was included as part of the 'Bulldog Skin' single.

Track eight: *'Jane Of The Waking Universe'*

This song is practically a reunion of the 'classic' lineup, with Tobin, Mitch, and Kevin all playing on it. It's an impressive track, with a fun tune, a classic title, inscrutable lyrics, and a melody that stays in your head for days. The initial track list for *Mag Earwhig!* had this as the record's last track, which would have been a fine choice. However, the final version of the LP has three more songs.

Track nine: *'The Colossus Crawls West'*

This is yet another song that was first intended for *Not In My Airforce*. It's just Pollard singing against an electric guitar. It's not bad, but coming as it does as song nineteen out of twenty-one tracks, it doesn't do much for the record.

Track ten: *'Mute Superstar'*

The late appearance of Cobra Verde on this song feels jarring, since we haven't heard from them in the past six tracks. It's okay, but does nothing to alter my view that the record would have been better served ending with 'Jane Of The Waking Universe.'

Track eleven: *'Bomb In The Bee-hive'*

This song has a great title, but not much else. The stop-and-start drums, and the fills, are right out of 'I Am A Tree.' It doesn't go anywhere, feels like filler, and again, seems like a curious choice in terms of ending the record.

11 DO THE COLLAPSE

nineteen ninety-nine

G BV didn't release anything in 1998—the first year in a decade that nothing was issued under the name Guided By Voices—but Bob was still busy. The year saw the release of Pollard's second solo record, *Waved Out*, which came out on Matador Records. It's a short album at fifteen tracks in thirty-four minutes. It has some lo-fi, ramshackle songs, and some that are just plain annoying ('Showbiz Opera Walrus'). But it's also home to some real Pollard gems, like 'Subspace Biographies.' *Rolling Stone*, in an article about Pollard that appeared around when *Waved Out* was released, called the record 'an obliquely epic album steeped in arena-worthy hooks.'

In an interview with the CMJ magazine, Bob described the difference between his solo stuff and what he released as GBV. 'With Robert Pollard, I'm allowed to crank it out with less production, and with Guided By Voices I'm expected to go up to the next level as far as sound quality is concerned.' It was a return to the way he'd made music earlier in the decade, Bob proudly declaring, 'I did probably 80 percent of it myself.'

This was done partly out of necessity, since the Cobra Verde lineup had dissolved at the end of the last tour. Pollard was once again without a band. Doug Gillard had stuck around—the only member from the previous incarnation to do so—but that left Bob looking for a drummer and a bass player. As usual, he didn't have to look for long. Drummer Jim Macpherson was someone Pollard had had his eye on for a long time.

Macpherson, who's also from Dayton, got his start in local band The Raging

Mantras. While playing around town, Kim Deal saw them and asked Jim to play on the demos for what would later become *Last Splash*. Macpherson was replacing Slint drummer Britt Walford. Walford had played on the first Breeders record, *Pod*, as well the *Safari* EP, albeit under pseudonyms. Macpherson was in the band during the '94 Lollapalooza tour, which also featured GBV. He'd also played in Kim Deal's short-lived band The Amps, along with former GBV roadie and future member Nate Farley.

Once The Amps were over, and Deal was struggling to resurrect The Breeders, Macpherson was back in Dayton and playing in a local group called Real Lulu. Pollard had the band open up for GBV in Indianapolis, partly as a way for Gillard to check out Macpherson. Jim was asked to join soon after. But before work began on any new GBV material, Macpherson played on a number of tracks on *Waved Out*, as did Gillard.

Now that Bob had a drummer and a guitarist, all he needed was a bass player. He managed to persuade full-time lawyer Greg Demos back into the fold. He now had a complete lineup, telling *Rolling Stone*, 'I'm happy with the new band. They do what I tell 'em.' Pollard was ready to tackle the next Guided By Voices record.

Before we get to the album, I want to address the narrative that's been built up around the LP. The shorthand for *Do The Collapse* is that Pollard ditched Matador, signed to a major, and got a big-shot producer to make a slick, commercial album. The reality is that Bob had been talking for years about making a 'big rock' record, something like *Who's Next*. 'I wanted to make a good-sounding record from the beginning,' he's said. 'We just never had the resources.'

He didn't want Toby's four-track to be a crutch, and he didn't want to be pigeonholed as lo-fi forever. So, in 1998, while he was still on Matador, he began looking for a producer who could help him achieve the big, heavy sound he'd always wanted. Ric Ocasek was the guy he turned to, Bob saying, 'I was exploring some possibilities for producers, and he was at the top of the list.' And while it may have seemed at the time like an opportunistic move to get Ocasek involved, the choice actually made a lot of sense. Ocasek's also from Ohio, and he loves music from the 60s and 70s. 'Bob and I like the same bands—and don't like some of the same bands,' Ocasek told *Billboard*, right before *Do The*

Collapse came out. Like Pollard, he wrote poetry and made collages, and he'd also produced a number of indie or alternative bands, including Possum Dixon, Bad Brains, Suicide, and a band that Doug Gillard would later join, Nada Surf. He also produced Weezer's super-successful first record.

Matador was fine with the choice, and the record was made for $90,000. According to Matador label-head Gerard Cosloy, this is when the trouble began. GBV's managers began breathing down his neck to release the record as part of the deal Matador had with the major label Capitol. In order for this work to everyone's benefit, *Do The Collapse* would have had to have sold 250,000 copies, something that Matador knew just wasn't going to happen. Once Matador balked at going the major-label route, Pollard began looking for a new record company.

Even though there weren't as many people interested in the band as there had been a few years prior, A&R executive Adam Shore—who'd also signed The Brian Jonestown Massacre—was a huge GBV fan. He'd seen them live about twenty times. Shore began to lobby them to join the label he worked for, TVT. But it was not, initially, an easy sell. Shore's boss, label founder and president Steve Gottlieb, didn't want to sign the group. Shore told me, 'He didn't really think that that was a sort of band that he wanted to have on the label. They were old and they were niche and he wanted things that could have a wider reach.'

Gottlieb had founded TVT in 1985. He's the same age as Pollard, and he holds a degree in literature from Yale and a law degree from Harvard. The label was launched with the double record *Television's Greatest Hits*, a collection of TV theme songs from the 50s and 60s. The original name of the label, Tee Vee Toons (later shortened to TVT), reflects its beginnings.

Shore, who had given his boss a copy of *Do The Collapse*, didn't let Gottlieb off the hook. 'I kept pressing him and pressing him on listening to the music and spending time with the music. I wrote him long e-mails about who they are and what they mean, and how they really are a forty-year history of rock music all condensed into one.'

Gottlieb still didn't budge, and Shore knew that time was running out. As a last resort, just before Christmas, he made a CD that contained just one song—'Hold On Hope'—and sent it to Gottlieb with a note that read, 'I think this song is a hit, let me know what you think.' It did the trick. Gottlieb called Shore over the holiday and the band signed to the label shortly after.

This is where we get into the whole myth of GBV jumping from an indie to a major, because Matador's not quite an indie, and TVT wasn't exactly a major. All throughout the 90s, Matador had relationships with major labels—first with Atlantic, from '93 to '96, and then with Capitol, from '96 to '99. When Matador made the switch in '96, it was, according to the *Los Angeles Times*, the object of a 'fierce five-month bidding war.' Capitol ultimately prevailed, paying somewhere in the neighborhood of $10 million for a five-year joint-venture agreement. Because of this, it seems odd that Matador always gets talked about in the same breath as Teen-Beat or K, which were truly one- or two-person DIY operations. And, for as big as TVT ever became, it was never a major label. The *New York Post* described it as 'one of the largest independent record labels in the country.' You could actually argue that GBV going to TVT was actually a step down from working with Capitol-backed Matador.

Another aspect of the deal that was different from Matador was that TVT didn't mind how many records Bob put out. Shore even went so far as to say, 'Matador felt that Bob's solo albums cannibalize GBV's sales—we don't.' The agreement was that TVT had a ten-day first-look option on all Bob's stuff, and, if they passed, Pollard was free to do whatever he wanted with it. The label was too busy working on GBV albums to bother with anything else Bob produced, and Pollard didn't seem to mind, since he'd just introduced his Fading Captain Series. This would open the floodgates in terms of new material. In 1999 alone, Bob released another solo LP, *Kid Marine*; the Doug Gillard collaboration *Speak Kindly Of Your Volunteer Fire Department*; and debuts from two new side projects, Lexo & The Leapers and Nightwalker.

Do The Collapse was recorded at Electric Lady Studios, the famous studio built by Jimi Hendrix shortly before his death. Located in New York's Greenwich Village, on the site of an old nightclub, it's a legendary facility that continues to draw bands from all around the world. A huge number of artists have recorded there, including a bunch that I'm sure Pollard admires, such as John Lennon, David Bowie, Led Zeppelin, The Clash, and The Rolling Stones. But while Ocasek was a good fit for the band, a few problems quickly emerged. For one thing, he was so famous that the guys were nervous to be around him. 'I was really anxious and scared to meet with him,' Pollard said, 'but he turned out to be really nice.'

Jim Macpherson felt the same way. 'When I actually got in the studio I freaked out and lost my shit. Looking through the control room glass seeing Ric Ocasek, who I idolized in high school.' To ease the drummer's nerves, and to show that he's just a regular guy, Ocasek took Macpherson for a walk around the city. It seemed to work, since Macpherson quickly completed his parts and returned to Dayton.

Another problem was that Ocasek didn't allow drinking in the studio. This was hard for Bob, who, as you may have heard, likes to have a beer or two. But even this wasn't too big of a deal, and the record was completed without much fuss. Only guitarist Doug Gillard was skeptical of the touches Ocasek was adding, but even he came around and later expressed admiration for the LP.

The cover was the first GBV sleeve in a long time that Bob didn't have a hand in designing. Instead, in-house designer Ben Wheelock came up with the art, which features a car crushed into a cube. I think the object in the photo is a brilliant representation of the 'collapse' of the title, and the white background makes it striking (although some of the fonts on the back look a bit 90s). When it came to the cassette, it was housed in an ingenious package that made it look like a box of cigarettes.

The LP spawned two singles, 'Teenage FBI' and 'Hold On Hope.' 'Surgical Focus' was also issued on a seven-inch, with cool packaging, to satisfy the hardcore fans and vinyl enthusiasts. TVT also managed to get 'Teenage FBI' on the soundtrack to the TV show *Buffy The Vampire Slayer*. Since Bob was formerly the Vampire On Titus, there's a certain symmetry to this.

After *Do The Collapse* had come out, TVT put out the *Hold On Hope* EP in 2000, which included eight B-sides, among them an instrumental called 'Do The Collapse.' Not to be outdone, that same year Pollard's Fading Captain Series issued *Daredevil Stamp Collector*. This vinyl-only release reproduced most of the *Hold On Hope* EP, and had a very similar design. The difference was that it added one more song, and, as if trying to erase the existence of Ocasek's version of 'Hold On Hope,' substituted the demo for the studio version.

Reviews for *Do The Collapse* were mostly positive. CMJ's Steve Klinge stated that the LP sounded more 'finished' than prior records: 'Where past

GBV albums each had standout tracks, gems that leapt out against the fragments and fuzz, *Collapse* is full of complete, fully realized songs.' In a short and shallow review, Marc Weingarten of *Rolling Stone* gave the record only three stars. 'Longtime fans may bristle at GBV's new slick tricks, but *Do The Collapse* is hardly a concession to commercialism.'

When all was said and done, the record—while selling more than any previous GBV release—didn't quite break the band the way that everyone had hoped. After being asked by *Rolling Stone* if he was surprised that *Do The Collapse* wasn't more successful, Bob answered, 'I was actually, because Ric did it, and he said, You guys are going to be really surprised what happens with this record. And it didn't really take off. So that surprised me, but I wasn't disappointed.'

SIDE ONE

Track one: *'Teenage FBI'*

Label and band both agreed that this would be the first single. And yet, as hard as TVT tried, it wasn't a hit, and it didn't get played on the radio. As Shore explains, 'Even though we were a very big independent label, we were still an independent label and there's not a lot of spots for independent labels on alternative radio. There's also not a lot of spots for indie artists on alternative radio.'

That's a shame, since 'Teenage FBI' was the most commercial song GBV had so far released. It starts with some weird synthesizer noise that reminds me of early Devo—specifically that breakdown toward of the end of 'Jocko Homo.' It quickly turns into, quite simply, one of the best GBV songs ever. And while Don Depew had done an incredible job getting a big sound from his sixteen-track studio on the previous album, it doesn't hold a candle to what Ric Ocasek has done for the band here. I also don't mind the little new-wave bits that Ocasek added to the song. They're also not quite as out-of-left-field as you might think. The first songs on both *Waved Out* and *Mag Earwhig!* had some Casio or keyboard elements to them, so this wasn't exactly the first time GBV had used those sounds. And, when you compare this version with the non-Ocasek version of 'Teenage FBI' that appears on the best-of, there's no comparison—the LP version is absolutely superior. Chris Ford, on

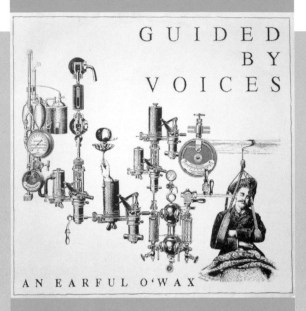

TOP LEFT At a time when no one in America had heard (let alone liked) any of GBV's self-released material, German label Get Happy!! issued this compilation of early tracks in 1993.

LEFT Unbeknown to Bob, 'manager for life' Pete Jamison sent out copies of 1992's *Propeller* to journalists and tastemakers. (Courtesy of Boris Schlensker)

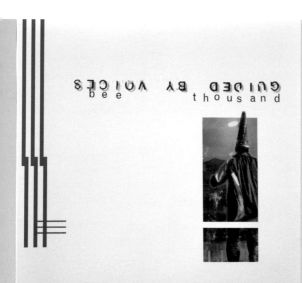

GUIDED BY VOICES
bee thousand

LEFT The main element from
the *Bee Thousand* cover
came from the October
1990 issue of *National
Geographic*. It was part of
the story 'The Cajuns: Still
Loving Life.'

RIGHT The special
'Director's Cut' edition
of *Bee Thousand* from
2004 featured the art
Bob intended for the
original cover.

PREVIOUS SPREAD
Robert Pollard in the
early 90s. (Photo by
Jason Thrasher)

GUIDED BY VOICES

bee thousand
the director's cut

ABOVE Coming off their biggest year ever, GBV appeared on the cover of *Magnet* in January 1995. In the issue, *Bee Thousand* was named best record of 1994.

OPPOSITE A press photo of the band around the time they signed to Matador. *Left to right* Mitch Mitchell, Kevin Fennell, Robert Pollard, Tobin Sprout.

ABOVE The wavy lines from 1995's *Alien Lanes* first appeared on Benny Golson's 1967 jazz album *Tune In, Turn On.*

GUIDED BY VOICES
UNDER THE BUSHES UNDER THE STARS

COBRA VERDE

"STRIPED WHITE JETS"

ABOVE As part of a tribute record, Cleveland band Cobra Verde covered the *Alien Lanes* track 'Striped White Jets' in 1997. That same year, everyone from the band would join Pollard in GBV.

LEFT The man on the cover of 1996's *Under The Bushes Under The Stars* was taken from the story 'Florida Rides A Space-Age Boom' in the December 1963 issue of *National Geographic*.

ABOVE A press photo of the 'Guided By Verde' lineup. *Left to right* Doug Gillard, John Petkovic, Robert Pollard, Don Depew, Dave Swanson.

RIGHT The first appearance of the rune, GBV's quasi-logo, was on the 1996 EP *Sunfish Holy Breakfast.* The rune was based on a sketch by Pollard. It's meant to be a paper football sailing through a goalpost.

ABOVE AND RIGHT The face in the collage for 1997's *Mag Earwhig!* came from the *Splendor Solis*, an illuminated manuscript from the 16th century.

the website *Diffuser*, wrote of this song, 'While it is undeniably commercial rock, "Teenage FBI" is at least a really good example of commercial rock.' Although, since Pollard has said that the song has roots in his teaching days, and that 'cleaning out the hive' refers to picking one's nose, this is not typical commercial rock territory.

Track two: *'Zoo Pie'*

Doug plays some great stuff on guitar, and when Pollard sings about wanting to 'be a man,' he's got that perfect 70s heavy-metal sound. Toward the end, with some background vocals, the song veers back into the group's usual Beatles-esque territory.

Track three: *'Things I Will Keep'*

This song starts with a synth sound that runs through the entire track, probably an Ocasek touch. Jim Macpherson sounds great on the drums, and Doug Gillard proves yet again what an asset he was becoming to the band; his flourishes throughout the track sound amazing.

The lyrics have a great cadence to them, Bob writing:

Coded ancient decrees
Oh brightness we shall see
Loaded up and at night when
We shall flee

The way he sings these lines, and knits them into the melody, is amazing. It's something he does in dozens of songs; Bob uses language for its effect rather than its meaning. English comedian Stewart Lee has talked about Pollard's songs being more about rhythm, and 'what words sound like,' rather than them having a literal explanation or some grand point. 'He's got a brilliant feel for where a consonant goes or whether to extend a vowel,' said Lee, adding that Guided By Voices and The Fall 'are the best bands of the last thirty years.'

It's a standout track from the record, and one of the best of the band's career. In fact, Pollard has said it's his favorite song from this LP, and that it inspired the sound of a lot of the songs on *Isolation Drills*.

Track four: 'Hold On Hope'

This is the most controversial song on the band's most controversial record. Bob's gone so far as to call 'Hold On Hope' his biggest mistake (this coming from the guy who'd released, just a year before, 'Showbiz Opera Walrus'). While I understand that it's a slow song—a ballad—and GBV's supposed to be this balls-to-the-wall drunken beast of a band, they'd recorded ballads before, and would do so in the future. Think of 'Liar's Tale,' 'Drinker's Peace,' 'Learning To Hunt,' 'Be Impeccable,' 'That's Good,' and many others. So why pick on this one? Bob's favorites, The Who, had plenty of ballads. One of Pollard's favorite albums, *Who's Next*, has 'Behind Blue Eyes.' That starts off as a ballad, but it doesn't mean it's a bad song, and it doesn't make that a bad record.

I think Bob's embarrassed by two aspects of the track, the first being its commercial appeal. It's a song that everyone pounced on—the label, Ocasek—as being the thing that would get them on the radio. (Don't forget that it was also the song that got them signed to the label; without 'Hold On Hope,' there's no TVT deal.) But Bob *wanted* to get on the radio. And, while he wanted to get there on his terms, I don't see this as being any huge betrayal of who he is as an artist. It's actually surreal and subversive, with lines like, 'One another, animal mother, she opens up for free.' It's not Whitney Houston.

The other thing he's embarrassed about is the song's sentimentality. 'It's not that I disagree with optimism or positivity,' Bob later said. 'It's just that I didn't like the treatment and some of the corny lines,' adding, 'I've got nothing at all against beautiful songs. You just have to be careful.' And while you can certainly go from pathos to bathos in a single line, or without meaning to, this song never does that for me. In fact, it's been a great comfort at times in my life when I have, quite frankly, reached out for a hand I couldn't necessarily see. So, if the *Village Voice* wants to be snarky and call 'Hold On Hope' 'the best Collective Soul song ever recorded,' I couldn't care less.

Something else that has no doubt colored Pollard's opinion of the track is the battle he had with the label when it came time to release it as the second single off the album. Initially, the group agreed. But Gottlieb, not wanting to replicate the failure of 'Teenage FBI,' wasn't going to take any chances. They wanted to bring in some professional help. 'At the time, there were two singles remixers that pretty much owned alternative and AOR radio,' says Shore. 'And if you had one of those two guys do a kind of "radio mix" of your song, then you had a much better chance of the song being a hit.' Shore dutifully relayed this request to GBV, and the band gave their okay for the remix.

TVT took the song to Jack Joseph Puig. Puig began as a bass player before turning to studio and engineering work in the late 70s. As an audio engineer and producer, he's worked with a number of prominent 90s acts, such as Hole, Weezer, The Black Crowes, Stone Temple Pilots, Goo Goo Dolls, and many more. He's won two Grammys, and he later became an executive at Interscope Geffen A&M Records.

Puig looked at his role as more than just a remixer. 'In this day and age,' said Puig, 'mixers are no longer dependent on what's given to them on a hard drive.' He felt free to add whatever he thought a song needed to become a hit. One of the things Puig added to 'Hold On Hope' was a new instrumental line, getting film composer and record producer Jon Brion to play a Chamberlin— a keyboard similar to a Mellotron—on the track.

What Puig created was radically different than what the band had recorded with Ocasek. The drums sound like a drum machine, and the acoustic guitar's been turned into a grunge-lite electric. It's truly horrid, and not at all representative of either the song or the band. Bob heard the remix and made it very clear to Shore that he did not want it to be released.

This left their A&R man in a tough situation. 'I went back to Steve Gottlieb,' Shore recalls, 'and said, Listen, I tried. I did everything I could. The band and management are not happy.' He suggested just releasing the album version, but Gottlieb refused. He'd invested a lot in the group, and it was time for GBV to play ball. He told Shore, 'You have to get their permission.' When Shore told him that they were on tour overseas, Gottlieb ordered Shore to get on the next plane. Shore dutifully flew to England, where he met up with the group before a gig at the Hop & Grape at Manchester Academy. 'We went to a pub, and it was the five guys in the band and me. I was wedged into the corner of a booth, and the five of them were circled around me as I made as persuasive an argument as I could.'

Shore was outnumbered, and a bit intimidated. It didn't help that he wasn't quite sure about the argument he was making. The band didn't buy it. 'They were furious that they were having to have this conversation, and they accused me of not understanding the band, not caring about the band, and not being a fan of the band, which was pretty crushing to me.' Shore had his answer. He stayed for the show, and then went back to New York to tell Gottlieb the bad news. 'Hold On Hope' was still issued as a single, but there was no marketing push. There was no campaign. TVT had given up on promoting the album.

As maligned as the song was at the time, it was redeemed in the eyes of a lot of people when—to everyone's surprise—Glen Campbell covered it on his 2011 record *Ghost On The Canvas*. The LP's release was accompanied by the news that Campbell, the voice behind classics such as 'Wichita Lineman' and 'Rhinestone Cowboy,' had Alzheimer's and was retiring from show business. This was to be his last record. The LP, a mixture of originals and covers, got a great response, with several reviews and write-ups singling out Campbell's emotional delivery of 'Hold On Hope' as a highlight.

Carlos Ramirez, on the website *Diffuser*, later placed it at sixth on a list of the ten best GBV songs, writing, 'While most Pollard fanboys dismiss it as his weak attempt at writing a "modern rock" hit single, when it comes down to it, the Ric Ocasek–produced "Hold On Hope" is GBV's finest pop moment. An aching ballad with swelling strings and layered vocal harmonies, it's admittedly not stylistically in the same universe as most of Pollard's work, but you'd be a fool to deny how great "Hold On Hope" truly is.'

Track five: 'In Stitches'

This is another slow and heavy song, similar to 'Zoo Pie.' Some of the lyrics are interesting, Pollard writing about 'permanent holy wars.' Since 9/11 was just a few years away—and would usher in endless conflicts that were often seen as proxy wars of religious faith—this could be seen as prescient. The lyrics also make reference to 'human amusements at hourly rates.' That would end up being the name of the GBV best-of that Matador put out in 2003. *Human Amusements* was also one of the working titles for the record, along with *When I Go North*.

Track six: *'Dragons Awake!'*

This song starts with just a simple acoustic guitar, but, by the end, there are some subtle strings and bass. It also features some surreal and funny lyrics. For example, Pollard alters the old saying about casting pearls before swine by writing, 'Sprinkle the pearls over the ham.' He also mentions 'softer tits' being 'tapped by suckers of the sap.' I don't know what it all adds up to, but it's a nice moment between two faster and harder songs.

Track seven: *'Surgical Focus'*

This is another great-sounding pop song, with everyone in the band sounding awesome. The subtle synth in the chorus adds a lot, and when Bob sings, 'Until I get it, I can't breathe,' it's a total highlight. An acoustic version was included on the *Plugs For The Program* seven-inch.

Track eight: *'Optical Hopscotch'*

This is the weakest song on side one. The opening lyric, 'Meet me at the market, where you bought me out,' goes back to some of the bitter lyrics Bob was writing around the time of *Propeller*. By the end, there's some effective use of backing vocals, as well as Bob saying, 'Look!' It's a good song to listen to on headphones.

SIDE TWO

Track one: *'Mushroom Art'*

This is one of the shorter songs on the record. The part that begins 'happy the universe' has some strong melodic twists to it. It also features some prog or fantasy lyrics, Pollard writing about 'a bejeweled crow on a quilted tent.' By the way, mushroom art is a real thing. Go to Etsy and you can get mushroom paintings, posters, prints, and a whole lot more. You can probably also get a bejeweled crow or a quilted tent.

Track two: *'Much Better Mr. Buckles'*

This song doesn't have any distinct melody to it, though the choruses are catchy, and there's some impressive guitar work by Doug Gillard. The overall sound is super-heavy, and the guitars absolutely crunch—the sound is lightyears ahead of anything Bob or the band had released before now.

Track three: 'Wormhole'

This is not about astronomical wormholes but rather regular, literal ones, Pollard starting the song by declaring, 'I am an earthworm.' He later crawls into a hole, hoping to be safe. It's an interesting premise, going back to the comparison of humans with flies on *Same Place The Fly Got Smashed*. We can be swatted by life just as easily as an insect can. And, whether you're a worm or a human, we're all going to end up in the ground, where, as Bob writes, 'the soil is rich and muddy in the riverbed' and the worms 'feed on the urgent promise of the dead tonight.'

It's reminiscent of the final stanza in the last of Wordsworth's Lucy poems, where he writes of the idealized, but deceased, title character:

> *No motion has she now, no force;*
> *She neither hears nor sees;*
> *Roll'd round in earth's diurnal course*
> *With rocks, and stones, and trees.*

And with, one can presume, Pollard's earthworm.

Track four: 'Strumpet Eye'

This short song takes a while to get going, but, once it does, it's a lot of fun. The lyrics are also vintage Pollard; he writes here that the title character 'can barely get into her own pants.' Also, now that we've had four songs in a row that are basically just straightforward rock songs, let me say that I don't get why people think that Ric Ocasek has his fingerprints all over the record. We're now a dozen songs in, and there have been only two or three minor touches that you could call new wave. Instead, it just sounds like a clear and clean representation of Bob's songs.

Track five: 'Liquid Indian'

I agree with Steve Soderbergh when he says that the chorus gives him goose bumps; it's definitely the best part. It also reminds me of the chorus to the early Devo song 'The Day My Baby Gave Me A Surprise.' And while the verses have some playful language, the song doesn't hang together. In fact, the album suffers a bit from its sequencing. Side one holds all three singles, and the second side doesn't have any truly memorable songs. So the LP starts to run out of steam at this point.

Track six: 'Wrecking Now'

This song features jangly guitar and discordant strings. It also foreshadows some of the emotionally raw songs on the next record, with Pollard writing, 'She's bleeding now' and 'I'm through with you.'

Track seven: 'Picture Me Big Time'

At four minutes, this is the longest song on the record. It lags a little, with a guitar solo that lasts too long, but otherwise it's a lot of fun, especially when Pollard does his best Big Rock voice to belt out the line 'I will deliver to you.' The song seems to be about Pollard's ambition as a songwriter, and how he perhaps felt conflicted by trying to reach a wider audience. He's tempted to 'keep it closer,' having the band remain a secret, like during the previous decade. Then again, he has 'words that speak to everyone,' which only he can deliver.

Bob's been fighting this battle for most of his career. He started GBV by making records he didn't want anyone to hear. Then he craved success, inviting people—like in this song—to 'picture' him in the 'big time.' And now, more than three decades into the band, he seems to be content in his own small universe, a place he's termed 'the littlest league possible.'

Track eight: 'An Unmarketed Product'

This fast song is reminiscent of 'Shocker In Gloomtown' or 'Game Of Pricks.' It's also the shortest on the record, at barely a minute. It seems like another track where Bob's commenting on his status as an object of commerce, something to be bought, sold, and indeed, marketed. This makes it similar to songs on prior records like 'I Am Produced' and 'Lord Of Overstock.'

Pollard not only had to sell records but recoup his advance. For someone who had often written about the inability to escape death, he's now writing about something just as inescapable: debt.

12 ISOLATION DRILLS

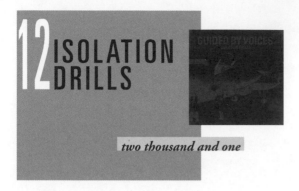

two thousand and one

n the previous decade, GBV had risen from obscurity and conquered the indie rock world. They produced a bona fide masterpiece (*Bee Thousand* or *Alien Lanes*, depending on your point of view). They signed a six-figure record deal and toured the world. They appeared constantly on MTV. It'd been an amazing ride for a bunch of drinking buddies from Dayton. But by the end of the 90s, things were starting to slip. The band's previous LP saw the band leave indie-cred powerhouse Matador for the much larger but significantly less cool TVT. They made a slick, commercial record with a big-name producer and toured longer and harder than they ever had before. All the strain of trying to get to that next level led to the ruin of Pollard's marriage of two decades, sending him into a depression.

Guided By Voices were a party band, and the party was taking a turn for the worse. As Bob said later, 'Life is a series of mistakes. You have to learn from them, and you can't dwell on them or condemn yourself. The biggest mistake I made was cheating on my wife while I was on the road. I didn't do that for six years but finally succumbed, and it cost me everything, including my happiness.'

Everything Pollard went through during this period bled into the music and lyrics he was writing. His experiences and circumstances fueled GBV's twelfth record, *Isolation Drills*, making for some of Bob's most poignant lyrics and one of the band's best albums.

But he wasn't the only one going through hard times. At the turn of the century, the record industry—the one Pollard had tried for so long to break into—was itself in a downward spiral. The introduction of the internet, along with Napster, was beginning to change everything. The web allowed music fans to trade their catalogues with both friends and strangers for free. At its height, Napster had eighty million registered users, and its growth sent shockwaves throughout the industry.

A whole new generation saw records and songs as something you didn't have to pay for. The heyday of the CD was over. By the time iTunes launched in 2003, this behavior was ingrained. According to cnnmoney.com, from 1999 to 2009 the revenue in the US from music sales was cut in half, shifting from $14.6 billion to $6.3 billion. And when people did spend money on music, it was usually to buy a single rather than the entire record. From 2000 to 2014, album sales tanked by 86 percent, while the sales of single songs increased by 718 percent.

It wasn't just the industry that was in decline. The musical scenes that Pollard had been associated with—lo-fi, indie rock, and alternative—had all lost steam by the end of the decade. *120 Minutes*, the MTV show that had played such a big part in breaking Guided By Voices, had gone off the air to make way for reality shows. Grunge was a completely spent entity, as was Britpop. Magazines like *Alternative Press*, and radio stations like KROQ in Los Angeles, went from profiling and playing alternative artists like Beck and The Breeders to featuring nu-metal or emo bands like Staind and Blink-182.

Radiohead, who'd produced one of the best records of the 90s with *OK Computer*, returned in the new decade with a pair of LPs that largely replaced guitars with electronic textures. They might have been pointing the way forward, but it wasn't much fun. And while bands like The White Stripes and The Strokes would soon lead a 'rock revival,' that was still a few years away.

The world Bob had always wanted to break into just didn't exist anymore. Which is probably okay, since the closer Pollard came to breaking through, the less he liked it. He hated playing the third stage at festivals at eleven in the morning. He hated waking up early to do in-stores or talk to a radio station. He hated when his label told him an LP lacked singles, or chided him for 'holding out' on them. They wanted hits, but Bob did, too. He thought he was supplying them, but nothing worked. 'I've come to the conclusion that maybe we're not capable of having a hit,' Pollard said. 'We're just not that kind of a band.'

While GBV didn't release anything in 2000, Bob released two records by two new side projects as part of his Fading Captain Series: an LP from Hazzard Hotrods, *Big Trouble*; and *Speedtraps For The Bee Kingdom* by Howling Wolf Orchestra. Both of these efforts are tossed off, even for Bob, so you have to wonder: if Bob wanted to be successful, why did he give any time at all to side projects like these?

The year 2000 also saw the release of the first *Suitcase* box set, *Failed Experiments And Trashed Aircraft*. Pollard had long talked about having a 'suitcase' full of songs, and with this release he proved to the world—not that there was much doubt—that he indeed had a mountain of tunes just sitting around in his basement. It was rumored to be a ten-CD set, but by the time it arrived, Pollard had culled it down to four CDs, twenty-five tracks per disc. The hundred songs span the entire history of the band, some of them even predating GBV. They range from alternate versions of tracks that had already been released to unheard gems or album outtakes.

Another unique feature of the box set is that Bob attributed each song to a different fictional group. At one time, Pollard was thinking of writing a book of band names, but he ran out of steam after coming up with a hundred or so. He puts them to good use here; there are some real classics among them: Huge On Pluto, Judas & The Piledrivers, Ceramic Cock Einstein, Arthur Psycho & The Trippy Warts, and Royal Japanese Daycare. At least one of the names would be revived for later releases, with Ricked Wicky (credited with two *Suitcase* songs, 'Messenger' and 'Invest In British Steel') going on to release three full-length LPs, and a number of singles, in 2015.

Matt LeMay, in a 7.9 review for *Pitchfork*, wrote, '*Suitcase* is crammed with classic Pollard moments—those unique occasions where poorly recorded, sloppily delivered songs somehow become transcendent pop genius.' Less charitably, the *AV Club* called it 'a must only for the hardest of the hardcore Pollard fans.' To date, three more volumes of the *Suitcase* series have been released.

When GBV went into the studio to record their new LP, the band had two new members. Doug Gillard and Jim Macpherson were back on guitar and drums, although Macpherson would leave the group right after recording to spend more time with his family. The new members were Nate Farley on guitar and Tim Tobias on bass. Both of them had strong ties to the band. Farley was the roadie who'd saved the day a few years prior, when Tobin Sprout had to bail on a West Coast tour to be with his wife, who was giving birth. A Dayton local, he'd also been in the short-lived Kim Deal band The Amps, along with Macpherson. Tobias had been in Doug Gillard's previous band, Gem, not to mention a group called 4 Coyotes who'd released a few seven-inches on Scat. Tim's brother is Todd Tobias, the producer and multi-instrumentalist who would go on to co-produce the next three GBV records. Todd also produced and provided the backing tracks for a number of Pollard solo records, not to mention he's the creative force behind the side project Circus Devils, who released fourteen records of fractured, Devo-inspired weirdness before calling it quits in 2017.

Pollard said of his new lineup, 'Technically, we're the best we've ever been.' He also admitted that they were a bad influence on him. Things were getting out of hand, even for GBV. To help right the ship, Bob called a band meeting and told the guys to tone down their partying. Coming from a guy who'd been known to hurl cans of beer into the audience, pass around bottles of tequila to the crowd, and who often got so drunk onstage he slurred his words, this was saying something.

To produce their new record, Pollard picked Rob Schnapf. Schnapf had worked on Beck's breakthrough single 'Loser,' and, right before working with GBV, produced Elliott Smith's second major-label record, *Figure 8*. Pollard, however, had no idea who he was. Schnapf was brought to Bob's attention by Adam Shore, his A&R rep at TVT.

The aim for the LP was simple. As Pollard put it at the time, 'I wanted our music to evolve to the point where it matched the way we sounded live.' As much as Pollard liked the results, *Isolation Drills* would mark the last time Bob or the band would use a big-name producer who received sole credit.

The LP was recorded once again in New York City, this time at Loho Studios. Loho began life as a rehearsal space before turning into a recording studio. Among the acts who have recorded there are Ryan Adams, Joan Jett, Blues Traveler, and Matador labelmates Yo La Tengo. The studio operated from 1983 to 2007. It has subsequently been purchased by the Blue Man Group, who use it for rehearsals and auditions. Rob Schnapf—unlike their previous producer—allowed GBV to have a drink or two while they were recording, and, by all accounts, the sessions went smoothly.

The original title of the record was *Broadcaster House*, after a song from their 1994 EP *Clown Prince Of The Menthol Trailer*. But Pollard changed the name because he felt it didn't fit the nature and feel of the LP. 'I looked at the dark nature of the record and how it was kind of personal and everything,' he said, so he changed it to *Isolation Drills*. (There's also a song called 'Isolation Drills,' which is a B-side of the 'Glad Girls' single.) The title referred to, as he put it, 'Looking at your life.' Pollard was doing a lot of that, and it wasn't a comfortable experience. His whole existence had been turned upside down, first on a national level by becoming a celebrity, then at home when his marriage fell apart.

He and his wife had been married for twenty years, and Bob was only forty-three years old. That meant he'd been married for almost half his life. Plus, a separation like that is never limited to just the couple. Family and friends inevitably take sides, and there are the kids to think about. By this point, Pollard's children were almost adults themselves, but that doesn't necessarily make it easier.

Pollard's also said that, around this time, fans started to get in his face at shows, challenging his integrity and looking for a fight. Others had found his phone number in Ohio and called his house, telling his wife what an asshole he was. Pollard must have been wondering, 'Is this what I've been striving for all these years? Is this what success looks like?'

The material that wound up on the LP came to Bob in a short, concentrated period. There would be no ransacking old tapes or bringing back songs from other projects or LPs. Instead, the lyrics came from a burst of poetry Pollard wrote while driving himself around for the tour for their previous LP. When he got home, he put the words to music. What he was writing about was his life, the mistakes he'd made, and where he currently found himself. 'When you're sad and you're having problems with the people that you care about in your life,' he said, 'it does put you in a seriously melancholy mood. But good stuff comes from it.'

What came from it was one of GBV's best records. Greg Kot of *Rolling Stone*, in a four-star review, wrote that '*Isolation Drills* makes the case more persuasively than ever that these indie-pop godfathers should matter to more than just the loyalists.' He also noted the more mature subject matter, saying that the songs on *Isolation Drills* 'dig behind the savant-slacker façade,' adding, 'Once slapdash with his talents, Pollard now turns even a ninety-nine-second fragment like "Sister I Need Wine" into a fully finished haiku of autumnal longing.'

Blender magazine's Joe Gross struck a similar tone. 'Pollard sounds grimmer, as if the former grade-school teacher suddenly realizes that touring in a van past age 40 isn't as much fun as he expected. And coming from a guy famous for having his own beer cooler on stage, "How's My Drinking" is one cold-eyed, self-critique.'

The sleeve for *Isolation Drills* was once again created by in-house TVT designer Ben Wheelock. The fighter jets on the cover are another in a long line of aerial and flight-related references in GBV's work. The addition of the rune on the side of one of the planes was a nod to the cover of *Secret Treaties* by Blue Öyster Cult, which featured a drawing of the band standing in front of a fighter jet that had on its tail the Blue Öyster Cult logo.

SIDE ONE

Track one: *'Fair Touching'*

You can hear immediately how the band's getting back to basics here: electric guitars, pounding drums, and that's about it. It's probably the most clean and straightforward the band had ever sounded. As Bob said of the LP, 'It's less keyboard-oriented and not quite as much gimmicky this time around.' The lyrics for this track aren't as introspective as ones found elsewhere on the album, probably because it's an older song. It first appeared on the sole release by side project Lexo & The Leapers on an EP entitled *Ask Them*, which came out in 1999.

Track two: *'Skills Like This'*

This massive song finally begins to capture the hurricane force of the band's live shows. For a band that had just come off their longest tour, the lines

'Reinvented nightly, wake up with skills like this' could be seen to represent what Pollard and the guys were going through. Every night they had to get onstage and throw that 'great party' they'd promised back on *Propeller*. That also meant waking up not just with skills but also with hangovers and strangers. As Bob's said, 'That line "I want to reinvent you" is just me [asking] myself, What do I do now?'

Track three: *'Chasing Heather Crazy'*

Pollard wrote this absolutely perfect pop song after TVT didn't hear a single on the batch of tracks Bob initially turned in. Even worse than that, label founder Steve Gottlieb said that Pollard was holding out on him, telling him, 'You have more hits in you, send us more stuff.' This seems incredible, since Pollard was the guy with the crate full of songs; it's not like there was any shortage of tunes. What Gottlieb meant (and wanted) was more commercial material. 'Think summer,' he told Bob. 'Think cars and girls.'

This was not necessarily where Pollard's head was at. Bob was thinking autumn, not summer. Anything having to do with cars and girls involved a man, alone, in a car, driving away from a girl. And the girl had just told him she never wanted to see him again. So it's to Pollard's credit that, despite the pressure under which this song was produced, it's a wonderful and amazing song. However, as poppy as it is, there are some clues in the lyrics as to Bob's emotional state. The girls Pollard invites you to visit are 'stumbling' around (they might be related to the 'glad girls' found later on the record who 'only want to get you high'). Plus, their world is 'crumbling down.' It's not as fun as it seems.

> *Staring out from otherworldly windows painted red*
> *Doesn't have to listen to the voices in your head*
> *That's a different lie*
> *Do you remember what was said?*

The bit about lies, and trying to get one's own facts straight, shows the extent of Pollard's confusion at the time. He was living almost a double life, and keeping it all straight, or in focus, was challenging. 'We tour all the time,' he said. 'It's hard on everything. You get this sense that you don't live anywhere. You're almost homeless … It takes its toll on the relationships in your life.'

And then there's that detail of the 'otherworldly windows' that are 'painted red.' The color red has long symbolized love and passion, but also blood and fire. And red, or rather scarlet, was the color of the *A* that adulteress Hester Prynne had to shamefully wear in Nathaniel Hawthorne's *The Scarlet Letter*. Pollard's admitted that it was infidelity on his part that broke up his marriage. All of which gives added depth to what Bob dashed off as a mere pop song.

Track four: *'Frostman'*

This short, rambling lo-fi song doesn't match anything else on the LP. A longer version, clocking in at 2:40, was the B-side of a Pollard solo single in 2008, released as part of the Happy Jack Rock Records singles series. The longer version is okay, but this one is just a snippet. If it was smashed up against a bunch of other shorter songs, maybe it would fit, but coming as it does, after three fleshed-out songs, its placement sabotages the flow.

Track five: *'Twilight Campfighter'*

Called a 'luminous folk-rock hymn' by *Rolling Stone*, this is another song that goes back to GBV's R.E.M.-influenced past. Showing that you sometimes can look too hard at Pollard's titles or lyrics, he said, 'The title means nothing. My friend said to me, "I got a title: 'Twilight Campfighter.'" I go, "That's fucking great, man."' He's also said that it's his favorite song on the record. Musically, it has a sense of yearning, and when Pollard longs to see 'your twilight eyes,' it takes me back to the swooning second half of 'Over The Neptune / Mesh Gear Fox.'

Track six: *'Sister I Need Wine'*

After four straightforward rock songs and one throwaway, this is a welcome track. The guitar sound was achieved by Pollard, Gillard, Farley, and Tobias, all playing the same guitar part simultaneously, crowded around a single microphone. It's a great effect, especially when some subtle strings come in.

The lyrics finally get at some of the darkness that's only been hinted at in earlier songs, Pollard saying he needs alcohol not just for a fun time but to give him, and his life, color.

The next lines, 'But I can see the light burn through, still it is the night brings me to you,' take the song to a whole other level. Light, which we'll see again in 'Glad Girls,' is a universal literary symbol. It stands for the divine or spiritual, not to mention it's the source of knowledge and goodness. Its opposite is, of course, darkness, something that Pollard hints at in the following line about 'the night that brings me to you.' He's writing about temptation and the ancient struggle between light and dark. If you consider that the 'sister' Bob's referring to might be a nun, the lyrics take on religious overtones as well. The song ends with Pollard proclaiming that he's going to 'drink the truth' and 'shed not one tear.' He's come to grips with what he's forfeiting, and he's declared what he's losing in exchange for the escape to be worth it.

Track seven: 'Want One?'

Any vibe created by 'Sister I Need Wine' is promptly squashed with this meathead rocker that puts me in the mind of 80s metal bands like Van Halen; the only interesting thing about it is the whistling.

Track eight: 'The Enemy'

This starts with a lo-fi snippet name-checking the original title for the LP, *Broadcaster House*, before going into another heavy rock song. The drums and the guitars sound huge, and there's even what sounds like some backward guitar at the very end.

While I find most of the lyrics to be impressionistic or cryptic, the final lines about lovers being statues in a 'ten-acre garden' are haunting. The idea of being turned to stone, and standing in a huge expanse, is a wonderful if depressing metaphor for the distance and inertia we can create between ourselves and the people we love. The phrase 'everlasting big kick' also makes an appearance in the song. This was going to be the name of a six-song solo EP around the time of *Sandbox*. It was listed on the Gotham City Music insert, but it never materialized.

Track nine: *'Unspirited'*

This is the most musically varied song on the first side, incorporating synth strings in addition to some great guitar work by Gillard and solid drumming from Macpherson. Pollard's said that the song's about how he felt at the time. 'Things were going on in my life where I kind of thought I was losing my shit a little bit. I felt like I was unspirited. The way to deal with it was just to become numb and not give a fuck about anything.' But there was another element to the song: his son, Bryan, who was around twenty at the time. 'He's a man now,' said Bob. 'And he's going to be in this whole fucking mess. The same mess that I'm in.' You can see this in the lyrics, Bob writing, 'Everywhere that you go, I'm with you now' and 'When you lose it all, you'll think of me.'

Underneath Pollard's admiration for his son is the knowledge that, no matter how mature Bryan is, he's going to be caught up in the heaviness of life. Marriages end, hearts get broken, children get left behind. Bob's also asking for a little understanding and forgiveness, writing, 'When you take the fall, you'll drink to me.' When Bryan realizes how hard it is to navigate true adulthood, maybe he'll look back with understanding on some of the choices his dad made.

SIDE TWO

Track one: *'Glad Girls'*

This song—immediately picked by the label as the record's first single— is one of the band's best, and most fun, ever. It's incredibly catchy and takes only about a half second to draw you in. That might be because, like 'Can't Buy Me Love,' it opens with the chorus. The website *Medialoper* calls this 'perhaps the most joyous-sounding song Robert Pollard has ever recorded.' And yet, even in this jubilant tune, which seems, on its surface, positive and like a celebration—the word 'glad' is right there in the title—we find the dark undercurrent that runs through the rest of the album. 'There will be no coronation, there will be no flowers flowing,' Pollard writes. 'There will be no graduation, there will be no trumpets blowing.' This evokes a passage from *The Crack-Up* by F. Scott Fitzgerald: 'There would be no badges of pride, no medals after all.' Pollard, once so celebrated and heralded for his talent, was seeing that maybe it all wasn't going to add up to much.

Bob again references darkness and light. 'With the sinking of the sun, I've come to greet you.' It's almost the return of the Vampire on Titus. And, of course, there's the line 'The light that passes through me.' I mentioned before the symbolic significance of light. The song even contains the idea of redemption, noting the 'good and bad men all around,' some of which are lost, while others have found the light. That goes right back to the eighteenth-century Christian hymn 'Amazing Grace.' In fact, Bob said the songs on *Isolation Drills* were all about 'sin' and 'being out there in the absence of everything.' We might be guided by voices, but it's sure as hell hard to be guided by God.

A video for the song was made by filmmaker Nol Honig. After stumbling upon a way to turn footage into vector art using a computer program, he sent a short sample of the technique to TVT founder Steve Gottlieb, whom Honig knew from doing some illustration work for the label. Gottlieb liked what he saw, which spurred Honig to create a spec video using the same technique for the *Bee Thousand* clip 'Ester's Day.' Gottlieb loved the video, but he initially wanted Honig to make a video for another band on the label, Sevendust. Honig balked, only wanting to work with GBV or Nine Inch Nails (the only bands on TVT he liked). Gottlieb agreed to a GBV clip and set a budget of $7,000. After Bob saw, and approved of, the 'Ester's Day' clip, he and Honig—along with longtime manager David Newgarden—brainstormed until they came up with the 'Magic Binoculars' concept. Honig later spent a day filming models in Brooklyn before flying out to meet up with GBV at a tour stop in to Seattle to shoot Bob and the band.

Track two: 'Run Wild'

While I'm not a fan of the way the verses sound—that palm-muted guitar style is too similar to bad heavy metal—the chorus absolutely soars. Whereas Pollard had once admonished his fans to just 'motor away,' he's now inviting them to 'leave your things in the streets and run wild.' His voice sounds amazing; it's a joy to listen to. However, even here, there's a hint of melancholy. No matter where you run to, or how you do it, you're going to end up somewhere. And your problems will still exist when you get there. Basically, you can run wild, but you can't run away.

Track three: *'Pivotal Film'*

Pollard said the inspiration for this song was the English glam band T. Rex, and that the results were exactly what he wanted. 'I think that's the best rock song that we've ever done.'

The song ends with 'scenesters' exiting 'into thin air.' This could be seen as a reference to the band's seemingly overnight success, and the ensuing backlash. Long touted as the 'next big thing,' GBV had to wonder what happened to all those early 'scenesters' who had supported them. To quote The Breeders, 'You loved me then. Do you love me now?'

Track four: *'How's My Drinking?'*

Bob's said that this song was a response to a nasty article in the *Dayton Daily News* that came after one of the band's famously drunken shows—one that saw Pollard stumbling around by the end. Even though he was stung by the piece, he promptly rejected any warnings or advice by the writer. Instead, he wrote this track. It's another in a long line of GBV songs that address not only alcohol and drinking but Bob's own attitude and feelings toward it. 'I don't care about being sober,' he proclaims. He's basically telling us to leave him alone when it comes to his drinking. It's funny that this record drew some comparisons to *Blood On The Tracks*, since one of the saddest lines on that record is Dylan's delusional promise, 'I can change, I swear.' Pollard here stubbornly refuses any sort of self-reflection or altered behavior, declaring flatly, 'I won't change.' Musically, it has a woozy, lurching feel, and he delivers his vocal as if he has indeed had a few beers.

Track five: *'The Brides Have Hit Glass'*

This is probably the most obvious song on the record, in terms of dealing with what was happening in Pollard's life during this period. The opening lines refer to Bob's double life of touring, and never fitting in anywhere:

I don't come around
Never call or let her know
I got a life of my own

But it's more than just his marriage that's falling apart. Bob's whole notion of himself, and the success of his band, is being challenged. But even though there's sadness, there's also hope, Pollard insisting, 'There's a better road ahead of me.' Of course, he then adds, 'I just don't know how to make it there.' He's not offering any easy fixes.

Track six: 'Fine To See You'

This slow song doesn't have a discernible structure; it just unwinds. The lyrics again reference how low Pollard was feeling at the time ('There is nowhere to go but up').

Track seven: 'Privately'

Much like the last couple of songs, this is a ballad laden with strings. The muscle and power from the opening couple of tracks have been left behind. The lyrics are a plea for privacy, Pollard wanting to keep 'bitter' and 'contagious' words a 'secret.' He writes, 'Don't post them for broadcast, keep them private and away.' It's ironic for Bob to ask for this, since he's making the request in the very public forum of a song that's going to be heard by tens of thousands of people. The ending, with Bob repeating 'privately' as the song fades out, is one of the best endings of any GBV album.

13 UNIVERSAL TRUTHS AND CYCLES

two thousand and two

After delivering the most mature records of their career with the TVT albums *Do The Collapse* and *Isolation Drills*, GBV stood at a crossroad. They'd done their best to reach more people, recording slick, commercial records and touring more than ever. Bob was writing what he thought were hit songs ('Glad Girls' and 'Chasing Heather Crazy'), and yet the records sold more or less the same, and radio play was still scant. That bigger audience never arrived. 'We just realized that we were flogging a dead horse,' Bob said of his time with TVT. 'The attempt was to try to sell more records and to get more radio play, but that wasn't happening.' After fulfilling their two-album deal, they left.

The band ended up back on Matador. As Pollard stated in a press release announcing the news, 'It's great to be reunited with our good friends at Matador, fellow rock geeks with the same basic philosophy on record artistry.' Matador's Gerard Cosloy added, 'We have long regretted the interruption of their tenure with the label and are grateful this partnership will recommence.'

Billboard characterized the return as unsurprising and referred to the switch as GBV being 'back home at the friendly confines of Matador Records,' adding that the New York–based label had 'lifelined the group out of years of regional obscurity in the mid-90s.'

First of all, it was Scat, not Matador, that discovered and broke the band. Also, GBV's 'obscurity' was such in the 80s and early 90s that the region

Billboard was referring to was planet Earth. Guided By Voices was an unknown entity, even in their hometown. This was not a situation where a local band, with a local following, suddenly gets a national audience. GBV were a group that, before Scat came along in 1993, weren't playing shows and had no distribution other than a few friends who got their homemade LPs into mom-and-pop stores (where they didn't sell). Remember also that the band had broken up; 1992's *Propeller* was meant to be their last release, and, if Robert Griffin had never called Pollard, it all quite possibly could have ended there. Also, how 'friendly' was Matador toward the band, or vice versa? It's obvious that Matador liked GBV and wanted them back. And Bob had long admired the label and stated he wanted to be part of it. But all the things that led to trouble with Matador previously were still there. It's like when you get back with an ex without solving any of the things that broke you up in the first place: it'll be fun for a while, but, in the end, you're headed for trouble.

To start with, even back during the first round with Matador, the label had been concerned about the band's drinking. In *Hunting Accidents*, Bob talks about a meeting that the label had set up to talk about the excesses of the *Mag Earwhig!* tour. And even though Pollard had tried to rein the band in on later tours, this is still GBV we're talking about. Drinking was always going to be an issue, which Matador had to have realized.

Also, Bob had no intention of having Guided By Voices be his only musical focus. The label execs had put their foot down and limited Pollard to one GBV record a year, and, while they'd released both Bob's and Tobin's solo records, they'd passed, and would continue to pass, on the more arcane side-project stuff (the same as TVT). During the second Matador phase, the label only released GBV material. It didn't put out anything by Toby or Bob, even though they both continued to release solo records. And it certainly didn't put out any Circus Devils or Acid Ranch or Lifeguards records, or anything else Pollard cooked up on the side.

In a 2003 *New York Times* article about GBV (the headline of which was 'The Band That Can't Stop Recording'), Cosloy called Pollard's massive musical output 'impressive but unwieldy.' I'll talk in a later chapter about what this means as a fan, but for a label head like Cosloy, this was a real headache. It meant he couldn't get as much coverage for the band, or even reviews. Bemoaning the 'downward spiral' of GBV's album sales, which began around the time of *Under The Bushes*—which is to say, when they first signed to Matador—Cosloy declared, 'Part of that is due to the volume of Guided By Voices–related product.'

So, going back to Matador seems a bit weird. The band was still the band, and the label was still the label. Neither had changed in terms of how they functioned or what they expected. The seeds of the end were right there at the beginning. Why did either side think that the results would be different than they'd been the first time around? It's also not like the group didn't have choices. At the time, GBV were talking to several independent labels, including Vagrant and Sub Pop. Guided By Voices signing to Sub Pop sounds absolutely right. The band's whole 'loud rock'n'roll' thing would fit in perfectly on the Seattle label. However, when his manager told him that Matador was also interested, Bob instantly jumped at the chance.

Around the time *Universal Truths* was made, there was a return to the guitar-based rock sound that was GBV's bread and butter. This rock revival was led by The White Stripes and The Strokes but also featured groups like the Yeah Yeah Yeahs, The Vines, and The Hives. Suddenly, playing guitar and being loud was fashionable again. Even Radiohead, who'd largely eschewed guitars around the turn of the century—focusing instead on Warp Records atmospherics—released a more guitar-based LP with 2003's *Hail To The Thief*.

Another thing these new bands had in common was their youth. These were young kids, barely out of their teens. GBV were always the odd group out due to their age; they were seen as old even when they burst onto the scene ten years before. By this point, they were elder statesmen. That was okay, since a number of these bands—including arguably the most important one, The Strokes—name-checked GBV and said what an influence they'd been on their sound.

Bob had now achieved yet another milestone in his artistic achievements—he'd lasted long enough to influence a new generation. His musical fandom had come full circle. He was having an impact on bands the way that the bands he'd loved growing up had had an impact on him. 'When you're younger,' said Strokes guitarist Albert Hammond Jr., 'you have your older idols. [GBV] were like my modern idols who made me feel like I could do it.'

Bob loved the attention, and he even boasted that he'd 'discovered' The

Strokes. The band had thrown their demo onstage during a show, and GBV actually listened to it on the ride to their next concert. They liked what they heard and invited the band to open up for them on a string of shows. 'After that they went over to England,' Bob said, 'and all of a sudden they were the biggest thing on earth.'

The relationship between the two bands lasted longer than just that initial string of dates. The Strokes and GBV played a pair of sold-out shows at New York's famed Apollo Theater, including one on New Year's Eve. The Strokes even joined GBV onstage for what *Rolling Stone* described as a 'boozy' encore of 'My Valuable Hunting Knife.'

The Strokes would later return the favor, bringing Pollard onstage at Reading to play 'A Salty Salute.' The Strokes even put GBV in the video for their song 'Someday,' squaring off against the band in the game show *Family Feud*. Pollard described The Strokes as his 'best buddies,' and, for a while, it seems they were.

Now that GBV were free from TVT, their first major decision was to not go with a big-name producer. They felt they could do this because they'd learned enough from the two prior LPs. Plus, they wanted to stay in Ohio, where they're more comfortable (and so they could keep costs down). However, they felt they needed a bit of help, so they drafted Todd Tobias, the younger brother of bass player Tim Tobias.

Todd was the musical mastermind behind side project Circus Devils, which was just getting started around this time. The way that group worked was that Todd —often along with his brother—would create the music and send it to Pollard, who would then lay down vocals over the tracks. The music Todd and Tim provided was often raw, weird, and angular—Bob's strange and fantastical lyrics were often the perfect accompaniment. It's safe to say that the Pollard who'd hoped to achieve mainstream acceptance, and a wider audience for his work, didn't have that in mind when embarking on the journey he'd take with Circus Devils over the next decade and a half.

Working on GBV's new album was a big change—not to mention a step up—for Tobias. 'This was my first assignment as a record producer working in a real studio,' he writes in *See You Inside*, his history of Circus Devils. The GBV LP 'would be released to the world on a prestigious indie rock label. It was a big jump from my rinky-dink home recording set up.'

Joining them in the studio, after the departure of drummer Jim Macpherson, was Jon McCann. Otherwise, the rest of the lineup was the same as on the last LP. Doug Gillard and Nate Farley on guitar, and Todd's brother Tim on bass. McCann had gotten to know the band when his previous group, American Flag, opened for GBV. His time in GBV didn't last long, however. This is the only album he's involved with.

As usual, the idea for the record changed and ballooned from Pollard's original vision. At first, he wanted to make a stripped down, twelve-song record. The dozen tracks were done and mixed, and then Bob wrote more songs. The new tracks were shorter than the longer tracks he'd intended for the twelve-track LP. While originally intending to place these songs on a solo record, Pollard instead went the *Alien Lanes* route and sprinkled the shorter songs among the longer ones, 'kinda like an old GBV album.' The short songs added to *Truths*, to my ears, often detract more than they add. If he'd indeed kept it at a tight dozen songs, the LP would be a classic.

In terms of titles, Pollard considered *From A Voice Plantation*, *All Sinners Welcome*, *Invisible Train To Earth*, and *Panic Revolution*. The eventual title, *Universal Truths And Cycles*, was chosen because, according to Bob, 'It's more applicable to the way the album feels. It's about daily struggle, daily existence, car rage, riding on a subway, and all that. It's about the things that everybody goes through daily. You're reborn every morning, and you get a new chance to get your shit together.'

Being back on Matador meant that Pollard once again not only had more say over the music but also the covers. 'On our last two records with TVT they did not let me do the album covers, ' Bob said, 'and I don't like those covers. They came up with the ideas and we accepted them, but they don't look half as good as the covers I do.' The cover that in-house designer Mark Ohe and Bob came up with stands out among the dozens of other GBV sleeves. It's also the only one where the material it's made out of—a heavy cardstock, with a rough texture—is part of the overall design and desired effect.

The album spawned two Matador-backed CD singles, 'Back To The Lake' and 'Everywhere With Helicopter.' Pollard's Fading Captain Series put out the seven-inch versions. Fading Captain also issued two more singles on vinyl, for the songs 'Cheyenne' and the title track. The singles were released in two-week increments starting that May, leading up to the release of the record in June, to drum up interest in the LP.

Matador also made a video for 'Everywhere With Helicopter.' Shot at New Jersey's Six Flags Great Adventure amusement park, it shows Bob lip-syncing the song while riding various roller coasters, interspersed with scenes of four kids walking around and enjoying the park. It's a fun video, especially when Pollard goofs around with the kids and eats burgers, fries, and cotton candy. After so many tales of Bob's drunken antics, it's sweet to see him play the family man. The only bad thing is that this was when Pollard was coloring his hair, plus his hair's awfully short, so it's not his best look.

Giving the record a 7.6, Matt LeMay from *Pitchfork* wrote, 'To make a long story short, it's the best thing Pollard's done since *Mag Earwhig!*' However, after acknowledging a few of the record's classic tracks, such as 'Cheyenne,' LeMay makes note of the LP's short song snippets, writing, 'Yet, other songs, like the minute-long "The Ids Are Alright" and "Factory Of Raw Essentials" meander in typical Pollard fashion without ever really registering.'

LeMay also makes mention of GBV's failed attempt to break into the mainstream, noting that, 'Whatever hopes [Pollard] might have had of bringing his sweet rock and roll to the masses have been crushed, trampled, and stomped into the ground.' The bits there about being 'crushed' and 'trampled' are a tasteless reference to a tragedy that happened in Cincinnati in 1979. At a sold-out Who concert at Riverfront Coliseum, eleven people were crushed to death, and twenty-six others suffered injuries, when the crowd rushed through the doors. The band wasn't told about the tragedy until after the concert, which went on as planned. Pollard was actually at this show, and in an era before cell phones and social media, there was a period where his family didn't know if he was dead or alive. History came full circle in 2006 when Pollard, as a solo act, opened up for Pearl Jam at the same arena (by then known as the US Bank Arena). He even joined the band onstage to play 'Baba O'Riley' in what has to be one of the ultimate tributes to his all-time heroes. There's footage of this on YouTube, and it's a joy to watch, especially when Eddie Vedder says that's Pollard's 'a big man' singing 'a big song.' A recording of Pollard's performance that night was released on Merge as the live LP *Moon*.

In his *AV Club* review of *Universal Truths*, Keith Phipps cited Bob's prodigious musical output at the time, writing that 'Pollard churned out so many footnotes under his *Fading Captain Series* aegis that even the most devoted fan would find it hard to keep track of them all, much less remember which ones housed the gems among the clutter.' Phipps also mentions Bob's resignation with his cult status. 'Pollard now seems less interested in converting the world population into Guided By Voices fans than in furthering his own vision of what rock'n'roll should sound like.'

Rolling Stone's Rob O'Connor, in a three-star review, also couldn't help but take notice of just how much stuff Pollard was releasing. 'Just like the 1960s British Invasion that unleashed records at a breakneck speed until Americans were drowning in vinyl, Guided By Voices leader Robert Pollard is determined to oversaturate the market all by himself.'

It's not a good sign when magazines start reviewing the amount of your output, instead of the quality. The year *Universal Truths* came out, Bob also issued a Circus Devils record; an EP of B-sides; a collaborative record with Mac from Superchunk under the name Go Back Snowball; an Airport 5 record with Tobin Sprout; four GBV singles; a full-length Guided By Voices record; and whatever the hell that thing was he made with Richard Meltzer. Critics were right to wonder if Pollard was spreading himself too thin.

SIDE ONE

Track one: *'Wire Greyhounds'*

We're back in *Alien Lanes* territory with this super-short song snippet that lasts just thirty-five seconds. It also contains Bob's most over-the-top English accent. I'm not a big fan of these fragments, especially here, as the start to what's actually a solid and mature record.

Track two: *'Skin Parade'*

This starts off in a similar vein to the first song, like one of the band's lo-fi tracks from the early 90s. Bob's singing over an out-of-tune acoustic guitar with room noises behind him (including laughter, conversation, and bottles clinking). But that portion's just another snippet. Once the song kicks in, as a full-band rocker, it sounds huge. There's also a constant sort of pounding or noise in the background that, along with the way the vocals are recorded, tie it to Pollard's side project Circus Devils.

Track three: 'Zap'

This acoustic song harkens back to 'Paper Girl' from *Same Place The Fly Got Smashed*. Bob's voice sounds great, and there are some strong melodic turns of phrase. The lyrics show Bob at his most mature, asking, 'Is it good for you to ask for assistance? And to ask for it for others also?' It's a far cry from 'I wish I could give a shit, just a little bit.' However, the song's a bit short, at not much more than a minute, so it feels like yet another fragment.

Track four: 'Christian Animation Torch Carriers'

This absolutely solid track finally, four songs in, kicks off the record in proper fashion. That being said, it has a spare intro that lasts a minute before the song finally gets going. But once it does, it sounds amazing. Todd Tobias does a great job producing the group, and Doug Gillard's guitar playing is spot-on; by this record, he's proved himself to be indispensable to the group's sound. At three minutes in, when the song's title makes its appearance, the track goes into overdrive. and it's glorious.

The lyrics don't have a ton of meaning, scanning more as poetry. The mention of Christians in the song, as well as the album's Roman-inspired cover art, makes me wonder whether Pollard's here referring to ancient history, rather than recent events. The Romans had of course banned Christianity, and Christians were persecuted for decades, sometimes being fed to lions or having to, like the illustration on the front of *Universal Truths*, fight for their lives against wild and dangerous animals. That being said, the whole idea of Romans screaming 'Christians to the lions!' is more likely than not overblown, and was a later creation of Christians, who were eager to cast their ancestors as martyrs.

Track five: 'Cheyenne'

This absolutely gorgeous track features amazing vocals by Bob. He can be a classic hard-rock singer, like Roger Daltrey, but his ability to hit high notes here shows his vocal range. Cheyenne is the capital of Wyoming and was also the name of a TV series that ran during Bob's childhood. It's also sometimes a girl's name. The production is just great, and the song features more amazing guitar work by Doug Gillard, here turning in probably my favorite GBV guitar solo ever. Jon McCann also does a great job on the drums. *Pitchfork's* Matt LeMay cited this as the record's standout track. 'Built around a lovely chord progression and developing toward an endlessly catchy finale, "Cheyenne" could easily be the most blissful Guided By Voices song since *Waved Out's* "Subspace Biographies."' The fact that *Waved Out* was a Pollard solo record, and not a GBV LP, shows that—with so much Bob-related merchandise available—it was hard to keep track of what song went with what project.

Track six: *'The Weeping Bogeyman'*

This short acoustic song has some atmospheric production by Tobias. It's a bit meandering, and doesn't seem to have much of a point, but a few melodic turns of phrase late in the song make it a nice listen.

Track seven: *'Back To The Lake'*

Everyone sounds amazing here, and even though it's fairly short, at just a few seconds past the two-and-a-half-minute mark, it feels like a fully fleshed-out song. I'll take the lyrics at face value and assume they're about Pollard trying to reach someone who just won't answer their phone, or 'pick up' (something you used to have to do when phones had two pieces and usually rested on tabletops). Plus, Ohio has about fifty thousand lakes, so I'm sure Daytonians, like everyone else in the state, spend a fair amount of time visiting lakes for vacations. When asked by *Spin*, in 2004, to rank his top ten GBV songs, Pollard put this at number six.

Track eight: *'Love 1'*

Although it's fun to hear Bob say 'crème brûlée,' this is not a satisfying song, and was most likely one Pollard added at the last minute.

Track nine: *'Storm Vibrations'*

At a second shy of five minutes, this is the record's longest track. It starts with arpeggiated electric guitar and sounds like a slightly faster 'Behind Blue

Eyes.' The song quickly expands and turns into a full-blown rocker. And when Pollard repeats, 'Does it hurt you? To love, I mean,' he's getting back to the emotion-laden songs on the previous LP.

The song also has the repeated refrain 'It will try to find you no matter where you may go' from an older song called 'Try To Find You.' A live recording of the earlier song (credited to the fake band Fat Change and recorded in 1984) was included on the first *Suitcase* compilation. Pollard might still be talking about love here, but I think he's actually talking about death. As he's said before, in songs such as 'Exit Flagger,' there's no escaping it; death will always find you. And, of course, death is one of the ways that love ends up hurting. When you lose someone close to you, it feels like you're losing a piece of yourself. It's one of the most painful things you can experience. As the poet and undertaker Thomas Lynch writes, 'Grief is the price we pay for being close to one another. If we want to avoid our grief, we simply avoid each other.' We don't want to feel grief, but we want to feel love. These could be the 'confusing emotions' Pollard references. It's a truly monumental tune that's made even more epic by ending with the sound of a jet engine. It would be a great way to end the side, except there's one more song.

Track ten: *'Factory Of Raw Essentials'*

This short acoustic track starts with a bad vocal by Bob, who's practically slurring. That being said, by the end it sounds quite striking. Of all the short songs on the record, this is probably my favorite. The phrase 'Factory Of Raw Essentials' is still in use today; you can see it at the top of the Rockathon website.

SIDE TWO
Track one: *'Everywhere With Helicopter'*

This amazing track shows that, despite some ups-and-downs for the band— label changes and varying lineups—GBV could still deliver powerful material. I love Bob's singing on this. Pollard has an incredibly versatile voice, and I'm always impressed when he finds interesting ways to use it. There are some strong cover versions of this song, including Jason Isbell's acoustic version from the *Sing For Your Meat* tribute record.

Track two: 'Pretty Bombs'

This song features strings and a Beatles-esque interlude toward the end. The last minute is just pure music, and it highlights what a strong band Bob had put together.

Track three: 'Eureka Signs'

This is just about the closest that GBV ever got to sounding like The Who circa 1971. For the first line, instead of singing 'You tell me you've come to your senses,' try singing 'I'd gladly lose me to find you.' The lyrics again hint at some of the unrest that was all over *Isolation Drills*: 'Every day it's the god awful same, I wanna go solo and drive.'

Track four: 'Wings Of Thorn'

This mainly acoustic song doesn't seem to be about anything, and, at just over two minutes, it's over pretty fast.

Track five: 'Car Language'

At 4:44, this is the second-longest song on the record. It's also a weird one: the drums don't kick in for two minutes, and, even when they do, there's no real beat. The lyrics seem like they could be right out of J. G. Ballard's infamous novel *Crash*, with Bob writing about the 'wild joy of traffic,' 'flashing metal interaction,' and 'auto-erotic satisfaction.'

Track six: 'From A Voice Plantation'

This is another song that doesn't go anywhere—there are a bunch of weird guitar noises and lyrics about 'smoke rings,' 'ghosts,' and 'onion fields'— bringing the momentum created by the first couple of songs to a standstill.

Track seven: 'The Ids Are Alright'

This acoustic track starts with a melodica, which is the first (and last) time the instrument's been used on a GBV album. It's short, at not much more than a minute. The title contains two references, the first being 'The Kids Are Alright,' a Who song that appeared on their first record, 1965's *My Generation*. It was released as a single, and, even though it wasn't a hit—it peaked at #41 in the charts—it became one of the group's best known and most loved songs. It also provided the name for the 1979 documentary about the group made by Who super-fan Jeff Stein. And the id is one of the three parts of the psyche that Freud identified, along with the ego and superego. However, I don't see much connection in the lyrics to these ideas. In fact, the final line, 'All things happen,' makes me think of Carl Jung's idea of synchronicity.

Track eight: 'Universal Truths And Cycles'

This song is a great example of how, quite often, Pollard's lyrics don't scan as song lyrics, with Bob resisting simple 'moon/June' kind of structures in favor of non-rhyming verses that read more as poetry. Pollard and the band played this mid-tempo tune on the *Universal Truths And Cycles* tour but never again. Recording-wise, Bob—like his hero, John Lennon—double-tracked his vocal here, and it sounds good. I wish he did that more.

Track nine: 'Father Sgt. Christmas Card'

This starts off very lo-fi, with Bob returning to the English accent found on the first song. But then the band kicks in, and the song gets fleshed out. The last thirty seconds of the track, and thus the record, consist of Bob repeating, 'Oh God, bless you.' Whether this is a sincere religious declaration, or someone in the studio just sneezed, I don't know, but it's a touching way to end the LP.

EARTHQUAKE GLUE

two thousand and three

M uch like the previous year, 2003 saw the release of not just a new Guided By Voices record but a whole mountain of Pollard-related product. First, Bob and Doug teamed up to form a new group, Lifeguards, whose debut was called *Mist King Urth*. (There would only be two Lifeguards records, the second one being 2011's *Waving At The Astronauts*.) There was also a new Circus Devils record called *Pinball Mars*.

Pollard also released a mini solo LP called *Motel Of Fools*; Matt Hickey of *Magnet* called it 'the soundtrack to a nonexistent film; a collection of mumbling noises, tape tricks, found sounds and some trademark pomp rock,' adding that 'it isn't always listenable in a traditionally direct way, but it's never less than interesting.' Hickey addressed all the other activity, too. 'Bob Pollard has been criticized for releasing seemingly every scrap of non–Guided By Voices material emanating from his hyper-creative being. The guy does crap an entire album after morning coffee, but what sometimes gets lost when slamming Pollard's prolific urges is that most of the stuff found on his flurry of platters is pretty good—and sometimes great.'

The key word in all that is 'urge.' To quote Devo, Bob has 'an uncontrollable urge.' He just can't resist releasing stuff. It's not that he needs an editor, as is sometimes suggested, it's that he needs some self-control. And while Hickey's right that there's quality stuff on some of these records, it's a chore to wade through the various projects just to find a couple of quality tracks.

In a short interview accompanying a review of three of the records listed above, the writer asks Pollard, 'I know you write songs all the time and you're doing other things, but are there times when you get bored doing what you do full-time?' And Bob's answer is illuminating. 'Oh, yeah, I get totally bored … I miss working a bit.' When he was working, he only had weekends and holidays to devote to writing songs or making collages. But songs and collages were now what Pollard did to simply pass the time, and he had a whole lot of it on his hands.

Something else that made its debut in 2003 was *EAT*. Billed as Bob's 'literary magazine,' its first issue boasted 'never before seen collages, poems and band names all done by Bob specifically for this magazine.' Pollard's since put out an issue of *EAT* more or less annually.

In 2003, the Matador box set came out, the full name of which is *Hardcore UFOs: Revelations, Epiphanies And Fast Food In The Western Hemisphere*. It was—and continues to be—an impressive package. It consists of five CDs, a DVD, and a handsome booklet. The CDs include a compilation of live tracks, a disc of demos and unreleased material, a CD of B-sides and compilation tracks, a copy of the best-of album *Human Amusements At Hourly Rates*, and a re-pressing of their very first record, the 1986 EP *Forever Since Breakfast*.

The best-of has the same tracks as the single disc edition that came out at the same time, only the box-set edition goes in chronological order. I actually prefer this version, since it's interesting to hear the band develop over time, not to mention go through their different eras and lineups; it reminds me of the Beatles compilation *1*. Also included is the Banks Tarver documentary *Watch Me Jumpstart*.

As if all that weren't enough, GBV released a new album. And, unlike the drama that went into other LPs of this period, putting together *Earthquake Glue* seems straightforward. Sure, there were the alternate titles—*Model Prisoners Of The 5 Sense Realm, Live Like Kings Forever, All Sinners Welcome*—but there weren't necessarily alternate versions, nor an alternate vision. Instead, it's just fifteen songs, clocking in at forty-five minutes.

It was produced once again by Todd Tobias, the first-time producer who'd done such a great job on the previous LP. It was also recorded again in Dayton. The only major change from the last record is that there's a new drummer, with

Kevin March replacing Jon McCann. March was a graduate of the Berklee College of Music, not to mention a veteran of a number of 90s bands. He got his start with Boston by way-of-Hawaii group The Dambuilders. They had a bit of a hit in '94, with 'Shrine.' March then joined the DC-based Shudder To Think. Shudder had started in the post-hardcore scene, releasing three records on ultra-indie Dischord before making the major-label jump to Epic. The band fell apart in 1998. Apparently, March was personally recommended to GBV by Dave Shouse from The Grifters and Bloodthirsty Lovers. Bassist Tim Tobias soon gave March the thumbs-up, telling an interviewer, 'Kevin is a great person to have on the road; he has a great sense of humor and keeps us all laughing.'

March proved himself to be an amazing asset; he would occupy the drummer's throne until the band broke up the following year, and he would be asked back in 2013, when Bob fell out with Kevin Fennell. And, like Doug Gillard, he remains with the band to this day. For *Earthquake Glue*, Pollard told March to be Keith Moon, requesting him to 'Go wild!' March recalled, 'Not many people tell you to do that in the studio, so I did!'

The record's cover featured a Pollard collage, which was the first time one had graced a GBV sleeve since 1997's *Mag Earwhig!* The back featured a photo of the band standing in the parking lot of a vacant strip mall in Dayton.

An interesting thing to note about the packaging is that it didn't come with a lyric sheet. This was because, according to Bob, 'I don't think it's lyrically as good as the last one. On *Universal Truths And Cycles*, most of the songs started off as poems, I wrote the melodies later. Whereas on this one the music came first, so it was a bit more difficult for the lyrics to be poignant.'

Earthquake Glue spawned two singles, 'My Kind Of Soldier' and 'The Best Of Jill Hives.' Videos were made for both songs. The video for 'Jill Hives' is about as nonsensical as they come, featuring a guy in a carrot costume singing the song's lyrics while a quartet of revelers dance in the background. The video for 'My Kind Of Soldier' was similarly simple, and also did not feature the band. Instead, it starred a guy nicknamed 'Beatle Bob' (real name Bob Matonis), and has him dancing to the song while facts about him are inserted in between shots. Matonis goes to concerts all around the country, not to mention festivals like South By Southwest, to do his crazy dancing thing. And while some people obviously find his shtick charming—as do GBV, I assume, since they put the guy in one of their videos, plus they had him be the emcee for their final shows—plenty of other people, including a whole bunch from St. Louis, where Bob lives, have had more than enough of him.

A fun thing Matador did for the release of *Earthquake Glue* was to give the owners of the first twenty-five thousand copies of the Digipak CD the chance to find inside a 'golden ticket.' Finding one entitled the owner to a signed copy of the *Hardcore UFOs* box set. The winning ticket had a picture of Pollard and the words 'In Bob we trust' at the bottom.

David Holmes of *Stereogum*, when ranking all of GBV's LPs, said of *Earthquake Glue*, 'It took them fifteen years, but Guided By Voices finally made a stadium record worthy of Cheap Trick. This is the purest form of Guided By Voices' "arena-rock" years, a big, polished, tightly constructed beast of a record that is too damn catchy to be hated, even by the lowest of the lo-fi purists.'

Spin was less effusive, giving the record only a C+ and calling it the band's '136th album,' writing that it 'feels like a gallery of napkin sketches—hazy, almost-there stadium anthems that don't quite fill the stadium.' Bob defended the record in an interview with Keith Cameron for *Mojo*, saying, 'Almost every song on the record could be on college radio. It's poppier, it's more melodic, I think. And the packaging's really cool.'

Before Pollard and the band headed into the studio to record the album, he put down in demo form almost all the songs that would eventually appear on the LP. This was what he gave to the guys in the band to teach them the songs. Pollard liked the results of what he recorded—reportedly it only took five hours—so he released them as *Edison's Demos*, a name that was a pun on an early contender for the LP's title, *Edison's Memos* (which was also the name of a song by Acid Ranch). Of the fifteen tracks that would appear on *Earthquake Glue*, twelve appear on *Edison's Demos*. Two, in fact, appear twice, in different forms. One song, 'Blasted But It's Easy,' was recorded at the time of *Earthquake Glue* but renamed 'Broken Brothers' and released on the single for 'My Kind Of Soldier.' The three songs not included are 'My Kind Of Soldier,' 'The Best Of Jill Hives,' and 'Of Mites And Men.' For some reason, Pollard—who loves to make up fake band names and record labels—released this himself, sort of anonymously. Only a thousand copies were released, which means it's a sought-out fan-favorite today.

SIDE ONE
Track one: *'My Kind Of Soldier'*

This absolutely fantastic song—one of the best tracks on the record—was actually a late addition to the LP. Bob wrote it after the rest of the record was finished, the band getting together to record it at Steve Albini's studio. Bob wanted it to end the record, but Matador placed it at the beginning.

Pollard's long used military imagery and phrases in his work. There are the LPs *Not In My Airforce*, *Kid Marine*, and *We All Got Out Of The Army*, not to mention the songs 'Back To The Navy' and 'The Military School Dance Dismissal.' This song follows in that tradition, with some of the lyrical imagery speaking to battles or war, Pollard mentioning 'shelled remains,' a 'strike brigade,' and 'fighting' for control. The track is also another of Bob's pragmatic admissions about the prices that must be paid in life, telling the unnamed soldier, 'You can ride on my shoulders when you've won.' You don't get anything for free. Win the battle, and then we'll talk.

Track two: *'My Son, My Secretary And My Country'*

The long intro to this song—it lasts for almost a minute—is played by a group of eighth-graders from Esther Dennis Middle School. The school is located in the Northridge section of Dayton, which is about five miles from where Pollard used to live on Titus. The lyrics contain some arresting imagery; I just wish the ideas were fleshed out a bit more so I knew what Pollard was singing about. The 'rah' at the end is credited to the Model Prisoners of the 5 Sense Realm, which is basically a bunch of Pollard's buddies, as well as his brother.

Track three: *'I'll Replace You With Machines'*

The title of this song may make you think of the Circus Devils record *When Machines Attack*, which was described as 'eighteen sonic postcards from a probable future forecasting civilization's approaching doom and the opportunities to cash in.' And yet, in the lyrics, I don't see much evidence of a robot uprising. What I think Pollard's talking about is his own inability to say no to people. He wants to replace someone with a machine not necessarily because they're incompetent, but simply because he can't 'face' them. The music is okay, though the background effect, which sounds a lot like the one on 'Skin Parade' from the last record, comes awfully close to drowning out everything else. The *Edison's Demos* version is softer, being just Bob on an acoustic guitar.

Track four: 'She Goes Off At Night'

New drummer Kevin March does his best Keith Moon impression on this track. In fact, the whole song sounds like The Who circa '67–'68. Lyrically, the song's about escape and trying to hide from one's own reality. It reminds me of Tobin Sprout's 'Ester's Day' from *Bee Thousand*. In that song, the eponymous character can't bear her life and just wants to escape, declaring, 'Let's just go, get out of here.' In 'She Goes Off At Night,' the character is 'hiding from the dreams,' because, if she were to face them, she'd realize just how many of them haven't come true. These are characters who, as Sprout puts it, can't 'bear to face their dreams.' Sometimes an unfulfilled fantasy is just as hurtful or damaging as your everyday reality. *Edison's Demos* actually has two versions of this song—one's a typical demo, but the other's a mix of just Pollard's vocals.

Track five: 'Beat Your Wings'

This is the record's longest song, at 4:48. The message seems to be almost an avian version of 'Motor Away.' Instead of getting in a car and just getting the hell out of there, Bob uses the metaphor of a bird: 'We'll beat our wings, we'll rise again.' And yet, as incredibly liberating as it must be to fly, all a bird is doing is following its instincts; it's not making a choice. It doesn't know how or why it can fly. As Pollard writes in the last lines, after acknowledging the 'perfect high' and the 'sweet seed growing' (allusions there both to flying and getting stoned), he adds, 'And never know why we feel anything.' You can run wild, you can motor away, you can beat your wings, but, as Alfred Montapert says, 'Don't confuse motion for progress.'

Track six: 'Useless Inventions'

This song sees Pollard play social critic, which is not something he does often. While his lyrics occasionally talk about politics and national issues, most often he writes about internal and psychological issues. Maybe this is because, as he puts it in 'The Other Place,' from GBV's debut EP, 'Who am I to argue the words of our prominent leaders?' But here, Bob's taking aim at a modern phenomenon that has only become more prevalent, and more annoying, since *Earthquake Glue* came out in 2003: the idea of solutionism. This can be defined as 'the belief that all difficulties have benign solutions, often of a technocratic nature.' This leads us to refrigerators with touch screens, and toasters with Wi-Fi. Basically, smart products that end up making us dumb. *Time* magazine's 2003 list of the best inventions of the year included a snorkel FM radio, a car boat, and bikinis made out of salmon skin. To quote Bob in this song, 'I'm getting tired of useless inventions.' The track's also an indictment of America's rampant consumerism. This is a country where department stores stay open all night on Thanksgiving so people can save a few bucks, and President's Day's all about watching bad actors pretending to be George Washington and Abraham Lincoln in car commercials. You have to keep up with the Joneses, and that includes buying all the latest gadgets, crap you don't need. The idea that you actually don't need any of this shit is an 'antiquated notion' in today's world.

Track seven: *'Dirty Water'*

There's no real tune here, and a lot of the production effects sink whatever melody gets established. It's only three and a half minutes, but it feels like it's twice as long. The *Edison's Demos* version isn't much better, although it's interesting to hear that the long guitar intro is even in the demo version.

Track eight: *'The Best Of Jill Hives'*

Pitchfork's Eric Carr, in his original review of *Earthquake Glue*, wrote, '"The Best Of Jill Hives" is a GBV classic by any measure, new or old.' Tim Tobias, whose bass line opens the song, has said of its creation, 'That one rolled out real easy. Bob came in the studio one day with it all written out and we just went ahead and did it.' The fact that GBV was able to create these modern classics with no real struggle or drama shows how comfortable Pollard was with his new band, and with Todd Tobias as a producer. The song's title came after Bob misheard the name of the soap opera *The Days Of Our Lives* when he was getting his car fixed.

The lyrics paint an Eleanor Rigby–esque portrait of a lonely woman named

Jill Hives. Unlike the invitation in 'Beat Your Wings' to just 'rise again,' Jill Hives is 'sad,' 'cursed,' and 'grounded.' She's not going anywhere. Worse than that, she's self-defeating, leaving the narrator to wonder, 'I don't know how you choose your words' since the ones she decides on are ones that 'suit [her] worse.' It's like the Radiohead song 'Just' where Thom Yorke writes, 'You do it to yourself, and that's what really hurts.' We're our own worst enemies.

Jill Hives seems to be a spinster; having 'been around,' she's now 'left flat.' But she rationalizes her loneliness, deciding that 'every child of god's a brat,' a decision that Pollard—a father of two—labels as tragic. The word 'deciding' there is key to understanding her. She wants to think that she's in charge; *she's* the one choosing the outcomes of her life. But then, in the next verse, Pollard references her 'punchdrunk history' and the fact that Hives is actually—like the characters in 'Ester's Day' and 'She Goes Off At Night'—looking for a way to 'exit her destiny.' She wants a way out. And yet, for all her rationalizations and justifications, the same as all of us, she knows she's not in charge of her own life.

But Jill Hives manages to get by, finding escape in a nine-to-five job and trying to find happiness in material objects, here alluded to by Pollard's utterly brilliant reference to 'trifle in the crystal bowl.' The word 'trifle' has a dual meaning. It can refer to a dessert made out of cake and fruit—that huge thing that shows up at the end of Blur's video for 'There's No Other Way'—but it also means 'a thing of little value or importance.' Plenty of people think that expensive objects can make them happy, while others try to forget their troubles with food.

What I especially love about the song is that Pollard doesn't condemn the character. There's real empathy here; for all her faults, Bob writes, Jill Hives is 'number one in all our souls.' This is probably because he realizes, the same way we do, that we're all a bit like her.

SIDE TWO
Track one: *'Dead Cloud'*

This is a solid song, with new drummer Kevin March indeed sounding a lot like Keith Moon. I tried to count all the cymbal crashes, but quickly lost track. The *Edison's Demos* version is just Pollard on an acoustic.

Track two: 'Mix Up The Satellite'

This song shows GBV's jangly side, the long outro having an R.E.M. if not Smiths vibe. It shows that Doug Gillard can paint with real color, in addition to providing blistering licks and solos. The *Edison's Demos* version could practically be on the record; it certainly sounds better than anything that was on *Vampire On Titus*.

Track three: 'The Main Street Wizards'

This is another absolutely gorgeous song, with Kevin March turning in another amazing performance, while Tim Tobias provides some great bass lines, and Doug and Nate deliver huge swathes of electric guitar. Todd also fills in the background with some keyboard parts and synth washes. Lyrically, it's a cynical song, with Pollard's eponymous wizards not being the kind you find in fairy tales, but rather those pundits or thinkers who get branded as such (like Bernie Madoff being dubbed the Wizard of Wall Street). Whereas Bob once proclaimed, 'Trust the wizard,' he's now more skeptical, asking, 'Can you exchange the past?' But then he quickly adds, 'Nothing is made to last.' Later in the song, Pollard asks, 'Can you explain the wrath on everyone's holy path?' Given that this song was written not long after 9/11, I think this refers to the ongoing discussion about the role that religion plays in violence—a subject that is dealt with in Karen Armstrong's devastating book *Fields Of Blood*.

Track four: 'A Trophy Mule In Particular'

The opening line, 'I wince when you map out how to get it together,' shows yet again that Bob just wants to do things his way. Plus, the line about 'the rock market crumbling' is just funny. The album's title, *Earthquake Glue*, gets a mention in the song; it's among the items found inside a 'freak bag.' In terms of the song's title, I assume that Pollard's using the word 'trophy' in the hunting sense, meaning what's kept from the kill, such as antlers or skin, versus the shiny plastic thing you get when you play soccer. That being said, mules aren't hunted for sport. The line then about being a soldier, in essence a 'trophy mule,' could then be seen as an antiwar comment. You're just a target, grist for the mill; nothing will be kept from your demise.

Track five: *'Apology In Advance'*

Bob's lyrics here hit a bit too hard on the rhymes: 'eyes' / 'ties' / 'despise' and 'plate' / 'wait' / 'contemplate' / 'fate.' He also puts in another reference to current events—remember that the year this record came out, 2003, is when America invaded Iraq, after having already invaded Afghanistan—by writing of a 'disabled vet.' Of course, this is still Pollard, so a few lines later he writes that's 'he's been around the block / I even threw up one street over.'

Track six: *'Secret Star'*

At 4:43, this is the second-longest song on the album. Most of that time is taken up by a long intro and the fact that the song just sort of stops for about thirty seconds. It also has a bunch of different parts, but it doesn't quite add up to a multipart epic the same as something like 'Over The Neptune / Mesh Gear Fox.' The final bit sounds a lot like 'Baba O'Riley,' a song the band have played extensively. Also, the line about a spinster who keeps 'checking for a special clock remover' is a callback to Jill Hives from side one.

Track seven: *'Of Mites And Men'*

Like 'The Ids Are All Right' from the previous LP, this title is a semi-clever pun. Pollard's referencing John Steinbeck's 1937 novel *Of Mice And Men*, substituting 'mites' for 'mice.' According to the Illinois Department of Public Health website, '"Mite" is a term commonly used to refer to a group of insect-like organisms, some of which bite or cause irritation to humans.' The song takes a while to get going, and once it does—with some fiery Doug Gillard guitar work that's similar to the soloing in 'The End' by The Beatles—it just sort of stops. I wish it were a bit longer, but other than that, it's a fitting way to end what's a solid mid-career record for the band.

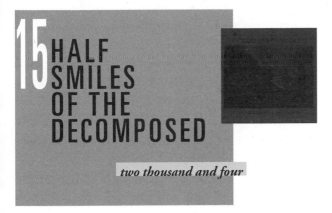

15 HALF SMILES OF THE DECOMPOSED

two thousand and four

This is the year Pollard came closest to breaking up GBV for good. While he'd broken up the band back in 1992, that only lasted a few months. And when he broke up the band for a third time in 2014, on the *Cool Planet* tour, fans didn't have to wait long: *Please Be Honest*, Guided By Voices' twenty-second record, came out just two years later. But in 2004, when Bob announced the end of GBV, he seemed to mean it. This was serious. The band was done. For almost a decade, that was it. As *Stereogum*'s David Holmes wrote, 'If *Half Smiles Of The Decomposed* had been Guided By Voices' final album, its maturity would have been a fitting swan song.'

Pollard cited two things that led to the end of GBV. He felt that Guided By Voices had run their course creatively, and he was tired of dealing with the baggage that came with releasing records under the name GBV. 'I'm doing this to get back to ground zero and challenge myself,' he said at the time. 'Get back in the studio so I can play more guitar and do more things. It got to the point where the band was so good it could pull off anything, and so I've become complacent.' It wasn't just that he was doubting the musical direction of the band. He was also tired of the expectations that came with releasing something under the name Guided By Voices, adding that it had 'gotten to be a bit too analytical. There's too much read into it, there's too much evaluation, too much comparison of this album with the last one.'

The catalyst that allowed Bob to finally pull the plug was the record he'd just made with the band. 'After I listened to [*Half Smiles*], it had kind of a sad, melancholy but uplifting feel to it, and it felt like a fitting wrap-up, and at that point I made the decision.'

Matador label head Gerard Cosloy said of Pollard's decision, 'It's a smart move, going out on top.' The body of work they'd already created meant that, as Cosloy put it, 'GBV will be regarded as one of the greatest bands of their era.' However, he also said, 'The band will eventually be known as just the first half of Pollard's artistic journey.'

That's not how things have turned out. Despite the fact that GBV records amount to just a quarter of what Bob's released, it's the thing he's best known for. Sure, people like Circus Devils, and some of the smaller side projects have their fans, but nothing can rival the attention, not to mention the love, that anything GBV-related receives. I can see how Bob could come to view that as an albatross around his neck. It's tough to escape an artistic legacy. Even David Byrne, who's had a successful solo career, has never managed to equal, or get out from under the shadow of, his first group, Talking Heads.

The breaking apart of GBV also meant severing ties to Matador. *Half Smiles Of The Decomposed* was the last thing that the band, or Pollard—not to mention Toby or anyone else associated with the group—released on the New York–based label. Even though Pollard considered GBV to be the 'Matador house band,' he actually had a short relationship with the company—just about a dozen records, if you include his solo LPs. Pollard's new creative home—for a few years, anyway—would be Merge Records, the North Carolina–based label started by Mac and Laura from Superchunk. Bob released five LPs and an EP on Merge. Then, starting in 2008, he released everything on one of his own labels: Guided By Voices Inc., Rockathon, or Happy Jack Rock Records.

For the recording of *Half Smiles*, Tim Tobias—who'd left the group in the middle of the *Earthquake Glue* tour in 2003—was replaced by Chris Slusarenko. Beyond being a veteran of a bunch of bands—starting with Deaf Midget before moving on, in the early 90s, to Sub Pop grunge band Sprinkler, the first Portland band to be signed to the Seattle label—Slusarenko also owned a record label for a while, Off Records. Off put out some Pollard-related projects, including an album and an EP by The Takeovers, a group Chris also played in. And, of course, Slusarenko was part of Boston Spaceships, along with drummer John Moen. Moen's played with The Decemberists as well as a bunch of other bands (including The Takeovers).

The seriousness and melancholy that Pollard heard in *Half Smiles Of The Decomposed* is evident even in the title. Normally, GBV records are called something like *Finalize The Paisley Circus Rainfall* or *Moose Bucket Triad Jamboree Comedown*. But not this one. Even the only other known alternate title I could find, *Dreaming Of Sleeping*, is still somber.

That's not to say the title is without Pollard's usual charm. The fact that the decaying corpses being referenced are wearing 'half smiles' is an acknowledgment that their time had come; whether or not they were complicit in their own death, they're more or less okay with it (the same as Pollard was with the ending of GBV). The decomposed people might even be happy about it—grateful, even—the title then becoming a wry stand-in for another group that, with their obsessed fan base, GBV was sometimes compared to.

The seriousness of the title is also conveyed in the cover art. Whereas the previous LP featured bright colors and thick orange and pink lettering, the cover to *Half Smiles* is dark and muted. In a total contrast to *Earthquake Glue*—a cover that contained a bright blue sky—the *Half Smiles* cover is all about night; there's even a sliver of moon in the upper left corner (and the back features a photo of a sunset). Since it features a bit of incinerated paper, the cover collage also hints at the state of the band. Bob, after fifteen albums, was feeling burned out and just needed a rest. And then there's the title of the collage: 'Ashes To Ashes.' That's a reference to the English Burial Service, which is itself derived from the Bible, specifically Genesis 3:19 ('In the sweat of thy face shalt thou eat bread, till thou return unto the ground; for out of it wast thou taken: for dust thou art, and unto dust shalt thou return'). Bob wasn't just killing GBV; he was burying it. You can't get more final than that.

Reviews for *Half Smiles* acknowledged the undeniable quality of the album. *Rolling Stone* gave the LP a three-and-a-half-star review, Greg Kot writing that 'it's packed to bursting with sometimes inscrutable pleasures: melodies with the whiff of half-remembered classics, misbegotten home-taping experiments' and 'arrangements that appear to collapse before resolving in brave choruses.'

Pitchfork gave the record a 7.0, reviewer Rob Mitchum noting that it had a 'pocketful of bright spots,' but that it was also filled with 'mediocre filler,' adding that 'slow, limp songs like "Window Of My World" and "Tour Guide At The Winston Churchill Memorial" can't come close to even the outtakes (*Suitcase*) of the outtakes (*King Shit & The Golden Boys*) from the band's classic lineup.'

This shows the peril that Pollard was talking about. Not only were his new songs getting compared to the classics on LPs like *Bee Thousand*, now even obscure compilations and anthologies were getting referenced. Bob had wanted to flood the market with product, and it was coming back to bite him.

A number of the reviews also took the opportunity to give GBV a valedictory lap around the indie rock racetrack. *Drowned In Sound*'s Alex Wisgard finished his review by writing, 'So ladies and gentlemen, grab a bottle of Miller Lite, and let's drink a toast to Robert Pollard, and his merry band of Voices; the Fading Captain has left the building, and my god, has he left it with style.'

Bob's breaking up of the band also meant that the tour for the record took on an even more celebratory tone than usual, since fans knew it would be the group's last. GBV shows are always a loud, drunken mess, but their farewell tour—dubbed 'The Electrifying Conclusion,' a phrase that appears in the song 'Murder Charge' off *Same Place The Fly Got Smashed*—took things to a whole other level. When it came to the final show, just to amp up the epic factor a notch, it took place on New Year's Eve, in Chicago, at the Metro.

After Tobin Sprout opened the show, GBV proceeded to play sixty-three songs over four hours. They also brought on a few guests and longtime associates, including Don Thrasher, Greg Demos, Jim Macpherson, and Toby, who joined Bob for '14 Cheerleader Coldfront.' *Pitchfork*'s Eric Carr wrote of the show, 'The farewell was beautiful, a little sad, and incredibly appropriate—a symbolically fitting close to another year and one band's monumental career.' In 2005, a DVD came out featuring the entire, uncut concert.

SIDE ONE
Track one: 'Everybody Thinks I'm A Raincloud (When I'm Not Looking)'
This starts by fading in, which is rare for GBV. It matches the last song on the record, which fades out. The lyrics paint a sad picture, with Bob acknowledging that perhaps the best days of the band were behind them:

'Cause this is not my day
And nobody really cares
Anymore anyhow
And nobody called again

The band that ten years before were everywhere now couldn't get anyone to 'really care' about them. Of course, GBV—even then—had a hardcore following, but it was never enough to take Pollard to that 'next level,' something that was abundantly clear to him by this point. Even though Pollard's 'hung over,' he's also hungry to 'fix' things. Then again, having just been called lazy in the previous verse, he admits to wanting a 'miracle cure' for his sorrow. Pollard put this at number ten when ranking his favorite GBV songs of all time for *Spin* in 2004.

Track two: *'Sleep Over Jack'*

With its seesaw bass line and weird voices in the background—which sound like a more demented version of 'Yellow Submarine'—this strange track sounds more like Circus Devils than GBV. The only interesting thing about it is that the name of the record makes an appearance, Pollard writing, 'Ragged enzyme horror shows, half smiles of the decomposed.'

Track three: *'Girls Of Wild Strawberries'*

This absolutely gorgeous song has to be a contender for the best track on the record. Bob's said that the lyrics don't mean anything, but that he was inspired to write it after seeing the 1957 Ingmar Bergman film *Wild Strawberries*. Pollard thought that the women in the movie were striking, and that led him to write this. The film, which was also written by Bergman, is considered to be one of his best. Derek Malcolm in the *Guardian* wrote that the film's theme is 'how life can become atrophied and sterile.' Since that's what Pollard was feeling about the band at the time, that was probably another connection he felt with the film. The only bad thing about the GBV best-of coming out the year before is that this song isn't on it. Also, on the *Electrifying Conclusion* DVD, there's some great footage of Pollard recording demos of this song and 'Window Of My World.' (You can also find this footage on YouTube.)

Track four: *'Gonna Never Have To Die'*

This is the shortest song on the record, at 2:18. According to GBV insider Rich Turiel, the solo that Gillard plays on the song is the same as the one Bob played on the initial demo he gave to the band.

Track five: *'Window Of My World'*

This is another absolutely stunning song that shows just how much Bob had grown as a songwriter. What I find interesting about Pollard's take on the idea of everyone's world having a window is that he's actually *outside* himself. He's not looking *out* through *his* window. He's removed from himself, looking in, like in an out-of-body experience. After all, *he* doesn't need a window to know what he's feeling or seeing; *he's* the one it's happening to. Instead, the song is removed and analytical, going back to the self-examining 'I Am A Scientist.' He's detached and seeing what it is he presents to the world, because of course any window, no matter how big, is going to conceal something. There's a whole lot of us that gets hidden from view. In fact, something once obstructed Pollard's view into himself; he even still has the 'bruises to prove it.' I think this refers to all those challenges that used to be thrown up between him and his songwriting: teaching, worrying about making a living, the disapproval of his parents. Stuff that kept him from doing what he really loved. He couldn't see clearly; it was like a fog, and he was lost inside it. The song ends with Bob feeling 'bold' and 'crashing through the world in my world.' He's not content to merely sit and watch his life; he's going to participate.

The fact that *Pitchfork* called this song 'limp' speaks to the expectations that GBV were held against. Bob was right; he'd painted himself into a corner. GBV was meant to be this heavy, party band, and that doesn't leave room for a beautiful song like this. A Muzak version of the tune was used as the soundtrack to a slideshow of photographs played before concerts on the band's final tour.

Track six: *'The Closets Of Henry'*

This is a perfect example of GBV's mature mid-period sound; it's an absolutely gorgeous song with jangly guitar, great drumming, and a spot-on vocal by Bob. It's almost unthinkable that—in less than a decade—Pollard would head back to the basement with Mitch Mitchell and Kevin Fennell. Since the lyrics name-check Charlemagne and make mention of 'an old king's secret files,' I think the 'Henry' of the title is any one of the eight King Henrys who reigned in England between the twelfth and sixteenth centuries.

Track seven: *'Tour Guide At The Winston Churchill Memorial'*

While there's not actually a Winston Churchill memorial (in America, anyway), there is a Winston Churchill museum. It's associated with Westminster College, which is located in Fulton, Missouri. It was established in the 60s and is housed beneath a church that dates from 1677. The church was reconstructed, stone by stone, from its original location in London. That it had been damaged during the London Blitz makes it the perfect site for a Churchill museum, since he was the British prime minister from 1940 to 1945, helping to see London, and the allied powers, to victory in World War II. Churchill's not buried there, though; he was laid to rest in 1965, just inside Westminster Abbey.

The National Churchill Museum is open daily and offers group tours, during which you're liable to have a tour guide. Pollard's second wife, Sarah, worked there as a guide right around the time she met Bob, which was in 2003, when GBV played a show in Missouri. This would fit the narrative of the song, since it seems to be about having a crush on a tour guide at the Winston Churchill museum. As she gives the tour, extending 'her knowledge,' the song's protagonist fantasizes about spending the rest of his life with her. Pollard says that the efficient female tour guide is 'on top of things,' while Bob then invites her to get 'on top' of him.

Pollard describes memorials like the one that's being visited as 'places that tremble and wish.' They shudder to remember the horrors committed in the acts they commemorate, but they simultaneously wish that their existence serves as a record and reminder so that such acts never happen again. If you've ever been to the Holocaust Memorial Museum, you know what an apt description this is. These places do their job, sort of, Pollard writing, with a shrug, 'So I guess some truth belongs to us.' Just because you educate people about the horrors of something, that doesn't mean they won't repeat or improve upon those very same horrors. As a former teacher, he knew that all too well. He's also smart enough to know that, even when touring a museum dedicated to defeating evil and eradicating the worst of human nature, it's easy to be distracted by the attractive woman leading the tour. That's human nature, too.

The song's lyrics contain an additional reference to World War II, Pollard writing, 'The longest day dying now.' June 6, 1944, the day the allies landed on the beaches of Normandy—in a military operation that's come to be known as D-Day—is referred to as 'the longest day.' There's both a book and a movie of that name, the latter being a huge Hollywood production featuring dozens of big stars, like John Wayne, Henry Fonda, and Sean Connery. The film came out in 1962, so Pollard probably saw it in later years on TV. The line in the song 'The longest day dying now' could be seen as a plea for remembrance; for people to not forget about the sacrifices that were made on that horrible day. People, and even history, can have short attention spans, which is exactly why places like the National Churchill Museum exist: to remind us and warn against repeating in the future the mistakes of the past. The line might also be a reference to the so-called greatest generation that, by 2004, was beginning to die out.

Musically speaking, this is a gorgeous song with some great jangly guitar; it could almost be a Smiths song (except that Morrissey despises Churchill). It's an all-around great example of mid-period, mature GBV. And, by the way, I think Pollard would have liked Churchill, since he once said, 'All I can say is that I have taken more out of alcohol than alcohol has taken out of me.'

Track eight: 'Asia Minor'

At under two and a half minutes, this is one of the shortest songs on the record. In fact, it takes about a minute for the drums to even kick in. The title of the song refers to a peninsula that used to be known as Anatolia; it now makes up the Asian part of Turkey.

SIDE TWO

Track one: 'Sons Of Apollo'

This track, which began life as a *Do The Collapse* demo called 'The Kissing Life,' starts with a martial beat, electric guitar, and a preacher railing against smut and pornography, saying that 'Satan is going to vomit filth out of hell.' He compares our depraved modern era to Sodom and Gomorrah, the cities that were destroyed by God for being wicked. This is heavy stuff. Where are the elves and wizards when you need 'em? But, when you keep in mind when this record was made, it makes a bit more sense. In 2004, 9/11 was still fresh in people's minds, and America was at war in Iraq and Afghanistan. George W. Bush, a devout Christian, was president. He called the United States' involvement in the Middle East 'a war between good and evil.' So overblown biblical rhetoric like this was common in both politics and the culture wars. The garbage spewed in the intro is still being heard today, only in place of 'old-fashioned moral standards' you hear 'Make America Great Again.' To paraphrase Bob's favorites, The Who: *Meet the new bullshit, same as the old bullshit.* Even though we're all 'coming of age' to a 'new day,' it's a dark new day filled only with 'running.' The dawn we're waking up to is one we all want to vehemently escape. Pollard, who has long advised us to 'run wild' or 'motor away,' is here giving us something deeply terrifying to escape: our own country.

Track two: *'Sing For Your Meat'*

The original title of this was 'Sing For Your Meat, Leon,' a reference to Kings Of Leon, the band out of Nashville who, at the time, were seen as protégés of The Strokes (they still get a mention in the song, in the first line of the second verse, Bob writing, 'Come here, Leon'). Pollard had heard that the Kings Of Leon weren't playing the game to get a bigger audience, and so this was Bob's way of advising, 'You gotta do it, man' ('sing for your meat' basically being the same as 'sing for your supper').

It's interesting that Pollard should admonish another band for not trying harder, since he was a guy who, by his own admission, hated to jump through the music industry hoops and wanted to do the least amount possible in terms of promotion (something he references earlier in the record, writing, "Cause they say that I'm too lazy'). Kings Of Leon must have listened because they indeed started to play the game, and, in not much time at all, were much bigger than The Strokes. As an RCA executive put it, 'If you're a couple of kids from rural Tennessee and your father is a whacked-out preacher and you have this opportunity, well, yeah, you're going to listen.' And it's ironic because The Strokes—who were, in a way, protégés of GBV—were the ones who didn't listen. Kings Of Leon quickly eclipsed them. This has been going on in rock'n'roll since rock'n'roll began; the line here about 'the boys' being dressed up 'in suits' could just as well apply to The Beatles.

Track three: 'Asphyxiated Circle'

The way Pollard sings this shows how versatile his voice is, not to mention how adept he is at melody. The lyrics seem to be a biting condemnation of something trying to suffocate Pollard; it must have been on his mind at this time, since, in another two songs, he'll be writing about feeling 'smothered.' The line 'You write me out, I reappear,' recalls *Bee Thousand*'s 'Smothered In Hugs,' where Bob mentions 'the textbook committee' deciding that 'you should be left out, not even mentioned.' But Pollard's not taking any shit. He declares, 'But I will say what I want to, and there is nothing you can do.'

Track four: 'A Second Spurt Of Growth'

This track finds Bob sounding more like Paul Simon than Pete Townshend. The 'spurt of growth' that Pollard's referring to here is most likely emotional growth. He'd met his second wife at a GBV show the previous year. They'd be married by 2006. His divorce from 2001 was probably still fresh in his mind at the dawn of this new relationship, something he seems to reference in the first line, 'Exhausted from the last escape.' And yet now he's in a new relationship, one that finds him 'leaving and returning now routinely.'

Pollard may also be referring to artistic growth, the song being a plea to his fans to stick with him. After all, *Decomposed* was supposed to be the band's final record. Bob would soon be a solo act. Would anyone care? Pollard's smart enough to know that the answer is out of his hands; he can't 'change the future.' This shows his pessimistic side. It's not just the past that can't be changed; we're not even in control of what hasn't happened. Think back to the characters from 'Redmen And Their Wives,' the ones whose existences were 'issued' rather than lived. Bob, who'd struggled for personal freedom all his life—whether it was from coaches, parents, or a spouse—knew all too well that, as he writes here, 'People want to keep you down.' Their efforts may 'make you weak,' with their attempts to have you remain 'fixed,' meaning static or unchanged. But Bob promises to be 'stronger.'

In the chapter on *Isolation Drills*, I mention the Bob Dylan line in 'You're

A Big Girl Now' where he promises, 'I can change, I swear.' And even though Pollard resisted such declarations on that album, here he seems to channel Dylan, writing, 'A second spurt of growth will come about me, don't doubt me.' It's a positive note. We all, no matter where we are in our lives, have the capacity for growth and for change.

Track five: '(S)mothering And Coaching'

This interesting song has at least four different parts; it's sort of a mini prog epic clocking in at just shy of three and a half minutes. The title alludes to a Freudian slip, blending 'mother' with 'smother.' Pollard—for a while, anyway—didn't have the best relationship with his mom. For years, neither of his parents believed in his dream to make a career out of music, and this left a wound that took years to get over. The song portrays his relationship to his family as dire:

You tear your childhood down from the cheekbone
You sell me down when you tell me you'll never
Spend days unphased not to tell me, 'I love you'

The reference to 'coaching' in the title is also interesting, as when Pollard writes about 'playing for the team.' While he'd been involved with sports most of his life, Pollard seemed to resent coaches. Bob then—like now—didn't like to be told what to do. Coaches are often parental surrogates, especially for fathers. You want to please them, you seek out their praise, you take the field in their name and promise victory. Even Lou Reed, an anti-authority rebel who had plenty of issues with his father, wrote in the song 'Coney Island Baby,' 'Believe it or not ... I wanted to play football for the coach.'

The last lines of this song seem to be in the voice of the mother, pleading with her child:

Baby don't go
We'll miss you so much
This is your home
Baby don't go

It's reminiscent of 'She's Leaving Home' from *Sgt. Pepper*, the tale of the self-absorbed parents who can't believe their daughter would choose adventure over her cloistered hometown and their oppressive love.

Track six: 'Huffman Prairie Flying Field'

GBV's flight and aerial references reach their absolute zenith with this song, named after a famed location just outside of Dayton. A century before, in 1904, when the Wright brothers returned to Ohio after their initial flights at Kitty Hawk in North Carolina, they needed a place to continue their experiments. A banker named Torrence Huffman came to the rescue, letting the Wright brothers use his pasture, rent-free. This became known as the Huffman Prairie Flying Field. The Wright brothers used this location until 1916. Today, it's a national historic landmark and part of the Wright-Patterson Air Force Base.

The song that Pollard named after this location is absolutely exquisite. The only downside is that some of Bob's vocal is a bit rough. Then again, maybe Pollard felt he was meeting the expectations of his fans who wanted lo-fi—who just expected mistakes: 'If that's what you want to feel, then that's what I will sell you.' But that kind of second-guessing what his audience wanted is also what led to the band's demise. He needs to throw off the shackles of those expectations, which is why he's referencing this legendary field where the Wright brothers chased their own dreams:

> *I've come to start up my head*
> *Been closed and locked up*
> *For far too long*

Guided By Voices had been a band for twenty years, and that was seeming, to Bob anyway, like 'far too long.' An added poignancy to referencing Orville and Wilbur Wright is Bob's relationship with his brother, Jim. Whether it's the Wright brothers or the Pollard brothers, it's two guys with a vision and a goal, against the world, sticking together. It's a fine feeling to know that each pair of siblings made their mark in history.

16 LET'S GO EAT THE FACTORY

two thousand and twelve

T he eight-year gap between this and 2004's *Half Smiles Of The Decomposed* has so far been, in the thirty years Bob's been releasing material as GBV, the longest stretch between albums. Not that getting rid of GBV stopped Pollard from releasing music. He kept up his usual hyper-productive pace during the hiatus, releasing dozens of LPs. This included albums by Acid Ranch, The Moping Swans, Psycho and the Birds, The Takeovers, Carbon Whales, Cosmos, Keene Brothers, Boston Spaceships, and Circus Devils, not to mention Robert Pollard solo albums. While each of these undoubtedly had their fans, none seemed to make the same impact as Guided By Voices. This is something Bob himself acknowledged when he chose the name *Crickets* for his fifty-song Fading Captain Series 'best of.' People just weren't paying attention. As *PopMatters*' Matthew Fiander wrote in a review of the double-CD set, 'If Pollard and his most devoted fans were honest with themselves, they'd realize that Bob's non-GBV side projects … may yield the occasional decent track, but are largely without merit.'

Pollard also wasn't playing nearly as many concerts as he had with GBV. He was burned out on the treadmill of record-tour-record. Staying off the road, and being out of the public eye, meant that his profile was the lowest it'd been since before the band broke in '93.

Where did all that leave Bob? He'd spoken in 2004 about 'painting myself into a corner' with GBV. Had he done the same thing all over again, painting himself into a different corner? If so, what was left for him to do except, as the old cliché goes, get the band back together? When his old label, Matador Records, called in 2010, inviting Pollard to play in Las Vegas as part of its twenty-first birthday party, that's just what Pollard did.

Not that it was an easy decision. Back when the band first broke up, Bob was asked, 'Can you see GBV doing a Pixies-style reunion tour in ten years?' Pollard's answer was, 'Right now I'm gonna say no but I might change my mind. Ten years from now if I need some money, I might have to go for it.'

A few years later, he was asked by *Magnet*, 'Now that indie-rock reunions are big business, have people started bugging you about getting Guided By Voices back together?' Pollard derided this as mere 'cashing in,' adding, 'I don't see Guided By Voices reforming.' He also admitted, 'I'm not selling as many records as Guided By Voices did.'

And then, it happened. On June 28, 2010, Bob announced on his website, 'GBV Classic Line-Up Reunites.' The guys who'd recorded LPs such as *Bee Thousand* and *Alien Lanes* would appear in Las Vegas on October 3, headlining the third and last day of what was dubbed 'The Lost Weekend.' The celebrations would see dozens of Matador bands take the stage, including Sonic Youth, Belle & Sebastian, Liz Phair, Yo La Tengo, Fucked Up, New Pornographers, and another iconic indie band from the 90s that had recently reunited, Pavement.

Getting everyone on board was surprisingly easy. Bob just picked up the phone and started calling. As Tobin Sprout said, 'It was one of those things that I never thought would happen. I mean, there was no reason for it to happen.' That Tobin had left the group on good terms assured his participation. 'I didn't even give it a thought,' he said. 'It's something I've missed ever since I left, and to be able to do it now, to be able to go out and have fun with it … I can't wait to do it.'

Mitch Mitchell and Greg Demos were still in Pollard's orbit, and so were easy enough to contact and get on board. Tracking down drummer Kevin Fennell, however, wasn't as easy. As Sprout put it, 'He had just moved around and nobody was really sure where he was.' But they soon found him, and then, poof, the classic lineup was together again for the first time since 1996. When they all got back together for that first rehearsal, Sprout said, 'It went great,' adding that 'if you've been friends that long, you just pick up where you left off.'

For the first song of the first rehearsal, the band played 'A Salty Salute.' At first the guys just stood around somewhat awkwardly, until Bob asked, 'Shall we?' Greg Demos then kicked in with that bass line, Kevin started pounding the drums, and bam—in just a few seconds, the club was open. The practices went smoothly, and, soon enough, they were off to play the Matador festival, which, by all accounts, was a huge success for GBV.

David Greenwald of the *Los Angeles Times* wrote, 'If Matador at 21 were a game, Guided By Voices would've won—they earned the most encores, the most fist pumping, the most singalongs, the most pushing against the stage and the most chanting of the whole weekend.'

Uncut's Michael Bonner wrote, 'The big draw was not the last ever Pavement reunion show, nor Sonic Youth's *Sister*-heavy set, nor even the possibility of finding yourself at the blackjack table with one of Superchunk. No, the biggest clamour of the weekend was reserved for the reformation of a greying, beer-swilling bar band from Dayton, Ohio.'

GBV did such a good job, and had such a fun time, they extended the reunion to two dozen dates all across the country. I saw them in New York, and they sounded awesome. People were overjoyed, not just to see the band once more, but to see *this* particular group of guys, onstage, together again. These were the heroes, the conquerors, the underdogs, the dreamers. As *Pitchfork's* Paul Thompson wrote in a review of *Let's Go Eat The Factory*, 'A reunion of … late-era Guided By Voices would've been nice, but it wouldn't have meant much.'

Pollard must have agreed on some level, because he decided to do a record. As he told an interviewer, 'I was sitting in a bar in Chicago with Toby, and we just kind of became inspired to do one. We started coming up with titles and art ideas immediately.'

Rather than take the lessons he'd learned on the big-budget records he'd made for TVT, or even the trio of mid-fi LPs made for Matador, Pollard opted to go back to the band's origins: the basement. 'We recorded the songs that

I had written for the album up at Toby's house in Leland, Michigan,' said Pollard. 'We recorded it big in the room and then fixed and fucked things up in the mixes.' Stuff was also recorded at Greg's and Mitch's houses. To get, as Bob called it, 'the old lo-fi feel of semi-ineptitude,' they occasionally switched instruments.

The result was a twenty-one-track record that clocked in a forty-one minutes. The LP lists two producers, Chief Runningmouth and the Soft Spoken Trout, stand-ins once again for Bob and Toby, respectively. *Factory* came out on the band's own Guided By Voices Inc. label, the name perhaps a nod to just what an identifiable business entity the group had become. No longer just a band, GBV was now a brand.

The cover for the LP —a series of photos of a record in a white sleeve—is just awful. Bob had complained about the packaging of the TVT releases, but they were miles ahead of what he came up with for this album. It is, in my opinion, the worst GBV cover. The back, featuring a Pollard collage—the same as on the singles for the record—showcased the usual GBV aesthetic, and they all looked much better.

Even though the band didn't produce any videos for the LP, there was such enthusiasm for their return that they managed to score an appearance on *The Late Show With David Letterman*. For a group who'd never had a hit, and weren't on a big record label, this was a huge coup. Forget being indie-rock icons, this was broadcast television, coast to coast. Even Pollard's parents now had to admit that Bob and the group had finally made it. That didn't stop the band from not taking it seriously; Greg Demos was so busy making rock-star moves that he slipped and fell right on his ass, prompting Letterman to later ask, 'You all right?'

The *AV Club* gave the new album a B+, Steven Hyden writing, 'It takes only a few seconds of hearing *Let's Go Eat The Factory* to recognize the exact right combination of guys who recorded the band's most beloved records.' And while the LP wasn't quite another *Bee Thousand* or *Alien Lanes*, the LP managed to capture 'a similar mix of in-the-moment inspiration, boozy camaraderie, and unhinged loopiness.'

In the *Guardian*, Maddy Costa gave the LP a four out of five and called it 'exhilarating, a kaleidoscopic burst of ideas and passion and absurdity. Songs tumble into each other, many lasting just a minute or two, yet each one distinct and compelling.'

Steve Kandell of *Spin* gave it an eight out of ten, writing, 'The 21 songs here are no more or less inscrutable than the hundreds of tunes Pollard has penned since he last played with this band, but they gel in ways that so many of those didn't, reveling in their limitations rather than trying to overcome them. It's the difference between The White Stripes and The Raconteurs.'

That last line is spot-on. Jack White plays in a bunch of bands, the same as Pollard, and he releases records under his own name. But nothing holds the public's attention more than The White Stripes. Bob was beginning to realize the same was true for him and GBV: his valuable hunting knife was turning into a double-edged sword.

An interesting thing to note is that a number of the reviews spent considerable space praising and welcoming the return of Tobin Sprout. As Spencer Grady wrote for the BBC, despite the focus being on Bob, 'It's the songs of Pollard's erstwhile sideman, Tobin Sprout, that threaten to steal this particular show.' Tobin's songs, according to Grady, shine the brightest amid *Factory*'s 'clutter,' with Sprout being the band member 'who has fully seized the opportunity afforded by this lineup's reformation.' The review actually calls Bob the record's 'biggest stumbling block,' deciding that 'many of his contributions here seem slight, half-finished approximations of former glories.'

Pitchfork struck a similar note. 'While Bob seems to be re-acclimating himself, *Factory* finds Tobin Sprout more ready to get back into it,' adding that the LP finds Toby 'quietly stepping out of the shadows and stealing the show.'

All the attention sent Sprout's way may have rankled Bob, who was used to being seen as the group's sole leader. But, for the time being, the band was back together, and they'd go on to release six LPs in just two years.

SIDE ONE

Track one: *'Laundry & Lasers'*

There's a scene in *The Force Awakens* when Han Solo and Chewbacca climb aboard the Millennium Falcon, and Solo says to his friend, wistfully, 'Chewie, we're home.' That's what hearing this song does to me every time, especially when the drums kick in. But it's more than just nostalgia. It's a comfort in knowing that Bob's home, too. He's with his buddies. They're in their basements, making music and having fun. It's just like old times, and there's nothing wrong with that. Because what was so great about this lineup reuniting is that, for a few years anyway, there was no animosity. It wasn't some cynical thing done for cash. It just sounds like they're having fun, and they're inviting us along. It's not unlike the invitation on 'Over The Neptune / Mesh Gear Fox,' except this time, rather than 'throwing a great party' they're just having us over for a couple of beers. The record's title also gets a mention, Bob writing, 'Let's go eat the factory, let's go running in there.' 'Laundry & Lasers' was also what they called Kevin Fennell's basement.

Track two: *'The Head'*

This is a fine example of one of GBV's short songs that actually works. I especially love the church organ, and the double meaning of 'head' is fun; it refers to the 'head' or 'boss' of the operation, but also means a person's head, which, in this case, seems to have been 'sawed off' from their body. It's all very *Barton Fink*. Jim and Mitch each get a co-writing credit. This shows that, after half a dozen LPs wherein Bob received sole credit on most of the songs, GBV were back to being a democratic group. Or, rather, it was as democratic as GBV ever were.

Track three: *'Doughnut For A Snowman'*

This track actually began as a jingle for the Krispy Kreme doughnuts that get mentioned in the song. Bob wrote it just for fun, making it, as he said, 'Sugary, like the donuts.' But when his manager actually got serious about sending Pollard's composition to the company, Bob got cold feet: 'I can't be remembered as the guy who wrote the Krispy Kreme theme.' Bob was also approached at one time to write a Budweiser commercial, but balked at having to sing the famous catchphrase, 'This Bud's for you.' Pollard's voice here sounds great, and Tobin adds some welcome atmospheric touches to the production. While I know that Bob had it as a lifelong goal to make some fierce-sounding records—which is why he hired big-name producers, not to mention got in the guys from Cobra Verde—this song is the perfect example of that lighter, more whimsical GBV we hadn't heard from in a long time.

Track four: 'Spiderfighter'

It's great to hear Tobin Sprout again on a GBV record. He'd been instrumental in not just the sound of the band but also the intellectual and emotional makeup of the group. He's a smart guy, and a painter. If this lineup was *Gilligan's Island*, he'd be the Professor. The comparison has been made to The Beatles, with Pollard being Lennon and McCartney (and, for good measure, Ringo as well), and Tobin being George Harrison. I think there's a lot to that comparison, and not just because Lennon and McCartney had twelve songs on an LP while George only had one or two. It's because Harrison was a soulful guy, a searcher. Music seemed to take second place to spiritual fulfillment. Toby seems similar in that respect. He could have said, 'Screw my family,' and jumped into the drunken excess of GBV headfirst, but instead he left the band, went back to painting, and made a couple of fine solo records. He seems to me, like Harrison, a whole person, on or off the stage.

This song is also a great example of just how versatile Sprout is. For the first two minutes, it's a stomper with a cool riff, feedback, and a straightforward drumbeat. But then, two minutes in, the song segues into a gorgeous piano melody that sounds like 'Let It Be,' with Sprout crooning, 'And now is the time I make up your mind.'

Track five: 'Hang Mr. Kite'

This song was meant to have guitars, but they were lost due to a technical glitch, so Sprout replaced them with keyboards. It's actually a welcome touch, showing that getting back together with this lineup, and recording on their own, didn't have to just mean kicking out the jams.

Track six: 'God Loves Us'

This fun track gives songwriting credits to Tobin, Bob, Mitch, and Jim Pollard. Sprout's repeated phrase 'We are living proof that God loves us' is a subtle rearrangement of the Benjamin Franklin quote about wine being 'a constant proof that God loves us, and loves to see us happy.' This quote often appears online, not to mention on T-shirts, as 'Beer is proof that God loves us and wants us to be happy.' The refrain of 'We are, we are, we are' reminds me of 'Whisper To A Scream,' the 1983 song by British band The Icicle Works.

Track seven: *'The Unsinkable Fats Domino'*

This was the first single from the record. It was also the first new music heard from this lineup since 1996, not to mention it'd been seven years since the last new material from GBV. It's a great song, and the perfect choice as a single. As Steven Hyden of the *AV Club* wrote, '"The Unsinkable Fats Domino" is the sort of punchy, to-the-point pop song Pollard rarely bothers with anymore, and can still write very well when he's motivated.' Born Antoine Dominique Domino Jr., Fats Domino was a singer-songwriter who had a bunch of hits in the early rock'n'roll era, including 'Ain't That A Shame' and 'Blueberry Hill.' One of the first artists entered into the Rock and Roll Hall of Fame, Fats Domino, unfortunately, finally did sink, dying in 2017 at the age of eighty-nine.

Track eight: *'Who Invented The Sun'*

This super-subtle and gentle song from Sprout sees him singing barely above a whisper. The lyrics seem to be a sort of mash-up between Plato's 'analogy of the sun' and the 'allegory of the cave,' since it deals with a caveman coming in from the cold, as well as the birth of the sun, which 'turns' and 'burns.' It's a great example of a track that's short but still sounds and feels fulfilling. Unlike the next song.

Track nine: *'The Big Hat And Toy Show'*

Tom Breihan of *Stereogum* called this one of GBV's 'obligatory mid-album songs where everyone just seems to be halfassing it.' That about sums it up.

Track ten: *'Imperial Racehorsing'*

At nearly three minutes, this is one of the few long tracks on the LP. It's a bit meandering but somehow manages to hold itself together. It's got some synth horns that are fun, and it ends with a long guitar solo, something we didn't often get with this lineup. This is a title that Bob's had for a while, since there's a different song, an instrumental, also called 'Imperial Racehorsing,' that was part of the aborted LP *Mustard Man & Mother Monkey*, which was an early version of *The Power Of Suck*.

SIDE TWO

Track one: *'How I Met My Mother'*

This is a fun song that gets its name by twisting what was a popular TV show at the time, *How I Met Your Mother*, which ran from 2005 to 2014. I don't know whether to take the song seriously, which is to say literally, and suggest that it's about the narrator's birth, or whether it's just a minute of Pollard nonsense. Either way, it's over fast.

Track two: *'Waves'*

Consequence Of Sound wrote that this song is 'well on its way to becoming a bona fide GBV classic.' I agree that it's another strong track by Tobin Sprout. In addition to waves in the ocean, Sprout's also referring to a variety of other kinds of waves—radio, cosmic, and invisible energy waves—'bouncing all around the atmosphere.' One of the things I love about the track is that the last minute of it is just music. GBV rarely stretch out instrumentally, or just let songs play themselves out, but they do on this one, and it's a welcome touch.

Track three: *'My Europa'*

This simple song features just Pollard singing against an electric guitar treated with a ton of tremolo. In Greek mythology, Europa—the sister of Cadmus—was a Phoenician princess who was kidnapped by Zeus. Europa is also one of Jupiter's moons. I'm not sure to which one Pollard's referring, but, either way, it's a pleasant track, foreshadowing 'Be Impeccable' from the next LP.

Track four: *'Chocolate Boy'*

This was the third and final single from the record (issued, it should be noted, on chocolate-colored vinyl). It's an absolutely stellar track, showing just how economical Pollard's songwriting could be. It's just a minute and a half, and yet it feels fully fleshed out and resolved. What I like about it is that, with Tobin Sprout back in the fold, and now that Bob's not having to consider Doug Gillard's shredding capabilities or Todd Tobias's art-rock sensibilities, he's free to create small gems like this. The lyrics also go back to the more whimsical nature of some of their early songs. With its mention of a 'paper man' and the 'chocolate boy' of the song's title, we're back in *Sgt. Pepper* territory. Speaking of, with all Bob's attempts to sound like The Who in the late 90s, and on the second run of Matador albums, he often eschewed the softer, more psychedelic sound of The Beatles, which this song harkens back to.

Track five: 'The Things That Never Need'

This interesting song is basically a spooky piano being played while some voices speak in the background. The voices sound warbly, almost like computers; it's basically GBV's version of 'Fitter Happier.' It lasts about a minute before segueing into the next song.

Track six: 'Either Nelson'

The opening lines to this are an instant Pollard classic:

> *I challenge you to rock*
> *I challenge you to proper drinking*

If GBV had a pledge of allegiance, those would be the opening lines. I'm not sure who's on the piano, but they have no idea what they're doing. But the guitar and the drums sound okay, and, if you can manage to block out the piano, it's not bad.

Track seven: 'Cyclone Utilities (Remember Your Birthday)'

This song has some cool riffs in it—Mitch Mitchell gets a co-writing credit, so those are probably his. What's funny to me is that the lyrics espouse a whole bunch of advice that Bob himself never takes. The opening line is 'Know the importance of timing your ideas.' For a guy who often releases two records on one day, or seven records a year, I haven't seen him worry much about the timing of his ideas.

The line 'Oceans of programs in a very useful age, more ways of getting your ideas across' seems to be about the internet. Pollard no longer had to rely on a record label, or distribution networks, to get his music to his fans. It's also highly ironic to hear a guy whom every publication or critic had admonished for his hyper-productive output sing, 'Not every voice needs to be heard.' The final line gives a clue to his real outlook, Pollard writing, 'Noble experiments spark positive reactions.' Bob counts everything he does in the column of 'noble experiments,' and whether the reactions they create are 'positive,' he figures that—as long as we're listening and feeling something—then he's done his job.

Track eight: 'Old Bones'

The *AV Club* called this song 'the album's strangest, prettiest track … which sounds like "Auld Lang Syne" sung by a dying android.' I don't agree with the robot part, but I do think this is one of the LP's most delicate and gorgeous songs (and does nod to the New Year's Eve staple). The lyrics are some of the most heartfelt in the entire GBV catalogue, Tobin declaring to his love that 'when you're old and gray, I'll still take your hand in mine' and 'when your bones are frail I'll still sleep soft at your side.' It's a tender and mature song. It's not the GBV of elves and wizards; it's the product of a band whose members were all past middle-age.

Track nine: 'Go Rolling Home'

Even though *Consequence Of Sound* wrote that '"Go Rolling Home" lingers too long, which says a lot considering it's a 37-second song,' I don't mind this short fragment, especially since it segues right into the next track.

Track ten: 'The Room Taking Shape'

This and the previous song basically feel and sound like one track, and they're both super solid, although I wish that Bob had taken another crack at his doubled vocal, since it's wobbly. Bass player Greg Demos gets a co-write, so maybe that's him playing acoustic guitar.

Track eleven: 'We Won't Apologize For The Human Race'

It's only fitting that this—the longest song on the record, at 4:02—should follow two of the album's shortest songs. When the band's comeback single, 'The Unsinkable Fats Domino,' was issued the previous November, it was actually branded a double A-side, with this song on the other side. So the band obviously thought highly of this track. It's certainly a great title, reminiscent of the Circus Devils song 'Love Hate Relationship With The Human Race.' The lyrics are interesting, with Pollard directly name-checking his original group of fans, writing, 'Generation X lies in its sleep, innocent as angels next to generation Z.' Also, the chorus of 'If you want some, if you need some' sounds striking with some call-and-response background vocals by Pollard. It's a fitting end to a fine record. While this comeback LP isn't a stone-cold classic, that's okay, because the sheer fact that it exists, and that GBV had released another record, is welcome news. This LP basically broke open the floodgates for more Guided By Voices records—and that means this record will always be special in GBV's discography.

17 CLASS CLOWN SPOTS A UFO

two thousand and twelve

f the release of *Let's Go Eat The Factory* surprised fans who thought they'd never get another GBV album, then the release less than a year later of a follow-up was absolutely amazing. No one seemed more shocked by this than the group themselves. When an interviewer asked Mitch Mitchell, 'Was the band planning to release two records in such quick succession?' he answered, 'That pretty much took us by surprise. I didn't expect even to do the first album!' The group kept writing, and so the records kept coming. There'd even be a third LP before the year was out.

The only thing that changed—from the first reunion album to this one—is that the group made a concerted effort to give the new songs a more polished sound. Pollard, sensing—the same way that he did in 1996—that staying in the basement was creative death, opted to head into the studio. *Let's Go Eat The Factory* would be the last time Bob released an LP full of home recordings. Even the lo-fi GBV album *Please Be Honest*, where Pollard played every instrument, was recorded in a studio. In addition to having a few songs recorded at home, a large number of these tracks were recorded in studios around Ohio, such as Cro-Magnon and Waterloo Sound, with former producer Todd Tobias doing a bit of engineering. The heightened fidelity means that it's a huge advance over the grab-bag nature of the previous album. This went a long way toward proving to people that a reunited GBV was no novelty. As Steven Spoerl wrote for *PopMatters*, 'It's not a rumor anymore, folks. Guided By Voices are back. In a big way.' *Consequence Of Sound*'s Justin Gerber struck a similar note, declaring, 'The reunion is over.' He didn't mean that the band had broken up. It was exactly the opposite. At a certain point, when you get back with your ex, they're not your ex anymore. It's just who you're with. That's what happened with the band.

Class Clown was the second GBV record to come out on the band's own Guided By Voices Inc. label. (Every record since *Let's Go Eat The Factory* has come out on this label.) For the first time in Pollard's career, his own label seemed and felt and acted like the real thing. He was no longer just coming up with weird names and slapping a logo on the sleeve. Instead, Guided By Voices Inc., and the band's management, was doing a good job of getting the group exposure. The label was doing marketing, the band were getting booked on TV shows, and songs were being premiered on music websites. GBV had managed to finally merge the autonomy of their early years—writing, recording, and releasing whatever they wanted—with the accessibility and profile of the years they'd spent on independent labels. They weren't getting played on the radio, but they didn't get played on the radio in the 90s, either. At least now they didn't have to worry about recouping an advance or getting charged for dinners or videos.

The cover for *Class Clown* features a striking Pollard collage, which is emphasized because there's so much blank space around it. Also, because it's sitting in a sea of black, with white type above a circular design that features mostly a creepy baby face, it makes for an arresting sleeve. It's my second favorite GBV cover of all time, behind *Mag Earwhig!*

Class Clown spawned three singles, 'Jon The Croc,' 'Keep It Motion,' and the LP's title track. 'Keep It In Motion' had a video featuring a magician backstage as he gets ready for his routine. The magician's name is Magic Stan, and he's played by Jon Glaser, a writer, comedian, and director. In a 2012 Q&A with *Magnet*, when asked about the role music plays in his life, Glaser answered that he listens to music every day and that 'Guided By Voices has been my main dishes-cleaning band as of late.' The video was directed by Todd Lamb. Lamb also directed the 2009 video for the Boston Spaceships song 'Let It Rest For A Little While' from their third LP, *Zero To 99*.

All the singles from this year had non-album tracks as B-sides, so if you add those tracks to the dozens that were on the three records that also came out in 2012, you get a picture of just how prolific the band were during this period.

Now that we're two records into the reunion, let's talk about how these and the ensuing albums fit into the GBV story and discography, not to mention how potent, and important, nostalgia is to these and the next couple of LPs the band would release.

When the initial reunion was announced back in 2010, it was seen by a lot of people as nothing more than a victory lap. A bunch of drinking buddies getting back together to relive fun times, the old lineup playing the old songs, and people loved it. For some bands, that's enough. But it wasn't good enough for Pollard, so he decided to record a new album. And, when he did that, the situation turned into something else. The band became, somehow—and against a whole lot of odds—Guided By Voices all over again. However, instead of going into a studio and knocking out a record, they returned to their basements. That made a lot of sense, since this lineup had never made a proper record. The closest they came was a week or so in Memphis with Kim Deal in the 90s.

This meant they weren't just singing songs from 1993 to 1996—they were trying to go back in time and re-create the working methods that had led to the *writing* and *recording* of those songs in the first place. And while it's real hard to have lightning strike twice in the same location, that's what GBV were trying to do. What's amazing is that it worked; some of these post-reunion records are quite satisfying.

In a story about the new music that the Pixies put out in 2014, *Pitchfork*'s Jayson Greene wrote, 'Many groups go away, then return to us diminished— Goodie Mob, Black Flag, the Stooges, Smashing Pumpkins. We have more or less reconciled ourselves to this phenomenon. But very few bands come back wiped clean of their basic essence, as the Pixies did.' In a review of that band's first full-length record since 1991's *Trompe Le Monde*, fellow *Pitchfork* writer Stuart Berman summed up the recent history of the Pixies, declaring 'what was once a valorous underdog-victory narrative has slowly turned into a cautionary tale about pissing away all the goodwill you've accrued.'

How did GBV escape this fate? Why didn't critics and fans say the same thing about them? Why wasn't *Class Clown Spots A UFO*, not to mention all the other LPs GBV put out around this time, just an 'increasingly mournful asterisk affixed to a beloved legacy' (as *Pitchfork* said of the new Pixies material)? Is Bob that much of a genius? Yes and no.

What spared GBV from those kinds of reviews, and accusations of sullying their reputations and ruining their legacy, was that the band pulled off a difficult trick: their new material was familiar, and yet it was also original. As Daniel Couch wrote in a review of *The Bears For Lunch* for website the *Quietus*, 'This post-reunion version of the band has been dislocated from its original meaning and reassembled into something distinctly new.' GBV managed to achieve the same feel and general approach of their earlier work without openly aping it. They were dealing, the same as the Pixies, in sounds they'd forged in the 90s but managed to somehow make contemporary. GBV's new songs retained the spirit of their original work—even, to some degree, the template—but managed to also be imbued with something open and fresh.

The band knew what it was doing. In marketing materials accompanying their first post-reunion LP, Guided By Voices Inc. wrote, 'Fans of GBV's iconic release *Bee Thousand* will recognize the same gloriously messy aesthetic in *Let's Go Eat The Factory*.' And the press release for *Class Clown* said it offered a 'generous helping of *Alien Lanes*–style snippets,' adding, 'In fact, the sequencing of *Class Clown* harkens back to that landmark LP.' They were explicitly comparing their new work to their previous classics—and yet they managed to make this not a bad thing.

What's even more remarkable about this is that Bob's never seemed like a nostalgia guy. Part of his whole 'short attention span' thing means he doesn't dwell on anything for too long. This can apply to the present, or the past. Here's what he told *Rolling Stone* in 2013: 'When I make an album, I tire of it pretty quickly. I may listen to it for a week after it's finished and then I put it away. Within another few weeks, I may have written ten or fifteen new songs. By the time one album comes out, I'm already tired of listening to it and [it's] on to the next.'

When it came time to review *Class Clown Spots A UFO*, Steven Hyden of the *AV Club* gave the record a B+ and wrote that 'As with *Factory*, the strength of *UFO* is that it sounds like a true GBV record, rather than simply a clandestine avenue for Pollard's solo material.' Hyden, too, singled out Sprout. 'If anything, Pollard's sidekick and sounding board Tobin Sprout is even more prominent this time around.'

Pitchfork fought against this idea. 'Tobin Sprout's age-defying voice and surplus of solid songs helped his return to the fold on *Factory* seem especially triumphant,' Paul Thompson wrote. 'This time around, it's Bob's show all the way.' He went on to say, 'Pollard seems the looser dude here, providing *Class Clown* with nearly all of its gnarlier rockers and oddball overtures.'

In terms of where the LP sat in the rest of the band's discography, Steven Spoerl of *PopMatters* called *Class Clown* 'one of the strongest LPs that Guided By Voices have ever released.'

SIDE ONE

Track one: *'He Rises! Our Union Bellboy'*

You can tell from this opening track we're already in different territory from the last record; it was recorded at a studio and sounds better than anything on *Let's Go Eat The Factory*. Plus, at three minutes long, it's one of the longer tracks on the album. Bellboys, also commonly known as bellhops, derive from the nineteenth-century word *bellhopper*, which—as you can probably tell—is someone who 'hops' into action when a bell is rung. They're most commonly found in hotels, where they take bags to rooms and do other assorted errands for guests. And, yes, some bellhops belong to unions, often under the umbrella of the Hotel Restaurant Institutional Employees & Bartenders Union. According to the Bureau of Labor Statistics, in Pollard's home state of Ohio, in 2017 there were 520 people working as baggage porters and bellhops, where they earned an average yearly salary of $21,350.

In terms of popular culture, there's a very silly Jerry Lewis film from 1960 called *The Bellboy*, that Pollard probably saw on TV while growing up. And, of course, The Who have a song—one of the few to feature Keith Moon on vocals—that's part of their 1973 rock opera *Quadrophenia*. In the 1979 film version, the bellboy is played by Sting. GBV's song seems to reference this, since Townshend's bellboy promised to 'keep my lip buttoned down,' while Pollard's promises being similarly obedient, 'No pulling on the leash.'

Track two: 'Blue Babbleships Bay'

This song, engineered by Todd Tobias, is a return to the mid-fi later records of GBV. This shows they weren't only striving for a return to the territory of *Bee Thousand* and *Alien Lanes*. The word 'babbleship' is mostly likely a Pollardian twist of 'battleship.' The song also mentions 'Cleopatra shoes.' This is used most often to describe a style of women's sandal that has lots of buckles and straps.

Track three: 'Forever Until It Breaks'

Whereas the track 'Waves,' on the previous LP, was filled with nightmare imagery of being surrounded and subsumed by the ocean, this Tobin Sprout tune finds him at his most idyllic, repeating—over a pastoral backing track—'We walked along the water.' It ends with Sprout repeating, 'I'll breathe.' It's really gorgeous, showing yet again how welcome his contributions were on GBV LPs.

Track four: 'Class Clown Spots A UFO'

This song has it all: faux horns, handclaps, great background vocals, an instrumental breakdown, and a jaunty beat that you just can't resist. It's not only a fine song for this record, or for this incarnation of the band; it stands up alongside the group's best work from any period. It also shows just how much was lost during the years when Pollard was focused on sounding like a hard rock band on record. 'Baba O'Riley' is great, but I also love to take a stroll down 'Penny Lane.' *Pitchfork* called the track 'one of those dizzyingly catchy Pollard songs that seems to sew two or three viable hooks together, its crisscrossing chorus the product of some serious craftsmanship on Pollard's part.' The song has a long history, first appearing as part of the almost-twelve-minute song-suite, 'Special Astrology For The Warlock Tour.' That epic track was eventually pruned down to just *Propeller*'s 'Over The Neptune / Mesh Gear Fox' and 'Circus World.' The next time it appeared was as 'Crocker's Favorite Song' on *King Shit & The Golden Boys* in 1995. As *PopMatters* wrote of that version, 'When it first appeared, it was a thing of absolute devastation, a song of heartbreak. Here, [on *Class Clown*] it's reworked into a warm celebration. That transition from bleak to utterly winsome seems to serve as a good metaphor for the recent change of fate for the band. It also serves as a persistent reminder of Guided By Voices' enviable versatility.' A different demo version appears on *Suitcase 3*.

Track five: *'Chain To The Moon'*

This short but absolutely gorgeous song finds Pollard singing against an acoustic guitar. The idea of extending some sort of chain all the way up to our moon goes back at least to 1938, when Buckminster Fuller published a book called *Nine Chains To The Moon*. The title refers to the concept that if all the humans of the world's population stood on top of each other, they would form a chain that would stretch from the earth to the moon, back and forth, nine times.

Track six: *'Hang Up And Try Again'*

This fun song has Bob sounding a bit country, like on the early records before he started employing an English accent. Anyone who grew up before the 90s probably recognizes the phrase 'Hang up and try again.' It's something you used to hear when you tried to reach someone on a landline, only to not have the call go through. It's something called an 'intercept message.' According to Wikipedia, 'an intercept message is a telephone recording informing the caller that the call cannot be completed.'

Track seven: *'Keep It In Motion'*

The title of this song, which sees Sprout and Pollard singing together for the first time since *Propeller*'s '14 Cheerleader Coldfront,' could be seen as the encapsulation of Pollard's whole career. As he's said, 'The point is to keep it in motion. Get it down and move on.' Because the opposite is inertia (defined as 'a tendency to do nothing or to remain unchanged'). That's just not Pollard's style. I consider this, along with 'Don't Stop Now,' to be both a great slogan for Bob and the group and a declaration of intent in terms of what he stands for as a person.

Track eight: *'Tyson's High School'*

If Black Sabbath tried to rewrite 'Be True To Your School,' it would sound like this. And while The Beach Boys often wrote about the pleasures of youth, as well as trying to regain the joy of being young in songs like 'Do It Again,' Pollard here takes a more fatal and unsentimental view, opening the song with 'You can't go back and enroll now.' School spirit is no match for old age.

Track nine: 'They And Them'

This is one of the few Tobin Sprout songs that doesn't work for me. It's just a minute long, and it consists of nothing but Sprout chanting, 'When the days are older ... they and them.'

Track ten: 'Fighter Pilot'

This is another Sprout song, and it's also slight. It's mainly just some garbled voices, until Tobin, at the end, mumbles something about a 'fighter pilot,' as well as name-checking his song 'Spiderfighter' from the previous LP.

SIDE TWO

Track one: 'Roll Of The Dice Kick In The Head'

This is the shortest song on the record. However, despite its brevity—and even though I was hard on the song snippets of *Alien Lanes*—I like this track. It's short but feels full, cramming a lot into its forty-six seconds.

Track two: 'Billy Wire'

Speaking of short songs, this one is an absolute masterpiece at just a few seconds past two minutes. With the exception of an odd middle-eight break, which finds the song sort of stop, this track gets back to the punk spirit found on the *Grand Hour*'s 'Shocker In Gloomtown.' The song's title may have been derived from the 1963 British film *Billy Liar*, starring Tom Courtenay and Julie Christie.

Track three: 'Worm W/ 7 Broken Hearts'

This short and ragged song name-checks 'Billy Wire' from the previous track. It's basically just Pollard singing two verses over some guitars that sound like a hurricane, pounding drums, and a lead guitar that sounds Middle Eastern. As ramshackle as the track is, there's an even more ragged version. A 'home-fi' version is on the B-side of the 'Class Clown Spots A UFO' single, 'home-fi' being Bob's name for the boom-box recordings he does at his house. Also, just for the record, worms don't have seven hearts; they've got five.

Track four: *'Starfire'*

This Tobin Sprout song is, I think, about an alien invasion and planetary destruction. If it is, it's the nicest song about an alien invasion and planetary destruction I've ever heard. By this point, Tobin was beginning to record his songs on his own, playing all the instruments and just delivering to Bob the finished results. Because of that, some of them sound a bit out of place with the songs Pollard was recording with the rest of the band. And while his later song on this record, 'Lost In Spaces,' perfectly complements the track right in front of it, this one doesn't sit quite as naturally between its neighbors, so you can begin to feel the band breaking into two branches. Whereas Sprout's songs on *Bee Thousand* and *Alien Lanes* were seamlessly woven into the overall structure, on the reunion records—as much as I love them, this one included—they're starting to stand out, and not in a good way.

Track five: *'Jon The Croc'*

Pollard sings in the chorus, 'Let him cry like a crocodile around you now.' The origin of the phrase 'crocodile tears' dates back to the sixteenth century, and is based on the notion that crocodiles cry when they eat their prey. However, it's a physical reaction and not an emotional one; they're not sad they're eating whatever they're eating, hence the use of the phrase to mean a faked or disingenuous emotion. That crocodiles cry while feeding was first reported by John Mandeville, in the fourteenth century, as part of his writing about his travels. The cover image of the cotton plant used on *Vampire On Titus* first appeared as part of these writings.

Track six: *'Fly Baby'*

This song features just acoustic and electric guitar and Bob's vocal. And while I love GBV's heavy rock songs, or their more whimsical or poppier side—like this album's title track—I also love Pollard in singer-songwriter/troubadour mode, like he is here. He has a great voice, and it sounds pleasant against a slowly strummed acoustic guitar. While he had at one point suggested creating, with Tobin Sprout, a sort of Simon & Garfunkel record, he later cast doubt on the idea: 'It's really hard for me to grow up. I still like to rock.'

Track seven: *'All Of This Will Go'*

The title seems to be a recasting of the ancient phrase 'This too shall pass,' or 'All things must pass.' The latter was the name of George Harrison's mammoth triple record from 1970, and the former is an old Persian saying. In this particular song, the 'this' Sprout seems to be referring to is a temporary setback or condition (if not just winter). His repetition of 'tap tap tap' is almost like the ticktock of a clock, as if the characters in the song are looking forward to time passing so much that they're watching it count down by the second.

Track eight: *'The Opposite Continues'*

This is a good hard rock song. The line 'Pretend to know the paradox within you' recalls The Who's line 'Don't pretend that you know me, 'cause I don't even know myself.' We're all mysteries, even to ourselves. As the song winds down, there's some major shredding, showing that just because Doug Gillard was no longer in the band, Pollard was still going to have heavy guitar licks in his songs.

Track nine: *'Be Impeccable'*

This absolutely stunning track is a prime example of how a song—and this is something GBV repeatedly prove—doesn't have to be recorded or played perfectly to be powerful. That's probably not how the guys in Steely Dan used to see things, and even I get impatient with Bob when things are purposefully sloppy, but this sounds raw and live and immediate. With headphones, like with a great Lou Reed song, you feel like Bob's sitting there just singing to *you*.

The lyrics are also touching, the narrator inviting someone to just be themselves and that, if they are, that'll be enough. Here's the chorus:

> *Be what you are*
> *Be impeccable*
> *The untrackable star*
> *I'll shine my flashlight to where you are*

I find that last line about the flashlight devastating. With it, Pollard's doing a number of things. First, he's showing the other person the way: he's a beacon; the object of the song can use the flashlight to find their way back home, or just to him. But it could also be a spotlight; Bob wants to celebrate and showcase this person. It's not just a signal; it's a tribute. And, lastly, it's a connection. Within the perpetual darkness in which we all must live, if I shine my flashlight at you, and you flash yours at me, we'll be touching, however faint the light.

Track ten: 'Lost In Spaces'

Similar to the previous track, this song by Tobin is beautiful. It's just Sprout singing against a piano with some synth strings; he's practically whispering, declaring that the song's subject makes 'great things better.' In terms of the title, *Lost In Space* was a TV series that ran for three seasons in the 60s. It was brought back, in 2018, as a series on Netflix.

Track eleven: 'No Transmission'

While it would have been fitting to end the LP with the previous song—thereby mimicking the twenty-track *Bee Thousand*, which similarly ended with a gentle song by Sprout—Pollard chooses to go out with a bang instead of a whimper. As *PopMatters'* Steven Spoerl wrote, this song 'expertly brings everything to a crashing close, re-igniting an energetic fire that'll leave the listener on an adrenaline high.' I agree—it's one of the best songs on the record. Musically, everyone sounds good. The drums are great, along with a solid bass line and some good lead guitar work. Bob's vocal melody, which on other songs can sometimes be at odds with the music he's singing on top of, is integrated here. I don't find a ton of significance in the lyrics, but to quote the previous song, 'I'm not sure what it means, but I like it.'

18 THE BEARS FOR LUNCH

two thousand and twelve

I n addition to this, the third GBV LP released in a year, Bob also released two solo records: *Mouseman Cloud* and *Jack Sells The Cow*. Every other month, it seemed, Pollard was putting out something new, and—thanks to the internet—you could have it delivered right to your door. Being into Bob was more like subscribing to a magazine. Since this ended up being one of Pollard's most prolific years, before I look at *The Bears For Lunch*, I want to address just how productive Bob is.

Because it's such a big topic, I'm actually going to break it into two subjects. In this chapter, I'll talk about why I think Pollard makes as much stuff as he does. In the next chapter, I'll talk about what this means as a fan.

The key to Pollard's work ethic lies in the fact that he was into sports before he was into music (in terms of music being his main pursuit). Because of this, he approaches songwriting from the point of view of an athlete more than as an artist. At Dayton's Northridge High School, Bob excelled at basketball, baseball, and football. This included being a star pitcher and quarterback. His participation in sports continued when he went to Wright State University. He pitched the school's first-ever no-hitter in 1978. 'In addition to the no-hitter in college,' Bob said in an interview with ESPN, 'I threw eleven others between the ages of ten and twenty.'

It must have been in the Pollard blood, because Bob's brother was also a star athlete. Both Bob and Jim have been inducted into their high school's Hall of Fame. Music, by contrast, was something that Pollard didn't get serious about until college, and this was only after—following an injury to his arm— it became apparent he wasn't going to have a career in sports. That's when he learned to play guitar and started writing songs. What I think happened at that point is that he approached picking up a guitar the same way that he picked up a bat; it was less about artistic inspiration than it was just swinging and trying to hit something.

Take a look at the opening lyrics to 'Keep It Coming,' the 2002 B-side of 'Everywhere With Helicopter.' Pollard writes, 'What's more important, the run or the finish?' Based on the rest of the song, and Pollard's subsequent career, I think his answer would be that the run itself—the pure act of being in the race and getting out there and trying—is more important than where you actually finish (or if you even get to the finish line). That's why guys like Cal Ripken Jr. are so celebrated: not necessarily for being the best players but for getting out there and playing every time. What's important is suiting up for battle and heading out onto the field. It might be raining, but you play. You might be in pain, but you play. You may even lose, but at least you tried.

So when *Pitchfork's* Saby Reyes-Kulkarni writes that 'Pollard's prolific output can be read as an obsessive quest to master the art of songwriting,' I think that's completely wrong. Same as when he says that Pollard's been 'in pursuit of the perfect song' for thirty years. There's no doubt in my mind that when Pollard finishes something like 'Have A Jug,' he doesn't think, 'Hey, one step closer to the perfect song!' He knows that the perfect song, just like the perfect painting or perfect book, or even the perfect chocolate-chip cookie, doesn't exist. What matters is getting out there and trying, each and every day. You don't always win, but that's not the point. (Then again, sometimes you pitch no-hitters.) That's why Pollard's written so many songs, not to mention it's why they contain so many mistakes. Any sport, by its very nature, is unpredictable. That's kind of the allure, right? If we wanted choreography, we'd go to the theater. Every game is different. Each stadium has its own quirks. Every time you play, any number of things can happen. All you can do is react in the moment and hope for the best. It's all instinctual; there's no time to think. And that's how Pollard puts down his songs.

In Bob's mind, you can no more plan out where your song goes than you can know whether you're going to make a free throw. Or throw a strike. You just get out there and try. So, when Pollard writes a song and it's thirty seconds long, that's the song. Or, if it's four minutes, then *that's* the song. And if it also happens to sound amazing, that's great. Or, if it sounds like crap, that's fine, too. He doesn't sweat the details. He just moves on, because the point isn't perfection. The point is playing the game.

Bob's interaction with a song is therefore more physical than mental. This makes the mountains of tracks he's produced more a show of stamina than intellect. This outlook is rare in rock'n'roll. Musicians mostly get lumped in with writers and painters. They may jump around in concert, but, when it comes to writing songs, they slave away in the garret just like all the other tortured artists. But Bob thinks that's silly. His attitude is you just get out there and do it. Because he's treating it like a sport. Pitchers don't wait for inspiration, nor do quarterbacks. Their only muse is to win, and their only chance to do that is to take the field. That's what Bob's doing every time he picks up a guitar. It's also why he's not necessarily hung up on each song sounding perfect.

Getting back to *Bears*, since this record capped a 2012 trilogy of sorts, a number of publications looked at them as a group and tried to find a common theme, or else make some sense of how they fit together. *Pitchfork* decided, 'It's clear now that *Let's Go Eat The Factory* was the weird one, *Class Clown Spots A UFO* the one with the most range, and *The Bears For Lunch* the flat-out catchiest.'

The band seemed to agree with this assessment, Tobin Sprout telling an interviewer, 'I see *Factory* as an abstract, where *Bears* and *Clown* have more of a polished feel.' Maybe that's why I like this one the best of the reunion records. The home-recorded, lo-fi fragments of *Alien Lanes*, which the band tried to re-create for *Let's Go Eat The Factory*, are nowhere to be found on *The Bears For Lunch*. Instead, the LP is a collection of great pop songs, with both Pollard and Sprout continuing to turn in great tunes.

Matthew Fiander of the website *Prefix* wrote of the album, 'It's the best record of this trilogy of new records, and also manages to top Pollard's great solo stuff from this year.'

Stereogum's David Holmes, making the same point as a number of reviews around the time of the reunion LPs, wrote that 'the secret weapon here, as is often the case, is Tobin Sprout, who brings his psychedelia flirtations to full fruition on "The Corners Are Glowing" and threatens to steal the whole show with the wondrously catchy, Led Zeppelin *III*–influenced "Waving At Airplanes."'

A few reviews took the band to task for releasing so much material in a single year, suggesting that their prodigious output could have instead been curtailed into one all-around-classic album. As *Pitchfork*'s Stuart Berman put it, 'You can't help but think the band's re-emergence would be that much more dramatic if they had pared down their three 2012 releases into one record stacked with the best songs from each.' At *Consequence Of Sound*, Justin Gerber struck a similar note, writing, 'One could argue that just taking the best material the band recorded this year would create a five-star LP, as opposed to three good-to-very-good ones.' While I wouldn't go so far as that, I do think each LP—as with most GBV records—could have used judicious pruning. I'd still prefer three albums, but each one could have had fewer songs. But that's a small complaint. GBV were back, and that's what matters.

SIDE ONE

Track one: *'King Arthur The Red'*

While the first reunion LP saw the band back in their basements, by now they'd returned to the mid-fi sound of the second round of Matador records. This song even brings Todd Tobias back as an engineer. The subject of King Arthur goes back to Pollard's elementary school days. He's said that a lot of the robot, wizard, and elf imagery that was found on *Bee Thousand* was because of the stories, tales, and myths he read to his students. Whether King Arthur was a real person or just a legend is not known. Anyway, the song doesn't seem to actually be about him. The line about 'needles buried in the red' sounds like it refers to the recording of the song. Either way, it's a fun track, and a great way to start the record.

Track two: *'The Corners Are Glowing'*

Even though this Tobin Sprout song is one of a handful of longer tracks on the album—it's a few seconds over three minutes long—the second half is almost purely instrumental, Toby just letting the music breathe and setting up a solid groove. By this point in the reunion, since Tobin no longer lived in Dayton, he was just recording his songs solo, playing all the parts himself. 'I send the songs to Bob and that's all I do.' It's hard to argue with the results, though I can see how Pollard might have, over time, resented this. It's one thing when they were in the same room together, or Tobin was recording the group on his four-track. But by this point, Bob was just sticking Sprout's solo songs on GBV albums, and since Pollard was hardly lacking songs of his own, I can see how he would have begun to feel that Tobin's place in the group was not entirely necessary. Plus, that so many reviews were praising Toby's songs over his probably didn't help things.

Track three: 'Have A Jug'

While I like to hear Pollard singing against just an acoustic guitar, this feels like a sketch or demo of what it could have been. In terms of what the song's about, since this is Bob, I'll assume that 'have a jug' is basically a synonym for 'have a drink.' The lyrics reinforce the idea that the song's about drinking: 'Have a jug and you will see your new personality.' Even though people claim—as Pollard seems to do here—that too much alcohol can change a person's behavior or personality, that's just a myth. As *Esquire*'s Katie Frost put it in a 2017 article, 'A study published in *Clinical Psychological Science* shows that there is little switch in character between sober and wasted. And although people tend to become more extroverted after drinking, this is just a louder version of their usual nature.' That 'new personality' that Bob's alluding to is actually something that's already there; it just needs a few drinks to bring it out.

Track four: 'Hangover Child'

This track—one of three singles GBV released from the record—features some strong drumming, a solid bass line, and a sea of guitars. Plus, Pollard's singing with a slight British accent, which is always fun. It was also recorded by former producer Todd Tobias, so it sounds good. The song's lyrics are more impressionistic than narrative, Pollard throwing around a bunch of great lines. The bit about 'check-out lines for the red light sales' is a callback to the crass consumerism Bob decried on 'Useless Inventions.' And the bit about burying 'your nose in the bookends' is funny as Bob references the world's worst reader. And, even though I can't get a clear picture of who or what the 'hangover child' is or what it's meant to be or represent   Pollard? His fans? Pete Jamison?— it's a great track. Plus, the last forty-five seconds, where Pollard sings against himself, absolutely soar.

Track five: 'Dome Rust'

This is another lo-fi song that sounds like it could have come right off one of the band's EPs from 1994, except there's no tape hiss. I don't know who's playing drums, but I don't think it's Kevin Fennell. The song's not horrible, but it doesn't add much.

Track six: 'Finger Gang'

This fun and freaky song makes me think of Pollard's other project, Circus Devils, not to mention one of that band's main influences, Akron's Devo. The lyrics are sparse, Pollard repeating over and over the song's title, as well as shouting, 'They put the finger on you!'

Track seven: 'The Challenge Is Much More'

This track gets Pollard back to the empathetic territory of 'Redmen And Their Wives,' Bob here writing of a senile relative who's being packed off to an old folks' home. It's a place where he's having to relearn behavior like dressing himself and combing his hair. While Pollard has written plenty of songs about death, this one's about something found along the way: old age. Bob calls facing this reality a 'challenge' that's nearly 'impossible,' because, just like the 'Exit Flagger,' it's hard to 'ignore.' Unless you pull a Jimi Hendrix or Kurt Cobain, and flame out brilliantly in your youth, the ravages of time will get you in the end. Also, the line about how 'patience holds the key to every door' is a welcome bit of wisdom from a guy known more often for absurd non-sequiturs.

Track eight: 'Waving At Airplanes'

This absolutely gorgeous Tobin Sprout song is probably his best GBV contribution since 'To Remake The Young Flyer.' And, just like that track, it's an homage to planes and flying, this time from the point of view of someone simply waving at one. Everything here just clicks—Sprout does some great harmonizing, there are some great bass slides, and the last minute of the song just stretches out, and it all sounds superb.

Track nine: 'The Military School Dance Dismissal'

Pollard in ballad mode is one of my favorites, and I love anytime he sings against a piano, so obviously I like this song a lot. And while it irks me that Greg Demos (I think he's the one on the piano) didn't try for a second or third take, the rawness of the recording—and the mistakes in the playing—don't detract from the overall power of the song. The way Bob delivers the lyrics against the melody is great, and there are a few fun lines. I especially like 'None of them or all of us will fight,' Pollard again preaching the solidarity that comes up often in his songs ('A Salty Salute' being the best example). The nod to 'military school' in the title keeps it in line with numerous other references Bob has made over the years to various branches of the armed forces. *Pitchfork* wrote that the song 'sounds like Pollard crooning a *Hunky Dory* piano ballad in some Dayton dive at the age of eighty-five.' I hope we don't have to wait that long to get more tracks like this.

Track ten: 'White Flag'

Even though Pollard's provocative in some of the lines, asking 'What's the agenda?' and 'What were you thinking?' this is mostly Bob putting up his hands and saying, 'You win.' He counters any skepticism the subject of the song might have about this by adding, 'I think you know this time it's real.' And, just for fun, the line 'You know how I feel' also appears on The Who's 'Bell Boy,' from *Quadrophenia*.

In terms of when and how white flags became a symbol for surrender, it reportedly goes back nearly two thousand years, with the first historical mention coming from ancient Rome. They were used because they were easy to obtain and to see, even in battle. The tactic is still used in modern-day warfare; it's part of the Geneva Convention, and was used in the first Gulf War by surrendering Iraqi soldiers. It also doesn't have to be a flag that gets waved. Soldiers have been known to wave white handkerchiefs, undershirts, even socks.

SIDE TWO

Track one: *'Skin To Skin Combat'*

This Tobin Sprout song is the LP's longest track, at 3:43. With his mention of 'combat' and a 'soldier,' Sprout keeps up the military theme of the previous two songs. It's an engaging tune, especially at the end, when Sprout—like Pollard at the end of 'Hangover Child'—sings against himself with two different vocal lines.

Track two: *'She Lives In An Airport'*

This is not only my favorite—and I think the best—track on this record, but it's one of my all-time favorite GBV songs. One of the reasons I love it is that it's a character song. Pollard usually serves up surreal lyrics, or bits of twisted poetry—we get a lot of fantasy imagery, but not a lot of people. But this song—with its whimsical tale of a woman who, well, lives in an airport—is right up there with any of the character songs that Ray Davies wrote. Plus, it's just a lot of fun, Bob writing, 'She lives in an airport, so I get to travel for free' and 'Her name is destiny, it's destiny calling.' The song also has a number of references and allusions to marketing and advertising, Pollard writing of 'special offers,' 'sales-pitch jargon,' 'faster service,' 'crossed-finger discounts,' 'false advertising,' and 'no money down.' He's equating the 'come-on' from the woman in the airport with the ads and sales pitches we're all bombarded with on a daily basis. A romantic request can be just as sleazy as an offer from a used car salesman; in the end, everyone just wants you to sign on the line that is dotted. Lou Reed echoed a similar sentiment on his LP *Mistrial*, writing, 'You're paying a price when there is no price to pay. Lovers trust, there's no money down.'

Track three: *'Tree Fly Jet'*

I'm not a huge fan of this song, and its inclusion on the LP baffles me, especially coming after one of the album's best songs. Plus, at just 2:46, it seems to last for twice that long.

Track four: *'Waking Up The Stars'*

This Tobin Sprout track is reminiscent of Paul McCartney's 'Blackbird.' Rusty Roberts of the website *Chunky Glasses* wrote that this is 'a country tinged, acoustic romp that is the best song here with Sprout finger picking on his six-string sounding nothing like anything GBV could have ever done in their bedrooms and basements twenty years ago.' Toby here is in dream territory, describing himself 'floating toward the ceiling' and 'flying over fields.' This usually symbolizes freedom and happiness. But Sprout then has an out-of-body experience, writing that his 'soul goes around and down,' and, in the process, he discovers 'things I'd never see.' It's an epiphany that leaves him with yet more questions, the song ending with Tobin—despite everything that's been revealed to him—'wondering once more.'

Track five: *'Up Instead Of Running'*

Pollard's use of 'sha-la-la' in this song actually drives home just how infrequently Bob resorts to those kinds of phrases. Whereas some songwriters use a whole lot of la-la-las or bah-bah-bahs to fill out their lyrics, Pollard never does that. He's a word guy, even if he's using those words mainly for emotion, or for the way they sound, and not for the literal meaning.

Track six: *'Smoggy Boy'*

This is the record's shortest track at just thirty-five seconds. It's basically just one verse, but it's a good one, and, in some crazy way, it sounds like a whole song. It's like those Napalm Death tracks that are just bursts of noise with a shouted phrase or two.

Track seven: *'Amorphous Surprise'*

This is the band in the angular, post-punk vein that they tried out on their first couple of records. Daniel Couch of the *Quietus* called the song 'a needling, repetitive throwaway' that 'even at just two minutes … goes on too long.'

Track eight: *'You Can Fly Anything Right'*

This track sees Bob in full-on singer-songwriter mode. The title, while yet another GBV allusion to flight and planes, also seems to be a bit of an homage to the 1943 Nat King Cole classic 'Straighten Up And Fly Right.' The lyrics find Pollard being both cynical and sweet, writing, 'I'll respect you when you're number one'—an echo of 'My Kind Of Soldier' where he'll only offer praise if the soldier wins. But later in this song he's more forgiving, proclaiming, 'They'll still love you if you drop the ball,' and adding, 'If you think so and will it, it's your night.'

Track nine: 'Everywhere Is Miles From Everywhere'

It's good to see that the jangly R.E.M. sound didn't completely disappear with Doug Gillard. The lyrics harken back to the eponymous royalty of the opening track, Bob writing, 'There is fornication, no consent, nor king.' The title itself is a fun Pollard phrase that is, I suppose, technically true. If you think about it, everywhere is miles from everywhere else. It's like what Buckaroo Banzai always said, 'Wherever you go, there you are.'

19 ENGLISH LITTLE LEAGUE

two thousand and thirteen

While this year saw the release of only one Guided By Voices full-length, there was also a six-track GBV EP, *Down By The Racetrack*, which came out in January. A few months later came the sole EP from a new side project called The Sunflower Logic. The year 2013 also saw the release of two Robert Pollard LPs, *Honey Locust Honky Tonk* and *Blazing Gentlemen*, not to mention two Circus Devils records (released on the same day). As if all that wasn't enough, Pollard debuted yet another side project: Teenage Guitar. Since this flurry of releases was business as usual for Bob, let's return to the topic of Pollard's prolific nature.

In the last chapter I gave my theory as to why I think he releases so much stuff. Now I want to talk about what that means as a fan. How do people like us, who love Pollard and think he's a genius, manage to deal with the sheer amount of stuff he puts out? What part does that prolific nature play in how we either negatively or positively look at Bob and his work? And, finally, is it possible to actually appreciate or even listen to the mountain of work he's produced? It's something you wrestle with every time you reach for a GBV record. That there are dozens of albums means you have to choose. And that's when all you're talking about is GBV. When you add in all of Pollard's other projects, it's more than a hundred. This gets mentioned over and over again in reviews and interviews. In *Magnet*, a publication so friendly to Pollard it's put him on the cover numerous times, writer Jonathan Valania framed it this way: 'People feel like they can't keep up. ... People were saying that … back in the early 90s and it's only gotten worse.'

Uproxx.com had a story about this called 'Can A Musical Artist Be Too Prolific For Their Own Good?' Setting up his argument, author Chris Morgan writes, 'The knee-jerk reaction may be to dismiss this question out of hand. How could more music from an artist you love be a negative? Can there be too much of a good thing?' His opinion, finally, is yes. He offers up this sober assessment: 'Not every Guided By Voices song is good. There is probably nobody who would argue otherwise.' This gets at the heart of the 'Bob's too prolific' argument. As Morgan writes, 'The main issue here is diminishing returns, or perhaps quality versus quantity.' *Paste* agrees, proclaiming, 'Robert Pollard is a classic example in confusion with quantity versus quality.'

Jay Parini, in an essay for the *New York Times Book Review* entitled 'The More They Write, The More They Write,' looked at this phenomenon in authors:

> Overproduction can also damage the quality of a writer's prose. Anthony Burgess, one suspects, would have been well advised to slow down; there is a frenetic, distorted quality to many of his novels that broadcasts the haste of their composition. Virtually every prolific writer, from Balzac to Joyce Carol Oates and Gore Vidal, has dull passages, even whole books worth tossing out. Nevertheless, telling these writers to slow down is like telling a bird not to fly. 'I write a lot because I'm a writer,' Mr. Vidal said in his lofty, mandarin voice. 'That's what I do.'

A lot of that could be applied to Pollard. Quite a few GBV LPs, including this stretch of reunion albums, could be trimmed down considerably. Entire records by some of Bob's projects are disposable (the Teenage Guitar stuff that started to appear this year being a perfect example). Bob, however, seems to agree with Vidal. 'My philosophy is, if you like to write and play music, why hold yourself back? I don't see it as being a diluting thing.'

No one's saying he can't write songs, let alone play music. He's an adult, and he can do whatever he wants. But if he's going to release three or five or seven records a year, and he expects anyone to pay attention to them, or listen to them more than once, that's a different thing. Because he is, by sheer definition, diluting both the market and the interest for his work. Pollard puts out an LP, and, before you know it, there's another. And another. There's barely any time to let one sink in before he comes out with something else. Pollard's actually said, 'If I could put out an album a month, that would be no problem.' That may not be a problem for him, but it would be for anyone who likes him and wants to acquire, not to mention digest, what he produces.

Bob and his label seem to disagree. The marketing materials for *English Little League* stated, 'The Guided By Voices project, as any fan knows, both requires and rewards effortful listening, and lazybones who dismiss the volume of Pollard's output as (basically) impossible misunderstand the care with which he assembles his dreamscapes.' It goes on to characterize such complaints as 'whining.' All of that is bullshit. It's impossible to reap the rewards from any sort of listening when there's a machine-gun attack of material. Great LPs do indeed pay dividends over time, but that's because fans are given the space to enjoy them. Not to mention those albums contain rich veins of material that invite listeners to dig in and discover hidden gems. Think of Bob's favorite albums; something deep and unwieldy like *The Lamb Lies Down On Broadway* by Genesis. That LP has layers. There's subtlety. There's a vastness. It contains details and touches you can only appreciate over time. It's like a five-course meal where you savor every bite. Pollard, by contrast, has turned the consumption of his music into a hot-dog-eating contest. When you add in the fact that a whole bunch of what Pollard puts out is dashed off, and that Bob's quality-control filter is somewhat lacking, it adds a whole other dimension to the argument. It's a chore to ignore or separate out the bad songs, or projects, from the good stuff. And, quite frankly, if Pollard was a keener judge of his own talent, we wouldn't have to.

You can indeed draw a direct correlation of quality to quantity. Because even though Bob may answer, in reply to the charge of being too prolific, 'That's what I do; I love to write songs,' where I find real fault is in releasing so many tracks that are just sketches. If he spent twice as much time on half as many songs, what he released would be of a higher quality. Because, whereas most musicians look at the composed song as merely a blueprint to what will eventually be recorded, Pollard usually takes the written—or just plain *documented*—song as the finished product. What if his favorite groups had done that? John Lennon's demo of 'Strawberry Fields Forever' sounds just like dozens of Guided By Voices tracks. What made it into an epic for the ages is that The Beatles kept working at it and developing new ideas to supplement, complement, and expand it beyond Lennon's original vision. It's rare for Bob to do that. He either just sticks with the basic instrumentation of the demo, or else he records his songs with a basic band format. When producers like Ric Ocasek have tried to add other touches, or instrumental flourishes, both Pollard his band—and even most of his fans—have cried foul.

Marketing materials accompanying the release of *English Little League* noted that 'Pollard has recently installed a studio in his house.' Rather than being some elaborate set up, the 'studio' consisted of not much more than a room, an eight-track tape machine, and some condenser mics. Bob christened his home studio the Public Hi-Fi Balloon, the same name he'd used for art show that ran in downtown New York the summer of 2010. A number of tracks from *Little League* were recorded there, the first of which was 'A Burning Glass.'

Pollard also used his home studio to record The Sunflower Logic's debut EP, *Clouds On The Polar Landscape*; some songs that ended up on *Suitcase 4*; a few tracks for his solo record *Honey Locust Honkey Tonk*, from this same year; and the first Teenage Guitar record. Everything that came out of the Public Hi-Fi Balloon sounds just awful, and Pollard stopped using it shortly after it was introduced. Even the records that feature just him playing all the instruments, like the second Teenage Guitar record, or the GBV LP *Please Be Honest*, were recorded in a studio rather than at home. This speaks to what I talked about in the *Bears For Lunch* chapter, about Pollard being a former jock. As much as he rebelled against coaches, team sports are in his blood. For as much of a singular genius as he is, Bob is—at heart—a team player. The idea of him spending days or weeks holed up in a studio chasing the perfect sound, like Tom Scholz making the first Boston record, was just never going to be the case.

The cover for *English Little League* is probably one of the most Pollard sleeves ever. The collage is done on a page of old college ruled paper. It's dirty and stained, and there's writing seeping through from the other side. The album and band name have been typed out on an old typewriter. The only thing that's disappointing about the package is that there's no lyric sheet. In the past, Bob's done that because he didn't think highly of the lyrics. That being said, the interior of the LP does have the lyrics to one song, 'A Burning Glass.' I'm not sure why he chose this song out of the others; perhaps it's somehow the most lyrically personal or significant on the album? It's sort of like how R.E.M., a band famous at the time for inscrutable vocals and not including lyrics with their records, printed the words to just one track, 'World Leader Pretend,' on their 1988 major-label debut, *Green*. They did this because, as singer and lyricist Michael Stipe said, 'I think to be able to read "World Leader Pretend" as well as listening to it will help clarify a lot of the intention behind *Green*.' I'm not sure if Pollard was thinking along the same lines. If so, it doesn't help a ton, since the lyrics to 'A Burning Glass' are baffling.

English Little League spawned four singles: 'Flunky Minnows,' 'Islands (She Talks In Rainbows),' 'Trashcan Full Of Nails,' and 'Xeno Pariah.' Their UK record company, Fire, compiled all the singles' B-sides into a seven-song EP called *Glue On Bicycle*.

In reviewing *English Little League*, *Pitchfork*'s Paul Thompson gave it a 6.8 and wrote that 'like so many GBV albums before it, [the LP] gathers a couple all-timers and a few respectably jagged pop-rockers together with several total trainwrecks and calls it an LP,' adding that 'while it's perfectly pleasant from moment to moment, the whole never congeals.' And while the *AV Club* gave the record a B, with reviewer Matt Wild saying that 'it remains a pleasure to hear GBV doing what it does best: cranking out song after song,' he also wrote that '*English Little League* is decidedly overstuffed at seventeen songs.'

For the website *Pop'stache*, Craig Bechtel wrote, 'A few of Pollard's numbers start out promisingly enough, like "Crybaby 4 Star Hotel" and "Know Me As Heavy," before the typically surreal lyrics veer into cringe-worthy territory ... and his baritone goes wildly out of tune, and not in a charmingly amateurish way.' The review also wondered whether Pollard having his own label is a good thing. 'Perhaps the 21st-century model of releasing records through one's own label has its downside,' Bechtel concluded, adding, 'Even after repeated spins, *English Little League* sounds like the perfect illustration of the law of diminishing returns—it's C-grade Guided By Voices at best.'

SIDE ONE
Track one: 'Xeno Pariah'

This awesome song has about twenty seconds of jangly guitar before Pollard and the power chords come in. *Pitchfork* called the track the 'best first-shot of GBV's second act, a sharp, clear-eyed rocker with a head-lodge hook all its own.' In terms of the title, 'xeno' is a Greek prefix meaning 'foreign.' This is why it appears in the word 'xenophobia,' which can be defined as an 'intense or irrational dislike or fear of people from other countries.' A pariah is an outcast, or someone who's been shunned by society. The song's lyrics are directly about this: someone being shunned for being different or foreign. But Pollard offers to help, saying, 'I'll tell you what to do.' Bob wants to show this person how to belong in his society. And yet, Pollard hints at the struggle that all immigrants face when they try to fit in: 'The smile on your face is leaving no trace of the something that hides in you.' Everyone who comes to this country for a better life has left something behind, sometimes entire worlds. That's not easy, and is something Bob acknowledges with the line 'There'll be no denying the tears that you're crying.' Looked at through this lens, 'Xeno Pariah' is a chilling song, because even though Bob admits that 'there's something good' inside the stranger he's writing about, that's not enough: the song's subject must 'change' before he's ultimately 'driven away.'

The B-side to 'Xeno Pariah' was a re-recorded version of 'Little Jimmy The Giant.' The original version of 'Jimmy,' released on the first *Suitcase* compilation, is the oldest Guided By Voices song in existence, having been recorded way back in 1974, when Bob was just seventeen. It's a very fun and touching song about his brother, then in the seventh grade, who wasn't being taken seriously in sports because of his small size.

Track two: 'Know Me As Heavy'

This is a fun song, although knowing the lyrics would go a long way toward helping make some sense of it. There are some good lines, I think, except Bob's slurring his words, and the vocals are deep in the mix; plus, someone who doesn't know the lyrics is singing along with Bob.

Track three: *'Islands (She Talks In Rainbows)'*

This is an absolutely stellar Tobin Sprout track that's a bit faster than most of his others. And, while some of his songs on the last couple of LPs saw him barely singing above a whisper, here he's almost back to the territory of the *Under The Bushes* gem 'Atom Eyes.' Sarah H. Grant at *Consequence Of Sound* declared it the album's 'best song' and wrote that 'the gorgeous two minutes feel like a warm beach blanket to curl inside.' It's so good that it was issued as a single, which is rare for a Toby track. It was originally written for his 2010 solo record *The Bluebirds Of Happiness Tried To Land On My Shoulder*, except it didn't make the cut. 'The song didn't strike me at first and so it got filed away,' Tobin has said, adding, 'Playing it with the band gave it new life. I did an acoustic demo for Kevin that I like a lot. I like Kevin's drumming on it, and Mitch played the power guitar.' That Toby has the rest of the band playing on the song, instead of recording it all himself, goes a long way toward having its sound match the others on the record; it doesn't stand out from Pollard's tracks like some of Sprout's did around this time. I especially like the last line, 'So tell her mother she's just fine.' It reminds me of the last line of 'Frank Mills' from the musical *Hair*: 'Tell him Angela and I don't want the two dollars back, just him.'

Track four: *'Trashcan Full Of Nails'*

Matt Wild at the *AV Club* described this song as 'the sort of tossed-off gem that Pollard excels at—weird, hooky, and completely nonsensical.' I agree that it sounds tossed off; it might work as a ninety-second song snippet, but, at well over three minutes, it quickly wears out its welcome. Since by this point Pollard had been writing, recording, and releasing songs like this for twenty-five years, he had no intention of changing his ways. As he writes here, 'Better try not to fix what fails.'

Track five: *'Send To Celeste'*

This track, which starts off with organ and Pollard singing against an electric guitar, slowly builds into what almost feels like a Broadway show tune. It ends up sounding absolutely huge—my only complaint is that I wish I had the lyrics to see what Bob's singing about.

Track six: *'The Quiet Game'*

This Tobin Sprout track sees him channeling Pollard from the second song, 'Know Me As Heavy.' The lyrics are mostly mumbled, indecipherable, and buried low in the mix. There's a riff that runs through most of the track, and, while it's not bad, it does nothing for me.

Track seven: *'Noble Insect'*

This is another one of the LP's singles that doesn't seem to rise to the level of a single. There's not much to it, and it's repetitive. *Pitchfork* called the song a 'dismal co-write from Pollard and Tobin Sprout that leaves neither side off the hook.' Whereas past collaborations gave birth to some great songs—'Hot Freaks' being probably the best example—they're not striking gold here.

Track eight: *'Sir Garlic Breath'*

This starts off as an acoustic song, similar to 'You Can Fly Anything Right' or 'Chain To The Moon' from prior reunion LPs. But the song gets lost after about thirty seconds, and then, instead of creating a true melody, Pollard resorts to just singing low and then high. The last minute of the song is almost hard to listen to, with Bob slurring and making up lyrics as he goes. It's a co-write with Greg Demos, so I guess that's him on guitar. It was recorded at Pollard's new 'home studio.'

SIDE TWO

Track one: *'Crybaby 4 Star Hotel'*

This song has a great title but not much of a tune. It name-checks actor and comedian Zero Mostel, a Tony Award–winning performer who appeared on stage and screen, perhaps most memorably in the original film version of *The Producers*.

Track two: *'Biographer Seahorse'*

This is another song where the title's almost the most interesting thing about it. That this is the fifth so-so song in a row goes a long way toward why this is my least favorite GBV record. That's not to say this is a bad song—there's actually a ton of potential. Bob's singing in a big and grand way, and the lyrics seems to hint at confusion and fear: 'People don't know what's happening.' But the execution of the track is just too fuzzy and unfinished. I have a feeling that if this had been fleshed out a bit more—if it'd been on *Isolation Drills*, and produced like those songs—it'd be a lot more effective.

Track three: 'Flunky Minnows'
This strong track gets back to some of the spirit of gems from the first side, like 'Islands' and 'Xeno Pariah.' *Pitchfork*'s Paul Thompson said the song 'is brimming with so many hooks, it spends its two minutes and change running around in circles, begging you to take them off its hands.' The lyrics are also cool, like when Pollard declares, 'Everything is wonderful and microscopes are fun.'

Track four: 'Birds'
It's interesting that this song is called just 'Birds.' On this LP alone we've been treated to noble insects, flunky minnows, and a biographer seahorse. It's another co-write with Sprout, and, again, it's just okay. There's some decent background vocals by Bob, but there's not much happening musically, and the mid-tempo nature of the song doesn't help.

Track five: 'The Sudden Death Of Epstein's Ways'
Matt Wild of the *AV Club* called this Tobin Sprout song 'undoubtedly *Little League*'s strongest moment.' The Epstein being talked about is The Beatles' manager, Brian Epstein, who discovered the scruffy band playing lunchtime sets at the Cavern Club. However, once the band stopped touring, Epstein didn't have much to do, and this, combined with some turmoil in his personal life—he was gay at a time when homosexual activity was illegal in the UK—led to his untimely death at the age of just thirty-two. Sprout's said of this song, 'I was reading about the sudden death of Brian Epstein and other things in the 60s, like Jesus freaks. The high that some people get when they find God, and how it can change people for the better.' And yet, Sprout's using Epstein here more as a symbol, Tobin explaining, 'It's not about Brian; it's about a generic lost person named Epstein who finds his way.' This ties it to past songs by Toby about similarly lost characters, such as 'Ester's Day.'

Track six: *'Reflections In A Metal Whistle'*

This is another of the tracks recorded at Pollard's new home studio. It sounds awful. The only other thing I can say about it is that a line from 'Noble Insect,' 'friction in Japan,' comes up again.

Track seven: *'Taciturn Caves'*

At almost four minutes, this is the LP's longest track. And while there's a riff that sounds a bit like Black Sabbath's 'Paranoid,' this song doesn't do much for me, especially toward the end, when it just limps along.

Track eight: *'A Burning Glass'*

This song is as good as any to use as an example for the 'quality over quantity' argument, as well as to cite just how bad some of these songs sound. It's hard to justify its inclusion on anything except maybe a *Suitcase* compilation, and even then I'd skip it.

Track nine: *'W/ Glass In Foot'*

Built around a guitar riff that sounds an awful lot like 'Can't Explain,' this is a welcome return to form after a long run of lackluster songs. *Consequence Of Sound* called this the record's best track. I agree that it's a fun song, and a good way to end what's otherwise a lackluster LP.

20 MOTIVATIONAL JUMPSUIT

two thousand and fourteen

I t was good to be a fan around the time this record came out. The old lineup was back together again, they were playing shows and were releasing records at a rate of two to three a year. It was like your divorced parents got back together and you didn't need to have two Christmases anymore. It was too good to be true. You just knew something bad was bound to happen.

In October 2013, drummer Kevin Fennell put on eBay a set of drums that he'd used on a number of GBV records. It was the kit he'd played on numerous tours, and at least one TV appearance, not to mention it was part of the sessions for the classic LPs *Bee Thousand* and *Alien Lanes* (in addition to the more recent reunion records). In an era of Kickstarter, or with websites like *Reverb*, bands and musicians often sell memorabilia—including their gear—directly to fans. Fennell's opening bid of $55,000, however, seemed to strike many people as being damned expensive, bordering on outrageous. But is it? An original *Propeller* sells for almost five figures, and Bob and Toby each command thousands of dollars for their artwork. Plus, Pollard's put out hundreds of LPs and singles, and none of them were free, so why is fifty-five grand so controversial? Either someone pays it, or they don't.

Pollard wasn't happy. He called Kevin to complain, at which point Fennell responded via an email wherein he laid out his various points and reasons for why he was doing what he was doing. Pollard responded with a nasty reply that left no doubt as to his current or future relationship with Fennell, Bob ending the message, 'Don't ever fucking bother me again.' The reason we know this is because Fennell posted the emails on Facebook. And while that is undoubtedly not a cool move—Bob intended for that exchange to be private—given everything that was being said in the press and around town, Fennell felt he had to get his side of the story out there. Even though Bob seemed to think Kevin was making some sort of dick move, trying to rip off fans for cash, that's not the way it seems to me.

Here's what Fennell wrote on a website he set up to sell the drums:

> So you might ask, why sell them if they are so great? Well you need to understand that I do so with great reservation, as I have sentimental feelings attached to them. Great memories of lugging them in and out of studios, bars, clubs, halls and stadiums, and always feeling secure that they could take a beating and sound great while doing so. I guess I believe that there is someone out there who will appreciate them as much as, if not more than, I do.

Drummers don't get the big advances or a share of the publishing. Kevin didn't have royalty checks coming in from a dozen different solo or side projects. While Pollard's earned every cent of what he's received, I find it hard to believe he wouldn't cut Kevin some slack. Yes, Bob owns the name Guided By Voices, but he can't claim to own, or be in control of, every aspect of its history. And I get that this is the guy who wrote 'leave my fucking life alone,' but doesn't that extend to others? Why not leave Kevin's life alone? But Bob didn't, and instead he sent Kevin an email in which he fired Fennell, in addition to berating him on a number of levels. I won't quote from it much, because it's just too depressing to do so, but one thing that stuck out to me the most is that Pollard criticized Fennell for being an 'amateur.'

I won't go into the dozens of examples where Bob's conducted himself, both live and on record, in a less than professional manner. Suffice it say that Pollard's on thin ice when he proclaims to be a standard bearer for musical professionalism. If this was Rush we were talking about, maybe, but GBV? And, yes, I get that Bob's the boss, and he gets to call the shots, but this just smacks to me of a double standard.

Pollard's other main point is that no one cares who's drumming for the band. 'Do not delude yourself, Kevin, that people gave a shit who was behind that drum kit.' I can only speak for myself and say that I care. And Bob cares, too. Because is he going to say he liked The Who, or got as excited by their records, or seeing them live, when anyone but Keith Moon was the drummer? And if Pollard extends that thinking to guys like Mitch Mitchell or Tobin Sprout, then he's the one who's deluded, since the overall charm, not to mention the musical output, of that early lineup is a huge part of why those records were so successful. Bob even referenced this when the guys got back together in 2010: 'I've been convinced that there definitely seems to be a unique chemistry characterized by everyone's individual approach and style. It sort of comes through when you hear it and one can identify it, for the most part, with this particular lineup.'

You cannot deny the charm, and the history, of the original lineup. Without them, and what they brought to LPs like *Bee Thousand* and *Alien Lanes*, there is no GBV. This is why Bob's reaction seems overblown, not to mention needlessly cruel. I also find it to be at odds with his jovial Uncle Bob persona.

So Fennell was out, and the previous drummer, Kevin March—who'd played on the last two LPs for Matador—was asked back. He would go on to tour with the band, and play on the next LP, before Bob killed the band yet again.

Motivational Jumpsuit followed the usual template of the recent run of records. It consists of twenty songs in under forty minutes, with some polished tracks sitting next to Bob's usual lo-fi snippets, as well as Tobin's mini-masterpieces.

Five singles were released from the record: 'Alex And The Omegas,' 'Planet Score,' 'Save The Company,' 'The Littlest League Possible,' and 'Vote For Me Dummy.'

A funny basketball-themed video was made for 'Planet Score.' It was directed by Mike Postalakis, an Ohio native who now lives in Los Angeles. He's a writer, performer, and filmmaker. He's also a very funny and interesting guy, not to mention a huge GBV fan. It would be the first of four star-studded videos Postalakis would make for Pollard, each one featuring actors who had been in some big movies or TV shows, the most well known being Matt Jones, who played Badger on *Breaking Bad*, and is also a big GBV fan.

Bob was open to any of the singles off the record being chosen for the video. The reason it was 'Planet Score' is because it seemed to Postalakis to work best as a kind of 'mini-movie.' The result is a lot of fun to watch, and, because it was produced by website *Funny Or Die*, the video was seen by tens of thousands of people.

Another cool thing about the song is that the line about Planet Score being a 'record store' came true in 2015, when friends Joe Stulce and Tim Lohmann opened Planet Score Records in Maplewood, Missouri. Stulce is a big GBV fan, so when it came time to name the store, he didn't have to look far, since *Motivational Jumpsuit* had just come out. After posting his idea online, months before the store actually opened, the news made its way to Pollard. Bob immediately gave his okay and then, less than a week after the store opened, he paid Planet Score a visit. He shopped, hung out, posed for photos, and signed all of Stulce's GBV vinyl.

The cover of *Motivational Jumpsuit* is curious in that it's barely a collage. We see a photo of a stack of half-open boxes as a poster for the *Tigerbomb* EP hangs on the wall. In the middle of the photo is a vintage-looking person we can only see from behind. Placing the figure in the contemporary photo makes it seem as if they're in the room staring at the boxes, and we're behind them staring at them staring. The self-referential nature of the cover reinforces the idea that all of Pollard's work takes place in a self-contained universe. It's Bob's world; we just live in it.

The album received mixed reviews. The *AV Club* gave the record a C+, calling it 'a ramshackle collection of 20 one- to three-minute songs raging with crunchy power chords, fragmented power-pop melodies, and impressionistic lyricism from the group's ageless anchor, lead singer-songwriter Robert Pollard.' Summing up the record, reviewer Patrick Bowman declared, 'It's difficult to find any song on *Motivational Jumpsuit* that GBV lifers can place among the group's most accomplished work.'

SIDE ONE

Track one: 'Littlest League Possible'

This is Pollard at his most meta, commenting not only on his jock past but also on the place in rock history in which GBV, after nearly thirty years of existence, found themselves. It starts off as an ode to baseball, the sport at which Pollard excelled, Bob writing, 'Gonna have a lot of fun, going to hit a home run.' He then provides the context for where all this fun is happening, and it's not at the major-league level (a somewhat-wistful admission, since Pollard was a gifted-enough athlete that he could have gone pro). Instead, this is all taking place in the 'littlest league possible,' which Bob defines as 'the most rudimentary division of competition.' Pollard then weighs the pros and cons of playing in such a league, asking rhetorically whether it's better to be 'the biggest fish in the smallest pond' or else to 'keep banging it out in the Texas league.'

It's a super-interesting discussion coming from Bob, since he'd once tried for a bigger audience. As a kid, he was groomed to be a professional athlete, and then, years later, he'd tried to achieve mainstream success with Guided By Voices. While he was never officially on a major label—or in the major leagues—he came close enough to both to realize what it would take to make it in each world. And he didn't want to do it. For his entire career, whether it was sports or rock'n'roll, he wanted to make his own decisions and do things his way. If that meant playing in the 'littlest league possible,' then that's a sacrifice he's willing to make. And by this point especially, Pollard seemed comfortable with that decision. The song is celebratory. He's not stewing or brooding, channeling the lament of Brando's has-been prizefighter who bitterly declared, 'I could have been somebody; I could have been a contender.' Instead, Bob's saying he's happy where he is. He doesn't care which league he's in; he just likes to play the game.

Track two: 'Until Next Time'

This short snippet hints at how the winners and losers of the previous song get chosen. Is it talent? Is it luck? As Pollard writes, 'Was it just not in your cards? It seems so unfair.' For a guy who'd seen his contemporaries, whether athletes or musicians, rise higher and go further than he did, this is an interesting idea: there's basically no rhyme or reason as to who succeeds and who doesn't. The greatness of some bands never gets recognized, and some people never get their due. And, in an upside-down world where talent is marginalized and mediocrity is praised, Bob wants to set things straight: 'The first shall be the last, and the last shall be the first.'

Track three: 'Writer's Bloc (Psycho All The Time)'

If the first song was Pollard at his most meta, this track—about writer's block, and the torture of creation—is Bob at his most ironic. The guy's a songwriting machine, so to hear him lament that it's taking him 'hours, days, weeks, months' and 'years' to finish writing something is the complete opposite of how Bob actually functions. And, since he's a guy who's never slaved after the perfect take, or getting just-the-right vocal sound, the line here about 'the last recording nearly killed me' is also ridiculous. The song's also funny, with Pollard twisting 'Publishers Clearing House'—that company with the sweepstakes—into 'publisher's screaming house.' With its talk of composition and publishers, the track harkens back to the 1966 single by The Beatles, 'Paperback Writer,' which saw a wannabe author, who'd worked on his book for years, begging an editor to 'take a look.'

Another interesting thing is that the title is actually 'bloc.' Pollard's spelling of the word with just a *c* provides a different meaning, defined as 'a combination of countries, parties, or groups sharing a common purpose.' You heard this a lot during the Cold War, countries in Europe being described as an Eastern Bloc. The pun's been used before; the English band Bloc Party have been around since the late 90s. I'm not sure why Pollard's using it here; maybe he just likes the look of it. Or maybe he's slamming the inherent cliquey-ness of writers, advising them to spend less time worrying over their work and just get it done. *PopMatters*' Mathew Fiander said that this song 'gives us an organizing tension for *Motivational Jumpsuit*,' writing, 'It's easy, as artists get older, to read some subtext of mortality into their work. Here, Pollard seems not so much concerned with that as with his reputation and his creative drive. If Pollard is not putting out six records a year, this song seems to ask, then who is Robert Pollard? If he can't keep up the impossible pace he's built, what happens then?'

Track four: *'Child Activist'*

We're back in *Vampire On Titus* territory with this short lo-fi track, which treats Bob's vocals with so much distortion you can barely make out what he's singing. But that's okay; the lyrics don't seem to have any distinct meaning.

Track five: *'Planet Score'*

This is probably the closest the band's ever come to capturing on tape the way they sound live. The sound's totally raw and in-your-face in a way that, for as much as it rocks live, a track like 'Cut-Out Witch' just can't match. It starts with a wallop of guitar and drums and doesn't relent for the duration of the song. It also shows how Pollard wrote to the strengths of the guys he had in the band at the time. It's definitely my favorite song on the record.

Track six: *'Jupiter Spin'*

This Tobin Sprout song has the same vibe as 'The Corners Are Glowing' from *The Bears For Lunch*. It also features some wah-wah guitar, along with lots of lyrics about a guy dancing (the word 'dancing' is used a dozen times in the track). The title of the song refers to the fact that, of all the planets in our solar system, Jupiter spins the fastest. A day on Jupiter lasts less than ten hours, and that's saying something, considering Jupiter is so large that 1,300 Earths could fit inside it.

Track seven: *'Save The Company'*

While *Bee Thousand* and *Alien Lanes* were mentioned over and over when this lineup got back together, this is one of the few songs to, in my mind, channel the spirit of those ragged classics; it has a sort of 'Queen Of Cans And Jars' vibe. Everything just fits here; it has a great tune, the lyrics are a lot of fun, and even though the sound is lo-fi, you don't care because it's absolutely gorgeous.

The lyrics are also classic surreal Pollard, Bob singing about running in the subway naked and 'ripening diamonds.' I don't know what it all means except that it sounds great against the chord sequence Bob's singing over. Pollard also makes a good joke late in the song, writing that 'he who controls the past is coming up soon from the rear.'

The track hews to a classic format of verse, chorus, verse, chorus, middle-eight break, chorus. This proves that Pollard knows all the parts to a song, even if he usually chooses not to use them. Even though the sound quality's not great, the choruses have that Phil Spector 'Be My Baby' drumbeat, complete with tambourine, and it just sounds awesome. While I don't glean any great meaning behind the lyrics, the title, along with 'West Coast Company Man,' from 2017's *August By Cake*, reflects Pollard's 50s upbringing. Because even though he's technically not a baby boomer, he was brought up in the aftershocks of the post-war America mentality, when fealty to a corporation was considered to be a good thing. You got a job at IBM or AT&T and you worked there for the rest of your life. Being a company man was considered a proper thing and so, as Pollard sings here, 'saving' the company would be considered an honor, a noble pursuit.

Track eight: *'Go Without Packing'*

This short track is a return to the bitter songs that made up side two of *Propeller*, Pollard here telling someone to 'go without packing,' meaning, basically, get out of here right now. It's sort of the song version of the note he wrote to Kevin Fennell. Pollard also squashes any hope that the person may have to try and get back in his good graces, mentioning 'hopeless language.' Basically, don't even try to talk your way out of it. And when Bob ends the song with 'Go love yourself,' but then quickly adds, 'Just go,' it seems like what he wants to say is 'Go fuck yourself.'

Track nine: *'Record Level Love'*

This short Tobin Sprout track, clocking in at just 1:16, is absolutely lovely. And while Bob would declare on the next LP that 'Bad Love Is Easy To Do,' here Toby's singing about the opposite, a 'record level love' that 'shines on everything' and 'makes you feel the way you want to be.' And to show that this isn't just hippie crap, Sprout starts the song by stating, 'It's not easy.' Record-level love may exist, but it's difficult to obtain. The song's just gorgeous, with jangly guitar and layered vocal harmonies. It's another great contribution, showing just how valuable Sprout was to the six-LP run of reunion records.

Track ten: 'I Am Columbus'

At nearly three minutes, this is the second-longest track on the album. It's a two- or three-chord stomper that brings back the tambourine from 'Save The Company,' as well as some organ and electric guitar. Pollard uses eighteenth-century explorer Christopher Columbus as a potent metaphor for someone who not only wants to take your time but your whole existence, writing, 'I seek the world.' *Pitchfork* called the song 'undercooked,' describing it as 'keyboard-jabbed psychedelic sludge.' The *AV Club* didn't like it much either, writing that it's 'clunky,' 'overwrought,' and a 'wince worthy' miss.

SIDE TWO

Track one: 'Difficult Outburst And Breakthrough'

Pollard does something on this track that rarely comes up in the thousands of songs he's written and recorded: he sings the first verse twice. It's rare for Bob—a man who's a mountain of words—to ever repeat himself. The tempo and sound are similar to other songs on the record, like 'Planet Score' and 'Vote For Me Dummy,' which shows that—five albums into the reunion—the formula was starting to wear a bit thin. As *Pitchfork* wrote in their review of *Motivational Jumpsuit*, GBV's 'recent albums have by no means tarnished their legacy,' but 'they haven't exactly expanded upon it either.' This song is a good example of that. It's not bad, but it doesn't exactly earn its place on a twenty-song record.

Track two: 'Calling Up Washington'

More than half of the twenty songs on *Motivational Jumpsuit* are under two minutes, with nine of those eleven songs clocking in at less than ninety seconds. This Tobin Sprout track is the album's shortest, at 1:12. And while I'm normally a big fan of Toby's stuff, 'Calling Up Washington'—while not sounding bad by any stretch—comes off as half-baked. Especially when you consider that Sprout owns his own recording equipment, and the band's on their own label. It's not like they're being rushed by their A&R guy, or that they simply ran out of time in the studio. They could have taken as much time as they wanted to get their songs and recordings right, and yet instead they took the opposite approach, releasing records that contained more or less sketches and first takes.

Track three: *'Zero Elasticity'*

This song sounds like a slower, sludgier version of Wire's 'Three Girl Rhumba.' It's also another song that, like 'Planet Score,' comes close to capturing the band's live sound. It's a fun track, with some background vocals from Pollard and lyrics that mention the album's title, Bob writing, 'I'll go second, you go first, in your motivational jumpsuit.'

Track four: *'A Bird With No Name'*

This title references 'A Horse With No Name,' which was a number 1 song in the US, and the first single, from the band America. The classic folk-rock song sounds so much like Neil Young that most people think it's actually Neil Young singing it, or that he wrote it, when in fact it's an original composition by America's Dewey Bunnell. That being said, the song replaced Young's 'Heart Of Gold' at the top of the American charts. 'A Bird With No Name,' since it's a mostly acoustic track, harkens back to the America track except that it's ominous and foreboding, whereas the earlier song is cozy and familiar (even if it is about heroin). The lyrics are mainly impressionistic, Pollard crooning about a 'forest of bars' and 'photographic cuisine.' But the last image, where Bob mentions flying on a 'bird with no wings' is striking. It's also a fitting juxtaposition with the opening line because, while it's fine if you're flying on a bird with no name, if the bird has no wings, there's going to be a problem.

Track five: *'Shine (Tomahawk Breath)'*

At a few seconds past three minutes, this Tobin Sprout tune is the record's longest. Like most of his tracks on the reunion LPs, it's slow and dreamy, with Toby delivering the lyrics in a croon. At two minutes in, the song peters out for a second, only to return with a long and lazy guitar solo that continues for the last minute. This makes 'Shine' yet another of Tobin's songs that contains a lot of music, which is always welcome. GBV songs are usually so lean and short that they have an intro (if one at all), a few verses and a chorus by Bob, and then they're over. There's no room to just stretch out and enjoy the pure act of listening, or experiencing, any music or melody that's *inside* the song. For example, on the track 'Bulletin Borders,' which appears later on this LP, Bob essentially sings throughout the entire 1:23 song; he starts before the music even kicks in. And while I love his voice, and his lyrics, sometimes I just want to hear the band stretch out, to just plain listen to and enjoy the music, which Sprout lets us do here for about a third of the track.

Track six: 'Vote For Me Dummy'

The chord progression on this song takes me back to 'Exit Flagger' off *Propeller*, except instead of starting with Pollard singing, 'I don't know where I'm going,' he croons here, 'Marry your uniform.' Also, even though the song's ostensibly about voting, it can't be about politics, since Bob writes, 'I'll tell you the truth.' Politicians just never do that. It's definitely one of the more fleshed-out songs on the record, with a verse/chorus structure and an outro where Bob sings, 'Please find me an island.'

Track seven: 'Some Things Are Big (And Some Things Are Small)'

This is another one of Tobin's songs that's very soothing and gentle. It could practically be on a kid's record (and I don't say that as an insult). The production is also stellar, with some subtle piano and layered vocals; it's Tobin's best track on the album. And even if the subject matter's a bit obvious—yes, some things are big, and some things are small—that doesn't matter because it's striking to listen to.

Track eight: 'Bulletin Borders'

This is another hard-charging song in the vein of 'Planet Score' and 'Vote For Me Dummy.' It sounds good, and almost takes me back to the *Mag Earwhig!* era of the band.

Track nine: 'Evangeline Dandelion'

This short, mostly acoustic song finds Bob singing about someone named Evangeline Dandelion before the song ends in crowd noise and a 'rah' that takes me back to the ending of 'My Son, My Secretary And My Country' from *Earthquake Glue*. The track has a promising atmosphere, but Bob's vocal is rough. I'd love to hear a more thoughtful version.

Track ten: *'Alex And The Omegas'*

One of the five singles released from the record, it's a great way to end the LP. The first minute of the song follows a verse/chorus structure, the lyrics being the usual surreal Pollard fare. But then the song switches into a start-stop section that's cool. *Pitchfork's* Stuart Berman wrote that it 'feels like it was designed as both a record and show closer, an amplified-to-rock charge that doubles as a victory lap.' And since the lineup that recorded the song, and this album, was no longer in existence, the song also acts as a final goodbye to the so-called classic lineup. It was fun while it lasted.

21 COOL PLANET

two thousand and fourteen

ool Planet marks the end of the reunion that began in 2010. Original drummer Kevin Fennell had been kicked out of the group, replaced by Kevin March. March was ecstatic when he got Pollard's call. 'To go back and do that again was unexpected, but I embraced it with open arms.' But while he was (and continues to be) a great asset, his addition to the band at this point threw the idea of GBV out of whack. This was no longer the *Bee Thousand/Alien Lanes* lineup. Instead, you had a hybrid that began to not make much sense.

You could sense this tension on the *Cool Planet* tour. There's a YouTube clip of them playing 'Authoritarian Zoo' at a club in Pennsylvania (which prompts Bob to introduce the song and sing the first line as 'Philadelphia Zoo'). And, while they sound fine, you can see the cracks that are starting to appear. Sprout stands mostly motionless, giving his Telecaster gentle strums. Mitch Mitchell's doing his usual power chord thing, while Greg Demos does his rock moves, which are the same moves he'd been doing for years. Meanwhile, new guy Kevin March is pounding away in the background, grinning and happy to be there. And Bob just seems stuck in the middle.

Pitchfork described a show from around this time as being 'workmanlike,' which is something you can see in the clip from the Philadelphia show. Writer Jason Heller also described the band as playing with a 'cold, canned efficiency,' which was a long way from the 'air of confusion and chaos that Robert Pollard and company once brought to their music.'

It's no wonder the band broke up during the tour. This meant canceling a dozen dates, including hometown shows in Dayton and Cleveland. As Bob said after he'd pulled the plug, 'It was tired, collectively. I don't know why, and I'm not blaming anyone specifically, but we seemed to be going through the motions toward the end. I couldn't see it progressing, getting any better or going any further, so I decided it was time to wrap it up.'

In addition to the two GBV records, in 2014 Pollard also released a Circus Devils album and another Teenage Guitar record. Since the previous year saw him release two solo records but there were none this year, he was also probably itching to go and do something on his own again, or just plain work with some other people. The following year, he'd keep Kevin March around and team up with Daytonian multi-instrumentalist Nick Mitchell for three Ricked Wicky records.

The reunion had also seemed to run its course with critics. *Pitchfork* gave *Cool Planet* the lowest grade of all the reunion LPs, a 6.2, down from the high of 7.3 awarded to both *The Bears For Lunch* and *Motivational Jumpsuit*. Jason Heller wrote, 'Where GBV's slovenly, dilapidated grandeur once felt vital and radical, it now putters along crankily, the sound of a band muttering to itself rather than playing to anyone in particular, themselves included.'

Paste's Garrett Martin wrote that the record had 'a few outright failures,' but that most of the album was 'pleasantly competent,' stating that 'most songs have at least one moment or part that stands out.' That seems to be either damning with faint praise, or just plain letting the band off easy. His review also calls the group 'essentially a nostalgia act.'

The return of Kevin March wasn't the only new thing about the record. For the first time since the band got back together, the LP—except for Tobin's stuff, which he recorded at his house in Michigan—was recorded in a studio, a new location in his hometown that Pollard had just discovered. As he told *Rolling Stone*, 'Cyberteknics has been around in Dayton for fifty years, and the guy who owns and operates it is Phil Mehaffey. He's great. He looks like George Martin. We just discovered him and his studio last year and that's a shame that it didn't happen sooner.'

The band would record *Cool Planet* at Cyberteknics, in addition to the Ricked Wicky records the following year. This is also where Pollard would record the all-on-his-own GBV album *Please Be Honest*. The studio features a ton of analogue gear, including an Electrodyne mixing console that used to reside at the famous Sigma Sound Studios in Philadelphia (which is where David Bowie recorded most of *Young Americans*).

Studio owner Mehaffey is a Dayton local who started playing music in 1953, as a session pianist for country artists. He sort of fell into owning the studio, and only later obtained his recording and engineering chops. Over the years, the studio's been home to sessions from all kinds of bands: funk, bluegrass, and a couple of local indie bands, such as Braniac.

In a 2015 article in the *Dayton Daily News*, written by none other than former GBV drummer Don Thrasher, Mehaffey said, 'A lot of musicians shoot themselves in the foot because they record at home. The sound is everything, but they spend way too much time on the computer trying to get things to sound right.'

While this may be true for some people, that's not at all Pollard's problem. But Mehaffey follows this up by adding, 'I'm not saying it's terrible, but there's a place right here in Dayton with a pro board and 2-inch tape recorder. As long as the band comes in here tight, I can knock out a whole album in a day.' That sounds more like Bob.

The cover for *Cool Planet* is effective, featuring a Pollard collage that, much like *Motivational Jumpsuit*, features a contemporary photograph—this time a picture of a store that had gone out of business—along with his usual vintage found art. The blue and pink of the top of the sleeve is also arresting. Matching pink shirts, with blue type, were sold on the subsequent tour.

The record's title comes from the fact that it was, according to the original release notes, 'Conceived during the sub-freezing Polar Vortex of 2014.' A polar vortex is basically when air from the north pole gets pushed south by a low-pressure system. Actually, there are two vortices, at the north and south poles, but you generally hear the term in the singular, meaning the vortex to the north (since that's the one that has an effect on the US). In the winter of 2013–14, huge swaths of Canada and America saw extremely cold weather, with the average temperature—across the US—sinking to seventeen degrees on January 6, 2014. Over two hundred million Americans were affected, and there were over a dozen deaths.

SIDE ONE

Track one: *'Authoritarian Zoo'*

Pollard's a bit out of tune on the verses, and the track doesn't get going until the chorus. But when it finally kicks In, the song sounds large and is a lot of fun. It's reminiscent of 'Mobility,' which would appear the following year as one of the first Ricked Wicky singles. One of the best things about the track is Kevin March's drumming, which sounds great; his fills add a lot.

Track two: *'Fast Crawl'*

The placement of this song as the second track is baffling, like when Pollard wanted to put 'Deathtrot And Warlock Riding A Rooster' as the second track on *Bee Thousand*. It kills any momentum the LP has gained from the first track. The lyrics are also standard fare. 'Have one for the road, big fall on your face' is not exactly parody, but it's certainly something we've heard before. And while 'fast crawl' is a clever oxymoron, it's not clever enough to save the song. *Pitchfork*'s Jason Heller, in his review of *Cool Planet*, said this track 'spoons out meandering sludge in unsavory lumps.' That captures the essence of this, and a few other tracks, on the album.

Track three: *'Psychotic Crush'*

The first Sprout song is a Bowie-esque ripper that's about as close as you can come to 'Ziggy Stardust' without putting on a unitard. But while it's a lot of fun, it's awfully short and feels a bit ramshackle. If Toby had made it a bit longer, and locked down the groove, it would have been a more effective song.

Track four: *'Costume Makes The Man'*

This is a gorgeous track that, while simple—it has just acoustic guitar, some droney church organ, and a bit of electric guitar at the end—is effective. Pollard sounds great, especially when he doubles his vocals. A couple of the tracks on this record have sloppy singing, but this one sounds great. It's also a fine example of how Bob creates so much melody on top of what are ordinary chord sequences, and the way he sings 'Killing the letter, I left' is downright magical. It's these little touches that transform what's a quiet, almost-folk song, to being something memorable. The title's also a clever variation on the phrase 'clothes make the man.' Pollard's implying that it's not how we dress that's important, but rather who we pretend to be that 'makes' or 'explains' us. 'Clothes make the man' has been around as a phrase for hundreds of years, going all the way back to the Middle Ages. Various writers have used some version of it in their work, from Shakespeare to Mark Twain, the latter quipping, 'Clothes make the man. Naked people have little or no influence on society.'

Track five: 'Hat Of Flames'

The *AV Club*'s Sean O'Neal wrote of this song that it 'feels most like it could have hailed from [the band's] heyday, 92 seconds of simple, razor-hewn pop about some mysterious, magical interloper coming through town in that titular hat. Guy Fieri, maybe?' I agree. If it had more tape hiss, and a snippet of another song at the beginning, I could see this being on one of the many EPs the band put out in 1994.

Track six: 'These Dooms'

The opening of this song is reminiscent of 'You Must Keep It Coming,' the B-side of the 'Everywhere With Helicopter' single. It's even linked with the theme of that song since, in it, Pollard asked, 'What's more important, the run or the finish?' Whereas here he snipes, 'You technically win the race.' It's also a bare song, with half being just Bob singing against an electric guitar. When the drums start, at a minute in, that's all that appears, so, even though the track gets a bit of life in its second section, it doesn't add up to much.

Track seven: 'Table At Fool's Tooth'

This short and punchy song was one of the singles from the record. It has a great Pollard title and sees Kevin March once again channeling Keith Moon with a whole lot of cymbal crashes. *PopMatters*' Matthew Fiander wrote that the track 'builds thick rock textures, back and forth between towering chords and rundown fills, but the stop-and-start song cuts off before it ever gets going.' The review also cites Bob's songs from the LP as being 'restless.' That seems an apt description since a whole lot of Pollard's tracks on *Cool Planet* disappear just as fast as they arrive, as if Bob was impatient to just get on to the next one rather than explore the possibilities of the one he's currently singing.

Track eight: *'All American Boy'*

This Tobin Sprout track is the record's longest, at 3:45. For the first two minutes it's a rocking track with piano and a lead guitar line that sees Toby singing and yelping like the last couple minutes of 'Hey Jude.' For a guy whose singing is usually barely above a whisper, it's a lot of fun to hear Sprout howl. The song's about the ability of rock music to offer an escape from a humdrum existence. But, of course, since this is GBV, you're going to need a little more than just music, so Toby pairs a rock tune with a stiff drink: 'I poured a shot into a paper cup, and washed down the tears as the Stones played.' Sprout's talking about the ability of rock'n'roll, and that 'special tune' that you love, to fill up your very soul. It's not just for fun, and it's not just loud; this stuff means something. What's also great about the song is that, two minutes in, we go from the end of 'Hey Jude' to the beginning of 'Let It Be.' All the instruments fall away until what we're left with is just Sprout singing and playing softly on the piano. He mostly repeats the first verse, except, this time around, he's tired and defeated. In the opening lines he was on his way 'to a better place,' whereas later his fate is 'sealed.'

Track nine: *'You Get Every Game'*

For the first minute of this two-minute song, Pollard does his usual lo-fi thing, singing nonsense over strums whose chords appear to have been chosen at random. But the last minute finds Tobin and Bob harmonizing over some droning keyboard and acoustic guitar. It's a fitting end to side one, though I can't say the whole song does much for the record.

SIDE TWO

Track one: *'Pan Swimmer'*

This is another great example of how a one-minute song can feel like a whole journey. That being said, I have no idea what it's about. The lyrics mention the Virgin Mary twice, and Pollard repeats 'looking at you' a bunch of times. I don't know what that all adds up to, but it sounds good. The song was played often during the tour that followed the release of the record, and with short tracks like this, you can easily see how GBV packs dozens upon dozens of songs into their marathon sets.

Track two: *'The Bone Church'*

This is a weird song that finds Tobin Sprout sounding more like Black Sabbath than his usual Beatles. It's built on another heavy riff, same as 'Psychotic Crush' from side one, except here it's slower and darker. The song's actually a co-write with Mitch Mitchell, who seems like he's learned a Sabbath riff or two in his time. It appears to be about fallen comrades, Sprout writing, in the opening lines, 'I am sad for my soldier friends, assuming this is last rights.' The 'bone church' of the title alludes to a place where these soldiers, if not being the site of their demise, will end up being their final resting place.

Later in the song, Tobin employs a Pollardian turn of phrase, mimicking both Bob's wordplay and his sometimes cynical outlook: 'Know your pieces of fate.' Pieces of eight used to be a form of currency. Made out of silver and originating out of Spain, pieces of eight were used all across the world. With Sprout's changing of the phrase to *pieces of fate*, he's acknowledging the erratic and often unfair nature of life. Who lives or dies, whether it's in war or peace, comes down to luck and the whims of fate. Tobin's narrator is the one standing in the bone church, while some of his fellow soldiers are buried in the soil, but it just as easily could have been the other way around. He's also, by citing a currency, saying that life—and death—is cheap.

Track three: *'Bad Love Is Easy To Do'*

PopMatters' Matthew Fiander wrote of this song, 'It's the band's most effortless pop song of the last four years, just pure hooks and perfect melodies, and Pollard and Sprout seem to delight in trading off through the track.' I agree that it's a fun track, although it's a bit thin. Kevin March's drums sound great, and he turns in a good performance, but it sounds like there's just one guitar, and the bass is either mixed so low or else there's no bass line at all. Lyrically, the song's subversive, since it turns a whole genre of pop music on its head: the love song. The charts are full of all kinds of tracks about romance and true love, but Pollard's having none of it. Here he's saying that 'bad love' is not only just as prevalent as good, or true love, but that it's 'easy to do.' I've compared Pollard, with his quick and cynical wit, more than once to Morrissey. This is another track that would fit right in—lyrically, anyway—on a Smiths record.

Track four: 'The No Doubters'

Even though Pollard's singing is flat in a few places on this slow song, March sounds great. With the lyrics, Bob's again making a hit of a political statement, writing that 'the no doubters are doers and shouters.' This brings to mind the famous Yeats line, 'The best lack all conviction, while the worst are filled with passionate intensity.' People who don't doubt, or who don't question their own beliefs or what's happening around them, are often—as Pollard says here—the ones who make the most noise. This can, in turn, end up causing the most trouble. Pollard's cynical side also shows here, since he offers no easy out from the situation, instead declaring, with resignation, 'It's always the same.'

Track five: 'Narrated By Paul'

This Tobin Sprout track is absolutely gorgeous. Like the second half of 'All American Boy,' the song finds Sprout channeling the Paul McCartney who wrote 'Hey Jude' and 'Let It Be.' The title, 'Narrated By Paul,' is probably a nod to McCartney. Tobin's obviously a fan of The Beatles, as is Bob. Sprout even has a much more overt Beatles reference on this record with the song 'Ticket To Hide.'

Track six: 'Cream Of Lung'

According to *Pitchfork*'s Jason Heller, 'Pollard barely shows up on "Cream Of Lung," a dull muddle that sounds as lively as if it were recorded while he brushed his teeth.' I agree. Even though the song picks up in the last thirty seconds, it's not enough to justify the first forty-five seconds, which sound like Pollard making up lyrics on the spot and not striking gold. For the record, Cream of Lung is Campbell's least popular soup.

Track seven: 'Males Of Wormwood Mars'

This is another track on which the band sounds like a three-piece. I can only hear one guitar, drums, and vocals. This isn't necessarily a bad thing, but it makes the song sound more like a demo than a finished song (although that line's always hard to find when it comes to GBV). The strides that the band had made on *Motivational Jumpsuit*, in terms of capturing their ferocious live sound—think of 'Planet Score'—have disappeared. I don't know if it's because they were in a new studio, or Mitch and Demos weren't around to add additional parts, but some of the rockier numbers here sound thin. The 'wormwood' of the title refers to an herb that is sometimes used for medical or, hundreds of years ago, magical purposes. It's also associated with the planet Mars, hence the 'Wormwood Mars' of the title. In a seventeenth-century handbook for physicians, wormwood is mentioned as being a cure for mice and rat bites, as well as for treating cholera, not to mention more arcane uses such as 'curing melancholy in old men, making covetous men splenetic,' and 'curing the right eye of a man and the left eye of a woman.'

Track eight: 'Ticket To Hide'

This is a bittersweet song, since it's quite possibly the last time Sprout will ever appear on a Guided By Voices LP. That's sad, since Toby was a large part of what made so many of GBV's greatest records great, especially the stuff from the early 90s. The title here is, of course, is a pun on The Beatles song 'Ticket To Ride,' which was a single from 1965. While that song was about the dissolution of a relationship, in this spare song Sprout's talking about a ticket to disappear from the world. It's about solitude, not heartbreak. Toward the end, Toby trades his acoustic guitar for an electric, repeating, 'It might get louder.' This ends up being ironic, since it never does get much louder. Instead, the song just fades out. It's a fitting way to say goodbye to the best foil Bob's ever had.

Track nine: 'Cool Planet'

This track is an absolute blast, and, even though the first twenty seconds are plain, when the song goes into the second section—Bob singing, 'In your strangled discontinuation, on the surface of the wall'—the song erupts. Even though I've compared some of Kevin March's performances to Keith Moon, here he's actually much more disciplined than Moon. His fills are precise, and he's right in the pocket. When, at a minute into the song, the instruments drop out and Pollard yells, 'Heroes do matter, insects do scatter,' I always get the chills. It's an absolutely fabulous moment. Toward the end of the song, as it begins to fade out, Pollard gives the LP's title a mention, crooning, 'It's a cool planet.'

22 PLEASE BE HONEST

two thousand and sixteen

This album marked the surprise return of Guided By Voices. Bob had shitcanned the band, and the name, in 2014 while they still had a dozen dates left on the *Cool Planet* tour. Pollard felt it had run its course, so he pulled the plug. He then spent 2015 making and releasing records, some of them as new bands. In just one year, Pollard put out a solo LP, *Faulty Superheroes*, as well as the Circus Devils album *Stomping Grounds*, along with three—count 'em, three—full-length LPs with his new side project, Ricked Wicky. Or rather, since GBV was no more, that was looking to be his main band. *Faulty Superheroes* would end up being the last solo record he'd make with longtime collaborator Todd Tobias. They would work on just one more Circus Devils record, 2017's *Laughs Last*. Tobias had been heavily involved in Bob's projects for a decade, working on dozens of Pollard albums and hundreds of songs.

When the fourth volume of GBV's *Suitcase* series, *Captain Kangaroo Won The War*, was released, it looked like it might be the last time the band's name would ever be used. But then, in 2016, Pollard announced that he was not only releasing a new Guided By Voices record but he was also playing all the instruments on the album. Mitch Mitchell and Greg Demos were no longer in the group, and neither, it seemed, was anyone else. This took people by surprise, and raised some eyebrows. It was like Paul McCartney calling *Ram* a Beatles record. At *Pitchfork*, Zoe Camp greeted the news by proclaiming, 'Guided By Voices are back … sort of.'

Confusing matters even more is that the GBV album came out just a month after Pollard's latest solo record, *Of Course You Are*. This prompted *Spin*'s Anna Gaca to write that this 'would seem to make [*Please Be Honest*] a solo record as well.' Why was one LP a solo album and the other a GBV record? Theories abounded, with *Stereogum*'s Tom Breihan surmising, 'Maybe he's reviving the name because the new songs fit the GBV tradition, or maybe he realizes that people care more when his old band's name is attached.' Pollard's admitted in the past that stuff released as GBV just sells more and gets more attention, so there's probably something to the theory.

What happened was that Bob had a batch of songs he liked and resolved to record them by playing everything himself. It's something he'd done before with GBV, around the time of *Vampire On Titus*. But this time, as he says, 'I came up with the notion that if I could pull it off and it wasn't too clunky, I would record it under the brand name Guided By Voices, which is really the flagship for all my projects. If not I was going to call it Teenage Guitar.'

I find two things interesting here. The first is that Bob acknowledges that GBV's a brand. In a Frankenstein's monster way, it's become bigger even than Bob, the man who brought it into the world. Because while Pollard doesn't need band members to be GBV, as he'd show on the next record, GBV doesn't even need *him*. After all, what makes 'Sudden Fiction' or 'High Five Hall Of Famers'—tracks on which Pollard doesn't appear at all—GBV songs, except that's what they're released or labeled as? The same goes for Tobin Sprout. What was the difference between a track Toby released as GBV versus on one of his solo records? Sometimes Sprout would even release the same song in a GBV version and a solo version.

The second thing that's interesting in Pollard's statement is that he admits that his previous work as Teenage Guitar was 'clunky.' I'm not a fan of those records, and it's simultaneously refreshing and frustrating to have Bob state that those LPs aren't of a high quality. It shows that he does have standards, that he can tell good work from bad. It also shows that he's willing to release a substandard record; he just won't call it GBV.

Please Be Honest was recorded at his new favorite location, Cyberteknics in Dayton. Working with studio owner and engineer Phil Mehaffey to set up various stations around the studio with different instruments, Pollard would just move from station to station, playing whatever was needed. The LP was also recorded in sequence, completing and mixing, usually, one song a day. Some days, Pollard recorded three songs. The LP was done in a week, at which point, Bob said, 'I thought it worked and sounded like a GBV album so that's what it is.'

While plenty of people, and publications, were skeptical about the LP, plenty were also won over by what's actually a decent record. As the *AV Club*'s John Hugar wrote, 'It's understandable to be a bit suspicious here, as this could just be an excuse for Pollard to release an album under the Guided By Voices moniker and attain more publicity in the process. But after listening to the album, it's hard not to agree with him. This album has all the elements of old-school GBV.' He even gave the LP a B+, a full grade higher than *Motivational Jumpsuit*.

PopMatters agreed with that general sentiment, with Magdalen Jenne writing, 'Regardless of lineup, GBV does have an aesthetic they stick to pretty closely.' However, by giving the album a four out of ten, she showed that she didn't think much of the aesthetic. The review ends, 'If you're deeply invested in the Guided By Voices catalogue this record won't disappoint you. You're getting exactly what they're selling.'

The collage that Pollard chose to be part of the cover is interesting. The majority of the image is taken up with a black-and-white photograph of the inside of a prison. A huge door is open, and at the opening to a cluster of cells stands a solitary figure, a man. At the end of this passageway is the rune, GBV's quasi logo. This could be read as a statement on both the solo nature of the record (Bob as a one-man band) as well as—since it was becoming obvious that the legacy of Guided By Voices was something he was never going to escape—that Pollard was about to enter, well, prison. GBV had become an albatross around his neck, and he was now thinking of the band as a literal jail cell (one that he was willingly placing himself inside of).

A color insert, above the prison photo, shows a bunch of businessmen. Two of them, in the foreground, are shaking hands. It's the kind of schmoozy glad-handing and deal-making that Pink Floyd satirized with their cover for *Wish You Were Here*, where one of the guys shaking hands is on fire. Was Pollard similarly commenting on the decision, or deal, he'd made when he revived GBV? Was bringing back the 'band' just a cynical business transaction? Did

Bob feel conflicted, or, at the very least, ambivalent, about what he was doing? A photo of shopping carts on the inside sleeve is another acknowledgment that GBV was now just another product, the same as toothpaste, something to be bought and paid for.

While Bob may have played all the instruments on the LP, for the subsequent tour he put together his usual and preferred five-piece-band setup: two guitars, bass, and drums, with him on vocals.

On bass he drafted in Mark Shue. Shue, who's originally from Virginia but now lives in Brooklyn, was a veteran of the band The Library Is On Fire, founded by Ohio native Steve Five in 2008. In a delicious act of foreshadowing, Mark and Steve met at a Robert Pollard art opening in New York. Also, the band's first LP was recorded by longtime Pollard collaborator Todd Tobias at Waterloo Sound back in Ohio. That Shue contributed songs to the group, and had started off playing guitar, meant that he was a great addition to the new GBV lineup. He would also end up as the youngest guy in the group, being nearly half Bob's age—something that Pollard seems to delight in pointing out while onstage.

Another new member was Bobby Bare Jr. Bare's father is a country-music singer and songwriter with a long career and a number of hits on the country and pop charts in the 60s and 70s. Bare Jr.—when he was just eight years old—even joined his dad on one of his biggest songs, the Grammy-nominated 'What If.' The song is a super-sweet and touching discussion between a father and son, the younger asking the older a series of 'what if' questions, such as, 'What if the sun stopped shining?' It's a great conceit since, as anyone with young kids knows, they never tire of asking questions. While it's a fun and good-natured song, the climax is devastating, as the son asks, 'What if I stopped loving you, what would happen then?' The father answers that it would be the end of his world. In its own way, it's just as emotional as 'Father And Son' by Cat Stevens, or Harry Chapin's 'Cat's In The Cradle.' Because Bare Jr. was surrounded by his dad's music, not to mention was part of show business at such an early age—he was also on *Hee Haw* as a kid—it's natural that he, too, would become a musician and songwriter. Whether solo, recording under his own name, or with his band, Young Criminals' Starvation League, he's released half a dozen records, starting in 1998, with *Boo-tay*. He was even, in 2015, the subject of a full-length documentary entitled *Don't Follow Me, I'm Lost*. Bare Jr.'s band opened for GBV on the *Cool Planet* tour, and, once the tour ended, Bare Jr began hanging out with Pollard and his wife. In terms of joining GBV, Bare Jr. says, 'I cried when he asked me.'

Bob brought back Kevin March on drums. March had recently played on all three of the Ricked Wicky records from the year before, so asking him to re-join a rejuvenated GBV made perfect sense. He's also a great drummer and, as we'd find out on *August By Cake*, a talented singer and songwriter in his own right.

An additional holdover from Ricked Wicky was Nick Mitchell. Mitchell had played guitar in the 2015 side project, as well as contributing songs. Mitchell had also played all the instruments on and produced Pollard's most recent solo record around this time, *Of Course You Are*, taking over those duties from longtime collaborator Todd Tobias. Mitchell's a Dayton local (and is not related to former GBV guitarist Mitch Mitchell). For over two decades, he's played in a band called Skeptical Cats, described by the website Dayton.com as 'one of the longest running and most established bands in the Midwest.' Mitchell's also similar to Pollard in that he has two kids, has done some teaching, and, for years, had a day job while trying to write songs and play shows in his free time. Pollard described Mitchell to *Premier Guitar* as 'a really good player,' adding that 'he can play almost any song.' Bob went so far as to compare Mitchell to longtime sideman Doug Gillard. Since Nick and Bob had just made four records together, inviting him to join Guided By Voices made sense.

At first, everything went great. Kevin and Mark flew in from the East Coast, and Bobby flew up from Nashville. The band practiced at Nick's house. As Mitchell told me, 'At those rehearsals, we played so loud and powerfully that my wife Pam had to remove the glass from the coffee table in the upper level of our house to keep it from rattling off and shattering on the floor!'

The newly formed lineup now had to learn all the songs. 'Bob would show up at the rehearsals with his set list written out on a large slab of cardboard, which he would prop up against the wall where we could all see it,' says Mitchell. 'In fact, the very first picture of all of us, which was used as the promo picture when the tour was announced, was in my garage next to the studio/rehearsal space, and you can see Bob holding a big piece of cardboard, cryptically turned away from the camera. That was the set list.'

The first leg of the tour, taking the group from Tennessee to Illinois, passed without incident. Everyone seemed to be enjoying themselves. However, after the second phase of shows—which kicked off with a hometown gig in Dayton, their first in four years—progressed throughout the Eastern Seaboard, Mitchell began to grow restless. Things came to a head during a concert that summer at the Grog Shop in Cleveland. 'The time away from our children and our (many) dogs, combined with some frustrations between myself and a couple of people involved with the tour, showed on my face, and affected my attitude and performance.' Pollard could tell Mitchell wasn't happy, and this didn't make *him* happy. 'Bob rightfully called me on it after our set, and that was the end of my tenure on the tour.'

Plenty of performers have come and gone from the band, but Nick's departure produced a particularly difficult situation. GBV were booked to play a festival in Cincinnati the very next day, and yet they were now down a guitar player. Would they cancel? Play as a four-piece? What Bob did is turn to the guy he'd compared Mitchell to: Doug Gillard. Bringing Doug back into the band made perfect sense. He knew the songs, he'd been present for big chunks of the band's best work, and he'd been a great collaborator with Pollard on projects such as Lifeguards and the recent ESP Ohio project. Gillard was also friendly with Mark Shue, having shared bills in New York with The Library Is On Fire (Shue had even played in Doug's solo band).

The only problem was that GBV were in Ohio and Gillard was in New York. Plus, when Bob initially reached out, Doug was asleep. 'I got calls and texts very late one night, but didn't see the messages until morning.' Once Doug and Bob spoke, Gillard got onto a plane and made it to Ohio in time to learn a few new songs at the band's hotel. Gillard saved the day. GBV would not have to perform a free-form jazz exploration in front of a festival crowd. After the show, Pollard asked Gillard to re-join the group, and Doug accepted. He's been back in the band ever since. It was a turn of events that even Mitchell, whose ouster paved the way for Gillard's return, welcomed. As he told me, 'Doug is a sweetheart of a guy, and a phenomenal player and writer. The world is right when he is standing stage left next to Bob. And I'm very grateful to Bob for letting me play a small part in his incomparable musical legacy, and we remain good friends to this day.'

SIDE ONE

Track one: *'My Zodiac Companion'*

Since I wasn't a fan of the Teenage Guitar records, I wasn't looking forward to the new Guided By Voices LP being basically a third Teenage Guitar album. This does indeed get off to a rough start with a flat vocal. But the guitar sounds good, and there's some synth, and, when the drums finally come crashing in, it sounds huge. Filmmaker Mike Postalakis almost made a video for the track. It would have featured a couple, seen via split screen, on the last day of their relationship. Chloë Sevigny would have played one-half of the couple, but when the guy who was asked to play the other half—a prominent podcaster— balked at appearing, the video was scrapped.

Track two: *'Kid On A Ladder'*

The fact that this song is built around a drum machine makes me happy. Imagining Pollard—this classic-rock guy with an aversion to technology— programming beats is just too fun. It's a good track, with some distorted guitar and a loping bass line. It doesn't hew to any sort of structure—it's just Bob singing verses throughout—but it sounds good. It's a great example of Pollard creating vocal melodies on top of chord structures. In terms of what those lyrics actually *mean*, Raj Dayal of the website *Pretty Much Amazing* wrote, 'Is it about our current state of affairs? The choices faced by today's youth? Maybe. I'm not sure deciphering Pollard's beguiling avant-garde poetry speaks to how beautiful it often is.' I agree with that. I like to listen to it, and that's enough.

Track three: *'Come On Mr. Christian'*

The instrumentation on this slower song is interesting. The electric guitar's playing single notes rather than chords, and Bob's actually playing a beat on the drums. There's also some keyboard synth. He's trying to give the songs color, and for the most part, he succeeds. The song also has an outro with some found sound—I don't know if it's Pollard speaking, or a clip from a movie—but it's slowed down and sounds trippy, like John Lennon saying 'Cranberry sauce' at the end of 'Strawberry Fields Forever.' My guess is the song's about *Mutiny On The Bounty*, with Pollard singing from Captain Bligh's point of view and addressing the man leading the mutiny, Fletcher

Christian. The references to drinking from a jug and a 'coward's salute' seem to reinforce this, not to mention the pun that Bob would be making in the final line by employing the phrase 'Shape up or ship out.' The original novel and subsequent film versions of *Mutiny On The Bounty* were based on actual events that occurred in 1789. A popular movie, with Marlon Brando as Christian, came out in 1962.

Track four: *'The Grasshopper Eaters'*

The record comes to a complete standstill with this annoyingly tuneless track. Not helping matters is that it's the record's longest (it's only about three and a half minutes, but it seems to go on forever). There are some decent acoustic guitar phrases, but everything is obscured if not just plain drowned out by what sounds like a plumber working on the studio's toilet while Bob howls nonsense in the background. It's Pollard at his most bewildering and, for me, frustrating. However, Ryan Reisert of the online zine *Treble* liked the song, calling it a 'highlight' that 'manages to marry the classic lo-fi aesthetic with one of those great Pollard melodies.'

Track five: *'Glittering Parliaments'*

The record gets back on track with this fast-paced song, which sounds the most like 'GBV.' Because, while I like 'Kid On A Ladder,' that feels more like a Pollard solo track than anything I've heard on a Guided By Voices album. Whereas this one has a flow and feeling, with a discernible bass line and a guitar that howls feedback, as well as a steady backbeat. It's one of the strongest tracks on the LP, and, if the record had gone from 'Come On Mr. Christian' right to this, it would have been better.

Track six: *'The Caterpillar Workforce'*

There were grasshoppers two songs ago, and now we have caterpillars. Bookworms also get a shout-out. It's decent, with some pleasant guitars and a droney organ, but there's not much to it; it's barely a minute and a half long, and it feels like a sketch. Which is a shame, since there are some impressive touches in it that I would have loved to see fleshed out. Like when Pollard sings, forty seconds in, 'At Ichabod Wood,' over a chiming acoustic guitar, it sounds great. But as soon as that moment arrives, it disappears, and it's on to the next song. Ichabod Wood is probably not a place but a person's name. The website findagrave.com lists an Ichabod Wood from New York who died in 1817 and another who lived in Massachusetts and died in 1798. Ichabod, while having recently fallen out of favor as a first name, must have been prevalent in the nineteenth and eighteenth centuries. The protagonist of Washington Irving's *The Legend Of Sleepy Hollow* was named Ichabod Crane.

Track seven: *'Sad Baby Eyes'*

This is the album's shortest song, at just thirty-five seconds. It was, however, originally part of a much larger suite called 'Peep Soul.' Pollard intended this to be a sequel to both his 2004 song 'Windows Of My World' and one of the last songs on *Bee Thousand*, 'Peep Hole.' The ambitious track—which Bob had been tinkering with on and off since the 80s—would have traced the life of a woman named Annabelle Gin Blossom Cartwheel, a spiritual sister to the spinster we met in 'The Best Of Jill Hives.' 'Peep Soul' would have given the listener a view into her existence, showing us pivotal moments of her life, as she experienced them, through the portals of her eyes.

Pollard had sketched out four more songs to go with this idea, among them, 'Curious Teenage Iris' and 'AARP Retina Blues.' At least one of those tracks had been considered for all three of the second round of Matador albums, but was always cut at the last minute. Bob tried these songs again for the reunion records, but he could never get the sound right. He ultimately scrapped the 'Peep Soul' idea and has so far released just this track, 'Sad Baby Eyes,' which would have been the first song in the suite, introducing us to the 'Annabelle Cartwheel' character just after she was born.

Actually, I'm lying. I have no idea what's going on with the track, or what led to it, except that Bob had a beer and someone pressed 'record' and afterward they all said, 'Hey, let's put that on the album!'

Track eight: *'The Quickers Arrive'*

This bare song—it's mostly just Bob and an electric guitar—is another one of the longer tracks on the record. Late in the tune there are some other guitar parts, including some bass that sounds almost like Joy Division, but it's not enough to keep this from feeling like a sketch or a demo. The *AV Club*'s John Hugar actually called this the record's 'strongest track,' writing that, even though 'we don't quite know who "the quickers" are, the song creates a vibe of impending fear,' adding that 'it feels as though the quickers are not literal monsters, but our own fears and anxieties.' That gets back to the idea of the 'fantasy creeps' found in an earlier GBV song—those hopes and dreams that 'hound' us and won't let us alone.

I also think that 'Quickers' could be a Pollardian twist on the religious sect the Quakers, who already got a shout-out in the earlier song 'The Grasshopper Eaters.' That would fit with some of the other eighteenth- and seventeenth-century references sprinkled throughout this album, in addition to other religious imagery: 'Please Be Honest' mentions a 'priest,' there's 'praying' in 'Defeatists' Lament,' and 'My Zodiac Companion' name-checks 'Magdalene,' which might be a reference to Jesus's disciple Mary Magdalene. That being said, since Quakers are teetotalers, I doubt Pollard's looking forward to their arrival anytime soon.

SIDE TWO

Track one: 'Hotel X (Big Soap)'

This lo-fi three-chord stomper starts off like a slower 'Planet Score.' The bass line's also reminiscent of 'Lethargy' off *Propeller*. At a minute and a half in, the song changes and gets a bit more acoustic. When Pollard sings, 'The trees outside are heavy with acorns, naked swimmers faking sleep,' it sounds good, except the guitar is sloppy. *Pitchfork*'s John S. W. MacDonald wrote of the track, 'And while musicianship is never the point with GBV, many of these tunes, like the lurching, proggy "Hotel X (Big Soap)," would have benefited from a bit more finesse. Too many of the drum and guitar tracks sound like they're being played with a hammer.' The song ends with a snippet of a marching band, which the liner notes credit to the 'Vandercook Lake Senior High School Band, under the direction of Arnold Kummerow.' The school's in Michigan, and Kummerow was the band director there for a long time, starting in 1968. He retired in 2012, at the age of sixty-seven.

BELOW *Daredevil Stamp*
Collector collects all the
Do The Collapse B-sides,
and includes the demo for
'Hold On Hope.'

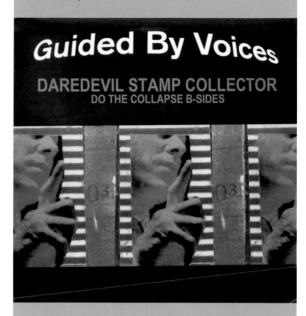

Guided By Voices
DAREDEVIL STAMP COLLECTOR
DO THE COLLAPSE B-SIDES

ABOVE To celebrate the
release of 1999's *Do The
Collapse*, TVT produced
promotional beer coasters.

RIGHT A promo copy of the
'Hold On Hope' single
containing the radio mix
that was ultimately nixed
by the band.

Guided By Voices
Hold On Hope

1. Ric Ocasek Radio Mix 3:31
2. Album Version 3:31
3. Jack Joseph-Puig Radio Mix* 3:40
4. Call Out Hook

From the album
Do The Collapse

Guided By Voices

Produced by Ric Ocasek
*additional production and mix by Jack Joseph-Puig

GUIDED BY VOICES
ISOLATION DRILLS

RIGHT The inspiration for 2001's *Isolation Drills* came from the 1974 album *Secret Treaties* by Blue Öyster Cult.

BLUE ÖYSTER CULT
SECRET TREATIES

OPPOSITE A press photo of the band around the time of the *Isolation Drills* tour. *Left to right* Doug Gillard, Tim Tobias, Jon McCann, Robert Pollard, Nate Farley.

GUIDED BY VOICES
LEAVING SOON

AUGUST 24TH

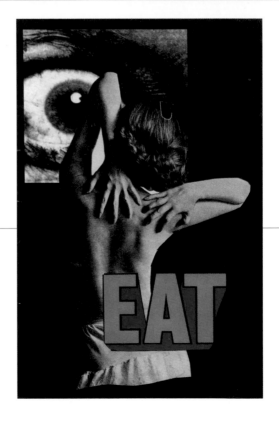

ABOVE After Bob declared that 2004's *Half Smiles Of The Decomposed* would be GBV's final record, the album's promotional campaign turned into a goodbye for the band.

RIGHT The first issue of Bob's literary magazine *EAT* made its appearance in 2003.

LEFT Demo versions of most of the songs from 2003's *Earthquake Glue* were released the following year as *Edison's Demos*.

BELOW In 2010, the so-called 'classic' lineup—Tobin Sprout, Greg Demos, Robert Pollard, Kevin Fennell, and Mitch Mitchell—reformed and hit the road. (Photo by Chris McKay/WireImage)

**GUIDED BY VOICES
PLEASE BE HONEST**

LEFT After disbanding during the *Cool Planet* tour, Guided By Voices were resurrected for 2016's *Please Be Honest*. The artwork—a man entering GBV jail—perhaps gives a clue to Pollard's feelings about the band being turned into an inescapable brand.

MAGNETIC FIELDS | IMELDA MAY | SPOON

MAGNET

REAL MUSIC ALTERNATIVE

GUIDED BY VOICES

ABOVE Bob on the cover of *Magnet* in 2017. The issue featured an interview between Pollard and punk legend Mike Watt.

EAT 15 - (DISLODGE) THE IMMORTAL ORANGEMEN

INCLUDES SIX SONG 7" ONE-SIDED EP

LEFT *EAT 15: (Dislodge) The Immortal Orangemen* came with a one-sided seven-inch and featured the artwork for *Sweating The Plague* and the front and backs of *Warp & Woof* and 2020's *Surrender Your Poppy Field.*

STREET PARTY · MOTOR · VERY SECOND · WILD
HOLY RHYTHM · NOW TO WAR · MY SON COOL · IRONMEN
CIGARETTE · JANE · TREE · THIMBLE
AS WE GO UP · EGO CENTRAL · BURY THE MOUSE · FAIR TOUCHING
DEAD LIQUOR · COOL JEWELS · ROBOT BOY · WRESTLING
HONS THE BEARD · LARGE HEARTED · ZODIAC · BLUE JAY
DOWNER · COBBLER · WEED KING · TEENAGE FBI
CUT OUT · BARCELONA · LIAR'S TALE · TROPICAL ROBOTS
SOME DRILLING · EXIT FLAGGER · YR LIGHTS · HEAVY
TWILIGHT · SHE WANTS · WRONG TURN · YOU OWN
END IT w/LIGHT · DRINKER'S PEACE · DOG SURPRISE · GOLD HEART
CHARMLESS · SPACE GUN · DEMONS ARE REAL · HUGS
RALLY BOYS · PLEASE BE HONEST · OVERSTOCK · SKILLS
SHOCKER · UNFUN GLITZ · CHEAP BUTTONS · TOWN OF MIRRORS
STRONG LION · YOURS TO KEEP · TIME REMAINS · PIMPLE ZOO
YOUR CRICKET · ECHOS MYRON · PEEP HOLE · PRICKS
SEE MY FIELD · WEST COAST RELIGION · MATTER EATER · SCIENTIST
CHASING HEATHER · AND I DON'T · IMMORTALS · DON'T STOP
10TH CENT · JILL HIVES · LITTLE LINES · GLAD GIRLS
SALTY · RAINCLOUD · HEY AARDVARK
HOT FREAKS · WHISKY SHIPS · SOLDIER
GOOD MORNING · CLOSER YOU ARE · LAKE
STEP OF THE WAVE · JAM WARSONG · THINGS
HUDSON RAKE · LITTLEST LEAGUE · HUNTING KNIFE
MY ANGEL · CHOKING TARA · COLD COLD
TRACTOR · COHESIVE · COMING BACK
KING 007 · LETHARGY

GBV NYE 2020

RECKATHON PRESENTS
A POLLARDIAN EXPOSITION
IN
DAYTON, OHIO.

3 DAYS OF BOB

heedfest X

AUGUST 30 · SEPT 1

ABOVE The setlist for the band's final show of 2019, on New Year's Eve, featured a whopping one hundred songs. (Courtesy of Matthew L. Leclaire)

LEFT The poster for Heedfest 10, designed by David Van McAleer, was an homage to Woodstock.

ABOVE The 'new classic' lineup
(*left to right* Bobby Bare Jr.,
Robert Pollard, Mark Shue, Kevin
March, Doug Gillard) onstage
at the Teragram Ballroom in Los
Angeles on January 31, 2019.
(Photo by Terrence McClusky)

Track two: *'I Think A Telescope'*

This is one of the most successful tracks on the record. It's just Bob singing against guitar, but it sounds big. There's even an impressive solo toward the end that shows how Bob can get by okay without Doug Gillard. Also, if you listen with headphones, you can hear the click track, or a metronome, in the background.

Track three: *'Please Be Honest'*

This is one of the record's best tracks, with Pollard hitting that *Vampire On Titus / Propeller* vibe. His singing's good, it sounds full with guitar and drums, and, unlike a lot of the other songs on the LP, it doesn't seem like a sketch or a demo. *Pitchfork* praised the tune for its seemingly lyrical clarity. 'Refreshingly, the song touches on a real-world subject (Pollard's attempt to get someone to level with him) rather than the usual carnival of GBV absurdities—the "cucumber guns," "shriveled artichokes," and "glittering parliaments"—that populate the rest of the album.'

Track four: *'Nightmare Jamboree'*

It's amazing that this song was recorded in a studio, because it sounds just awful. Anybody singing into a cheap laptop would sound better than this. I guess Bob wants it to sound this way; he figures this is the 'GBV aesthetic.' Even though I love some of the lo-fi stuff, I always figured that the poor sound quality was the side effect of the process instead of the main attraction, which it seems to be here. Either way, there's nothing coherent enough in the lyrics, or the melody, to make me enjoy this.

Track five: *'Unfinished Business'*

The drum machine is back on this short song, which has an ironic title for a guy with a hundred full-length LPs under his belt—he's not someone you would expect to have any 'unfinished business.' Yet a whole lot of songs on those records were recorded in a way that make them seem or feel 'unfinished.' Like, basically, half the tracks on this LP. This gets back to the first part of the argument I made when talking about Bob's prolific nature: that he views songwriting as an athletic versus artistic pursuit. As he writes in this song, 'I won't know all the words, but I'll finish what I started.' What's important isn't necessarily the finished product, it's a matter of just getting out there and doing it.

Track six: *'Defeatists' Lament'*

In this spare song of just acoustic guitar and piano, Pollard reminisces about his jock past, lamenting that there will be 'no more shots in the arm' and 'no more comebacks.' Continuing the sporting analogy I talked about in the last song, Bob seems to be saying here that you lose if you don't try. That's the lament of the defeatist. If your attitude is, 'Well, I'm going to lose,' then you've already lost. Whereas Bob sees glory in merely participating, in getting out there and giving it your all.

Track seven: *'Eye Shop Heaven'*

This song takes a while to get going—the drums don't enter for almost a minute—but, when it finally does, it's not bad. It has a strong melody and full-band sound, and, since the LP contains more than a few half-baked and just plain awful tunes, it's good that the record goes out on this high note.

23 AUGUST BY CAKE

two thousand and seventeen

uided By Voices, with their first of two records from 2017, finally partook in that most hallowed of rock'n'roll traditions: the double record. While previous GBV albums like *Alien Lanes* and *Bee Thousand* had been compared to crazy, quilt-like records such as *The White Album*—sprawling double LPs that cover a dozen different styles in twice as many songs—here GBV finally delivered the real thing: thirty-two tracks, clocking in at an hour and eleven minutes. It's the band's longest album, pushing fifteen minutes past the fifty-five-minute running time of the twenty-four-track *Under The Bushes Under The Stars.*

As a format, the double LP stretches back to the 50s, and releases such as a Carnegie Hall concert by big band leader Bennie Goodman. In terms of the rock'n'roll era, and the double record as an original, artistic statement, most people think that Bob Dylan's *Blonde On Blonde* was the first double album. The first double LP released by a rock band was *Freak Out* by Frank Zappa's band The Mothers Of Invention. *Freak Out*, which was also the group's debut, beat *Blonde On Blonde* to market by about a week. *Rolling Stone* called the appearance of these records 'a historic moment.' Because while The Beatles, along with Dylan, had proved the artistic value of the album—they were no longer just one or two hit songs along with a bunch of filler—the double LP allowed artists not only to express themselves over a large number of songs but also to write longer songs (think of Dylan's eleven-minute 'Sad-Eyed Lady Of The Lowlands'). While this would lead, in the 70s, to prog-rock excess—

with bands having long jams or 'song suites' that took up an entire side of a record—in most cases, double LPs just meant a whole lot of songs. That was not always a good thing.

In an article for the *Daily Telegraph* looking at the reissue of a double album by Led Zeppelin, Neil McCormick wrote that 'doubles too often prove to be acts of creative hubris exposing the limitations of an artist's ability, an egoistic failure to comprehend that not every single note they play deserves to be heard.' He summed up the problem with most of these releases by asking, 'What do most double albums lack? An editor.' Pollard's been accused on numerous occasions of needing an editor, and yet I don't at all feel that *August By Cake* suffers from having too many songs. Whereas I would have gladly cut three or four tracks from each of the reunion records, and I advocated in my *Alien Lanes* chapter for removing about half of the album's songs, here—astonishingly—all of it works. It could have been—given some of Pollard's worst propensities—indulgent, or half-baked, or just plain bad, but *August By Cake* is none of those things. Instead, it's an absolutely kickass record.

How did GBV pull this off? The answer's simple: Bob had put together a powerful new band, and each of the members was a talented songwriter in their own right. Whether this was part of his plan all along, Pollard was shrewd in the construction of the group, since each of the members could sing and had fronted bands or contributed songs to prior groups. In this way, at least for *August By Cake*, GBV became like The New Pornographers, an indie-rock supergroup consisting of a number of talented songwriters, with each of them taking turns at the mic. Not that Pollard ever meant for that to happen. 'It was initially just a batch of songs for a new album but at some point,' Doug Gillard said, 'Bob decided it should be a double album and we set out to do that.'

'I originally intended for it to be a single album,' Bob said. 'I had seventeen songs ready to record in New York with the band, but then I recorded six songs at a studio in Dayton that I really liked, so then I had too many songs for a single album and not enough for a double album. I asked each band member to write and record two songs each, which they did, and they were all really good songs. So that's what made it work.'

The other guys only had a few days to record and, in some cases, write their songs. Bobby Bare Jr.'s 'High Five Hall Of Famers' was written 'on the spot,' since Bob wanted the song almost immediately. Such a short deadline meant that the band members recorded their own songs by themselves. 'We didn't plan it this way,' said Gillard, 'but each one of us plays drums on our songs. [Bassist Mark] Shue played drums on his songs. Bobby Bare played drums on his. Myself on mine. We all pretty much did everything on our own songs. So it's a very diverse record that way.'

It's the strength of that diversity that goes a long way toward making this such an amazing record. I've said in prior chapters that, as much as I love Bob's songs, I've also appreciated when Tobin Sprout's spritely tracks were interspersed with Bob's heavier material. Here there are *five* different voices in the mix, not just two. That's not to say that Pollard's not contributing a lot of songs too. Bob wrote twenty-two songs for *August By Cake*, and almost all of them are good.

Another secret weapon of the group, and something that's greatly contributed to the success of this and the rest of the LPs covered in this book, has been the addition of Travis Harrison as engineer. Harrison was already a GBV super-fan—something he admitted to Doug Gillard when Travis's band at the time, The Unsacred Hearts, played with Doug's band at Pianos in New York City. They kept in touch, and Harrison later asked Gillard about Lifeguards, the Pollard/Gillard side project from 2003. Gillard and Bob were both open to doing another album if a label was interested in releasing it. Travis told them, 'I have a studio, a label, the [recording] skillset, and I'm a huge fan. Let's do this!' Travis not only engineered and released 2011's *Waving At The Astronauts* but also played drums on five of the songs. Harrison's studio, Serious Business (also the name of his label), was founded by Travis along with his friend Andy Ross, the guitar player in OK Go.

Pollard worked again with Harrison on 2016's ESP Ohio album *Starting Point Of The Royal Cyclopean*. Once again, Harrison engineered and played drums. With Doug Gillard on guitar, along with Mark Shue on bass, you can see the new GBV lineup beginning to take shape.

Something else that made *August By Cake* special was that it was Pollard's one-hundredth studio record. Rockathon celebrated this milestone by releasing a handsome hardcover book, *100*, which reproduced all hundred sleeves, front and back. It's a super-solid package, and a must for any fan.

After the somewhat-curious album *Please Be Honest*—which confused critics and fans alike, who wondered whether it was a GBV record or just a solo LP in disguise—*August By Cake* received mostly enthusiastic reviews. Critics were glad to see the band back in action, and operating at full force.

Author Nicholas Carr wrote on his blog *Rough Type* that '*August By Cake* is the most approachable Guided by Voices record since 2001's *Isolation Drills*, the most relaxed since 1995's *Alien Lanes*, and the most topical ever. Robert Pollard once divided humanity into two camps: Sad Clowns and Happy Motherfuckers. He was, he confessed, in the former category, but he envied those in the latter. *August By Cake* is a Happy Motherfucker record, but it's shot through with a Sad Clown sensibility.'

And while *PopMatters*' Dave Heaton declared that the album had fallen short of becoming the 'crown jewel of Pollard's career,' describing it as 'more like a chest overflowing with strange baubles, memories, and mysteries,' he also noted that the LP contained many 'brilliant, beautiful moments.' The *AV Club* gave the record a B, reviewer Katie Rife stating that 'the music barely hangs together at times, but the potential for the roller-coaster to go flying off the tracks is, as always, part of the fun.' *Under The Radar*'s Aug Stone, giving it an 8 out of 10, proclaimed that 'the album is so strong that it's possible had this been released instead of *Bee Thousand* at the time, it would've had the same impact.'

A curious thing about the LP is that no singles were issued either before or after it was released. Even though each of the reunion records from just a few years prior saw multiple singles—*Motivational Jumpsuit* alone had five—*August By Cake*, the same as *Please Be Honest*, stood alone as an album.

A video was made for one of the LP's thirty-two tracks, with 'Planet Score' and 'Bad Love Is Easy To Do' director Mike Postalakis asked back to direct his third GBV video (and a fourth overall for Pollard, since he also directed the clip for Ricked Wicky's 'Poor Substitute'). The video for opening track 'Five Degrees On The Inside' saw Postalakis take a more documentary approach. He shot in and around Dayton, re-creating various iconic shots from *Watch Me Jumpstart*. Footage was also shot at Rockathon, with Postalakis and pal Kyle Sowash (from the fine group The Kyle Sowashes), holding up various bits of Pollard merchandise. It's a great clip, serving as a wonderful visual postcard of Dayton.

The album's cover was the first since *Sandbox* to feature an original photo, and the first since the TVT releases to be *just* a photograph (rather than some sort of Pollard collage). The cover star was new bassist Mark Shue. Shue's drinking a beer, using the 'Calgarian method,' which is something Pollard came up with after a show in Calgary. There, he said to the band—taking a sip using both hands and holding the neck of the bottle with scissored fingers, 'Man, I bet this is the official method of drinking beer in Calgary.' It caught on as an in-joke and, over the next couple of months, they'd send photos to each other of themselves employing the 'Calgarian method.' The shot that became the LP's cover was taken by a friend of Shue's named Erin Weckerle, an accomplished visual artist from New York. She and Mark were having dinner at a Vietnamese restaurant in Brooklyn when he requested she snap a picture with her iPhone of him drinking via the 'Calgarian method.' Mark sent the photo to Bob who, just a few days later, decided to use it for the cover of the album.

SIDE ONE

Track one: *'Five Degrees On The Inside'*

Preceding the song is a bit of spoken word by Bob, where he announces, 'Ladies and gentlemen, I present to you, *August By Cake*.' Author Nicholas Carr describes this as a 'circus barker's come-on. A brassy fanfare. The curtain rises, and the show begins.' There are other circus references on the record, for example the tracks 'Upon The Circus Bus,' 'Circus Day Holdout,' and 'Amusement Park Is Over.' References like this can be found throughout GBV; art for the early LP *Same Place The Fly Got Smashed* is rife with imagery of clowns and the big top. *PopMatters'* Dave Heaton tied the song to another record, though, likening 'Five Degrees on the Inside' to 'a song that also has a bit of a regal progression to it, in a *Sgt. Peppers* way.' Much as the opening track on that seminal Beatles album invited the listener to sit back and 'enjoy the show,' Pollard's here doing something similar. The trumpet was played by Dennis Cronin, a New York City–based musician who also played on the ESP Ohio record. Pollard and the rest of the guys sound great on the track. There's a striking bass line, a melodic twin guitar attack, and the drums sound amazing. There are even some handclaps, and a very clever line from Bob: 'The sweet spot bled out to stain your life.'

Track two: 'Generox Gray®'

After the fast tempo of the opening song we get this slower, down-tempo track. This is reminiscent of another great double record, *The White Album*, which opened with the blistering 'Back In The USSR' and then followed it with the slower 'Dear Prudence.' It's also a bit more lo-fi than a lot of the tracks on the record, but it still sounds good. It actually reminds me, sound-wise, of 'Pencil Rain' by They Might Be Giants. Lyrically, the track seems to be a commercial for a make-believe product, something called Generox Gray, which can help you, as Bob writes, 'Complete the transition on your most sensational day.' This is the Pollard of 'Useless Inventions,' in which he decried mindless consumerism. Here, he's saying that you not only buy this thing but 'take the oath.' It's more than a product; it's a way of life.

Track three: 'When We All Hold Hands At The End Of The World'

This track, a reworking of 'Home By Ten,' which appeared in a much faster version on *Suitcase 2*, shows what a transitional record this is for the band. Even though Pollard had put together this amazing group of talented musicians, they wouldn't begin appearing on every track until the next LP. Instead, *August By Cake* featured some full-band stuff, some stuff Pollard had recorded on his own, and the tracks that the new members recorded. This track actually resembles the previous record, *Please Be Honest*; it's a slower 'Kid On A Ladder.' It was even recorded at the same studio, Cyberteknics. It's a fun song, with the final line, and image, of everyone standing and holding hands 'at the end of the world' being both a warm nod to solidarity and a chilling reminder that everything could all just disappear.

Track four: 'Goodbye Note'

This Doug Gillard song is the first on the LP not written by Bob. It's a strong track, once again showing what an asset Gillard is to the band. He's not just a great guitar player but also has a cool voice and knows his way around a good pop song (don't forget that he's the one who wrote 'I Am A Tree'). The song's subject, the heartbreak that comes with having to temporarily leave someone you love, has long been a subject in pop music, whether it's 'Leaving On A Jet Plane' or KISS's ballad 'Beth.' 'Goodbye Note' seems more tied to the latter than the former, since it's written in the voice of a musician who's leaving, most likely to go on tour. Whereas in the KISS song Peter Criss sang, 'Me and the boys are playing, and we just can't find the sound,' Gillard here suggests putting the object of his desire into a 'carrier' so he can 'take [them] to the shows.' It's a funny line. This is then followed by, 'What you think is not work is work, the insiders know.' Doug seems to be saying that if you work in an office, or sell cars or whatever, that job is you even when you're not at the office and you're not doing it. You carry it around in your head and your heart, even when you think you're supposedly off the clock.

Another fun thing about the guys in the group writing songs for the album is that they often played these songs live. This track was performed almost two dozen times on the subsequent *August By Cake* tour. The same way that hearing the other guys' voices gives this record diversity, these tracks perform the same function in a live setting. Plus, it's great to see Pollard by the side of the stage, rocking out, or providing background vocals. He becomes, in those instances, just like us: an audience member enjoying the band.

Track five: 'We Liken The Sun'

This starts out sounding a bit rough and lo-fi, but by the time it's over, it's gorgeous. With all the guitar work in the background, you begin to realize how much Doug Gillard's been missed on the past half-dozen or so records. In keeping with the circus theme, the lyrics mention 'the boardwalk clowns.' Pollard then mentions 'saints,' giving an already heavy and portentous song religious overtones. Since the final line includes 'Burn your face with your gun,' we're back in 'end of the world' territory.

Track six: 'Fever Pitch'

At 1:01, this song snippet is the shortest on the record. It's also one of the few songs that feels like it belongs to the previous incarnations of the band; you could easily envision this fitting on *Please Be Honest* or one of the reunion LPs. *PopMatters* called this one of Pollard's 'home-recorded surrealist numbers lo-fi enough that they'd seem like mistakes if we didn't know better.' It's not great, but the second half doesn't sound too bad, and it's blended nicely right into the next song.

Track seven: *'Absent The Man'*

This is Mark Shue's first song on the record, and it, too, kicks ass. It's a heavy track, and Mark's voice and playing fit in well with the rest of the GBV material. This is not only important but probably harder than it seems. If you think back to the Ricked Wicky project, while I liked some of Nick Mitchell's songs, I found them jarring when placed next to Bob's. Whereas, on this first side, we have a song each from both Mark and Doug, and they fit in perfectly alongside Pollard's. Speaking of Gillard, he provides a blazing solo here.

Track eight: *'Packing The Dead Zone'*

The placement of this song at the end of side one is a great bit of sequencing. Pollard began the record with an outstanding full-band track, but his next four songs are mostly lo-fi affairs. Doug's and Mark's tracks are solid, and the first side then ends with this awesome tune featuring the whole band. The voice at the beginning of the song, declaring 'We're creating a society of cell-phone-crazed, marijuana-smoking zombies,' belongs to Steven Stefanakos. He's listed in the liner notes as 'Detective Steven Stefanakos, GBVPD.' In addition to helming the official Twitter feed of the GBVPD (a division, I think, of the Teenage FBI), it turns out that he is indeed a detective. Stefanakos is a thirty-year veteran of the NYPD, with twenty of those years spent as part of the Emergency Services unit. He's had a distinguished career on the force, including being a 9/11 first responder. He's also a huge GBV fan, going all the way back to the 90s, when he heard the *Vampire On Titus* track 'Expecting Brainchild' playing in an East Village record store. When he asked who the band were and the clerk told him, Stefanakos wanted to buy the record, but it was the clerk's personal copy. Undaunted—this a New York City cop, after all—Stefanakos offered to buy it anyway, paying double the list price. After attending of bunch of shows in the New York area, Stefanakos introduced himself to Mitch Mitchell and Pollard, striking up a friendship that's now lasted decades. When Pollard was in town in 2016, to record *August By Cake*, he called Stefanakos, telling him, 'I have a line for you; I'd love for you to say it.' Steven went out to Serious Business in Brooklyn and ended up on the record. It's a fun way to open the song, especially when, after Pollard says, somberly, 'Life is hard,' Stefanakos answers back, 'Ask easier questions.'

SIDE TWO

Track one: 'What Begins On New Year's Day'

This simple, mostly acoustic track was actually written and recorded well
before the *August By Cake* sessions, having originally been released as a Robert
Pollard solo track in 2015, as part of an Amazon playlist that featured twenty-
five bands and musicians writing songs or offering new versions of holiday
classics. That this was once a Pollard solo song and yet now was a GBV track
shows just how fluid the line is between the two (if one even exists). Pollard's
song appeared alongside others by artists such as Yacht, Langhorne Slim, and
GBV fans Rogue Wave.

Track two: 'Overloaded'

This, the first of two songs written and performed by drummer Kevin March,
is absolutely stellar. It's one of the best tracks on the album, and not just
when compared to the songs written by the other guys; it's as good as Bob's
compositions on this LP or anywhere else. When the drummer is coming up
with gems like this, you know you have a strong lineup.

March—unlike the rest of the band, who had to scramble to write their
songs for the album—had his already recorded and all ready to go. He's said
that, after he sent the songs to Pollard, 'Bob came back and said, "You're done.
I like them just the way they are." So I was really flattered and honored that he
picked those two songs and thought they were done.'

In terms of whether a bit of Pollard had rubbed off on him over the years,
March added, 'I'm always influenced a little bit by Bob, just because he's an
influential writer. I had written "Overloaded" a while ago, but I remember
being inspired by the song "Fair Touching," which is an old Guided By
Voices song.'

The lyrics, though, seem to hint at another song from that same album,
'Unspirited,' with March writing about self-doubt and 'feeling overloaded.' It's
heavy stuff, and yet it's a super-fun and gorgeous song, with March sounding
like Hüsker Dü. It's one of the best tracks on the LP, and the album's biggest
revelation.

Track three: 'Keep Me Down (Slower Version)'

This is another recycled song, having first appeared almost ten years prior as a Boston Spaceships track, on the 2009 record *The Planets Are Blasted*. Since we've already seen a previously released Robert Pollard solo song become a GBV track, that a Boston Spaceships song is remade on a GBV LP only further reinforces the notion that Pollard can basically call anything he wants Guided By Voices. As noted in the track's subtitle, it is indeed slower than the original. Pollard also plays down the English accent he employed the first time around. It's a more ragged version, too, with a guitar solo that seems pasted on from another song. The sloppiness of the track actually gives it a lot of charm, with the cowbell making it feel like a barroom jam. The line 'I'm driven to you, I'm driven to drink' is also classic Pollard.

Track four: 'West Coast Company Man'

This is a fun song that has a few different parts, which is the kind of thing that didn't crop up much on the reunion LPs. The majority of those tracks were short and straight-ahead, whereas this one tackles three different styles in under two minutes. With its talk of a 'company man,' it harkens back to *Motivational Jumpsuit*'s 'Save The Company.' These songs seem to be a remnant of Pollard's post-baby-boomer/Eisenhower-era upbringing. Bob was raised at a time when men got a job at a factory or a company and that's all they did for the rest of their lives. Nowadays you're expected to have lots of different jobs, and you're looked at askance if you stay at one place too long, but, in the 50s, the opposite was true.

Track five: 'Warm Up To Religion'

Musically, this song is large and majestic. By the end, it's practically a doo-wop song with its cooing background vocals. The lyrics are also interesting. Pollard's included a lot of religious imagery in his work, and this, again, is an homage to his Midwest upbringing. In a 2014 Pew survey, 57 percent of Ohioans said that they prayed daily, while 67 percent said that they believe in God with absolute certainty. Bob, however, has always seemed—like he is about most things—a skeptic, which is something that shows in this song. For example, the opening lines, which seem to be about Pollard stumbling into a church to witness an emotional and ecstatic scene, find him asking, 'Why are they screaming? What did they win?' The mention a line later of 'hammer and nails' could be seen as a reference to Christ's crucifixion.

What I find most interesting about this song is that, for as much as a cynic as Pollard is, 'Warm Up To Religion' finds him, well, warming up to the idea of worship and belief. He even suggests, 'Maybe I'm in.' Later in the tune, Pollard imagines his own conversion and presence in the activities, writing, 'Why am I screaming? What did I win?' Even though he's now caught up in the moment, and hollering for Jesus along with everyone else, he still can't quite shake the notion that the whole scene is ridiculous.

The final line is total Pollard brilliance: 'A happier face in stained glasses.' Stained glass has been around for over a thousand years, and is often associated with churches and religious imagery. But with Pollard using 'glasses' instead of just saying 'glass,' he's implying that he's wearing glasses with religious scenes in the lenses, and that seeing the world this way has made him 'happier.' He seems to be implying that religion can indeed lead to happiness, but only at the expense of surrendering your own individuality and blocking out anything that doesn't gibe with the teachings of the church.

Track six: 'High Five Hall Of Famers'

This is Bobby Bare Jr.'s first song on the record. Unlike Kevin March, who'd recorded his songs prior to Bob's request and had them all set to go, Bare was tasked to come up with a song in just a couple of hours. The title refers to GBV, because, as he's said, 'We high-five a lot when we're out and we're laughing. A friend of mine would refer to restaurants he didn't want to go to and say, "There are way too many high-fivers there. I don't want to go hang out there." I never even thought of it as a thing. Still, my buddy pointed that out and I was like, "Yeah, we are high-fivers."'

Track seven: 'Sudden Fiction'

This is Mark Shue's second song on the record. It's also a track that was played extensively on tour in 2017 and 2018. It's a fun song, with some great guitar work from Doug Gillard and, I must say, some solid drumming from Shue.

Track eight: *'Hiking Skin'*

This short song sees Bob put in an incredible vocal performance. The high note he hits on the line 'Be careful on the highway' has got to be his best singing since 'Cheyenne' from *Universal Truths And Cycles*. The band also sounds great, and it's the perfect way to end side two. What's also interesting about the track is that it has a long single guitar outro, which is essentially the opening to the first track on side three, 'It's Food.' This more or less knits those two sides together, making for a fun experience when you listen to the record on vinyl. It creates the illusion that you're hearing the two sides uninterrupted. On CD, or if you stream it, it just gives you a sense of déjà vu.

SIDE THREE

Track one: *'It's Food'*

This track features solid guitars and another strong vocal from Pollard. I also like that you can hear buzzing coming off the amps; it shows that the band's retained some of their lo-fi spirit while also delivering songs that sound huge.

Lyrically, Bob's asking important questions and forcing us to confront the grisly reality that comes with the large-scale, industrialized slaughter of animals. That Pollard's now a vegetarian gives the message even more bite. At one point he writes, 'We can kill them, but we can't film them.' This might be a reference to those whistle-blower films that sometimes emerge of gruesome industrial farm conditions. And then, in the next line, 'We can can them, but we can't scan them.' Again, do you really know what's being jarred up and presented to you as food? This idea goes all the way back to 'Ambergris' from *Same Place The Fly Got Smashed*, where Bob asks, 'What's that you're eating? It might be misleading. You don't want to know.' All that being said, this is *not* 'Meat Is Murder.' It's a fun song.

Track two: *'Cheap Buttons'*

The opening line, '10 billion Ringo fans can't be all wrong,' is a reference to an Elvis Presley record that came out in 1959. It was a singles compilation officially named *Elvis' Gold Records, Volume 2*. However, at the top of the sleeve, in big red type, it says, '50,000,000 ELVIS FANS CAN'T BE WRONG.' The sleeve also features a bunch of pictures of Elvis wearing a gold suit. In 2004, The Fall released a greatest hits record that cheekily nodded to their cult status by being named *50,000 Fall Fans Can't Be Wrong*. The cover featured multiple pictures of a scowling Mark E. Smith wearing a jumper. And while it's funny that Pollard has upped the Elvis number from fifty million to ten billion, that they're fans of Ringo—instead of Paul or John—gives the line that much more charm. The next line, however, seems to be more about GBV: 'Target your audience, then write them a song.' This is reminiscent of 'If that's what you want to hear, then that's what I will tell you,' from 'Huffman Prairie Flying Field.' Indeed, the song seems to be about music and fandom, if not even a larger topic like politics: all you need to succeed is a cheap button and a catchy phrase that says 'something simple.' We all want to feel that we have discerning taste, or that we think for ourselves, but in the end all it takes is an inexpensive piece of tin to make us change our minds. But Bob's line about mass fandom does something more; he's indicting mob mentality, because *of course* ten billion Ringo fans can all be wrong. If something sucks, or is dangerous, it doesn't matter how many damn people like it. It still sucks and it's still dangerous. A number, no matter how large it is, doesn't bestow respectability on anything or anyone. It might just do the opposite.

Track three: 'Substitute 11 (An Educational Nightmare Teleplay)'

This track is a flashback to the years Pollard taught fourth grade. The first part's told from the point of view of a principal admonishing a substitute for not controlling their classroom. The second is from the point of view of a director describing what's happening to the hapless teacher as his day, and maybe his life, dissolves into chaos. It's a remarkable track, perfectly capturing the essence and tone of an anxiety dream. In its theatricality, it's similar to songs off *Tommy*, or Bowie's 'Space Oddity.' It also makes me think Pollard could, if he wanted to, pull off a rock opera or true concept album.

Track four: 'Chew The Sand'

This song written by Mark Shue, at 3:44, is the longest track on the record. It's also my least favorite. Shue's other two contributions to this LP are truly stellar, but this one—a meandering instrumental that Pollard shows up to hum on top of—doesn't do much for me. I'm not sure why it was included, except that Bob wanted the symmetry of eight songs per side. Then again, this is Robert Pollard; the guy has boatloads of songs. I don't understand why he didn't use something else in this song's place, because it doesn't do much for the record as a whole, and it's not a lot of fun to listen to.

Track five: *'Dr. Feelgood Falls Off The Ocean'*

This co-write with Bob's brother is a remake of the track 'Something For Susan In The Shadows' off of *Suitcase 2*. Similar to the other stripped-down tracks on the record, it harkens back to the bare sound of *Please Be Honest*, consisting of just a drum machine, Pollard's voice, and a single electric guitar. Doug Gillard shows up late in the track to provide a welcome solo, but by then the rest of the instruments are out of sync and it's a bit disorienting. *Spin*'s Winston Cook-Wilson wrote of the track, 'There's a vaguely Celtic feel to the melody and backbeat, and like any GBV song that's worth its salt, the band seems to be barely holding it together.' Despite this, it's a fun song. Plaintive lines from Bob, such as 'I never can be what you want me to be now,' sit right next to details of everyday life, Pollard telling someone that a plant needs to be watered. The song ends with a bit of wisdom: 'If you could have any object desired, you'd grow tired.' Just because you have a whole bunch of stuff, and all your wishes come true, it doesn't mean you'd be happy. The song's title is a reference to British band Dr. Feelgood, and may also be related to the name of their debut LP, *Down By The Jetty*.

Track six: *'The Laughing Closet'*

This gorgeous song sounds a lot like a Tobin Sprout track until Bob comes in with the vocals. It has jangly guitar and strong drums, and there's even some synth strings. It's good to see that this band, who can be ferocious live, can also sound this tender. Although, for as sweet as the song is, the last line, 'Gathering black masses,' seems to be a reference to the opening line of 'War Pigs' by Black Sabbath: 'Generals gathered in their masses, just like witches at black masses.'

Track seven: 'Deflect / Project'

Doug Gillard's second song shows him railing against a consumerist culture, as well as how people in power get away with all the awful things they do. The title describes the way the forces that are doing all this bad stuff protect themselves: by deflecting any criticism and instead projecting it back onto the person who's making the accusation. It's a classic defense mechanism of narcissists. Late in the track, Gillard writes, 'Evil things have come to light, tasting apples with parasites.' The idea of an apple being a symbol of either death or downfall appears in contexts as varied as *Sleeping Beauty* and the Bible. But what Gillard's doing here is laying out something subtler: the apple doesn't kill you, but, without you knowing, delivers evil that will grow inside you, unseen but always lurking. If you try to confront it, all it will do is deflect and project. It's a chilling vision.

Track eight: 'Upon The Circus Bus'

Bobby Bare Jr. has said of this, his second track on the album, 'I wrote [the song] acoustically while we were in Canada. I think we were in Montreal. I wrote it about a picture from *The Rolling Stones Rock And Roll Circus* where I was taking everybody that was in the film—I just did a list of all the people and all the things that were in that.' The song is just Bare Jr. singing and playing, with ambient noise and discussion in the background (maybe the GBV tour bus?). Whether or not he means to, the song connects The Rolling Stones' literal circus with GBV's own variation of it in real life. The background sounds add a lot to the song, giving the listener a good fly-on-the-wall feeling, much like Lou Reed's song 'Kicks' from *Coney Island Baby*.

SIDE FOUR

Track one: 'Try It Out (It's Nothing)'

This short song begins like your standard GBV tune, until some Beach Boys harmonies come in toward the end. This, along with Dennis Cronin again on the trumpet, saves it from feeling like a throwaway (this is, after all, track twenty-five on a thirty-two-track album).

Track two: 'Sentimental Wars'

Kevin March's second song on the record is, I have to say, tied with 'Overloaded' as being one of the best songs on the LP. It's just gorgeous, hitting the same winsome and emotional territory that Tobin Sprout excelled at contributing to the group.

The lyrics start with March asking a number of questions, including, 'Do you ever want it all?' and 'Do you ever find yourself?' The song resolves, with the 'sentimental wars' of the title hopefully won or at least over for now, and the narrator telling someone, 'Just take my hand, I will be with you always.' The final line, 'I've got this feeling inside of me,' is reminiscent of 'I'm waiting for that feeling' on the Blur track 'Tender,' which mines a similar territory (both lyrically and musically). On an LP stuffed with references to circuses, religion, and politics, it's refreshing to get what appears to be a simple love song.

Track three: 'Circus Day Holdout'

This song tells of, well, a circus day holdout: someone, maybe one of the several clowns referenced elsewhere on the album, who refuses to perform. After declaring that 'life isn't fair,' he says to tell the 'guys' (presumably his co-workers at the circus) that—even though he's leaving—he still 'cares.' His final kiss-off is a not-so-fond farewell, the big-top version of 'Take this job and shove it': 'Crank up your monkey and organ without me.' It's a funny line, and it fits with the kinds of statements that Pollard's been making for decades.

Track four: 'Whole Tomatoes'

At 1:12, this is the second shortest of the album's thirty-two tracks. *PopMatters* called it 'absolutely gorgeous, imagistic nonsense.' I agree with that. I also think Pollard wrote it after a visit to the grocery store.

Track five: 'Amusement Park Is Over'

This song sits in the middle of the stark sound of *Please Be Honest* and the full-band stuff found elsewhere on this record. It's basically just Pollard at Cyberteknics, except Doug Gillard adds some extra guitar that brings the track to life. I can't tell from the lyrics what the song's about, but the appearance of an 'amusement park' in the title ties it to the circus imagery found elsewhere on the album.

Track six: 'Golden Doors'

This super-spare song features just Pollard and a slowly strummed guitar. It's lo-fi, harkening back to the more stripped-down songs on the reunion LPs. It doesn't have much of a tune, but it's short at under two minutes, so it doesn't wear out its welcome.

Track seven: 'The Possible Edge'

This track showcases another great vocal performance by Pollard. The song's subject seems to be how you can gain an edge and how that edge, presumably over someone else, will put what you wish to obtain 'within reach.' The character Jake in the Orson Welles film *The Lady From Shanghai* describes having an edge as simply being 'something the other guy ain't got.' For example, 'A set of brass knuckles, a stripe on the sleeve, a badge that says cop on it, a rock in your hand, or a bankroll in your pocket. That's an edge, brother.'

Track eight: 'Escape To Phoenix'

This stomper has almost a glam vibe. Nicholas Carr wrote that it 'feels like the missing link between the Velvet Underground and the Bay City Rollers,' adding, 'I'm not sure it was a link that needed to be discovered, but it does end this fun and satisfying album with a rush.' It's indeed a fun song, especially since the last twenty seconds are taken up with a group of voices repeating the rebellious refrain from 'Circus Day Hold Out': 'Crank up your monkey and organ without me.' It gives the impression that, after the solo nature of *Please Be Honest*, and the increasingly fractured fraternity of the reunion albums, GBV are back to being what they were always meant to be: a team, a gang, a bunch of buddies drinking beer and cranking out righteous tunes. The boys are back in town, and the results are amazing.

24 HOW DO YOU SPELL HEAVEN

two thousand and seventeen

While this was recorded with the same group of guys who'd toured behind and recorded *August By Cake*, it's a totally different album from the prior LP. *Cake* was a double album, stuffed with thirty-two tracks of sonic goodness that saw—for the first time in the thirty-year existence of GBV—all the band members contributing songs. Yet the record before *Cake* featured just Pollard, with Bob playing every instrument. So what would the next record be? What would it sound like? Were we in for 'Sad Baby Eyes Part 2,' or more exquisite pop tunes from Kevin March? Would it be lo-fi, eclectic, or something else entirely?

Because GBV had been dinged over and over for producing quantity over quality, the fact that *Heaven* followed so closely on the heels of the previous record was not a good sign (*Cake* came out in April and *Heaven* was released just four months later). But I shouldn't have worried, since the fifteen-track *How Do You Spell Heaven* is a fantastic LP. Bob and the band produced one of the most focused GBV albums in over a decade. You have to go all the way back to *Earthquake Glue* to find a Guided By Voices record with only fifteen songs. The band were also doing a great job fleshing out Pollard's demos. Only three of *Heaven*'s tracks are under two minutes, and only one, 'They Fall Silent,' is the kind of lo-fi fragment that littered past albums. Instead,

Heaven shows Bob and the band—as well as engineer Travis Harrison—firing on all cylinders.

How Do You Spell Heaven is similar to David Bowie's *The Man Who Sold The World*. Because, while that was technically Bowie's third record, it's where he finally hit on the band, and the sound, that he would perfect over the next couple of years. And which, of course, would culminate in the classic *Ziggy Stardust And The Spiders From Mars*. As writers Roy Carr and Charles Shaar Murray put it, *The Man Who Sold the World* 'is where the story really starts.' The same goes for this album and GBV, in terms of this new era of the band.

Similar to that Bowie LP, *Heaven* is a heavy record. It's GBV's most out-and-out 'rock' album since *Isolation Drills*. Whereas *August By Cake* was just a taste of what this lineup could do, *Heaven* delivers on the full promise of Pollard's new band to such a degree that March, Gillard, Shue, and Bare Jr. now constitute a New Classic lineup. This is not a pickup band, or just some gaggle of guys Pollard threw together. This is something special, and the work these four guys have done together—whether it's been onstage, or on record—has been truly impressive.

As a longtime fan of the group, and a diehard for that early lo-fi stuff, I was blown away by the quality of the songs and LPs the band released around this time. To give some context, in terms of where I'm coming from, I bought *Vampire On Titus* when it first came out, and I was in my early twenties when I did so. This means I've not only liked GBV for a long time, but I've liked a lot of bands for a long time, following them decade after decade. What shocks me about Guided By Voices is that their new stuff is just as good as their old stuff. And while I've been critical of some of the band's moves, and what Bob's released—and I actually do subscribe to the 'Bob's too prolific' argument—the quality of the music Pollard's released in the past couple of years is high. This is a guy who, past the age of sixty, has managed to stay relevant and is releasing some of the best stuff of his career.

I can't say I've experienced this with any other band. There are other groups I've been following for three decades, and while I'm glad that some of those bands remain together, and release new music, I have a hard time getting as excited for their new stuff as I do the old stuff. And when I see those groups live, I'm usually itching to hear an older song. That's something that most bands that have been around for a while, or that get back together, have to deal with. If Oasis ever reunite, you just know that crowds would roar like crazy for anything off those first two records, then sit politely through an album cut off *Dig Out Your Soul* or *Don't Believe The Truth*. In fact, when Oasis put out a two-CD best-of in 2006, they ignored their third record completely. Even GBV's spottiest LPs have at least a few gems.

Then there's the Pixies. While they continue to release new material, I haven't heard anyone say it's on par with their early stuff. Instead, they're increasingly seen as a nostalgia act whose greatest artistic achievements are well behind them. They seem to know it, reveling in anniversaries and reissues and playing their old classic albums, in full, onstage. In 2018, the Pixies even toured with Weezer, a band who find themselves in the same situation. But with GBV, when they play live, their new songs sound as good as the old stuff. I actually prefer to hear more recent material, and that's kind of nuts.

In his review of *Cool Planet* for *Paste*, Garrett Martin, talking about GBV's staying power, wrote, 'Think of how bad the records from the Stones or The Who were in the 1980s, when they were twenty years removed from their peak.' Those bands continued to release records even in the 90s and beyond, but I don't think any casual or even hardcore Stones or Who fan would call those albums their best work. When those bands play live today, it's basically a parade of their greatest hits. They know what the crowd wants, and they give it to them.

Plus, as much as I love the players from previous incarnations of GBV— whether that means *Alien Lanes*–era guys like Mitch Mitchell or Toby, or even later members like Nate Farley and Todd Tobias who became, in their own way, fan favorites—I never think of Guided By Voices as 'incomplete' or 'less than' just because they no longer feature a founding or long-standing member. That's something I can't say of a group like New Order, a band that—without Peter Hook—doesn't make much sense. But Bob's managed to, with GBV, transcend any sort of adverse effect when it comes to whom he has in the group.

How Do You Spell Heaven was recorded the way that Bob's done a number of solo records, with Pollard providing demos to be fleshed out and recorded by the band, on their own, and then later putting vocals on top of the final instrumentals. This is the template they followed for the next LP, *Space Gun*, too, and, since these are both super-tight records, it's evidently a formula that works well with this group of guys.

The cover for the record is striking, and awfully reminiscent of the one for *August By Cake*. The photo's of Pollard leaning into a lamp, his face illuminated, while the background is mostly black. It's a cool image, with Bob looking both ghostly and serene, his red shirt providing a striking counterbalance to the dark background and Pollard's pale complexion. That the photo was taken by Mark Shue leads me to believe that it was a candid or impromptu shot, and—the same as with the photo on the cover of *August By Cake*— that Bob later saw it and said, 'We gotta use that for the cover.'

What also makes it a striking sleeve is that there's no type. Because as fun as the *August By Cake* sleeve was, I'm not a big fan of the font they used for the album's name. Whereas *Heaven* keeps things clean by relegating the names of the band and the record to the back. The back cover also has a cool, blurry photo of Kevin March, along with a handwritten track listing. The inside features the usual GBV aesthetic of found photos, handwritten lyrics, and collages.

It's also amazing that it's been more than thirty years since Bob had appeared on a GBV sleeve. He was part of the band photo for 1987's *Sandbox*, but ever since then—despite being the main creative force in the band, and the sole constant member for three decades—he's chosen to have either a collage or art grace the sleeves of Guided By Voices records. Even on his twenty-three solo albums, he appears on fewer than half the covers. This is something that can't be said for artists like David Bowie or Lou Reed, who appeared on almost every one of their two-dozen-plus releases.

A single was issued for *How Do You Spell Heaven*, the first time the band had done so since *Cool Planet* a few years prior. It was the last song on the album, 'Just To Show You.' Keeping with the democratic nature of *August By Cake*, the B-side, 'Knife City,' was a co-write between Doug Gillard and Mark Shue.

Reviewing the album for *Exclaim!*, Jenna McClelland exclaimed, 'Guided By Voices maintain their knack for bright, chaotic pop movements on new album *How Do You Spell Heaven*, complete with angular chord patchworks, abrupt melodic transitions and deliriously honest storytelling all held together with glue.' She added, however, that the LP 'suffers from a lack of consistency,' noting that 'there isn't enough here to make *How Do You Spell Heaven* stand out from Guided By Voices' deep catalogue. GBV rookies would do well to start by looking back; seasoned listeners are probably already here.'

The *AV Club* gave the LP a B–, reviewer Katie Rife declaring that 'keeping up with all things Guided By Voices is a full-time job.' Rife longed for the variety found on *August By Cake*, stating that '*How Do You Spell Heaven* suffers from having a tad too much of Pollard's lone influence, and as a result, it's overloaded with the kind of mid-tempo filler that takes a few listens to really stand out.'

Stuart Berman, writing for *Pitchfork*, gave the record a 7.4. 'With Pollard reassuming all lead-vocalist duties, this handsomely crafted record strikes a balance of crystalline jangle, authoritative swagger, and Wire-schooled crunch reminiscent of 2001's (way underrated) *Isolation Drills*.'

SIDE ONE

Track one: 'The Birthday Democrats'

This song is an absolute blast. The sound is just amazing; all the instruments sound great and so do Bob's vocals. Travis Harrison's also done a great job with the mix, since you can clearly hear Kevin March's hi-hat amid all the other stuff going on. Whereas the drums on some GBV tracks, especially in the early days, sounded like somebody pounding on cardboard boxes, here they sound great. You have to go back to *Isolation Drills* or *Do The Collapse* to find the band sounding this good. That may rub some fans the wrong way—not everyone liked the band's hi-fi sound, or even the mid-fi era of the second run of Matador LPs. Arguments about aesthetics aside, this is just how this band *should* sound. It's how these guys play, and to not capture it well, the way it's done here, would be a disservice to the group and to the song.

Track two: 'King 007'

This starts off with a kind of bossa nova feel, which is a lot of fun; a whole lot of Pollard's songs rock, but they don't always swing. However, by the time Bob gets to the line 'Catalogued in the high hills,' the band's launched into full-on classic-rock territory. Doug Gillard also provides some tasty guitar licks that give it a hard rock, 70s feel. This touches on something interesting about the band, namely their continued inclusion in the indie-rock scene. This is a group that's always worshipped The Beatles and The Who—GBV never had that affected, slacker vibe that so many bands from the 90s had. Bob doesn't do irony. Instead, what you see is what you get. (Let's also not forget that, due to his age, Bob was hardly a Gen Xer.) And yet, despite their semi-retro vibe and obvious influences, GBV have also managed to avoid looking like nothing more than a tribute band—something that can't be said for other bands who clearly have the same influences.

Track three: 'Boy W'

The record's sequencing pays off, since this is the third fast song in a row, not to mention that the first three songs run into each other. This makes the opening stretch of the album strong, with each track complimenting the other. The structure of this song is interesting, too, since it's basically four verses followed by two choruses, Pollard once again eschewing the more traditional structure of verse, chorus, verse. While the drums sound like a drum machine (albeit one light-years ahead of what was heard on *Please Be Honest*), it's all Kevin March. The guitars sound great, and Gillard provides little licks in the background that add a lot.

I can't quite tell from the lyrics if the song has any real meaning, although the phrase 'maximum high kick' is certainly a good description of Pollard's stage persona (not to mention it alludes to The Who's own early description of their music as 'maximum R&B'). Otherwise, I'll just take the lyrics to be a simple observation of childhood, a world filled with '*Z*s and *ABC*s,' meaning a lot of sleep and learning how to talk and write. Bob finally concludes, 'It's so damn fine to be six years all of the time.' The song's title, 'Boy W,' reminds me of 'Bill W.,' the co-founder of Alcoholics Anonymous. Since alcohol plays such a large part in the band's existence, not to mention shows up frequently in their songs, I would bet that Pollard has at least a passing familiarity with AA (if only because he's turned it down one or twice in the face of friendly advice).

Track four: 'Steppenwolf Mausoleum'

This is the second-longest song and the only one in the three-minute range on the entire album. While a lot of people remarked upon how, the week this record came out, the founding member of the band Steppenwolf,

Goldy McJohn, passed away—giving this tune an eerie sort of prescience—I think what Pollard's referring to is Hermann Hesse's novel from the 1920s. *Steppenwolf* came out in its original German edition in 1927, with the English translation appearing two years later. Due to the novel's psychedelic nature, and its seeming approval of drug use, the book—along with *The Doors Of Perception*, *Tropic Of Cancer*, and *Gravity's Rainbow*—became part of the literate rock'n'roll scene of the 60s and 70s. The song does indeed seem to deal with scenes from the book. At the novel's conclusion, the main character visits what's called a Magic Theater, experiencing a number of fantasies by entering through a series of doors. This song mentions doors with magical qualities, along with fantasy imagery that matches the tone of the novel. Musically, the song's also a lot of fun, with some psychedelic production touches and Beatles-esque background vocals. It's a great track.

Track five: 'Cretinous Number Ones'

Although the repeated line here, 'I dream of drinking,' is vintage Bob, it's also depressing—who dreams of drinking? However, the same way that I found the word 'rapists' a drag to hear in '(I Wanna Be A) Dumbcharger,' Pollard inserting the word 'abortion' here has much the same effect. If he were using the word in a way that made sense, or to make a point, I'd have no problem with it. But to just toss it in the lyrics, not to mention make it part of the phrase 'lucrative abortion,' feels jarring, and not at all fun to hear in a pop song.

Track six: 'They Fall Silent'

This acoustic track, at under a minute long, is the shortest on the record. It's similar to 'Frostman' off the otherwise-ultra-polished *Isolation Drills*. The same way that track felt out of place with the rest of the album, 'They Fall Silent' doesn't seem to match anything else on *How Do You Spell Heaven*. The song also feels lyrically incomplete, with Pollard sketching and outlining some interesting ideas, but then not fleshing them out. The opening verse, 'At the age of birth they learn to talk, at the age of death they learn to listen,' goes back to Simon & Garfunkel's 'The Sounds Of Silence,' in which Paul Simon describes 'People hearing without listening.' But the idea doesn't go anywhere, and the song is soon over.

Track seven: *'Diver Dan'*

On a record full of good songs, this is one of the best. While it definitely rocks, there are also some strong harmonies and background vocals on the chorus. In terms of the title, Bob's admitted in the past that he uses mishearing things for inspiration. I wonder if—for 'Diver Dan'—he got the title from the expression 'diver down.' In addition to being the name of Van Halen's not-so-great fifth record, scuba divers use a flag that means 'diver down' to let other divers know where and when someone's under the surface. (If you think that's not important, just watch the film *Open Water*.)

Track eight: *'How To Murder A Man (In 3 Acts)'*

Much as how *August By Cake*'s 'Substitute 11' was subtitled 'An Educational Nightmare Teleplay,' this song is similarly dramatic, with its three sections being likened to different acts in a play. The three parts don't cohere from a storytelling point of view, but it's amazing that Pollard and the guys manage to pack in so many different musical styles and tempos into a song that's under three minutes. In that regard, it's indebted to The Who's mini-opera, 'A Quick One,' which 'How To Murder A Man' resembles, the end of the first section sounding a bit like the 'cello, cello' section. Some of the lyrics are also a lot of fun, such as when Pollard writes of 'Salvation Army Beatle boots.' Beatle boots were named after the band, who popularized them in the 60s. They were basically a variation of Chelsea boots, which were black and leather with pointed toes and what's called a Cuban heel. They were popular for a while, but you don't see them much anymore, which is why you'd find them in a Salvation Army thrift store. However, by choosing that particular institution (instead of, say, Goodwill), Bob's making an allusion to regular old GI-issue army boots. Since his work is rife with military references and imagery, it's not a stretch to think that Pollard likens a band, and perhaps their fans, to a military organization. They wouldn't be the first; KISS call their legion of fans the KISS Army.

SIDE TWO

Track one: *'Pearly Gates Smoke Machine'*

This co-write with Doug Gillard is the record's longest song, at 4:01. It's also, somewhat bafflingly, an instrumental. It starts off as being awfully reminiscent of T. Rex's 'Bang A Gong' before turning into a full-blown stomper with guitar licks all over the place. It's not exactly annoying to listen to, unlike *August By Cake*'s instrumental 'Chew The Sand,' but I don't get a kick out of hearing instrumental classic-rock music. It also seems perverse to include a track with no vocals on a GBV album. After all, Pollard's the guy who loves coming up with words and melodies so much he does it for songs that aren't even his (think of the *Phantom Tollbooth* LP). The inclusion of this track is a bit weird—it doesn't ruin the record, but it doesn't make a lot of sense.

Track two: 'Tenth Century'

The first minute and a half of this track is quiet, with Pollard singing against an acoustic guitar. In its musical makeup, not to mention its lyrical tropes—Bob's singing about shadows melting 'in the high temples'—it goes back to the *Bee Thousand* era, when Pollard often used fantasy imagery. But the song soon turns, in its second part, very majestic and grand in a 'Save The Company' way, before turning into a heavy rock song for the last thirty seconds. The lyrics take a look at what life was like in, well, the tenth century. There's a grim determination about the characters in the song, 'knowing the halfway point to the new millennium'; as if they—or, rather, their ancestors—hang on long enough, all their desires will be answered. And yet, here we are, deep into the twenty-first century, and most things—like who gets fed and who goes hungry—still come down to just luck.

Track three: 'How Do You Spell Heaven'

This song, clocking in at just under two minutes, doesn't have a chance to develop any of its lyrical or musical ideas. That being said, there are some good lines, Pollard asking rhetorically, 'How do you spell heaven?' and 'Is bookshelf one word?' This is similar to the Insane Clown Posse song 'Miracles,' where the duo asked, in a much-mocked song, 'Fucking magnets, how do they work?' In an age of a hopefully solid basic education, not to mention Google, the answers to these—and a myriad of other questions—are right at your fingertips. Pollard seems to allude to this: 'Information machines closing the casket.' Is having too many answers going to kill us? Is the internet just another 'useless invention'? The answers to these questions are still up for debate.

Track four: *'Paper Cutz'*

This song gets back to the hard-rock template found earlier on the record. I also think some of the song might be literal, Pollard writing, 'I'm a paper man, and I love my hands.' As a guy who works almost daily with photos and illustrations for his collages, I can imagine that he gets his fair share of paper cuts. If the song has any deeper meaning than that, I'm not sure. Bob may not even be sure, since he sings, late in the song, 'And we don't even understand.'

Track five: *'Low Flying Perfection'*

This song has some welcome production touches, including ethereal background vocals. It starts with a single electric guitar line, before the drums and the rest of the instruments come crashing in. In this way, the song's similar to 'Don't Stop Now.' The reference to 'flying' makes it right at home with GBV's dozen other flying and plane references. *Pitchfork's* Stuart Berman called the track 'a harmony-gilded, country-dusted ballad from a band that's often in pursuit of high-flying imperfection.' There are also a couple of evocative—if not depressing—lines late in the song, Bob describing 'overfed vultures' who are 'robbing us.' It's a chilling vision; the vultures aren't circling—they're not flying high in the sky—they're right there, sitting next to us. There's no shame in what they've done—they're gloating as they 'admire' their handiwork and the age of greed and avarice they've brought forth.

Track six: *'Nothing Gets You Real'*

This song has a super-laid-back vibe, featuring some folksy strummed acoustic guitar and a spritely beat by Kevin March; it almost swings in a 'You're Going To Lose That Girl' way. Lyrically, though, the song is super-heavy, with Pollard making a very big—and depressing—point, stating that, as the title says, 'Nothing gets you real.' Or, rather, nothing can *make* you real. There's no quick fix, no easy answer. Not only that but the path to any kind of actualization will probably hurt: 'Sorrow lets you feel.' Most people don't realize this, or don't want to acknowledge this, Pollard quickly adding, 'No one gets this part.' People try to feel real by participating in movements, whether they're musical or political, something Pollard references: 'The scene is dying now, and you are taking shape.' It's only when you get out from under the shadow of groupthink that you will truly become yourself.

The song also references the lengths that people will go to feel real, including 'Slashing at your arm.' The quest to become real, to feel a true and genuine emotion, can quickly lead to self-destruction (on either a personal or national basis). In 1991, after being challenged with the idea that he and his band weren't serious, Manic Street Preachers member Richey Edwards slashed '4 REAL' into his arm with a razor blade, requiring eighteen stitches. Edwards disappeared in 1995, at the doomed rock-star age of twenty-seven. While his body has never been found, he has long been presumed dead. The drive and desire to find and experience true emotions, or to prove one's self as real, is a universal emotion and theme. This has only been heightened in the current political climate, where just about everything you see and hear is fake.

Track seven: *'Just To Show You'*

This short song—under two and a half minutes—was the only single issued from the album. Fans of the band's faster material might think this track is too slow or just middle-of-the-road, but it's a great example of the late-period maturity of the band. It fits alongside other recent examples of this sound and style, such as 'The Possible Edge' from the prior LP. It's a great track wherein everyone sounds good, and there are some welcome harmonies in the background—touches that show up repeatedly on this record but are scarce throughout GBV's discography.

25 SPACE GUN

two thousand and eighteen

This is a truly remarkable album, a late-period classic that's almost unheard-of in indie rock. Like the last couple of records, it began as a series of demos that Bob recorded and then delivered to the band via a burned CD. The demos consisted of the entire record, in order, with Pollard bashing out the songs on an acoustic guitar and recording them straight into a vintage boom box.

In terms of *Space Gun*'s fifteen tracks, fourteen were completely original. Only one, 'That's Good,' released previously on *Suitcase 3*, is an older tune that Bob wanted to rework. Two other *Suitcase* songs were considered for the album but were later dropped.

The cover for *Space Gun*, after two LPs that featured a single photograph, sports a vintage Pollard collage that draws inspiration from Russian Futurist Alexander Rodchenko. That the cover screams GBV only adds to the idea that this is a truly classic Guided By Voices album.

Another thing different about *Space Gun* is that Bob made a point to not release a whole bunch of competing material in 2018. Whereas, just a few years prior, you might get two Circus Devils LPs, a new side project, a Pollard solo album, and then two or three GBV records on top of all that, this time around Pollard wanted to focus his and the band's efforts on one project. He wanted the fans to be able to focus on one thing as well. 'We're all very proud of *Space Gun*,' Bob said, 'so I decided to not give it any distractions or competition for the entire year of 2018 other than a couple of very minor, non-GBV studio releases. I want to let people just chew on that one for a while and see if it has sustaining power.'

This seems a very interesting, not to mention somewhat damning, admission in terms of the 'Bob's too prolific' debate. Pollard's here basically copping to the fact that when he releases six or seven albums in a year, they do 'compete' with each other. It also just plain confuses people, not to mention making it hard to keep track of so much stuff. When work is of a high quality, people want to live with it, to savor it. If a work is deep enough, as *Space Gun* is, then one record a year is plenty.

In the last chapter I compared *How Do You Spell Heaven* to Bowie's breakout third record, *The Man Who Sold The World*. I want to keep that comparison going, since Bowie's follow-up, *Hunky Dory*, saw main sideman and guitarist Mick Ronson begin to expand his role in Bowie's band. Ronno was no longer just providing heavy-metal licks and power chords. He was also contributing intricate arrangements and playing Mellotron, the same as Doug Gillard does here on many occasions. On *Space Gun*, Gillard's touches, on the guitar and elsewhere, help make the record a success.

Three singles were issued from the album: the title track, which came out in December 2017; followed by 'See My Field' and 'That's Good,' both of which came out a few weeks before the LP was released the following March. 'See My Field' had two B-sides, one by Kevin March and one by Mark Shue. 'That's Good' featured tracks written by Doug Gillard and Bobby Bare Jr., while 'Space Gun' had only one B-side, a song called 'Kingdom Of Cars,' which, in a reversal of the 'I Am A Tree' scenario, Bob wrote but Doug sang.

Videos were made for 'Space Gun' and 'See My Field' by filmmaker Hunter Christy. Christy had been in a band in the early 2000s with Mark Shue. Knowing Christy's interest in film and video, Mark asked Hunter—in 2016—to make a video for a pair of New Year's Eve shows in Philadelphia and Brooklyn. Though just a minute long, the short clip that Hunter produced perfectly captures the essence of the GBV aesthetic. The grainy quality of the film matches the band's lo-fi sound, and the use of Cold War–era NASA footage makes it look like a Pollard collage come to life. It's easy to see why the band dug his stuff and asked him to eventually make videos for the new record.

Christy was initially tasked to create only one video, and it was actually the second of the two to appear. As he recalled, 'Days before I was set to film the narrative sequence of ["See My Field"], the team asked if I could shoot a video for "Space Gun" really quickly.' Christy then filmed, edited, and completed the video in under a week, adding on the coda of the kid in the space suit ejecting the VHS tape, thus connecting the two clips.

Both videos are a lot of fun, with my favorite being 'Space Gun,' because I love the way the graphics—partly inspired by Kubrick's *2001*—perfectly match what's happening in the song. Plus, the woman dancing looks cool, and there's a fun 3-D effect with the heads of the guys in the band. And when the rune shows up at the end, it gives me the chills.

'See My Field' is also an impressive clip. It features a boy, who's a GBV fan, rocking out in his room as he tries to master Bob's moves. The clip alternates between Bob doing the real thing in concert and the kid trying to replicate Pollard's performance in his room. There's a great touch when the video goes from Bob holding a microphone and a beer to the kid holding a toy microphone and a juice box.

Reviews for *Space Gun* were ecstatic, the majority of them saying that the record was an instant classic, not to mention the best music Bob had put out in a long time. *Rolling Stone* called the album 'pretty great,' reviewer Jon Dolan adding that 'it'd totally make sense coming out after 1996's *Under The Bushes Under The Stars*.'

At the website *Neon Filler*, grading the album a nine out of ten, writer Dorian Rogers called *Space Gun* 'the best thing [Pollard's] recorded under the GBV moniker since he resurrected the band back in 2012.' Rogers also praised the LP for its 'uncharacteristically consistent songs,' saying that 'there is little in the way of filler here and none of the half-formed snippets that can frustrate the casual listener.'

Musician Kristin Hersh, from Throwing Muses and 50 Foot Wave, in an essay for *Talkhouse* entitled 'Guided By Voices Are Still The Masters Of Creepy Cool,' wrote that 'listening to *Space Gun*, Guided By Voices' newest album, is like discovering a classic that you somehow missed out on when it first hit.'

SIDE ONE

Track one: *'Space Gun'*

At 4:18, this is the record's longest song. It kicks off with the sound of an electric paper-towel dispenser, which drummer Kevin March recorded on his phone at an airport in Phoenix, at Bob's request. The guitars on the track sound amazing, going right up to the edge of feeding back. There's also some great synth washes, or electronic squiggles; that's a sound that doesn't get used much in GBV, and here it adds a lot. Pollard's voice also sounds great, especially during some call-and-response lines. Lyrically, there are some great bits, Bob stating in the first verse, 'Doesn't matter what you do, you know what you've done.' He's stated in lots of songs, going back to 'Exit Flagger,' that there's no escaping death. Here, he's saying you also can't escape your conscience. Late in the song, he seems to put in a plug for the more outré examples of his past work, writing, 'Experimental exercise, but that's not so wrong.'

The song takes a break around the 1:40 mark. On the reunion LPs, a whole lot of tracks are about that long, but 'Space Gun' makes a great case for pushing past not only the two-minute mark but also the four-minute mark, because this one just keeps going and going. I would argue that the last thirty seconds or so, with Pollard repeating 'All day long,' and Doug's riffage in the background, are what simply make the song. While it'd be a good track without that last section, with it the song becomes truly great. I'd even say that it's the second-best GBV opening track ever, behind only *Propeller's* mighty 'Over The Neptune / Mesh Gear Fox.'

Track two: *'Colonel Paper'*

This short track—exactly two minutes—is a perfect companion to the longer opening track. It's heavier than a lot of Beatles tracks, but it's still similar to their work (with a bit of a 'Savoy Truffle' vibe), plus it names and creates a character. That places it alongside Beatles songs such as 'Mean Mr. Mustard,' 'Doctor Robert,' and 'Polythene Pam.' The song was inspired, as Doug Gillard has said, by 'a close friend and ex-bandmate who bought a bucket of KFC when his wife went away for the weekend, ate one or two pieces, then threw away most of it in the master trash can in the cold garage and passed out. He woke up hungry in the middle of the night and remembered he threw away the bucket. So he went back out to the garage, rummaged around in the trash can, reaching past the other garbage, paper and cigarette butts, and proceeded to eat that remaining extra-crispy-coated cold bird muscle and tendon.' You can just imagine Bob's eyes twinkling when he heard the story, thinking to himself, *Hot damn, that's a song*. Musically speaking, Doug said that he 'tried to have a super-thin guitar sound and still make the song muscly.' He certainly succeeded, because it's a fun track, perfectly placed as the second song on the album.

Track three: 'King Flute'

At 1:22, this is the record's shortest song. Drummer Kevin March goes crazy during the entire track—there are just too many fills and cymbal crashes to count, and yet it doesn't overpower the song. Lyrically speaking, with its tale of squires and kings, this sits firmly in the category of Pollard's fantasy songs.

Track four: 'Ark Technician'

This slower song is similar to the kinds of tracks that were on the second run of Matador albums. A lot of GBV's fans prefer the band to just rock out, but I appreciate these quieter tracks that feature acoustic guitar and a slower tempo. With its line about gathering 'in pairs,' the 'ark' of the title may be Noah's ark. Late in the song, Bob turns from religion to consumerism, citing meals purchased from 'Best Bought,' a fun twist on the big-box chain store Best Buy. Jared Dix of the website *Echoes And Dust* described the song as 'particularly early R.E.M.-like, almost like a lost outtake from *Reckoning*.'

Track five: 'See My Field'

For the opening of this song, Bob asked for a sitar, the Indian instrument that came into prominence thanks to George Harrison. Doug Gillard replicated the sound of a sitar after finding a tutorial on YouTube. To do this, he attached a paper clip to the bridge of his electric guitar and laid it over the strings. Lyrically, the song's another declaration of intent from Bob, a peek into his personal philosophy. In the opening line, Pollard—using language that goes back to his jock past—taunts the listener, writing, 'Go on, be a spectator.' Bob, meanwhile, is on the field, a place where he's so comfortable he proclaims, 'It's my field.' It's mid-game, and the old quarterback is telling someone to 'go long' and 'run so far' that they can receive what Bob's offering.

This is what Bob considers real: being on the field and giving your best effort. For him, creating art is athletic. It's physical, primal, spiritual. It's no wonder that Bob—a renown technophobe who still doesn't own a computer or send email—writes, 'It's no fun being lost in a make-believe city.' Why be in virtual reality when you could get on some grass and experience real life? The next line's amusing because of its cultural reference and because it shows Pollard to be self-aware, noting that 'the *Star Wars* people just look and laugh.' This is a crowd that has only seen what Bob's talking about 'in a photograph.' He knows he's old fashioned, maybe even a dinosaur; he knows that people may even laugh at him, but he doesn't care. As he writes in the final line, 'I'll keep my field, this is my cartoon.' Both the field and his way of life are things he's chosen for himself.

The message evokes Teddy Roosevelt's famous speech from 1910, which he delivered in Paris. It's come to be known as the 'Man In The Arena,' and here is the most-quoted passage:

It is not the critic who counts; not the man who points out how the strong man stumbles, or where the doer of deeds could have done them better. The credit belongs to the man who is actually in the arena, whose face is marred by dust and sweat and blood; who strives valiantly; who errs, who comes short again and again, because there is no effort without error and shortcoming; but who does actually strive to do the deeds; who knows great enthusiasms, the great devotions; who spends himself in a worthy cause; who at the best knows in the end the triumph of high achievement, and who at the worst, if he fails, at least fails while daring greatly, so that his place shall never be with those cold and timid souls who neither know victory nor defeat.

This idea is not only contained in 'See My Field'; it's the foundation of Bob's whole outlook on life and art. Whether you call it being in the arena or being on the field, Pollard believes in getting out there and trying. Art's not about inspiration, but instead has to do with the 'dust and sweat and blood' that Roosevelt describes. You fail only if you don't engage, if you don't even try.

Bob lives by this idea every day, waking up and putting himself in the arena. It doesn't always work, and it's not always pretty, but he succeeds by repeatedly taking on the challenge. And we, in our own lives, have a choice: Will we join him on the field, or will we just be spectators?

Track six: 'Liars' Box'

Similar to both the preceding song and the first track, 'Liars' Box' opens with a single-note guitar line. Pollard delivers the first verse over this sparse accompaniment until the rest of the band come in thirty seconds into the song. And while 'Liar's Tale,' from 1989's *Self-Inflicted Aerial Nostalgia*, told a story about the dissolution of a relationship, this track is much more abstract. Pollard writes of a 'city of paper' and 'gusts of lust.' I'm not sure, lyrically, what it all adds up to, even though musically it's a lot of fun. In the last minute or so, where Pollard repeats 'Summons of a glass to a sad, sad heaven,' it's beyond sublime. I have to go all the way back to the wonderful 'words of smoke' section in 'The Finest Joke Is Upon Us,' from *Mag Earwhig!*, to find something that's comparable.

Track seven: 'Blink Blank'

This starts with a chorused bass that sounds an awful lot like something Peter Hook would have played in Joy Division. Since one of Bob's favorite bands is Wire, this is right in line with Pollard's love of post-punk. There are also some synth washes, in addition to a solo late in the track that mimics the main melody.

The opening lines are classic Pollard, with Bob writing what seems to be a cheap 'moon/June' rhyme until he delivers a great punch line:

> *Lighthouse black*
> *Coffee can blue*
> *I lost an umbrella*
> *Looking for you in a shit storm*

The next verse seems to be tied to what he talked about in 'See My Field,' Bob saying that he and the band 'are the champs' when it comes to 'quests for new triumphs.' He's out there every day facing down foes and coming up the victor. Meanwhile, all the 'intellectuals are scratching their heads,' mere academics 'pondering a lost monocle.' These are the 'cold and timid souls' Roosevelt described, the critics who don't count. But all that effort comes at a cost, and sometimes even Pollard's mind gets emptied of ideas, as he admits in the song's chorus: 'I'm going blink blank in the think tank.'

SIDE TWO
Track one: *'Daily Get-Ups'*

This is one of many tracks that lands well shy of the two-minute mark. While I'm critical of a lot of the songs off the reunion LPs, where Bob just starts singing without any sort of musical foundation, this one at least starts with Doug laying down a cool riff. Lyrically, it's a throwaway—the refrain, 'Put on your make-up, got to have it,' is so macho it's practically a parody that should sit alongside the Cash Rivers track 'You Know She Thinks I'm Sexist.' In that song, Pollard, posing as an aging country star, croons, 'You know she thinks I'm sexist when I get up in the morning and I tell her to make me some eggs.' That must have been right after he told her to put on her makeup.

Track two: *'Hudson Rake'*

This expands upon songs from the two prior albums. Whereas *August By Cake*'s 'Substitute 11' was an outline for a TV show and 'How To Kill A Man' off *How Do You Spell Heaven* was structured like a three-act play, here Pollard writes a scene in which he names more than half a dozen characters. The lines that he sings are supposed to be coming from these characters, or else from news accounts describing the events. 'Earthquake shock to the head' is meant to be from an article in the *Carpe Diem Gazette*, while 'There was a terrible accident last night' is being spoken by an anchor from a local TV station. As a one-act play it doesn't work, mainly because the song's under two minutes, and Pollard doesn't do much to differentiate his voice from line to line. Maybe he's actually satirizing works like *Tommy*, where Pete Townshend sings in the voice of numerous characters and yet it all sounds like Pete Townshend. Still, it's amazing to see Pollard, thirty years into writing songs, pushing beyond the boundaries over and over again of what a pop song is or should be. Kristin Hersh, in the *Talkhouse* essay mentioned above, wrote of the track, 'Land on

"Hudson Rake" and stay a long, long time. Play it again and again. This is what happens when you cram a dozen songs into the body of one. It's another planet. The elegant movements are a water slide rather than a narrative, and yet … it all makes sense. Nobody else can do this.'

Track three: *'Sport Component National'*

The first half of this almost-three-minute song sounds like a jingle for imaginary cable channel SCN (Sport Component National). Pollard sings of 'getting ready to run' and a 'night game breaking out.' There might even be a bit of Bob's original demo at the twenty-four-second mark. While that's all fun, the last minute of the song is an absolute blast, with Pollard and the guys creating one of the most anthemic passages in recent history. There are also funny sports-related lines, including Bob writing of an overly muscled athlete, 'He's oh-so ripped, you'll recognize the scars.'

Track four: *'I Love Kangaroos'*

This very fun song is basically what you'd expect from Pollard with a title like 'I Love Kangaroos.' According to Doug Gillard, 'Apparently it was inspired by a clip Bob saw of a person pushed into water by a kangaroo.' But there's more to the song besides just a mad marsupial. Pollard, just after mentioning 'Penguin books,' talks of scratching a rash until it's 'well red.' That's damn clever. Later, Pollard describes the tune as a 'travelogue song,' which he's 'happy to compose.' He also admits not knowing how to end the song or where to take it next, figuring that nobody cares anyway. It's a fun meta touch. The music, meanwhile, perfectly fits the song's subject matter; it's fun and jaunty. The track is made even more playful by starting out with the sound of a cat toy, which Gillard has said was placed there for 'no reason,' adding, 'It makes a chirpy animal sound when touched. My cat ignores it, but at least I put it to use for the album.'

Track five: *'Grey Spat Matters'*

This is a slight song that, at just a minute and a half of chugging guitar, is probably my least favorite on the album. It also, combined with 'Daily Get-Ups,' shows that side one is much stronger than side two.

Track six: 'That's Good'

This was the third single issued from the album. It was also the only track on the LP to have been based on preexisting material. It was resurrected because, as Bob explained, 'I've just always thought that "That's Good" was very pretty and deserved more attention and better treatment.' That 'better treatment' means another string arrangement from Doug Gillard. The results are spectacular; it's definitely the best song on the album's second side, and one of the best ballads the band's ever produced. When Pollard writes, 'What's inside a head? Come and take a look around,' it's similar to *Bee Thousand*'s 'Peep-Hole,' in which Bob tells someone, 'I'm looking inside your brain, and Christ it's a cluttered mess.' He also writes here that 'You could fall down, but that's good.' This goes back to the sentiment of 'See My Field.' Do you want to be in on the action, or will you continue to sit on the sidelines, a mere spectator? Because—as long as you're in the arena—even if you lose, you win.

Track seven: 'Flight Advantage'

In this song, which was recorded as a band, Pollard mentions a number of natural phenomena: trees, birds, ants, dancing spiders. He sings about all this in a Southern accent. It's okay, but not terribly strong, again highlighting how the album starts to run out of steam as it winds up.

Track eight: 'Evolution Circus'

Having opened with its longest track, *Space Gun* closes with the second longest, at 3:37. While it's super-heavy and sounds good, I have to say it doesn't do much for me. The lyrics hint at topics that are grandly religious and historical, with its talk of Columbus and 'biblical ghettos,' but there's no clear theme or point. The band still sounds great, but overall this feels like a bit of a lackluster ending to what starts out as a truly stellar album.

26 ZEPPELIN OVER CHINA

two thousand and nineteen

This is the band's most consistently enjoyable record——an hour and fifteen minutes of pure rock. Prior double album *August By Cake* followed the *White Album* template. It was a crazy quilt of sounds, with all band members writing and contributing songs. This time around it's all Pollard, all the time. Each of *China*'s thirty-two tracks was written by Bob. It's the biggest chunk of new songs Pollard's ever delivered in one GBV release. And when you factor in that most of the album is a high- to mid-fi affair, this becomes even more impressive.

The album's name dates all the way back to before the band even existed. As Pollard explains, 'It was originally the title for a song that I wrote back in the late 70s called "Zeppelin Over China (And Everybody Thinks It's A Raincloud)."' The subtitle was used for the 2004 track 'Everybody Thinks I'm A Raincloud (When I'm Not Looking).' The original 'Zeppelin Over China' had been written for a short-lived, and mostly imaginary, band Pollard was in called Dash Riprock & The Hairspray Boys. They later changed their name to Dash Riprock & The Atomic Boys, which became just The Atomic Boys, until, finally, they were Rex Rock & The Clocks. All of that being said, the group never played live or recorded anything. They did, however—in true Pollard fashion—have a photo shoot. The phrase also appears in the Circus Devils song 'Thelonius Has Eaten All The Paper,' from the album *Five*, which contains the line 'A zeppelin over china filled with flies.'

Zeppelins—they're also called rigid airships —were invented in the late

1800s by Germany's Count Ferdinand von Zeppelin. Zeppelins are different from blimps. A blimp is just a big balloon, whereas a zeppelin has a metal frame. In the 1930s, zeppelins were used to ferry passengers on transatlantic trips. These would last anywhere from three to five days, depending on the winds. The *Hindenburg* made seventeen of these flights before blowing up in New Jersey in 1937, killing thirty-six passengers.

China has a striking sleeve featuring a great piece of Pollard artwork, a black background, and an elegant purple sans serif font. The collage featured on the cover is entitled *Twice Providing Once*, an apt name for a double album. The artwork is a collage sitting in the middle of a pool of blue fingernail polish that's been poured onto a mirror housed in a golden frame. Before gracing the cover of *China*, it was featured on page 120 of *EAT* 14.

Travis Harrison is back to not only record and engineer the record but also, for the first time in four LPs, receive sole producer credit. Harrison's work with Pollard and the band over the last couple of years—he also now travels with them, handling their live sound—has been truly exceptional.

'Travis has completely changed the picture and method of making an album,' Pollard has said. 'He makes it easier for me, as do the rest of the guys, and allows me to focus on pumping out songs.'

Once again, the band recorded at Harrison's New York studio Serious Business, as well as at the Magic Door out in Montclair, New Jersey. Vocals were recorded at the Stillwater River Lodge, located just northeast of Pollard's hometown of Northridge. When Harrison first began recording Pollard's vocals—after the band had laid down the instrumental tracks—he brought a whole bunch of gear. But now he just checks in to the Stillwater River Lodge with a laptop and microphone, and Pollard then proceeds to sing all the songs, in order, over the span of just a couple of days.

A number of *Zeppelin*'s songs were played throughout the 2018 *Space Gun* tour, including 'The Rally Boys,' 'Charmless Peters,' 'My Future In Barcelona,' and the album's first and only single, 'You Own The Night.' The latter song came out in July of 2018, and was originally going to be one of seven singles issued from the record. One single was going to be released a month, leading up to *Zeppelin*'s release the following January. And while this would have meant an abundance of B-sides, and a lot of cool artwork, Pollard ended up shitcanning the ambitious idea, which explains the six-month gap between 'You Own The Night' and the eventual LP.

The overall sound of the record is absolutely stunning. In the past, ultra-anthemic tracks would have rocked, but that's about all they would have done. Prior GBV albums either aimed to capture the sound of the band's ferocious live shows (a record like *Isolation Drills*), or else they were all about preserving the experimental nature with which they were recorded (Jimmy dropping amps and Pollard singing in his basement). Whereas here, 'The Rally Boys' has all the power of 'Game Of Pricks,' but with additional subtle touches like strings and synth washes. It rocks *and* it's polished.

Another sign of Bob's maturity can be found in the album's vocabulary. Just glancing at *Zeppelin*'s tracks, you see words such as 'carapace,' 'bellicose,' 'anathema,' and 'vertiginous.' If the Cash Rivers project is Pollard at his most lowbrow, a fair number of the tracks on *Zeppelin* are among the most sophisticated songs Bob has ever written.

China's reception was almost uniformly positive. Mark Deming, writing for the website *AllMusic*, gave the record a four out of five and said that it signaled 'an unexpected but very welcome late-career renaissance.' Kirsten Inneski, in the online magazine *Spill*, called the record 'dizzying' and wrote that 'it would be easy to get lost in the wide range of styles, but the measured sequencing ensures that the whole thing sounds smooth rather than sprawling.' David Haynes declared the LP 'all things to all people' on the website *Post-Trash*, stating that 'Thirty years into his residency as an indie-rock icon, Robert Pollard is still asking the same question he has always asked us: Are you amplified to rock?'

SIDE ONE

Track one: 'Good Morning Sir'

At 1:09, this is the second-shortest song on the record. But unlike 'Wire Greyhounds,' the thirty-five-second snippet that opened *Universal Truths And Cycles*, this doesn't feel incomplete or too short. It's a great way to open the album, especially since it starts with Pollard saying 'Good morning.' It's as if Uncle Bob's meeting us at his kitchen table, cup of coffee in hand, playing for us his latest tunes. The song speaks of a 'Mr. Redbird.' Pollard here is probably referencing a cardinal, a red bird that can be seen year-round in Ohio (on another song, he refers to a starling). Or it could be a reference to the baseball team, the Cardinals, based in nearby Missouri. But I also wonder if 'Mr. Redbird' might be a pun on the title character from Herman Melville's fourth novel, *Redburn*. The book tells the story of Wellingborough Redburn's journey to Liverpool with a bunch of seedy sailors. It was based on a trip Melville himself had taken as a young man. Early in chapter three, there's the following exchange:

> 'Good morning, sir,' said my friend.
> 'Good morning, good morning, sir,' said the captain.

Track two: *'Step Of The Wave'*

Out of the thirty-two songs on the record, only ten are three minutes or longer, with this track, clocking in at three minutes exactly, being the first to appear. It's a good thing, since the song sounds a bit tentative for the first 1:20, not quite finding its groove. But when Bob starts to repeat the song's title and the band kicks in, it just takes off. The sound is absolutely massive, with Kevin March's cymbal crashes and Doug Gillard shredding all over the place until the song ends in a huge crescendo.

Track three: *'Carapace'*

On this fun track, Bob introduces some interesting language, using the words 'panoply,' 'carapace,' and 'sarcophagus.' A panoply is a suit of armor, or anything worn that's protective. A carapace is, basically, a natural panoply, such as a turtle shell (which Pollard mentions in the song), or the shell of a lobster or crab. And, finally, a sarcophagus is a stone coffin, a similar—but longer-lasting—shell. Pollard uses all three of these as metaphors for how we both hide from life and try to shield ourselves from its various attacks: 'And you hide a lot, out of sight.' He also alludes to these shields perhaps turning into traps from which we can never escape: a carapace can become a sarcophagus if you're not careful. Despite sounding like a depressing song, it's a lot of fun, with an icy, post-punk guitar, a lot of cowbell, and Bob sort of scatting at one point as he riffs on the word 'sarcophagus.'

Track four: *'Send In The Suicide Squad'*

Bob turns in a powerful vocal performance on this track. There are also some strong background vocals, and Doug adds guitar phrases that sound vaguely Indian or Middle Eastern. Bob's said that the title came from his band Dash Riprock & The Hairspray Boys. Some of the original lines were 'Oh, what a lovely day on the Ferris wheel / I found a spider in my soup today.' Bob's described the song as being 'real goofy and kind of doo-wop.' The phrase itself, 'Suicide Squad,' could have originated from a couple of sources. The DC Comics Suicide Squad, a team of different super-villains, made their debut in 1959, as part of the series *The Brave And The Bold.* They've made various appearances throughout the years, most recently as a lurid 2016 film. 'Suicide squad' is also a sports term, referring to the set of players deployed during kickoff. Wherever the title came from, I think what Bob's writing about is the opioid crisis gripping Dayton, not to mention the entire country. As *Time* magazine declared in the opening to its special issue 'The Opioid Diaries,' from February of 2018, 'The opioid crisis is the worst addiction epidemic in American history. Drug overdoses kill more than 64,000 people per year, and the nation's life expectancy has fallen for two years in a row.' Pollard's hometown of Dayton has been hit hard by the crisis. In 2017, it had the highest rates of overdose fatalities in the state, as well as one of the highest in the country. Even though deaths have dropped since then, drug abuse is still a huge problem. Bob seems to be speaking about this, telling hopeless addicts, in a bid of solidarity, 'I'm hanging on for you.' ('Hanging' could also be a reference to a form of suicide.) He then tells them that he's been where they are: 'I've known of no tomorrow.' And while he's offering hope, he also tells them it won't be easy, advising, 'And you should know, it's a long way home.'

Track five: *'Blurring The Contacts'*

This starts with some backward audio taken from *The Dave Ramsey Show.* Ramsey is an author and radio personality who offers financial advice. The song itself is mostly just a slow, two-chord riff paired with a sludgy bass line— it's sort of Guided By Voices in Jesus Lizard mode. Meanwhile, Bob chants surreal lyrics that never quite land. It's not horrible, but coming after a run of strong songs, this is the first weak tune on the album.

Track six: *'Your Lights Are Out'*

The opening to this song sounds a lot like 'See My Field.' However, it soon takes on a life of its own, and, when it does, it's an absolute blast. The band sounds great, with Mark Shue providing some great bottom end against another icy guitar part from Gillard. In the song's last minute, Gillard's guitar provides the counterpoint to Bob's vocals, mimicking an earlier call-and-response section in the song. It's a great touch, showing just what can happen when GBV stretch out a track to the three-minute mark, as they do here.

Track seven: *'Windshield Wiper Rex'*

This short song—it's just a second under a minute and a half—is positively perverse, with Bob singing about 'wet sex' and an 'orgasm theater.' Based on those bits, I don't want to think too hard about what Rex's 'windshield wiper' might be a metaphor for.

Track eight: *'Holy Rhythm'*

This heavy song has witty lyrics that make it a lot of fun to listen to. For example, Pollard labels 'drunken ghosts in the dance hall' as 'boogeymen.' Bob's said that the track 'has to do with the spookiness or spiritual ghostliness behind a lot of religious institutions in general. And maybe the morbidity surrounding churches, cemeteries and funerals.' Pollard also uses the metaphor of a 'holy rhythm' to show how a person can get out of step with life: 'Broken dreams of broken men … got no holy rhythm.' Life has a cadence, a flow, and if you're out of step with that, you're out of step with the world. It's why Pink Floyd kicked off *Dark Side Of The Moon* with the sound of a heartbeat; there's a primal pulse to life, and if you can't latch onto that, you're in trouble.

SIDE TWO

Track one: *'Jack Tell'*

This begins as a bare, two-chord track, with Pollard singing against just an electric guitar and bass. But then, at a minute in, there's a bit of synth, and Bob sings softly, accompanied only by an acoustic guitar. Shortly after, the others come in, and, when they do, the song sounds huge. Kevin March adds amazing fill after fill, and Doug Gillard turns in great melodic phrases on the guitar, especially at the end. Another thing to note is that Bob's singing, as it is throughout the album, is a return to his slow-drawl country voice of the late 80s (rather than the English accent that was all over his stuff in the 90s). It's interesting to hear him, after thirty years, return to the sound of some of the pre-Scat LPs.

Track two: 'Bellicose Starling'

Something I noticed while listening to this record is just how often GBV songs feature a relentless downstroke on the guitar. Even on tracks that have more of a folk vibe, with an acoustic guitar, Pollard still hammers with downstrokes (as opposed to a combination of down- and upstrokes). You can hear it not only on GBV's straight-ahead rock songs but also on their quieter tracks, like this one. The prototype for this kind of playing goes all the way back to Led Zeppelin's 'Communication Breakdown,' and Johnny Ramone played that way for the entirety of his band's existence. This instills more than a bit of stiffness in GBV's playing and sound. I'd love to hear more looseness in Pollard's right hand when he strums, especially in slower and softer songs, where it's definitely warranted. If you have any doubt that Pollard can swing, give a listen to his solo track 'Zoom (It Happens All Over The World),' a super-fun tune that shows just how loose Pollard can be. This song seems to be, at least in part, about starlings, mentioning the bird's 'annual migration.'

Track three: 'Wrong Turn On'

The first line, 'For a digital eternity,' is yet another case of Pollard poking fun at modernity (as in when people complain that their phone or computer is slow). The idea of a 'wrong turn on' is also witty, and a classic pun. The music consists of a whole bunch of fast downstrokes on an acoustic guitar while Kevin March goes nuts on the drums.

Track four: 'Charmless Peters'

This starts with the line 'I'm tired of watching the child, the insane child.' This poor tyke joins others from recent Pollard LPs, such as the 'Hangover Child' and the 'Child Activist.' There are a number of references to childhood in the song, including school and being given a bottle (not to mention the kid being throttled, echoing 'Beat On The Brat' by The Ramones). Bob also references the classic Mother Goose rhyme 'Little Jack Horner' when he tells the child in the song to 'just sit in the corner with Horner.' The song's chorus, 'Smoke them if you have them,' has a colorful history. It got its start in World War II, where weary soldiers, when they were given brief breaks, were told, 'Smoke 'em if you got 'em.' The fact that soldiers were issued tobacco as part of their day—four ounces, along with ten rolling papers; this was later replaced with mass-produced cigarettes—was not just by chance, or because a majority of soldiers were smokers. Instead, tobacco companies lobbied to have direct access to soldiers, aided by politicians from states or regions where tobacco was grown. The military wasn't catering to the needs of smokers; it was—instead—creating them. This went on for years, the military and big tobacco working hand in hand to give soldiers exposure to cigarettes and to keep them in a steady supply of tobacco products. Even as late as 1990, during the first Gulf War, tobacco conglomerate Philip Morris sent ten thousand packs of Marlboros to an air-force base in North Carolina, where they were distributed to different branches of service.

Track five: 'The Rally Boys'

This song, which Pollard's called a 'fight song' and a 'pep rally for anyone's club or group of people,' is an instant classic. It sports a rousing and anthemic chorus that's up there with, not to mention a bit reminiscent of, 'Glad Girls.' Also, the 'Hey, hey' snuck into the chorus—the same as in 'Glad Girls'—gives it a sort of Monkees vibe. The structure of the song is interesting, since it basically has three opening verses, which take up the first forty seconds of the song; then four choruses comprise the last minute. The final line of the song transforms 'the Rally Boys' to the 'Rand McNally boys.' Rand McNally is a company that began in 1868, which became famous in the following century for making maps. It still exists today, publishing atlases and travel books.

Track six: 'Think Be A Man'

Following on from my point earlier about all the downstrokes, as you can hear in the opening of this track, when that's all the guitar's doing—setting the beat of the song—it limits Kevin March's options, rhythm-wise, so he mimics those downstrokes by pounding on his drums with the same beat. Here, Pollard seems to be offering some sort of advice on masculinity and maturity, telling men, 'Don't feel so vastly important.' The last line, 'The little girls do not understand,' is a refutation of Willie Dixon's classic blues track 'Back Door Man,' which states, 'The men don't know, but the little girls understand.' The song was covered by The Doors on their 1967 debut, and the power-pop band The Knack named their 1980 LP *But The Little Girls Understand*.

Track seven: *'Jam Warsong'*

This begins, 'When it's bad, fix it. When it's fixed, find a destroyer.' Since Pollard's spent a career doing everything he can to deliberately imprint on his songs and albums a sheen of imperfection, this could be seen as a comment on the way he makes music. More lines seem to further this idea, Bob writing, 'Jamming it out, making no sense.' Musically, the song's a lot of fun, with a sort of seesawing beat and some expertly double-tracked vocals from Pollard. And while Kevin March is usually asked to sound crazed like Keith Moon, which he does on a few tracks on this album, the slow pace here means he's allowed to breathe. His slow fills on the toms remind me of Ringo Starr's restrained playing on *Abbey Road*'s classic ballad 'Something.'

Track eight: *'You Own The Night'*

At 3:24, this is the second-longest track on the record. It's sort of an odd choice for a single, since it has a mostly acoustic middle section that brings the whole track to a halt. After an intro that sounds a lot like the one-string guitar riff from 'Space Gun,' Bob asks, 'What's it like being all that?' He then paints a vivid picture: 'Beneath a cloak of trees that run for cover over shadows.' Bob's vocal during this section is great; we're a long way from the neo-basement recordings of the still-recent reunion LPs. After the acoustic middle section, the track returns to the full band, and it sounds amazing. The music is led by a great bass line and is buoyed by strings and Kevin March's relentless cymbal crashes. It's hard to make out any sort of guitar in the mix, which is something I appreciate, since a guitar is the lead instrument in most GBV songs. This is another sign of how confident the band had become in their sound, and how Bob is okay if not just plain eager to redefine people's expectations of what GBV can be.

SIDE THREE

Track one: *'Everything's Thrilling'*

This bare-bones song finds Bob singing against an electric guitar that's being strummed fast. It sounds a bit rough all around, so I wouldn't be surprised if this was Bob's original demo. If it's not, I don't know why some of the other band members didn't flesh it out a bit more. At one point, Pollard sings, 'Sin is a powerful ally to everything thrilling.' Whereas Blake's famous proverb, 'The road of excess leads to the palace of wisdom,' shows what can be gained from indulgence, Bob here says that sin—while obviously bad—has an upside. He's right. You usually don't get a thrill from doing the right thing.

Track two: *'Nice About You'*

This track sways back and forth from jangly electric guitar to sawing downstrokes until, at 1:20 in, it gets poppy, with Pollard repeating the word 'nice' as synth strings are added to the mix. Lyrically, it seems to be an attack on critics who try to judge or even understand Bob. He references 'nodding consultants' with their 'piggly earlobes pressed to the wall.' Well, they can all 'rest assured,' because, as Pollard insists, he's nice. However, when he repeats the word late in the song, over and over, you wonder who he's trying to convince: us or himself.

Track three: *'Einstein's Angel'*

This slow song is a perfect example of how good Bob and the guys sound in this new era of the band, and how effortlessly amazing tracks just seem to come to them. Even though Bob's vocal feels a little flat throughout, at the end there are some background vocals that take the track to another level. It's also, at 2:37, a great illustration of how much music the band can fit into a short track.

Track four: *'The Hearing Department'*

This slow burn of a song is utterly gorgeous. Mark Shue turns in some slinky and sinewy bass lines, Kevin March's drumming is restrained and perfect for the tune, and Doug Gillard channels his inner Johnny Marr. The whole vibe of is stunning, and you can easily envision this being on *Strangeways, Here We Come*. While I often praised Tobin Sprout's songs—especially during the run of reunion records—for having passages that let the tracks breathe, Bob does the same here with an instrumental break late in the song. And whereas some GBV ballads—think of 'Don't Stop Now'—explode into catharsis, this one becomes more subdued. Lyrically, it's potent and powerful, documenting one of the most difficult aspects of a relationship: listening. Bob presents a couple, saying that 'he went out, he got lost' while 'she's not so good' and 'very poor in the hearing department.' Between them, they have a 'total lack of communication.' As Deborah Tannen writes in her 1990 bestseller *You Just Don't Understand: Women And Men In Conversation*, 'We all want, above all, to be heard. We want to be understood—heard for what we think we are saying, for what we know we meant.' Here, Pollard's couple deal with this same issue.

Track five: 'Questions Of The Test'

More than almost any song, besides maybe *August By Cake*'s 'Substitute 11,' this track calls back to Pollard's past life as a teacher. The lyrics, at first glance, are a sort of pep talk to a student who's taking a quiz. But Bob also offers advice, telling the pupil to 'make a guess' and 'concentrate, do your best.' There's even, at the bottom of the song's lyrics, a space that says 'your score,' as if this is a test we're able, or meant, to take. However, as usual with Pollard, all is not quite as it seems. The song starts with the student being woken from a coma and then being 'pushed' to wherever the test's being taken. There are then two mentions of a 'robot voice,' not to mention a final warning that 'your life depends' on the test's results. This might just be Pollard's idea of modern education (sleepy kids dragging themselves to school only to be subjected to standardized exams run by a computer), or it might be a sort of sci-fi fantasy. The song's also a blast musically, since, at forty-five seconds in, the track slows down to a bluesy dirge that reminds me of the back half of 'I Want You' by The Beatles. There's also some great backward guitar while Pollard's spacey vocals pan back and forth. The song shifts back into rock mode before slowing down and then ramping up again for a gonzo final thirty seconds that sound, in their last moments, like something by Devo. It's an awesome musical journey, and it's hard to believe it all happens in just three minutes. It's one of the best examples of the band's musical chops, and one of the best showcases of Travis Harrison's ability as an engineer and producer. It's also another song wherein Pollard sounds more Southern than he has in a while.

Track six: 'No Point'

This sparse song is just Pollard singing against a plucked acoustic guitar, with an electric guitar strummed underneath. That gives it a sort of 'Sister I Need Wine' vibe. The message at first seems pessimistic, Bob writing, 'There is no point in fixing it, out of your hands.' Basically: *don't even try to remedy the situation, because fate is stacked against you.* However, in the next line he's reassuring, promising, 'You'll get back in again, I know.' The lyrics also have some religious imagery and overtones. Pollard's flirted with religious subject matter throughout his career, as recently—and probably most explicitly— on *August By Cake*'s 'Warm Up To Religion.' And yet, however tempted or curious Bob may be, he's too much of a skeptic—not to mention a realist—to completely buy what religion is selling.

Track seven: 'Lurk Of The Worm'

Pollard seems to be fascinated with worms of all types. He's mentioned them in a number of songs: 'Wormhole,' 'Worm W/ 7 Broken Hearts,' 'Dusty Bushworms,' 'Inchworm Parade,' 'Ironrose Worm,' 'Males Of Wormwood Mars,' and 'Ringworm Interiors.' Musically, this song is rooted in Pollard's love of prog. You can imagine Peter Gabriel wearing a worm costume and singing this with Genesis at the Roundhouse in 1973. And if it tends toward excess, this is Guided By Voices we're talking about: most of their career has been based on excess on some kind—too many songs, too many drinks, too many high kicks. If the whole album were like this, I wouldn't be a fan, but for one track, it's okay.

Track eight: 'Zeppelin Over China'

At thirty-nine seconds, this is by far the shortest track on the album. It's also the only song snippet on the record, not to mention the only instrumental. It's a brief acoustic-guitar sketch played by Bob and recorded in the tour van, probably on someone's phone (you can hear keys being jangled in the background). It's not annoying to listen to, but it's puzzling for it to be the last song on the side, especially since it sticks out from the rest of the tracks on the album. However, it was said that David Bowie always had one track on a record—usually the last—that looked forward to the sound of his next LP.

For example, 'The Secret Life Of Arabia,' off *Heroes*, was a teaser for the exotic tracks found on the next album, *Lodger*. Maybe that's what GBV were doing here, giving listeners a sign of what to expect on the next LP, *Warp & Woof*, since that album was recorded quickly, in hotel rooms and tour vans.

SIDE FOUR

Track one: *'Where Have You Been All My Life'*

If the band Chicago, in the late 80s, had released a song called 'Where Have You Been All My Life,' you'd have been in for a sappy power ballad. That's not what Pollard and the guys serve up here. Instead, it's Bob spitting out rapid-fire lyrics over a one-chord guitar riff, until—three-fourths of the way through— the guitar becomes more start and stop (sort of like Franz Ferdinand's classic 'Take Me Out,' except without the disco feel). Pollard writes of the 'man behind the curtain' who is a 'well-known coward.' He's taking aim, as he did on the *Earthquake Glue* song 'Main Street Wizards,' at the people in charge, offering advice, when, in reality, they have no idea what's going on.

Track two: *'Cold Cold Hands'*

This mid-tempo rocker is a caustic put-down in the tradition of Dylan's 'Idiot Wind.' It begins, 'You're going to alienate the flowers with your cold, cold hands.' This is a person who's so chilly that even nature turns away from their icy touch. There are guitar flourishes throughout that flirt at becoming a solo, and yet one never quite develops. Doug Gillard's an amazing guitarist, and I would have welcomed twenty or thirty seconds of shredding, but— since the song's under two minutes—that never happens. Despite this, it's a strong song.

Track three: *'Transpiring Anathema'*

This begins with Bob growling 'I've got news for you, punk' over a simple guitar line. When the whole band join in, it sounds massive, and you can imagine how good this would be live. I mentioned before how Pollard's using a bunch of interesting words on this record, 'anathema' being yet another. While the most common usage means someone or something intensely disliked or loathed, or something that is considered completely wrong and offensive, the word also has a religious connotation. It's used in the New Testament to mean, essentially, 'God's curse.' I don't know which meaning Bob favors, or if he even means the word literally—he may be using it purely for poetic effect.

Track four: 'We Can Make Music'

This is a gentle and gorgeous track that breaks out of the band's usual hard-rock template. Instead, it features acoustic guitars and synth strings. The subject matter fits with Pollard's proggy side, with the lyrics being basically a paean to nature and the interconnectedness of all things. He writes that it's because of the trees, or rather nature, we create art: 'We write for them, I really believe.' Earth Bob is a refreshing change from Miller Lite Bob.

Track five: 'Cobbler Ditches'

The complaint that most people make about double albums is that because they contain so many songs, some just end up as filler. While I think *Zeppelin Over China* is a strong record, not all thirty-two songs can be gems, so if you had to point to one that feels like double-album filler, it'd be this. It's based on a downstroked, single-note guitar line—the kind that's cropped up a whole lot in Bob's recent work, and that appears throughout this album. His vocals are also high in the mix, and there's no real structure to the song—it's just six verses, and there's no real tune to latch onto. One fun thing is that a vintage *Alien Lanes* track gets a mention late in the song, Bob writing, 'Candy bar mars playing "Motor Away."'

Track six: 'Enough Is Never At The End'

This short track, with a title that sounds like it could be a James Bond movie, clocks in at just 1:14. It's the last of a number of brief songs. Of the first six tracks on side four, only one, 'Transpiring Anathema,' is over two minutes long, and even that one, at 2:03, barely qualifies. Instrumentally, this is interesting, with piano, synth strings, and violin. However, Bob sings it in a sort of shouty way, bellowing when the instrumental backing would seem to call for more of a croon. So, instead of it being an understated classic, like 'The Military School Dance Dismissal,' it comes off as not much more than a classier 'Sad Baby Eyes.'

Track seven: 'My Future In Barcelona'

At 3:49, this is the longest track on the album. It's also one of the most accomplished. The title proved prophetic, since the band went to Spain as part of the Primavera Sound festival the same year *China* came out. The lyrics seem to be a sort of tongue-in-cheek nod at the recording industry and the band's place in it, Pollard writing about 'moving units.' And, if he moves enough of them, he can retire in a glamorous foreign setting like Barcelona. Musically, the track's absolutely fabulous—Bob turns in one of the album's best vocal performances, the guitars soar, the drums sound huge, and there's a great sing-along chorus. The tune has a bunch of different sections, and yet it never meanders or gets lost the way some of Pollard's songs that lean toward prog have a tendency to do. Instead, it's a complex journey disguised as a pop song. It's also an instant classic, as good as anything the band delivered in their 90s heyday.

Track eight: 'Vertiginous Raft'

The first line here, 'Now is the time for all good men to come to the aid of their party,' is not a political call to arms, but was instead created by typing teacher Charles E. Weller in the nineteenth century. It was later changed to 'Now is the time for all good men to come to the aid of their country,' because if you substitute 'country' for 'party' and add a period at the end, it's exactly seventy characters long, which is a full line when typed. Pollard riffs on the line throughout, at one point changing it to 'Party now is the time for all good men.' Musically, the track sounds a lot like 'Circus Day Holdout' from *August By Cake*. And while there are some effective touches with synth strings and what sounds like bells, since the song's under two minutes and doesn't have much of a structure, it seems a bit strange to end the record here, rather than with something triumphant and fleshed out, like the previous track. But this is something that Pollard often does when it comes to sequencing records. He'll start an LP with a short song, or one that seems to start right in the middle. This acts to throw the listener off (think of *Universal Truths* or *Under The Bushes*). He does the same thing with last songs, too. This leaves the album feeling unresolved, but also like it's still sort of in motion. It's a tactic that Pollard often uses to great effect, as he does here.

27 WARP & WOOF

two thousand and nineteen

his album is different from any other GBV record. Each of its two-dozen songs was issued on a series of six-song seven inches over the course of half a year. The first two EPs, *100 Dougs* and *Winecork Stonehenge*, came out in 2018. The second two were issued in early 2019, as *1901 Acid Rock* and *Umlaut Over The Ozone*. These EPs were paying homage, as Pollard wrote in a note posted to social media in July of 2018, to the 'format that was so prevailent [*sic*] for GBV in the early slash mid-'90s.' The songs were then 'compiled and re-sequenced with new artwork' before being released as GBV's second LP of 2019, *Warp & Woof*.

The past releases Pollard was referring to were sloppy but super-fun seven-inches such as *The Grand Hour*, *Fast Japanese Spin Cycle*, and *Clown Prince Of The Menthol Trailer*. And even though those EPs contained tracks that were later reworked or provided inspiration for future albums ('Marchers In Orange' appeared first on *Spin Cycle*, while 'Broadcaster House' and 'Scalping The Guru,' from *Menthol Trailer*, would provide—temporarily, anyway—album titles, while *The Grand Hour* supplied the name of both *Bee Thousand* and *Alien Lanes*), GBV's EPs from that era were more or less standalone creations. The same way that The Beatles, and later The Smiths, released singles that weren't on their records, GBV's EPs were removed from their other work; the albums were the albums, and the EPs were the EPs.

So, then, what does that make *Warp & Woof*? Is it a compilation or a studio record? Is Bob striving once again for *Who's Next*, or is this just *Odds*

& *Sods*? It's somewhere in the middle. The four EPs are one thing—they have their own art and song sequence—while the LP is yet something else. And when you think about Pollard, and the history of the band, it makes perfect sense.

Bob's a guy who loves to make things. He has songs coming out of his ears, he's a prolific visual artist, and he loves to make up phrases and titles. That's why EPs are the perfect way for him to scratch his artistic itch. As a standalone album, *Warp & Woof* is a great listen, offering everything there is to like about GBV. It deserves to be considered alongside LPs such as *Space Gun* and *Earthquake Glue*. It's also the first record in a long time to capture some of the lightning-in-a-bottle essence that made *Bee Thousand* the band's pinnacle achievement. Because, as much as later records like *Let's Go Eat The Factory* served up short and ragged songs, that's all they were; they weren't sewn together into any sort of connected or consistent whole. But *Warp & Woof* really does get back to the ragged and rough quality that was the highlight of the lo-fi years, while retaining some of the best examples and impulses of late-period Pollard.

The record's raggedness is due to the fact that—unlike the past couple of albums, which were tracked at producer Travis Harrison's New York studio—much of *Warp* was recorded during 2018's *Space Gun* tour. Bob recorded his vocals in hotel rooms and small studios, while the guys recorded their guitars in the back of the tour van. I don't mean in the back of the van as they were parked at a Ramada Inn while waiting to play in Winnipeg; I mean in the back of the van as it sped down the highway between gigs. This results in a super-laid-back and catchy record that sounds amazing. It was also the perfect move for the guys to make after a trio of polished and accomplished albums.

The songs were short in order to squish them onto a seven-inch. According to Doug Gillard, he and the rest of the band rallied behind the challenge: 'I dig having those parameters to work within, and I think we all had fun doing things this way.' Of the twenty-four tracks, Bob wrote all of them, except side two's 'It Will Never Be Simple,' which is by Gillard.

The cover for the record's also strong, featuring a striking Pollard collage in black and yellow. The yellow is super bright, reminding me of past GBV sleeves like *Vampire On Titus* and *Self-Inflicted Aerial Nostalgia*. The only downside to the package is that there are no lyrics.

Another difference between the LP and the EPs is that the sides are named. Side one is 'Warp,' and side two is 'Woof.' The sides are also named, parenthetically, 'Cincinnati' and 'Cleveland.' For a band so closely identified with Dayton, it's fun to see Bob reference other Ohio cities like this.

In terms of the album's title, while sounding like the usual bit of Pollard nonsense, *Warp & Woof* is both a real thing and a phrase that gets used a lot. It derives from weaving, and was coined centuries ago. Here's the website dailywritngtips.com on the phrase:

> Weaving is the process of crossing threads or yarns to create a woven fabric. Picture an old-fashioned loom: a large wooden frame. One set of threads is fastened from top to bottom of the loom. These vertical threads are called the warp. Threads that cross from side to side, over and under the warp, are called the weft or the woof. Together, the warp and the weft (or woof) are the substance of the web thus created.

Pollard's collage for the album, with its series or horizontal yellow and black lines, seems to reference this idea. And yet, that's just the woof. He'd need a series of corresponding lines going up and down to act as the warp. This gives a clue, I think, as to the naming of the two sides. Pollard's saying that the songs together form an integral whole, with each one supporting the other in a tapestry of music, which only when listened to side by side will be complete.

The names of the cities may also play a part here, too, since Cleveland and Cincinnati are the most northern and southern points of the state, respectively. Perhaps these up and down points are meant to complement the side-to-side images of the album's cover, thus indeed forming the warp and woof of the title.

Reviews for the record were again positive, with critics amazed that the band could follow up a double album so quickly with such a solid record. 'For most artists, releasing a twenty-four-track album just three months after the drop of the previous LP would be a heroic feat,' marveled Sophie

Brzozowski, writing for *Exclaim!*, 'but then again, what's another couple dozen songs after you've written hundreds?' Michael James Hall, writing in magazine *Under The Radar*, described the LP as being filled with 'kaleidoscopic snapshot songs evoking swiftly passing moments of absolute musical and lyrical glee, bafflement and, sometimes, jaw-popping wonder.' Sean Kitching, on website the *Quietus*, declared *Woof* to be the 'pinnacle so far of the current GBV reformation,' before comparing the record favorably to past classic LPs by the band such as *Alien Lanes* and *Under The Bushes Under The Stars*.

SIDE ONE

Track one: 'Bury The Mouse'

There's some ferocious guitar work by Doug Gillard on this opening track. He's shredding left and right, and, while his playing is badass, even more astounding is the fact that Gillard played his guitar, to quote press materials for the record, 'in a van hurtling at sixty-plus miles per hour.' You get the feeling that the mention there of 'sixty-plus' is to protect the driver, who was probably going much faster. Bob, in the final moments of the track, references an early GBV record, writing, 'Bubbles will bump him around in the same place the fly got smashed.' *Same Place The Fly Got Smashed* was one of the last albums self-released by the band before they signed to Scat in 1993. 'Bury The Mouse' was also the opening track on the first side of the *100 Dougs* EP.

Track two: 'Angelic Weirdness'

Most of this track is just acoustic guitar and some subtle drums. Pollard's voice is again heavily treated, which I like, since the sloppy vocals were the only thing I didn't like about *Zeppelin Over China*. This song seems to be another of Pollard's commentaries on religion, a subject he's tackled on dozens of prior GBV tunes. Here, he's saying that he's experiencing 'angelic weirdness,' because an angel is walking with him. And yet, even though that should 'comfort him,' he can't get over feeling that, well, it's weird. Mark Shue recorded his bass line while balancing on a bench seat in the aforementioned speeding tour van.

Track three: *'Foreign Deputies'*

At just 1:01, this is the album's shortest song. It doesn't have much of a structure—it's just a long verse that doesn't rhyme or seem to make much sense. Toward the end, you can hear a voice talking about 'excrement' and a 'wastepaper basket.' This was taken from a recording of a commencement speech that John Wayne gave in the early 70s. In the recording, Wayne—clearly inebriated—slurs his speech, curses, and rails against college demonstrators.

Track four: *'Dead Liquor Store'*

For the first minute of this minute-and-a-half song, it's a straight-ahead stomper, with Pollard singing standard rock'n'roll lyrics against a driving beat ('When you held my baby, you pushed me right out the door'). But then the music's replaced with some spiky guitars that sound like the main riff to 'Queen Of Cans And Jars' before the song kicks back in and Pollard returns to the sort of scatting that showed up on 'Carapace' from *Zeppelin Over China*.

Track five: *'Mumbling Amens'*

This song starts, appropriately enough, with mumbling. When it finally gets going, it's slower and more jangly than the preceding tracks. The music is just gorgeous, especially when, late in the tune, Pollard croons, 'My childhood is through.' The word 'amen' is often said after a prayer—it means 'it is so' or 'so it be.' It's used in Muslim, Christian, and Jewish worship. Bob, speaking here of someone mumbling the word instead of saying it clearly, could be referring to the respectful murmur that usually pervades praying, or he might be indicting the empty lip service that most people give to religion—they go through the motions, but don't really believe. Either way, the track is a small gem.

Track six: *'Cohesive Scoops'*

This flat-out classic is everything you want from the band: it's anthemic, it's fun, it's got a great title, and it's a bit absurd. And while I'd praised 'Space Gun' for its four-minute-plus running time, 'Cohesive Scoops' loses absolutely nothing by clocking in at a mere 1:30. It's absolutely perfect, and kind of a miracle that it sounds so complete for a song so short. Lyrically, the line 'I know the world is the love you do' seems to reference Paul McCartney's 'The End,' wherein he famously declares, 'The love you take is equal to the love you make.' Otherwise, the lyrics seem to be about pet ownership, Bob asking, 'Tell me what's in the bowl now,' and 'Hey, did you let the cats in?' The track's title could also refer to kitty litter.

Track seven: *'Photo Range Within'*

The key to this jaunty song is Mark Shue's bouncy bass line. The overall vibe reminds me of the stomping T. Rex classic 'Metal Guru.' Once again, the mix is perfect: Bob's vocal is low, allowing his voice to be just another instrument rather than the main focus. The track's short, at 1:14, but it feels complete. The lightness of it is also welcome—I can't say it sounds like any other track in GBV's vast catalogue.

Track eight: *'My Dog Surprise'*

After the cats that got mentioned during 'Cohesive Scoops,' we now meet a dog (speaking of, shouldn't this be on the 'Woof' side?). The title refers to the misheard lyrics of Cream's 'Sunshine Of Your Love,' in which most people hear 'my dog surprise' in the first verse instead of the correct 'my dawn surprise.' There's also a bit of fun when, about halfway through, Gillard's guitar screeches and yelps, mimicking the barking of the eponymous dog. The real star of the song is drummer Kevin March, who gives an amazing performance. March's drums seem to be the only instrument to have been recorded in a proper studio, at the same New Jersey spot he's used for the past couple of records.

Track nine: *'Tiny Apes'*

Cats and dogs were mentioned in the last couple of tracks; we now have tiny apes in this tune, which is a bit absurd but also a lot of fun. The drums again sound awesome, with a gated reverb snare that reminds me of 'Modern Love,' and the guitar does a bunch of cool stuff, especially at the end. It's a short track that totally works.

Track ten: *'Blue Jay House'*

At 2:03, this is the record's second-longest song. It features keyboard stabs that are right out of Devo's 'Big Mess.' The lyrics, however, are boring. For Pollard, who has a mastery of words unparalleled in his contemporaries, to pen lines like 'The night was long, the night was black' seems lazy. His singing also consists of a method he often employs in place of a real vocal melody, which is just singing high and then low, and going back and forth throughout those two registers for most of the song.

Track eleven: *'Down The Island'*

This song is cross-faded with the preceding track, and there's a field recording of rain, giving the quiet, acoustic tune a pastoral feel. The opening reminds me an awful lot of 'That's Good' off *Space Gun*. The lyrics seem to be about longing and wanting to get back to an idyllic island paradise, Pollard declaring that he wants to 'speed this motor back to you' in order to be together once again with the object of his affection.

Track twelve: *'Thimble Society'*

This tune has a great vibe, with stop-and-start guitars and a good vocal melody, along with Bob hitting some high notes, but—like some of the other tracks on the record—it never gets fleshed out; it stops rather than ends. Pollard here seems to acknowledge the push/pull of GBV fandom, writing, 'I'm wearing you out.' Keeping up with him, he knows, is almost impossible (not to mention tiring). And yet, he follows this by slyly saying, 'I'm pulling you in.' Try as we might, we just can't resist his charms, no matter how frustrated by him we get.

SIDE TWO

Track one: *'My Angel'*

While not quite as catchy as side one's 'Cohesive Scoops,' this is another instant classic—a straight-up rock'n'roll song that wouldn't have been out of place in the repertoire of any 60s garage-rock band. Like 'Cohesive Scoops,' it's another *Warp & Woof* track that was played extensively on the *Space Gun* tour.

Track two: 'More Reduction Linda'

This joins other GBV tunes that mention a woman's name in the title, such as 'Choking Tara' and 'Jane Of The Waking Universe.' The music's kind of fun, with a cool guitar riff and a drumbeat that's mostly all toms. There's also background noise of what sounds like kids on a playground. Some harmonies toward the end are effective. My main problem with the track is Bob's vocal, which is silly and all over the place, verging on Cash Rivers–level absurdity.

Track three: 'Cool Jewels And Aprons'

Once again, great guitar work saves this from being yet another relentlessly downstroked song. The fun vocal harmonies call back to Pollard's love of British Invasion pop. I have no idea what the lyrics mean, or even what Bob is singing about, other than some references to 'Aspen' and 'UFOs.' This puts it in the same sort of space as a lot of the songs on *Warp & Woof*: they're short and simple; Pollard's not looking to say anything too heavy or deep. The genesis of the record was supposedly a half-hour songwriting session that yielded six songs. When you hear a track like 'Cool Jewels And Aprons,' you can believe that he writes six tunes in thirty minutes. Pollard can be deep and insightful when he wants to be, but that just doesn't seem to be the aim here, and that's okay. The true measure of any record is whether it's fun to listen to, and *Woof* succeeds when looked at through that lens.

Track four: 'Even Next'

This is a song wherein Pollard's technique of singing high and then low, back and forth, works. Some subtle but effective synth strings also add a lot. It's a good track, although I would have liked for it to last longer.

Track five: 'It Will Never Be Simple'

The catalyst for this instrumental is that—for the *100 Dougs* EP—Bob asked Gillard to make a song that had one hundred guitar tracks. At 2:32, it's by far the longest song on the album. It's a pleasant listen, even if the idea of an instrumental on a GBV record doesn't make a whole lot of sense.

Track six: 'The Stars Behind Us'

This is one of the more lo-fi tracks, with Pollard's vocal competing against some random background noise. Once again, great drumming and guitar work make the song rise above something you might find on a Teenage Guitar LP.

Track seven: 'Skull Arrow'

At 1:04, this is the second-shortest track on the album. It's also one of the more dispensable songs, even if it's fun to hear Bob rhyme the title with 'Camaro.' Pollard also writes, 'One hundred monkeys can't be wrong.' This harkens back to the *August By Cake* track 'Cheap Buttons,' which started with 'ten billion Ringo fans can't be all wrong.' It could also be a reference to the infinite monkey theorem, the idea that if you get enough monkeys together and give them typewriters and enough time, they'll produce Shakespeare. Or the lyrics to a few good songs.

Track eight: 'Out Of The Blue Race'

Pollard does more talking than singing on this track. It's not my cup of tea, and when he does sing, he uses an affected, faux-metal voice that's just annoying. That makes this one my least favorite tracks on the record.

Track nine: 'Coming Back From Now On'

This song is fun, since it opens in a fake concert setting, with Pollard announcing it to an adoring crowd (a callback to 'Over The Neptune / Mesh Gear Fox'). That plus the 1970s power chords makes it sound like something off *Frampton Comes Alive!*

Track ten: 'The Pipers, The Vipers, The Snakes!'

With this track, we can add pipers, vipers, and snakes to the birds, apes, cats, and dogs found elsewhere on the LP. Also continued is the power-pop vibe from the previous song. It's a fun track, made most memorable by Doug Gillard's riffs.

Track eleven: *'Time Remains In Central Position'*

Bobby Bare Jr. recorded his guitar part for this song in the greenroom of Baltimore's Ottobar club before a gig in August. It's an okay song, although it falls apart toward the end. Pollard's vocals are again a bit rough, especially when he announces, 'You don't see how it works.' The word 'works' is pronounced so flatly it could slide under a door. There's a great song in here, which the band could have achieved if they'd just worked on it a bit more.

Track twelve: *'End It With Light'*

This was also the last track on *Umlaut Over The Ozone*, from the second batch of four EPs, so, similar to 'Bury The Mouse,' which opened one of the EPs, Bob most likely had his eye on this song all along for the LP's final one. Doug recorded his guitar tracks at the soundcheck before the same Ottobar gig mentioned above. It's a super-solid song, and a great way to end the record, except it feels too brief at just 1:11. If it was reworked and expanded a bit, it might be a classic, but here it feels like just a sketch.

28 SWEATING THE PLAGUE

two thousand and nineteen

This LP brought an end to an enormously productive year for Pollard, not to mention capping a decade that saw the reformation of his most important band. Back in 2010, Pollard's main creative focus seemed to be a new group, Boston Spaceships, which he'd formed in 2008. They'd released their fourth LP as the decade began, *Our Cubehouse Still Rocks*, but would go on to release only one more record, a double album (the excellent *Let It Beard*), the following year. Boston Spaceships toured, made videos, and were in the process of gaining fans all over the world. Guided By Voices, by contrast, hadn't played live or released any new albums since breaking up in 2004. The only GBV material that appeared was archival: the third installment of the *Suitcase* series, which came out in 2009. It looked like Guided By Voices had bitten the dust, and that Bob was pulling a David Byrne—there was no way Pollard was ever going to resurrect the group that made his name. All that changed when 2012's *Let's Go Eat The Factory* marked the surprise return of GBV. Pollard and the band have been at it—mostly nonstop—ever since. Twelve more records have been made, and even more are on the way.

In 2019 alone, GBV released a whopping sixty-eight songs. What's even more amazing is that all the material—three records, including a double album—was of a super-high quality. Gone are the lo-fi experiments, the self-recorded snippets, and the half-baked concept records. Instead, Bob and his new lineup continue to create incredibly interesting and engaging work, albums that deserve, and are destined, to stand up against the group's best.

One of the reasons for the high quality is that GBV continue to be Pollard's chief priority. The only other original material Bob released in 2019 was a seven-inch that came with the latest issue of *EAT* magazine, and a low-key Cash Rivers album called *Loose Shoes*, which came out over the summer. *Shoes* was billed as an 'unofficial unapproved bootleg,' and was only released on vinyl in a short run of five hundred copies. It was apparently compiled out of leftovers from 2018's epic sixty-nine-song *Do Not Try To Adjust Your Set I Am The Vertical And The Horizontal*. And while I get that the whole point of the project is to be tasteless—earlier LPs were awash with dick references and sophomoric humor—on *Loose Shoes* none of it lands (I quickly lost count of the number of Cialis and Viagra puns). Bob seems to have gotten a bit tired of the shtick himself, since *Loose Shoes* bumped off the announced double CD of Cash Rivers material and no other releases are on the horizon. The seven-inch that came with *EAT* was even worse, consisting of fragmented boom-box recordings. It's useful only as documentary evidence of how Bob works.

The year also saw the re-release of two fan favorites, 2019 marking the twentieth anniversary of Pollard's third solo album, *Kid Marine*, and the first full-length collaboration with Doug Gillard, *Speak Kindly Of Your Volunteer Fire Department*. Both LPs are from a particularly eventful time in Pollard's career. In 1999 the band put in a bid for mainstream acceptance with their first polished album, TVT's *Do The Collapse*.

Collapse was a focused, high-fidelity collection of rock songs produced by Ric Ocasek, the power-pop legend who passed away in September of 2019 at the age of seventy-five. This was followed two years later by *Isolation Drills*, probably the band's most consistently solid rock record. *Drills* also failed to break the band beyond their group of core and ardent admirers, and, ever since then, GBV have been a cult group. Pollard may have worshipped The Beatles and The Who, but his own band were turning out to be more like Wire. Which was maybe fine with Bob, because he loved Wire, too.

In a review of the group's first UK shows in over a decade, which the band played the summer before *Sweating The Plague* was released, James McMahon of the *NME* lamented the fact that the band's legacy is just a footnote. After comparing them favorably to Nirvana and the Pixies—two bands with considerably higher profiles than GBV—McMahon summed things up by stating, 'Truth be told, with a bit of editing, Guided By Voices could have been enormous.'

I join McMahon in asking, 'What if?' And even though, as the novelist Richard Ford notes, 'It's revealing—though perhaps only of oneself—to think of people in terms of what might have been better for them,' I can't help but think about it. Imagine if something resembling *Do The Collapse* had been released in '95—when the band's profile was at its peak—instead of the abrasive and shambolic *Alien Lanes*. What would have happened?

I think everything would have turned out differently. GBV would have gotten a huge audience. They would have sold a lot of records and gotten on the radio. They would have had a hit. Pavement scored big with 'Cut Your Hair' and then quickly squandered their artistic capital on the meandering and unfocused *Wowee Zowee*; GBV did the same thing when they followed up *Bee Thousand* with *Alien Lanes*. By the time *Do The Collapse* arrived in 1999, the opportunity had passed. The group's course for the next two decades had been set.

Sweating The Plague was announced by Bob back in July of 2018 as an LP called *Street Party*, which was due to be released in February 2020. Later in the year, the album's title had changed to *Rise Of The Ants*, and it was now pushed up to October of 2019.

Plague is very different from the previous LP, *Warp & Woof*. Even though that LP had two dozen songs, it clocked in at a sleek thirty-seven and a half minutes. *Sweating The Plague* has a comparatively brief twelve songs but is *longer* than *Woof*, at thirty-eight minutes. Only four tunes on *Plague* are in the two-minute range, and two even flirt with five minutes.

GBV hadn't made a twelve-track LP since their second album from 1987, *Sandbox*. And while Pollard's promised in the past to deliver a streamlined set of songs, he usually can't control himself, and he ends up overstuffing LPs with tune after tune. *Universal Truths And Cycles* was supposed to be just such a record. As Bob said at the time, 'I intended to make a proper twelve song album … because we haven't done that, just twelve songs. So we did that, finished it and mixed it, and then I wrote a bunch of new songs.'

Plague's cover is also a departure. Eschewing Bob's usual style, it's bifurcated into a mostly white section and a mostly black section. The top seems to be paint streaks, while the bottom has a remnant of newsprint that recalls Pollard's collage past. The whole image is reminiscent of the color-field paintings of the 50s done by artists such as Mark Rothko, Barnett Newman, and Clyfford Still. The cover being in two parts also reminds me of R.E.M.'s fourth album, *Lifes Rich Pageant.*

The back of the record is also more sparse than usual. It features what seems to be a vintage photo of some sort of banner, atop which is a blank space containing the name of the songs, written out by hand. The LP has a gatefold sleeve, although the interior's also spartan, with one side showing a photo of a wall and the other what seems to be a picture of some brown mini-blinds. It's awfully bland. Similar to *Warp & Woof,* neither the CD nor the LP come with lyrics. However, the LP has a one-page full-color comic, entitled, appropriately enough, 'Sweating the Plague.' The artwork has a serious Gilbert Shelton or R. Crumb vibe. The way the album's lyrics are referenced in the panels makes it awfully similar to the sleeve that Crumb did in 1968 for *Cheap Thrills* by Big Brother & The Holding Company. The comic was done by Matthew Cutter, author of the Pollard biography *Closer You Are.*

Before *Sweating The Plague* came out, GBV gave English comedian Stewart Lee an advance copy and had him write his thoughts for their website. Lee got into the band back in '93, when a record-store owner on London's Portobello Road hipped him to the German compilation *An Earful O' Wax.* He's been a fan ever since. In the piece, he likens being a fan of Bob and the band to 'standing in a ticker tape parade and reaching out to grab at stray releases as the endless flurry of output from the Needmore Songs publishing house billows around you.' He sums up *Plague* as 'an uncharacteristically concise rock'n'roll record, with lush gems tucked in amongst the hooks and hits, and with a sprinkling of prog rock moves.'

I agree that it's a strong record. *Sweating The Plague,* while not quite achieving the highs of the super-solid *How Do You Spell Heaven,* or the instant-classic status of *Space Gun,* is a fine LP.

Critics also agreed. Thomas Wilde, writing for online music magazine the *Fire Note,* declared *Plague* to be the best of the band's three 2019 releases, stating that the LP 'represents one of the most cohesive twelve-song sequences the band has released.' Paul Rowe, on *PopMatters*, awarded the album eight out of ten stars and wrote that 'on *Sweating The Plague*, Guided By Voices relish their cult status as one the most impeccable live rock bands to hit the stage through an album that is designed to be played on stage in front of dopamine-stimulated crowds at blistering volume.' And Michael Joshua Rowin of *Slant* magazine acknowledged—and liked—the prog leanings of the record, deciding that 'many of *Sweating The Plague*'s best moments find Guided By Voices in near-prog terrain.' The restrained and economical scope of the album was also attractive, giving the 'impression that frontman Robert Pollard is finally displaying a human-scaled canvas on which to present his work.'

SIDE ONE

Track one: *'Downer'*

The record begins with a Gibson ES-330, a hollow-body electric. What makes it distinctive is that the strumming is coming from behind the bridge, which gives it a high-pitched and brittle sound. When the song kicks in, there are more effective production touches, especially on Kevin March's drums. And when Pollard chimes in with the repeated background vocal of 'cry, cry, cry,' it's a welcome touch. That being said, some of Bob's vocal sounds a bit rough and uneven. But there are some funny lyrics, like when he writes, 'What won't kill you,' and you're expecting him to end the line with 'makes you stronger.' Instead, Pollard sings, 'What won't kill you ... killed me.'

Track two: *'Street Party'*

This is the album's shortest track, at an even two minutes. The subject seems to indeed be a street party, one where 'the heat is insane.' This sets the crowd on edge to the point where Pollard offers, 'How can we help you settle them down?' Where the Kaiser Chiefs once predicted a riot, Bob here seems to be trying to avoid one. Musically, I love the guitars on the verses. And while I've been critical of Bob's style of composing on the last couple of albums, bemoaning the nearly constant right-handed downstroke, here some space is left between the strums. This gives the tune a welcome stutter effect.

Track three: 'Mother's Milk Elementary'

This starts with Pollard singing unaccompanied, and he sounds good. It's something he hasn't done often in thirty years of releasing records, and it's an arresting way to open the song. And since the opening words are 'Wake up,' the effect is as if Uncle Bob were gently rousing you from golden slumbers after one-too-many Miller Lites. When the band join in after two a cappella verses, the track transforms into a ballad in the vein of 'That's Good.' Lyrically, Pollard's admonishing someone to be mature and come to terms with who they are: 'Make like a grown-up … face it, embrace it.' But he's also trying to pin someone down on their own beliefs, demanding, 'Come in or stay out.' Basically, decide on where you stand. But Pollard's not letting them off the hook, asking for 'honesty or nothing.' The title 'Mother's Milk Elementary' is also evocative. As a former fourth-grade teacher, Bob must have often felt like little more than a babysitter overseeing coddled kids who looked to him for the same pampering and praise they received from their parents.

Track four: 'Heavy Like The World'

This is one of two songs on the record that were created from preexisting material. It's based on a track called 'I'd Choose You,' which appeared on *Suitcase 2*. The original features different lyrics, as well as slightly different instrumentation. What's also odd is that the opening is identical to 'Wormhole,' off *Do The Collapse*. That's either a sly homage, or Pollard's just copying himself. The track—which was the album's first and only single—features strong vocal harmonies, blazing guitar by Doug Gillard, and an overall stellar production by Travis Harrison. The band sound tight all around, and it's a gorgeous song. The flow of these first four songs is also effective. They're edited closely together and make for a cohesive and satisfying listening experience—it's almost as if Bob's going for the effect of a rock opera/concept album.

Track five: 'Ego Central High'

The title of this sludgy rocker continues the education theme found elsewhere on the album, the young students of 'Mother's Milk Elementary' now having graduated to 'Ego Central High' (after a brief stopover at Postal Blowfish

Middle School). The song even starts like a pep rally, Pollard declaring, 'Here's a fight song for everyone to ever improve your game.' But then he turns more circumspect, advising the listener to 'throw out the ring that will bring you more and forever enshrine your name.' Basically, don't worry about having everything and trying to be famous. While I've been critical about some of Pollard's vocal performances on the past couple of LPs, he sounds amazing here. The tune splinters just before the 2:00 mark, with the last sixty seconds including some prog changes that don't quite work before returning to the main melody for the last couple of bars.

Track six: 'The Very Second'

This opens with an acoustic guitar. However, just because GBV are not plugged in doesn't mean they've gone folk. The noodling soon transforms into a ferocious downstroked riff that culminates in the whole band joining in. Later in the song, the acoustic reappears, playing the same angular figure from the opening, and it's an effective reprise. This is one of the record's longer tracks, at 4:43. To me, this shows that Bob and the band are thinking about the song. They're considering what the tune needs, and what can be done with the arrangement. When tracks start with Bob's vocal, and are over in a minute and thirty seconds, the only thought is to get to the end. But when the band stop and consider the ingredients of a tune, and then come up with interesting ways of assembling those ingredients, I think they create moments of true beauty—which they do here.

SIDE TWO

Track one: 'Tiger On Top'

This is another track that leans into Pollard's proclivity to go prog, with lots of little snippets and different tempos. Unfortunately, the various pieces don't cohere into a whole, and it just feels like random bits. And while I admire musicians who can jump from tempo to tempo and part to part, to the listener, it's jarring. The song comes to a complete halt halfway through when two sludgy notes are repeated for twenty seconds. When the tune finally kicks in again, you've sort of forgotten what song you were listening to. Pollard's done this a lot in his career, trying to marry the multipart epics that often stretch out to one side of vinyl with the short and spiky post-punk statements of bands like Wire. Sometimes it works, and sometimes it doesn't. This one doesn't work.

Track two: *'Unfun Glitz'*

The guitars here sound amazing, sporting just the right amount of crunch. The drums are also placed perfectly in the mix so that you can hear them clearly even amid all the distortion. March does some rolls on the tom, which is something that doesn't crop up much in GBV—Bob's songs are usually pile-driving rock anthems, without much room for fills, but they add a lot of color here. The title 'Unfun Glitz' points out that all that glitters is not, well, fun. It hints at the irony that was found in Fellini's *La Dolce Vita*. That title translates as 'the sweet life,' and yet the lives the characters in the film led were empty and devoid of meaning. It all *looked* glamorous, or, as Pollard writes here, glitzy, but it was actually depressing. Musically, this is yet another song with prog leanings—it has a bit of that start-stop that crops up elsewhere on the record. The problem I have with that is it means the musicians are spending most of their time counting instead of putting real feeling into their performance. This can result in cold slices of sound that are merely academic—'calculated' in the most literal sense. Math rock was called that not just because the structures of its songs looked good on graph paper, but because listening to it often felt like doing your algebra homework. I prefer the band to sound much looser than they do for most of *Sweating The Plague*.

Track three: *'Your Cricket (Is Rather Unique)'*

This is another track that is based on older material, with a demo version appearing as part of *Suitcase 4*. The most significant difference is that Bob sang on the demo, but here drummer Kevin March takes on vocal duties. What's interesting is that Kevin—when he sings the low notes in the verses—sounds an awful lot like Bob. I don't know if that's on purpose, or else he just naturally sounds like him. On the choruses, however, March sounds like himself, and the distinction of his vocals versus Pollard's from the rest of the record provides an aural palate cleanser, in the same way that Tobin

Sprout's songs used to. That might be why I like the song so much. The track was initially reworked because Bob wanted to release a whopping seven singles in the lead-up to *Zeppelin Over China*. All those seven-inches meant the group would need a whole lot of B-sides. And while you wouldn't think that would be a problem for Bob, or for this band, the rate that Pollard has been releasing stuff over the past couple of years left the group scrambling for material. This is where 'Cricket' comes in. It had been earmarked by producer Travis Harrison a few years prior as a possible ESP Ohio B-side. He chose it after combing through *Suitcase 4* for suitable material. This is why Travis plays drums on the track and not March—Kevin wasn't part of ESP Ohio. Harrison had recorded the drums for 'Cricket' at the same time as the ESP Ohio B-side 'Hit Me With Tonic.' When the band opted to go with 'Tonic' for one of the two B-sides of the *Royal Cyclopean* seven-inch, in place of 'Cricket,' 'Cricket' was indefinitely shelved.

Cut to a few years later, when the group were scrambling for tunes to fulfill Pollard's seven-single mission leading up to *China*. Harrison remembered he had the drums already recorded for 'Cricket.' Bob and the band liked the idea of bringing it back to life, so the current lineup provided the instrumental backing. Since the drums were already recorded, they thought it'd be fun for Kevin March to do the vocals. Around the time all that was happening, Bob had already recorded and given to the guys the demos of what was then known as *Street Party*. Pollard liked what they'd done with 'Cricket' and wanted to include it on that future album, which they were planning on working on that winter. This is why it's mentioned on the back of the 'You Own The Night' sleeve as being part of the forthcoming LP.

Lyrically, I have no idea what type of 'cricket' Bob's referring to. The insect? The game? In the end, I guess I don't care, since the song is so good. What helps make the chorus absolutely fly is the instrumental buildup right before it kicks in; this creates a tension that's cathartically released when March finally begins to sing. The quasi-archaic language also gives the chorus an oddly formal but ultimately distinguished feel. It's an absolute classic, and my favorite song on the album.

Track four: 'Immortals'

The band sound great, once again, on this mid-tempo rocker. *Isolation Drills* has long been the standard-bearer in terms of GBV's muscular sound, but on the last couple of records, Travis Harrison has perhaps best captured the band's hard-rock side.

For the last minute of the song, Bob repeats:

When she crashes the party, that would be a pity
When everyone has gone, you and I will still be here

Pollard's lyrics here are vague in a fun way. Since the song's called 'Immortals,' that bit about 'when everyone has gone' could refer to an apocalypse—perhaps the 'plague' of the album's title. Or he could be referring to the party in the previous line, and the whole thing just might be about outlasting uninvited guests. It's kind of hard to tell, and that's part of the fun.

Track five: 'My Wrestling Days Are Over'

It's interesting that the last song was called 'Immortals' and yet, just a track later, Bob's addressing mortality of a certain kind, declaring that his days of wrestling are over. Athletes have to often walk away from their careers—sometimes sacrificing millions of dollars—because of the accumulated wear and tear on their bodies. For some sports, this can happen ridiculously early; for example, it's not uncommon for gymnasts to retire as teenagers. Even in the world of basketball, football, and baseball—three sports Pollard excelled at in high school—most athletes don't play much past thirty. It's intriguing that Pollard uses 'wrestling' for the song's subject, since it's one of the few sports he didn't play when he was young. I wonder if he chose it because of its metaphorical quality, as if Bob's 'wrestling' with the decision of when he should start changing the way GBV operate. What would that mean for him as a performer? What would that mean for us as fans? Musically, the song's a bit rough, since the band's playing on top of Bob's initial demo of vocals and acoustic guitar. The whole thing feels brittle in a wholly unnecessary way. Jeff Lynne dealt with a similar situation on 'Free As A Bird,' but that's because John Lennon was dead and couldn't do a second take. I don't know what the reason is here, except that it's just the effect Pollard's going for. Which is a shame, because I'd love to know Bob's thoughts about aging and facing the inevitable decline of physical prowess, but it's so muddy I can't make out many of the lyrics beyond the title of the song.

Track six: *'Sons Of The Beard'*

This song—the album's longest, at almost five minutes—starts off spare, with just down-strummed acoustic guitar and sparse drumming. The instrumentation soon gets more interesting, with some cool keyboard washes that remind me of the electronic squiggles that popped up on 'Space Gun.' After a lengthy and quiet instrumental passage halfway through, it returns with a vengeance with some great shredding by Doug Gillard. Lyrically, I can't get an exact fix on who the 'sons of the beard' are, or what they're meant to represent. In the cartoon insert included with the LP, there's an illustration showing a group of bedraggled and bearded figures marching with a banner that reads 'SONS OF THE BEARD.' A caption to the illustration quotes some of the song's lyrics: 'Into the world, with nowhere left to go.' Pollard also sings about 'fixing the game' and 'selling out the show.' However, without all the lyrics, or a more coherent point of view, it's hard to tell what it all adds up to. And, since the back half of the track never quite congeals—there are so many starts, stops, and tempo changes, not to mention there's no discernible chorus or tune to latch onto—it doesn't add up to a satisfying listening experience. It's another of the album's mini-prog songs that ends up sounding more like an exercise than a composition. The last twenty seconds consist of a tinny, quickly strummed guitar that slowly fades out. It's the same guitar that opened the record, forming the first four seconds or so of 'Downer.' This is an impressive and welcome bookending touch, as well as a fitting ending to a fine album, and an incredibly productive year and decade. *Sweating The Plague* is yet another testament to the power and skill of GBV's most accomplished and productive lineup ever. It's an amazing feat, and the only real question it brings to mind is: what's next?

AFTERWORD

The club is open-ended

Guided By Voices began as a dream. Music only came later, as did records, listeners, fans. Over time, it's turned into more things. A brand, an institution, a way of life. And now, more than thirty years after the release of their first LP, it seems as good a time as any to ask: Will Pollard ever stop? Seeing how Bob has come to the realization that Guided By Voices is what the world wants from him, and he seems happy to supply it, what happens now? In 1995, Pollard declared, 'The club is open.' Will it ever close?

That's not to say the plug hasn't been pulled before. *Propeller* from 1992 was supposed to be the band's last album. In 2004, Pollard announced the end of GBV, had a farewell tour, and then, for the rest of the decade, he recorded and toured as either a solo artist or with his new group, Boston Spaceships. In 2010, Bob reunited GBV's original lineup, but after a handful of records and numerous live dates, he fired everyone and devoted the following year to a new band (Ricked Wicky). It looked as if GBV had bitten the dust yet again, and maybe for the final time. Yet Pollard resurrected the name in 2016, with an odd album on which he played all the instruments. In 2017, he recruited a new lineup and began to unleash a slew of late-period classics. GBV are back and seem to be here to stay.

That's mostly a good thing. The twenty-eight records covered in this book form an important and lasting body of work. No band has approached this level of productivity, and, since more records are on the way, that number's just going to grow. But will another five or ten (or even twenty-eight) albums add to the band's reputation, or will that be too much for fans to take?

Other performers, even those who began as brash rock'n'rollers, have mellowed with age and embraced their elder-statesman status. Ray Davies and Elvis Costello explored new sounds and styles as the years went on. They turned down the volume, wrote books, expanded their musical palette. Pollard, by comparison, has just kept on going down the path he started on in the 80s. He won't be donning a blazer and fedora anytime soon, singing against soft strings or a piano. In the wee small hours of the night, Bob's still bashing out arena-rock anthems.

Not that anyone wants middle-of-the-road Pollard. There's not a GBV fan anywhere who's pushing for Bob to become staid and schmaltzy, turning in anodyne crap like 'Ebony And Ivory' or 'Silly Love Songs' (tracks that show how even a Beatle is fallible). But, certainly, as Guided By Voices approach their fourth decade, something's going to have to change.

But can Bob change? David Bowie provides the best and perhaps final example in terms of transforming not just from character to character or style to style, but in mellowing with age and being able to go from being a rocker to something more quiet, more intimate, more mature. On the other side of the spectrum there's Morrissey, a once-brilliant artist who seems to only get crankier and less interesting with age. Early in Pollard's career, on the band's fourth record, he predicted, 'We'll be middle-aged children, but so what?' Bob, now well past middle-aged, seems content (if not hell-bent) to retain his childlike outlook for even longer. Should our response be the same as his: 'So what?'

Another issue beyond GBV's albums is their live show. Since the beginning, the band's concerts have been all about amps turned to eleven and (high)-kicking out the jams. Where does this leave Pollard, who's now well into his sixties? While it's ageist to say that someone of advanced years shouldn't be in a rock group, there's no arguing with the physical reality of getting older. As we age, our bodies change. Bob, a former athlete, has to know that—at some point—GBV live shows can't continue to be sweaty three-hour marathons. Maybe this realization has already begun.

The band's final concert of 2019 was a New Year's Eve blowout that saw them play a whopping one hundred songs in Los Angeles. It ended up being the longest GBV set ever, clocking in at four and a half hours. It was a great show. The band sounded amazing and the crowd was pumped and happy to be there, but Pollard—who was suffering from, as he told *Rolling Stone* a week later, a 'bum hip'—had to rest in a chair at various points. Over the course of the evening he only twirled the microphone a handful of times. His other theatrics, such as high kicks and the *Karate Kid*/Jethro Tull pose, were also in short supply.

The performance took its toll on Pollard, who fans have long viewed as indestructible. About two hours into the show, Bob started feeling pain. But he didn't hold back. 'The songs are what they are, and I really belt them out. There's no way to really pace yourself or hold anything back. We just kept going toward the finish line.' Even though Pollard thought he might puke as the clock struck midnight, he kept on going, giving us all a night to remember. And while this is a heroic and just plain kickass expression of Bob's dedication to his craft, it also points to the fact that something is going to have to change. Perhaps that's a good thing.

TVT A&R executive Adam Shore likens seeing the band in concert to 'going to church.' He's right. You're with people who share your beliefs, in a place filled with ecstasy and worship. But that space is also becoming perilously filled with complacency and ritual. Because when you see GBV live, you know certain things are going to happen. There will be a cooler onstage. Bob's going to break out a bottle of tequila and pass it around. It will be loud. Pollard will shit-talk other bands. You even know certain songs are going to be performed: 'Cut-Out Witch,' 'Gold Star For Robot Boy,' 'Game Of Pricks.' As much as I love these tracks—live and on record—the audience shouldn't be expecting them. Concerts aren't a midnight showing of *The Rocky Horror Picture Show*, where moviegoers know what's coming and act accordingly. A certain amount of routine's always been part of performance (whether it's the perfunctory 'thank you' after each song or the charade of pretending the concert is over before returning for an encore), but celebration can turn into ossification if you're not careful.

With their rabid fans and the ritual of their live shows, Guided By Voices have been compared to another long-standing rock group, with the *Washington Post* calling GBV 'the Grateful Dead equivalent for people who like Miller Lite instead of acid.' By the end of their career, a Dead concert seemed to exist only to provide an excuse for what was happening in and around the stadium. Music was no longer the point. The band had turned into a brand, an institution, a way of life.

So how does the story end? After all these years, what's going to happen? Well, from past experience, we know a few things. Eventually—whether it's six weeks or six months from now—someone's going to leave the band. This will be a momentary setback. New collaborators will soon join. Pollard will always be able to find four guys willing to back him onstage and on record. Albums will be released. Lots of them. Some will be great, most of them will be good, and one or two just might suck. What will always remain is Bob's fractured sensibility, and his adherence to what he calls the 'four *P*'s' of rock: pop, punk, psych, and prog. Add one more *P* to that list—Pollard himself—and you get the recipe for the band. Because Guided By Voices are Bob. The same way they're Dayton. And Dayton's a city that's been around for a long time. It's taken some punches, and yet it keeps on going. It's seen good days and bad, fortune and misery. Even though it may not resemble today what it was in the past, that's okay. It will always remain in our hearts and minds, not to mention on the map. No matter what.

ACKNOWLEDGMENTS

Thanks to everyone who listened to the *Self-Inflicted Aural Nostalgia* podcast or reached out to me during its initial run. Thanks to Tom and everyone else at Jawbone for publishing and producing this book. Thanks to Paul Palmer-Edwards for his amazing cover, to Carrie Wicks for her careful editing, to Jeff Warren for creating and maintaining the Guided By Voices database, and to Jules Gray for keeping me honest in terms of GBV history. Thanks to everyone associated with the group who spoke to me for the podcast: Robert Griffin from Scat Records and Adam Shore from TVT Records provided insight into critical periods for the band, and Mike Postalakis and Travis Harrison shed light on how the group operates today. Finally, I want to give a huge thanks to Robert Pollard. Guided By Voices have been a large part of my life since I first heard them in 1993. They mean the world not only to me but to fans all over the globe, which is why this book exists. None of it could have happened without Bob, a guitar, and a boom box. And for that we're all grateful.

ENDNOTES

Introduction

'My entire family watched … ,' Robert Pollard interviewed by Mike Watt, *Magnet*, April 2017.

1. Devil Between My Toes

'Arizona State signed … ,' John Feinstein, *Washington Post*, June 8, 1980.

'I've got a devil … ,' Robert Pollard quoted in James Greer, *Guided By Voices: A Brief History: Twenty-One Years Of Hunting Accidents In The Forests Of Rock And Roll* (Grove Press, 2005).

'Yelling and hitting … ,' Pollard in Greer, *Hunting Accidents*.

2. Sandbox

'Lacking a scene … ,' Matthew Cutter, *Closer You Are: The Story Of Robert Pollard And Guided By Voices* (Da Capo, 2018).

'One of the sharpest … ,' Byron Coley, *Spin*, January 1989.

3. Self-Inflicted Aerial Nostalgia

'It might have been … ,' Pollard in Cutter, *Closer You Are*.

'Well, a few years back … ,' Robert Pollard interviewed by Phil McMullen, *Ptolemaic Terrascope*, September 1993.

'Reich believed that … ,' Marsha Anderson, naturalnews.com, February 4, 2012.

'You probably know … ,' Mark Mothersbaugh, fecalface.com, January 3, 2008.

4. Same Place The Fly Got Smashed

'I'll tell you what … ,' Pollard in Greer, *Hunting Accidents*.

'Not quite a … ,' Justin Gerber, consequenceofound.com, June 13, 2012.

'The band is drunk … ,' Nick Mirov, pitchfork.com, August 8, 1999.

'It seems reasonable … ,' Tom Dardis, *The Thirsty Muse: Alcohol And The American Writer* (Tickner & Fields, 1989).

'Pollard would go on … ,' Morgan Enos, *Glide Magazine*, April 4, 2017.

'Apparently somewhere in … ,' Rich Turiel, gbvdb.com.

5. Propeller

'Final statement,' Pollard interviewed by McMullen, *Ptolemaic Terrascope*.

'There were people … ,' Robert Pollard in Mark Woodworth, *Guided by Voices' Bee Thousand* (Continuum, 2006).

'I realized that we … ,' Pollard in Woodworth, *Bee Thousand*.

'From note one … ,' Robert Griffin, everygbvlp.com, April 15, 2018.

'It's so anthemic … ,' Griffin, everygbvlp.com.

'Fatally flawed,' Robert Pollard, gbvdb.com.

'The warm, fuzzy … ,' Larry Crane, *Tape Op*, March/April 1997.

'We took it to … ,' Pollard interviewed by McMullen, *Ptolemaic Terrascope*.

'We weren't even a live band … ,' Robert Pollard, robertpollard.net.

'I've always said … ,' Robert Pollard interviewed by Eric Miller, *Magnet*, October 2007.

'One of the greatest … ,' Pollard in Cutter, *Closer You Are*.

'We went down to my … ,' Tobin Sprout in Greer, *Hunting Accidents*.

'Look at the fourteen … ,' Pollard in Greer, *Hunting Accidents*.

6. Vampire On Titus

'I don't expect everything to make money … ,' Robert Griffin, agitreader.com.

'At least you don't … ,' Kim Pollard in Greer, *Hunting Accidents*.

'The noisiest, messiest … ,' James Greer, *Hunting Accidents*.

'I was definitely taken … ,' Griffin, everygbvlp.com.

'I can't think of anything … ,' Griffin, everygbvlp.com.

'They were very connected … ,' Griffin, everygbvlp.com.

'At least half of those … ,' Griffin, everygbvlp.com.

'It was a really organic … ,' Griffin, everygbvlp.com.

'Like a vampire on Titus … ,' Jim Shepard, belakoekrompecher.wordpress.com, February 24, 2014.

'Where in God's name … ,' Craig Marks, *Spin*, November 1993.

'It's a low-fi … ,' Tom Sinclair, *Entertainment Weekly*, December 24, 1993.

'We did like 20 … ,' Robert Pollard interviewed by Mark Deming, *Boston Phoenix*, December 21–28, 2000.

'Even at that early date … ,' Robert Griffin, email to the author, September 2019.

'It was with the … ,' Robert Pollard interviewed by Bradley Bambarger, *Musician Magazine*, September 1997.

'Lo-fi sound is essential … ,' Stephen M. Deusner, pitchfork.com, November 7, 2005.

'He was playing … ,' Albert Hammond Jr., consequenceofsound.com, April 2, 2015.

'Portable Magnus chord organ … ,' Griffin, email to the author.

7. Bee Thousand

'Around the time … ,' Pollard in Woodworth, *Bee Thousand*.

'Fitting a puzzle together … ,' Pollard in Woodworth, *Bee Thousand*.

'This original sequence is … ,' Eric Carr, pitchfork.com, December 6, 2004.

'It was very much … ,' Griffin, everygbvlp.com.

'Insanely brilliant songs,' Griffin, everygbvlp.com.

'I plucked up my courage … ,' Robert Griffin, *Bee Thousand: Director's Cut* liner notes, 2004.

'The band's cassette masters … ,' Griffin, email to the author.

'Bits of the beginnings … ,' Griffin, email to the author.

'If Bob had sent … ,' Griffin, email to the author.

'The weird image … ,' Griffin, email to the author.

'To communicate visually … ,' Griffin, everygbvlp.com.

'I always felt *Bee Thousand* … ,' Griffin, email to the author.

'Shit started to … ,' Griffin, everygbvlp.com.

'It did really well … ,' Griffin, everygbvlp.com.

'Batty lyrics … ,' Mike Rubin, *Spin*, July 1994.

'Remarkable,' Michael Azerrad, *Rolling Stone*, August 11, 1994.

'I wasn't sure if it was the best … ,' Griffin, everygbvlp.com.

'More of a Devo feel,' Griffin, email to the author.

'Afterwards I went off … ,' Pollard interviewed by Deming, *Boston Phoenix*.

'I'm not trying to … ,' Robert Pollard interviewed by Jonathan Valania, *Magnet*, September 2014.

'Death's coming to … ,' Pollard in Woodworth, *Bee Thousand*.

'Watching interesting possibilities … ,' Pollard in Woodworth, *Bee Thousand*.

'As far as learning … ,' Matt Berninger, vulture.com, February 22, 2008.

'I wrote … ,' Pollard in Woodworth, *Bee Thousand*.

'He had dollar signs … ,' Pollard interviewed by Valania, *Magnet*, September 2014.

'The shortest songs … ,' Griffin, *Bee Thousand: Director's Cut* liner notes.

'I included this track … ,' Griffin, email to the author.

'Star spangled elf shit,' Eric Davidson in Woodworth, *Bee Thousand*.

'Boldest statement,' Pollard in Cutter, *Closer You Are*.

'About nationalism and … ,' Pollard in Cutter, *Closer You Are*.

'Kind of a self-analyzing song … ,' Pollard in Woodworth, *Bee Thousand*.

'Might be the record … ,' Garrett Martin, Paste, June 21, 2014.

'After *Bee Thousand* I think … ,' Tobin Sprout in Woodworth, *Bee Thousand*.

8. Alien Lanes

'One of the great long-shot … ,' Marc Woodworth, *Bee Thousand*.

'In the mid-'90s … ,' Albert Hammond Jr., consequenceofsound.com, April 2, 2015.

'The world's best record collector,' Eothen Alapatt, dustangrooves.com, May 28, 2017.

'A lot of the labels … ,' Robert Pollard, robertpollard.net.

'Insane,' Chris Lombardi, *New York Magazine*, May 8, 1995.

'I write all the songs … ,' Robert Pollard interviewed by Craig Michael Gurwich, *Mean*, July 2001.

'A kind of indie-rock … ,' Matt Diehl, *Rolling Stone*, March 23, 1995.

'So heroically DIY … ,' *Uncut*, February 1, 2004.

'Four vinyl sides … ,' Anthony DeCurtis, *Lou Reed: A Life* (Little, Brown, 2018).

'Help make *Alien Lanes* … ,' Craig Rosen, *Billboard*, February 25, 1995.

'We were asked by … ,' James Greer, theweeklings.com, January 12, 2013.

'For a lot of commercial … ,' Rosen, *Billboard*.

'I enjoy collaborating … ,' Mark Ohe, 930club.tumblr.com.

'There are definitely … ,' Alex Ross, *Spin*, April 1995.

'Pop for perverts,' Robert Christgau, robertchristgau.com.

'Duds,' Christgau, robertchristgau.com.

'Create a double album's … ,' Robert Pollard quoted by Rosen, *Billboard*.

'Kim Deal hated … ,' Robert Pollard, exclaim.ca, January 1, 2006.

'The narcoleptic truck driver,' Robert Pollard, robertpollard.net.

9. Under The Bushes Under The Stars

'We kind of Were,' Pollard interviewed by Valania, *Magnet*.

'We rehearsed in Kim's … ,' Mitch Mitchell in *CMJ New Music Monthly*, May 1996.

'Why would Albini … ,' Pollard interviewed by Valania, *Magnet*.

'The thing about … ,' Robert Pollard in *CMJ New Music Monthly*, May 1996.

'We went to Europe … ,' Robert Pollard, robertpollard.net.

'We have to stop them … ,' Patrick Amory, *Billboard*, February 24, 1996.

'*Under The Bushes* searches … ,' Michael Corcoran, *Rolling Stone*, February 2, 1998.

'*Under The Bushes* manages … ,' Chuck Stephens, *Spin*, May 1996.

'Although *Under The Bushes* … ,' Lorraine Ali, *Los Angeles Times*, March 30, 1996.

'I didn't fire Kevin … ,' Pollard in Greer, *Hunting Accidents*.

'The good ship Guided By Voices … ,' Robert Pollard interviewed by Laura Dempsey, *Dayton Daily News*, September 20, 1996.

'Cut-outs took their name … ,' Greg Adams, musicweird.blogspot.com, September 1, 2014.

'Maybe the best opening … ,' *Magnet*, February 2009.

'Your heart's desire … ,' Cormac McCarthy, *Blood Meridian: Or The Evening Redness In The West* (Random House, 1985).

'They told me … ,' Robert Pollard interviewed by Tim Perlich, *NOW*, October 19–25, 1995.

'Have kids, have a family … ,' Pollard in Greer, *Hunting Accidents.*

10. Mag Earwhig!

'When it was just … ,' Robert Pollard interviewed by Eric Miller, *Ptolemaic Terrascope*, November 1997.

'The only band … ,' Thom Yorke, *Los Angeles Times*, July 3, 1999.

'Both bands sacrificed … ,' Jon Pareles, *New York Times*, June 27, 1994.

'I knew that finally … ,' Robert Pollard interviewed by Michael Jolly, *Daily Texan*, May 6, 1997.

'It was a little scary … ,' Pollard interviewed by Miller, *Ptolemaic Terrascope.*

'It was weird … ,' Don Depew interviewed by Larry Crane, *Tape Op*, November/December 1997.

'It was not real … ,' Pollard interviewed by Miller, *Ptolemaic Terrascope.*

'We just had a cassette … ,' Depew interviewed by Crane, *Tape Op.*

'Make it good,' Pollard interviewed by Miller, *Ptolemaic Terrascope.*

'We weren't getting along … ,' Pollard interviewed by Miller, *Ptolemaic Terrascope.*

'I don't think any … ,' John Petkovic, mtv.com, November 4, 1997.

'It just didn't … ,' Robert Pollard interviewed by Gail Worley, ink19.com, April 26, 2001.

'It isn't a concept album … ,' Pollard interviewed by Worley, ink19.com.

'Simply [rocked] harder … ,' Ben Kim, *Rolling Stone*, May 23, 1997.

'*Mag Earwhig!* sounds like … ,' Stephen Thompson, avclub.com, March 29, 2002.

'The thing about … ,' Jeff Terich, treblezine.com, August 19, 2016.

'Pollard turned in … ,' Brian Wolowitz, spectrumculture.com, May 3, 2012.

'Stigma about nonsensical lyrics,' Doug Gillard in *Magnet*, August 2014.

'You have to have … ,' *Magnet*, February 2009.

'Pollard can do prog … ,' *Magnet*, February 2009.

11. Do The Collapse

'An obliquely epic album … ,' Jonathan Perry, *Rolling Stone*, July 10, 1998.

'With Robert Pollard, I'm allowed … ,' Robert Pollard in *CMJ New Music Monthly*, June/July 1998.

'I'm happy with … ,' Pollard in Perry, *Rolling Stone*, July 10, 1998.

'I wanted to make … ,' Pollard interviewed by Worley, ink19.com.

'I was exploring some … ,' Robert Pollard interviewed by Jeff Stratton, avclub.com, July 28, 1999.

'Bob and I like … ,' Ric Ocasek interviewed by Bradley Bambarger, *Billboard*, July 10, 1999.

'I think this song … ,' Adam Shore, everygbvlp.com, June 24, 2018.

'Fierce five-month … ,' Chuck Philips, *Los Angeles Times*, May 31, 1996.

'One of the largest … ,' Brian Garrity, *New York Post*, June 19, 2008.

'Matador felt that … ,' Adam Shore interviewed by Bradley Bambarger, *Billboard*, July 10, 1999.

'I was really anxious … ,' Pollard interviewed by Perry, *Rolling Stone*, July 10, 1998.

'When I actually … ,' Jim Macpherson in thebestdrummerintheworld.com, September 13, 2013.

'Where past GBV … ,' Steve Klinge, *CMJ New Music Monthly*, September 1999.

'Longtime fans may … ,' Marc Weingarten, *Rolling Stone*, September 2, 1999.

'I was actually … ,' Robert Pollard interviewed by John D. Luerssen, *Rolling Stone*, April 4, 2001.

'Even though we were … ,' Shore, everygbvlp.com.

'While it is undeniably … ,' Chris Ford, diffuser.fm, August 17, 2014.

'What words sound like … ,' Stewart Lee, thequietus.com, May 25, 2011.

'It's not that I disagree … ,' Robert Pollard interviewed by Brenna Ehrlich, read.tidal.com, February 7, 2018.

'The best Collective Soul … ,' Scott Seward, *Village Voice*, August 31, 1999.

'At the time there were … ,' Shore, everygbvlp.com.

'In this day and age … ,' Jack Joseph Puig, soundonsound.com, November 2007.

'I went back to … ,' Shore, everygbvlp.com.

'We went to a pub … ,' Shore, everygbvlp.com.

'They were furious … ,' Shore, everygbvlp.com.

'While most Pollard fanboys … ,' Carlos Ramirez, diffuser.fm, May 10, 2013.

12. Isolation Drills

'Life is a series of mistakes … ,' Pollard in Greer, *Hunting Accidents.*

'I've come to … ,' Robert Pollard interviewed by Mike McGonigal, *Bomb*, July 1, 2001.

'*Suitcase* is crammed … ,' Matt LeMay, pitchfork.com, August 31, 2000.

'A must only for … ,' Keith Phipps, avclub.com, September 19, 2000.

'Technically, we're the best … ,' Robert Pollard interviewed by Peter Botham, *Rockpile*, June 2001.

'I wanted our music … ,' Pollard interviewed by McGonigal, *Bomb.*

'I looked at the dark … ,' Pollard interviewed by Worley, ink19.com.

'Looking at your life,' Robert Pollard in *CMJ New Music Monthly*, May/June 2001.

'When you're sad … ,' Pollard interviewed by McGonigal, *Bomb.*

'*Isolation Drills* makes the case … ,' Greg Kot, *Rolling Stone*, March 5, 2001.

'Pollard sounds grimmer … ,' Joe Gross, *Blender*, June/July 2001.

'It's less keyboard oriented … ,' Robert Pollard, exclaim.ca, January 1, 2006.

'That line "I want to reinvent you,"' Pollard interviewed by Worley, ink19.com.

'We tour all the time … ,' Pollard interviewed by Luerssen, *Rolling Stone.*

'Luminous folk-rock hymn,' Greg Kot, *Rolling Stone*, March 5, 2001.

'The title means nothing … ,' Pollard interviewed by Botham, *Rockpile.*

'Things were going … ,' Pollard interviewed by Worley, ink19.com.

'He's a man now … ,' Pollard interviewed by Botham, *Rockpile.*

'Perhaps the most joyous-sounding … ,' Jim Connelly, medialoper.com, June 9, 2016.

'There would be no … ,' F. Scott Fitzgerald, *The Crack-Up* (New Directions, 1945).

'Sin,' Robert Pollard interviewed by Eric T. Miller, *Magnet*, April/May 2001.

'Being out there … ,' Pollard interviewed by Miller, *Magnet.*

13. Universal Truths And Cycles

'We just realized that … ,' Robert Pollard in kindamuzik.net, June 17, 2002.

'Back home … ,' Jonathan Cohen, *Billboard*, June 22, 2002.

'Impressive but unwieldy,' Gerard Cosloy, *New York Times*, November 17, 2003.

'When you're younger … ,' Albert Hammond Jr., consequenceofsound.com, April 2, 2015.

'After that they … ,' Robert Pollard in kindamuzik.net, June 17, 2002.

'Boozy,' David Fricke, *Rolling Stone*, February 14, 2002.

'This was my first … ,' Todd Tobias, See You Inside, 2019.

'Kinda like an old … ,' Robert Pollard, robertpollard.net.

'It's more applicable to … ,' Robert Pollard in kindamuzik.net, June 17, 2002.

'On our last two records … ,' Robert Pollard in kindamuzik.net, June 17, 2002.

'To make a long story … ,' Matt LeMay, pitchfork.com, June 23, 2002.

'Pollard churned out … ,' Keith Phipps, avclub.com, June 25, 2002.

'Just like the 1960's … ,' Rob O'Connor, *Rolling Stone*, June 18, 2002.

'Built around a … ,' LeMay, pitchfork.com.

14. Earthquake Glue

'The soundtrack to … ,' Matt Hickey, *Magnet*, June/July 2003.

'Oh yeah, I get totally … ,' Robert Pollard interviewed by Matt Hickey, *Magnet*, June/July 2003.

'Kevin is a great person … ,' Tim Tobias, robertpollard.net.

'Not many people … ,' Kevin March interviewed by Eli Zeger, jerseybeat.com.

'I don't think it's … ,' Robert Pollard interviewed by Keith Cameron, *Mojo*, August 2003.

'It took them 15 years … ,' David Holmes, steregoum.com, March 13, 2013.

'Feels like a gallery … ,' *Spin*, September 2003.

'Almost every song … ,' Pollard interviewed by Cameron, *Mojo.*

'Eighteen sonic postcards … ,' gbvdb.com.

'More than a third … ,' Samantha Masunaga, *Los Angeles Times*, March 24, 2017.

'That one rolled out … ,' Tim Tobias, robertpollard.net.

'A staggering 45 percent … ,' Marilynn Marchione, *Boston Globe*, May 28, 2012.

15. Half Smiles Of The Decomposed

'If *Half Smiles Of* … ,' David Holmes, stereogum.com, March 13, 2013.

'I'm doing this to … ,' Robert Pollard interviewed by Mark Maske, *Washington Post*, September 10, 2004.

'Gotten to be a bit too … ,' Pollard interviewed by Maske, *Washington Post.*

'After I listened to … ,' Pollard interviewed by Maske, *Washington Post.*

'It's a smart move … ,' Gerard Cosloy, *Boston Globe*, September 8, 2004.

'Matador house band,' Robert Pollard interviewed by Allie Roxburgh, cwas.hinah.com, Autumn 2002.

'It's packed to bursting … ,' Greg Kot, *Rolling Stone*, September 16, 2004.

'Pocketful of bright spots … ,' Rob Mitchum, pitchfork.com, August 23, 2004.

'So ladies and gentlemen … ,' Alex Wisgard, drownedinsound.com, September 3, 2004.

'The farewell was beautiful … ,' Eric Carr, pitchfork.com, January 17, 2005.

'How life can become … ,' Derek Malcolm, *Guardian*, June 10, 1999.

'Limp,' Mitchum, pitchfork.com.

'You gotta do … ,' Pollard in Greer, *Hunting Accidents.*

'If you're a couple of … ,' Dave Gottlieb in Lizzy Goodman, *Meet Me In The Bathroom: Rebirth And Rock And Roll In New York City 2001–2011* (Dey Street, 2017).

16. Let's Go Eat The Factory

'If Pollard and his … ,' Matthew Fiander, popmatters.com, July 15, 2007.

'Painting myself … ,' Robert Pollard interviewed by Mark Maske, *Washington Post*, September 10, 2004.

'Right now I'm … ,' Robert Pollard, robertpollard.net.

'I don't see Guided By Voices … ,' Robert Pollard in *Magnet*, October 2007.

'It was one of those things … ,' Tobin Sprout interviewed by Spencer Patterson, *Las Vegas Sun*, September 30, 2010.

'He had just moved … ,' Sprout interviewed by Patterson, *Las Vegas Sun.*

'If Matador at 21 were … ,' David Greenwald, *Los Angeles Times*, October 4, 2010.

'The big draw was not … ,' Michael Bonner, *Uncut*, March 7, 2012.

'A reunion of … ,' Paul Thompson, pitchfork.com, January 4, 2012.

'I was sitting in a bar … ,' Robert Pollard interviewed by Steven Hyden, avclub.com, December 5, 2011.

'We recorded the songs … ,' Pollard interviewed by Hyden, avclub.com, December 5, 2011.

'It takes only a few seconds … ,' Hyden, avclub.com, January 3, 2012.

'Exhilarating, a kaleidoscopic … ,' Maddy Costa, *Guardian*, January 12, 2012.

'The 21 songs here … ,' Steve Kandell, *Spin*, December 20, 2011.

'It's the songs of Pollard's … ,' Spencer Grady, bbc.co.uk, 2012.

'While Bob seems to … ,' Paul Thompson, pitchfork.com, January 4, 2012.

'Sugary, like the donuts … ,' Pollard interviewed by Valania, *Magnet.*

'The Unsinkable Fats Domino … ,' Hyden, avclub.com, January 3, 2012.

'Obligatory mid-album … ,' Tom Breihan, stereogum.com, January 3, 2012.

'Well on its way … ,' Justin Gerber, consequenceofsound.com, January 2, 2012.

'Bouncing all around… ,' Tobin Sprout, email to the author.

'The album's strangest … ,' Hyden, avclub.com, January 3, 2012.

'"Go Rolling Home" lingers … ,' Gerber, consequenceofsound.com, January 2, 2012.

17. Class Clown Spots A UFO

'The pretty much … ,' Mitch Mitchell interviewed by Zach Schonfeld, *Wesleyan Argus*, February 9, 2012.

'It's not a rumor … ,' Steven Spoerl, popmatters.com, June 13, 2012.

'The reunion is over,' Gerber, consequenceofsound.com, June 2012.

'Guided By Voices has been … ,' Jon Glaser, *Magnet*, March 2012.

'Many groups go away … ,' Jayson Greene, pitchfork.com, January 10, 2014.

'What was once a valorous … ,' Stuart Berman, pitchfork.com, October 6, 2016.

'Increasingly mournful asterisk … ,' Greene, pitchfork.com.

'This post-reunion version … ,' Daniel Couch, thequietus.com, November 27, 2012.

'Fans of GBV's iconic release … ,' gbvdb.com.

'When I make an album … ,' Robert Pollard, *Rolling Stone*, December 5, 2013.

'As with *Factory* … ,' Hyden, avclub.com, June 12, 2012.

'Tobin Sprout's age-defying … ,' Paul Thompson, pitchfork.com, June 27, 2012.

'One of the strongest LPs … ,' Spoerl, popmatters.com.

'One of those dizzyingly catchy … ,' Thompson, pitchfork.com, June 27, 2012.

'When it first appeared … ,' Spoerl, popmatters.com.

'The point is to … ,' Pollard interviewed by Hyden, avclub.com, December 5, 2011.

'Expertly brings everything … ,' Spoerl, popmatters.com.

18. The Bears For Lunch

'In addition to the … ,' Robert Pollard interviewed by Daniel Dodd, espn.com, January 31, 2014.

'Pollard's prolific output … ,' Saby Reyes-Kulkarni, pitchfork.com, April 11, 2017.

'It's clear now that … ,' Paul Thompson, pitchfork.com, May 1, 2013.

'I see *Factory* as an abstract … ,' Tobin Sprout interviewed by Mark Toerner, ghettoblaster.com, December 10, 2012.

'It's the best record … ,' Matthew Fiander, prefixmag.com, November 13, 2012.

'The secret weapon … ,' David Holmes, stereogum.com, March 13, 2013.

'You can't help but … ,' Stuart Berman, pitchfork.com, November 12, 2012.

'One could argue … ,' Justin Gerber, consequenceofsound.com, November 16, 2012.

'I send the songs … ,' Sprout interviewed by Mark Toerner, ghettoblaster.com.

'A study published … ,' Katie Frost, *Esquire*, May 17, 2017.

'Sounds like Pollard crooning … ,' Stuart Berman, pitchfork.com, November 12, 2012.

'A country tinged, acoustic … ,' Rusty Roberts, chunkyglasses.net, November 20, 2012.

'A needling, repetitive … ,' Couch, thequietus.com.

19. English Little League

'People feel like … ,' Jonathan Valania, *Magnet*, September 2014.

'The knee-jerk reaction may be to dismiss … ,' Chris Morgan, uproxx.com, April 22, 2016.

'Robert Pollard is a classic … ,' Beca Grimm, *Paste*, April 30, 2013.

'Overproduction can also damage … ,' Jay Parini, *New York Times*, July 30, 1989.

'My philosophy is … ,' Robert Pollard in *Billboard*, February 22, 2002.

'If I could put out … ,' Robert Pollard interviewed by Ed Condran, *Bucks County Courier Times*, October 6, 2016.

'The Guided By Voices project … ,' gbvdb.com.

'That's what I do … ,' Robert Pollard, *Magnet*, September 2014.

'Pollard has recently installed … ,' gbvdb.com.

'I think to be able to … ,' Michael Stipe, *Atlantic*, November 8, 2013.

'Like so many GBV albums … ,' Paul Thompson, pitchfork.com, May 1, 2013.

'It remains a pleasure … ,' Matt Wild, avclub.com, April 30, 2013.

'A few of Pollard's numbers … ,' Craig Bechtel, popstache.com, May 23, 2013.

'Best song … ,' Sarah H. Grant, consequenceofsound.com, May 1, 2013.

'The song didn't strike … ,' Tobin Sprout interviewed by Matt Messana, popmatters.com, April 28, 2013.

'The sort of tossed-off gem … ,' Wild, avclub.com, April 30, 2013.

'Dismal co-write … ,' Paul Thompson, pitchfork.com, May 1, 2013.

'Is brimming with … ,' Thompson, pitchfork.com, May 1, 2013.

'Undoubtedly *Little League*'s strongest … ,' Wild, avclub.com, April 30, 2013.

'I was reading about … ,' Tobin Sprout interviewed by Matt Messana, popmatters.com, April 28, 2013.

20. Motivational Jumpsuit

'So you might ask … ,' Kevin Fennell, kfennell1.wixsite.com/gbvdrumauction/story, 2013.

'Amateur,' Robert Pollard interviewed by Josh Kurp, uproxx.com, October 24, 2013.

'Do not delude yourself … ,' Pollard interviewed by Kurp, uproxx.com.

'I've been convinced … ,' Pollard interviewed by Hyden, avclub.com, December 5, 2011.

'Mini movie,' Mike Postalakis, everygbvlp.com, October 14, 2018.

'A ramshackle collection … ,' Patrick Bowman, avclub.com, February 18, 2014.

'Gives us an organizing … ,' Matthew Fiander, popmatters.com, February 16, 2014.

'Undercooked … ,' Stuart Berman, pitchfork.com, February 19, 2014.

'Clunky,' Patrick Bowman, avclub.com, February 18, 2014.

'Recent albums have … ,' Stuart Berman, pitchfork.com, February 19, 2014.

'Feels like it was designed … ,' Stuart Berman, pitchfork.com, February 19, 2014.

21. Cool Planet

'To go back and do that again … ,' Kevin March interviewed by Eli Zeger, jerseybeat.com.

'Workmanlike … ,' Jason Heller, pitchfork.com, May 13, 2014.

'It was tired, collectively … ,' Robert Pollard interviewed by Brian Baker, citybeat.com, July 13, 2016.

'Where GBV's slovenly … ,' Heller, pitchfork.com, May 13, 2014.

'A few outright failures … ,' Garrett Martin, *Paste*, May 13, 2014.

'Cyberteknics has been … ,' Robert Pollard interviewed by John Gentile, *Rolling Stone*, December 5, 2013.

'A lot of musicians … ,' Phil Mehaffey, *Dayton Daily News*, January 22, 2015.

'I'm not saying it's terrible … ,' Mehaffey, *Dayton Daily News*.

'Spoons out meandering … ,' Heller, pitchfork.com, May 13, 2014.

'Feels most like it … ,' Sean O'Neal, avclub.com, March 13, 2018.

'Builds thick rock textures … ,' Matthew Fiander, popmatters.com, May 13, 2014.

'It's the band's most … ,' Fiander, popmatters.com, May 13, 2014.

'Pollard barely shows up … ,' Heller, pitchfork.com, May 13, 2014.

22. Please Be Honest

'Guided By Voices are back … ,' Zoe Camp, pitchfork.com, March 10, 2016.

'Which would seem to make … ,' Anna Gaca, *Spin*, March 11, 2016.

'Maybe he's reviving the name … ,' Tom Breihan, stereogum.com, March 10, 2016.

'I came up with the notion … ,' Robert Pollard interviewed by John Wenzel, *Denver Post*, April 29, 2016.

'I thought it worked … ,' Pollard interviewed by Wenzel, *Denver Post.*

'It's understandable to … ,' John Hugar, avclub.com, April 22, 2016.

'Regardless of lineup … ,' Magdalen Jenne, popmatters.com, April 25, 2016.

'I cried when he asked me,' Bobby Bare Jr. interviewed by Mike Bell, *Calgary Herald*, June 22, 2016.

'One of the longest running … ,' Dayton.com, May 14, 2016.

'A really good player … ,' Robert Pollard interviewed by Ted Drozdowski, *Premier Guitar*, February 3, 2015.

'At those rehearsals … ,' Nick Mitchell, Facebook message to the author, December 2019.

'Bob would show up … ,' Mitchell, Facebook message to the author.

'The time away … ,' Mitchell, Facebook message to the author.

'I got calls and texts … ,' Doug Gillard interviewed by Mike Vanderbilt, avclub.com, July 28, 2016.

'Doug is a sweetheart … ,' Mitchell, Facebook message to the author.

'Is it about our … ,' Raj Dayal, prettymuchamazing.com, April 21, 2016.

'Highlight … ,' Ryan Reisert, treblezine.com, May 5, 2016.

'Strongest track … ,' John Hugar, avclub.com, April 22, 2016.

'And while musicianship … ,' John S. W. MacDonald, pitchfork.com, April 2016.

'Refreshingly, the song touches … ,' MacDonald, pitchfork.com, April 2016.

23. August By Cake

'A historic moment,' Andy Greene, *Rolling Stone*, January 8, 2014.

'Doubles too often prove … ,' Neil McCormick, *Daily Telegraph*, February 19, 2015.

'It was initially just … ,' Doug Gillard interviewed by Jeff Niesel, clevescene.com, May 1, 2017.

'I originally intended … ,' Robert Pollard interviewed by Nathan Poppe, oklahoman.com, April 7, 2017.

'On the spot,' Bobby Bare Jr. interviewed by Brenna Ehrlich, read.tidal.com, April 7, 2017.

'We didn't plan it … ,' Doug Gillard interviewed by Erhlich, read.tidal.com, April 7, 2017.

'I have a studio … ,' Travis Harrison, sonicscoop.com, January 20, 2011.

'*August by Cake* is the … ,' Nicholas Carr, roughtype.com, April 16, 2017.

'Crown jewel of Pollard's … ,' Dave Heaton, popmatters.com, April 6, 2017.

'The music barely hangs … ,' Katie Rife, avclub.com, April 7, 2017.

'The album is so strong … ,' Aug Stone, *Under The Radar*, April 12, 2017.

'Man, I bet this is … ,' Robert Pollard interviewed by Ehrlich, read.tidal.com, April 7, 2017.

'Circus barker's come-on … ,' Carr, roughtype.com.

'A song that also has … ,' Heaton, popmatters.com, April 6, 2017.

'Home-recorded surrealist … ,' Heaton, popmatters.com, April 6, 2017.

'I'm always influenced … ,' Kevin March interviewed by Ehrlich, read.tidal.com, April 7, 2017.

'We high-five a lot … ,' Bobby Bare Jr. interviewed by Ehrlich, read.tidal.com, April 7, 2017.

'There's a vaguely Celtic … ,' Winston Cook-Wilson, *Spin*, March 14, 2017.

'I wrote [the song] acoustically … ,' Bobby Bare Jr. interviewed by Ehrlich, read.tidal.com., April 7, 2017.

'Absolutely gorgeous … ,' Heaton, popmatters.com, April 6, 2017.

'Feels like the missing … ,' Carr, roughtype.com.

24. How Do You Spell Heaven

'is where the story … ,' Roy Carr and Charles Shaar Murray, *David Bowie: An Illustrated Record* (Eel Pie, 1981).

'Think of how bad … ,' Garrett Martin, *Paste*, May 13, 2014.

'We gotta use that … ,' Pollard interviewed by Ehrlich, read.tidal.com, April 7, 2017.

'Guided By Voices maintain … ,' Jenna McClelland, exclaim.ca, August 11, 2017.

'Keeping up with all things … ,' Katie Rife, avclub.com, August 11, 2017.

'With Pollard reassuming … ,' Stuart Berman, pitchfork.com, August 11, 2017.

'"Low Flying Perfection" is ... ,' Berman, pitchfork.com, August 11, 2017.

25. Space Gun

'We're all very proud ... ,' Robert Pollard on his Facebook page, February 7, 2018.

'Days before I was set to film ... ,' Hunter Christy, facebook.com, December 19, 2018.

'Pretty great ... ,' Jon Dolan, *Rolling Stone*, March 23, 2018.

'The best thing [Pollard's] recorded ... ,' Dorian Rogers, neonfiller.com, March 23, 2018.

'Listening to *Space Gun* ... ,' Kristin Hersh, talkhouse.com, May 16, 2018.

'A close friend and ... ,' Doug Gillard, consequenceofsound.com, December 8, 2017.

'Tried to have ... ,' Gillard, consequenceofsound.com, March 5, 2018.

'Particularly early R.E.M-like ... ,' Jared Dix, echoesanddust.com, March 25, 2018.

'Land on "Hudson Rake" ... ,' Kristin Hersh, talkhouse.com, May 16, 2018.

'No reason ... ,' Gillard, consequenceofsound.com, December 8, 2017.

'I've just always thought ... ,' Pollard interviewed by Brenna Ehrlich, read.tidal.com, February 7, 2018.

26. Zeppelin Over China

'It was originally ... ,' Robert Pollard, gothamist.com, January 29, 2019.

'Travis has completely ... ,' Pollard, gothamist.com.

'An unexpected but very ... ,' Mark Deming, allmusic.com.

'It would be easy ... ,' Kirsten Inneski, spillmagazine.com.

'Thirty years into ... ,' David Haynes, post-trash.com, February 27, 2019.

'Real goofy and kind of ... ,' Pollard, gothamist.com.

'Fight song ... ,' *Time*, February 22, 2018.

'Travis has completely ... ,' Pollard, gothamist.com.

'We all want, above all ... ,' Deborah Tannen, *You Just Don't Understand*, 1990.

27. Warp & Woof

'Format that was so ... ,' Robert Pollard, guidedbyvoices.com, July 11, 2018.

'I dig having ... ,' Doug Gillard, offshelf.net, April 26, 2019.

'For most artists Robert Pollard ... ,' Sophie Brzozowski, *Exclaim!*, April 23, 2019.

'Kaleidoscopic snapshot songs ... ,' Michael James Hall, *Under The Radar*, May 15, 2019.

'Pinnacle so far ... ,' Sean Kitching, thequietus.com, May 8, 2019.

'In a van hurtling ... ,' gbvdb.com.

28. Sweating The Plague

'Unofficial unapproved bootleg ... ,' gbvdb. com.

'Truth be told ... ,' James McMahon, *NME*, June 7, 2019.

'It's revealing ... ,' Richard Ford, *Between Them*, 2017.

'I intended to make ... ,' Robert Pollard, robertpollard.net.

'Standing in a ticker tape ... ,' Stewart Lee, guidedbyvoices.com.

'Represents one of the ... ,' Thomas Wilde, thefirenote.com, October 24, 2019.

'On *Sweating the Plague* ... ,' Paul Rowe, popmatters.com, October 23, 2019.

'Many of *Sweating the Plague*'s ... ,' Michael Joshua Rowin, *Slant*, October 24, 2019.

Afterword

'The songs are ... ,' Robert Pollard interviewed by Brenna Ehrlich, *Rolling Stone*, January 7, 2020.

'Going to church,' Adam Shore, everygbvlp.com, June 24, 2018.

'The Grateful Dead equivalent ... ,' David Malitz, *Washington Post*, September 28, 2009.

INDEX